una storia segreta

A project of the California Civil Liberties Public Education Program

The editor of this book and the publisher and staff of Heyday Books extend our gratitude to the California Civil Liberties Public Education Program (CCLPEP) for making available the funds to complete *Una Storia Segreta*. In addition to its goal of sharing information and education about the Japanese American incarceration experience of World War II with the California community, the CCLPEP works to provide linkages and parallels with other communities and individuals. Education regarding past injustices will hopefully prevent individuals from ever committing them in the future.

The California Civil Liberties Public Education Program was created through legislation known as the California Civil Liberties Public Education Act, or AB 1915 (Chapter 570 Statues of 1998). The legislation was introduced in the California State Assembly in 1998 by Assemblymember Mike Honda of San Jose.

In one of the most public and far-reaching of the reparation activities, the CCLPEP provides grants for the development of public educational materials and activities to ensure that the forced removal and incarceration of U.S. citizens and permanent resident aliens will be remembered.

CCLPEP is administered by the California State Library under the leadership of State Librarian Dr. Kevin Starr. With this program, California has taken the initiative in recognizing the need for further education and materials on this important chapter in our nation's history. For more information on the CCLPEP, contact Diane M. Matsuda, Program Director, California Civil Liberties Public Education Program, (916) 653-9404, dmatsuda@library.ca.gov.

una

The Secret History of

storia

Italian American Evacuation and

segreta

Internment during World War II

Edited with an Introduction by Lawrence DiStasi
Foreword by Sandra M. Gilbert

Heyday Books, Berkeley, California

Library of Congress Cataloging-in-Publication Data

Una storia segreta : the secret history of Italian American evacuation and internment during World War II / edited with an introduction by Lawrence DiStasi ; foreword by Sandra Gilbert.
     p. cm.
  ISBN 1-890771-40-6 (pbk.)
  1. World War, 1939-1945—Italian Americans. 2. Italian Americans—Relocation—History—20th century. 3. World War, 1939-1945—Prisoners and prisons, American. I. DiStasi, Lawrence, 1937-

  D769.8.A6 W35 2001
  940.53'08951—dc21
                                      2001001793

Cover Photographs: Internment camp at Missoula, Montana; Josephine and Angelo de Guttadauro with their father in Reno, where the family lived to comply with Nino de Guttadauro's exclusion order, 1943.
Cover/Interior Design: Rebecca LeGates
Printing and Binding: Publishers Press, Salt Lake City, UT

Orders, inquiries, and correspondence should be addressed to:
Heyday Books
P. O. Box 9145, Berkeley, CA 94709
(510) 549-3564; Fax (510) 549-1889
www.heydaybooks.com

Printed in the United States of America

10 9 8 7 6 5 4 3 2 1

This book is dedicated to all those who lived this story
but never had the chance to tell it.

Contents

Acknowledgments

My deepest thanks go to the California Civil Liberties Public Education Program, without whose generous grant this book would not have seen the light of day. I am also indebted to my old comrade Malcolm Margolin, in on the idea from the beginning, and his superb staff at Heyday Books, for bringing the project to completion. The editing of Jeannine Gendar and Rina Margolin, always timely, precise, and thoughtful, deserves particular mention. So does the design of Rebecca LeGates, the steady direction of Patricia Wakida, and the production help of Devon Shaw.

Many of those I would like to acknowledge already appear in these pages: Rose Scherini, for her persistence in pursuing the people and the records that made the *Una Storia Segreta* exhibit possible; Stephen Fox, for the book and articles which first made an unknown story public; Guido Tintori, for the research that brought heretofore unknown documents on the internees to light. Equally important are those who first put our wartime exhibit together—Adele Negro, Eli Shahideh, and Rose Scherini—and those who supported it financially and morally early on: Neno Aiello, Andrew Canepa, Bill Cerruti, Maria Gloria, the National Italian American Foundation, the Italian American Federation of the East Bay, the Italian American Cultural Foundation, the Italian Heritage Foundation of Monterey, and countless others who made it possible for *Una Storia Segreta* to become a national event. Because of their efforts, the Wartime Violation of Italian American Civil Liberties Act—conceived and drafted by John Calvelli; introduced in the House of Representatives by Eliot Engel and Rick Lazio, and in the Senate by Robert Torricelli; and driven to completion by determined individuals like Anthony LaPiana—has now become Public Law 106-451.

Finally, I am most grateful to those whose stories, either about themselves or about their families, comprise the heart this volume. They are the ones who lived with the legacy of those fearful days, the ones who kept their memories alive until the moment was ripe for their release. Their generosity in sharing their stories can never be repaid, except in small measure by having a portion of them memorialized in these pages.

Foreword

Once upon a time, when I was a little girl, there were three terrible villains who made trouble for everybody: Hitler, Hirohito, and Mussolini. These three villains, like evil characters in a comic book, were causing a world war that threatened to rage everywhere. Schoolchildren like me didn't understand exactly why they were doing this; we certainly didn't grasp the subtleties of political movements like Nazism and Fascism and were obviously not going to learn the horrifying consequences of such movements until after the war. But we did know about air raids and blackouts; we had heard of the Blitz in England and admired the brave English children who didn't, like us, just have to hide under their desks when sirens sounded, but had to huddle in cellars and subway stations.

To be honest, I would have to say that the scariest of the three villains was definitely Hitler, with his little mustache, his goose-stepping soldiers, his barking and howling speeches. But for a child with an Italian last name and Italian-born or Italian-speaking relatives on both sides of the family, a child whose father was a Mortola and whose mother was a Caruso, the most disturbing of the three was unquestionably Mussolini. Noticing the Italianness of my name, with its vulnerably open vowel ending (so different from the clipped decency of an Anglo-Saxon consonant), other kids did kid me, implying that Mussolini had something to do with *me*. And it didn't help that everything about the culture in which I was growing up made me want to be a "real" American—what we'd now call a WASP—instead of a weirdly "foreign" outsider. I lived in New York City and at least superficially agreed with my parents and teachers that this was the greatest city in the world, yet in my heart of hearts I dreamed of happy days in an all-American movie-set small town: shady streets, a newsboy on a bicycle, a milkman clinking his bottles on a real front porch with a real porch swing.

Within not much more than a decade, of course, I would come to appreciate my Italian heritage, to savor its richness and complexity. But in those wartime days—well, it was hard enough to worry that the comic capers of Chico Marx might reflect something stupid about my Sicilian uncles, or that the pathetically helpless Italian family in *It's a Wonderful Life*, with their goats and chickens, might mirror something hopeless about my own family; hard enough to worry about such comparatively trivial popular images without having to defend myself against being seen, in some secret way, as related to Mussolini! And why should I have to defend myself, when I knew that I was a patriotic American who could sing "The Star-Spangled Banner" as well as anyone else, who could recite the "Pledge of Allegiance" better and faster than half my classmates, who collected cans and newspapers for victory drives and planted a victory garden too?

When I (very rarely) mentioned these anxieties about what we'd now call my ethnicity to my foreign-born parents, they fervently reassured me. My mother was a schoolteacher, my father a civil engineer who worked for the city. They insisted that I shouldn't worry about being identified with Mussolini, noting that my mother's older brothers had fled Sicily early in the twentieth century because they were socialist freedom fighters, even then opposing the kind of tyranny of which the Fascist dictator was now an embodiment. Besides, they told me, America was a melting pot in which we were all citizens together, in which everyone was equal, as they could testify—look how well they'd done on public service exams, where merit, rather than birth, was the factor that determined advancement. We took trips to the Statue of Liberty and the Empire State Building. We rejoiced that we were here in the home of the brave and the land of the free, rather than in any of the bad countries ruled by the world war's three villains.

The powerful testimony proffered in *Una Storia Segreta* demonstrates, alas, that my well-intentioned parents were misguided or naive, and that I was misled. Even though we were Italian Americans, we couldn't escape the long shadow of Mussolini, and certainly those who were "merely" Italians living in America—even those waiting and longing to be "naturalized"—couldn't escape that shadow.

The word "naturalized" is perhaps of some interest here. According to the *American Heritage Dictionary*, "to naturalize" means not just "to grant full citizenship to (one of foreign birth)," but also "to adapt or acclimate (a plant or animal) to a new environment; introduce and establish as if native," and "to cause to conform to nature." This is the paradox of naturalization: to be naturalized is to be inherently unnatural; a native, or "natural," American doesn't need to be naturalized; only a nonnative, not-natural American can in fact be acculturated as a naturalized, and therefore unnatural, American.

Such a paradox no doubt informs one of the most distressing comments that Lawrence DiStasi quotes in the introduction to this book. Addressing the Joint Fact-Finding Committee on Un-American Activities in California as they investigated disloyalty among Italian Americans, one Dr. Kellems speculated about these "aliens" that "there are a special group of people whose culture and background is so different from ours [that] it will be possible for them to forget that only if they will enter the American way of life." How eerily this passage echoes the xenophobia that has all too often characterized moments in our country's history when the very waves of immigration from which the nation is constituted were seen as threatening rather than enriching, painful rather than rife with possibility.

The twentieth century's two major wars were especially marked by such xenophobic backlash, with America firsters excoriating "hyphenated Americans" during World War I and authorities "quarantining" countless naturalized or even American-born citizens during World War II, from (most notoriously) Japanese Americans to German Americans and, as this book fully documents, Italian Americans. But even today, of course, a revulsion against what is foreign, what is "un-American" or "naturalized" (and therefore unnatural) informs quotas, statutes, and ballot-box propositions directed against immigrants.

For me, as an Italian American student of American literature, one of the most unnerving formulations of the feelings that shaped and still shape these phenomena appears in Henry James's 1907 *The American Scene,* wherein the supposedly Italophile master's magisterially elegant prose gives an especially abhorrent tone to his sneering description of strolling workers "of the simpler sort" that he observed on Boston's Beacon Hill one Sunday afternoon in 1907: no "sound of English, in a single instance, escaped their lips; the greater number spoke a rude form of Italian, the others some outland dialect unknown to me....No note of any shade of American speech struck my ear....The people before me were gross aliens to a man, and they were in serene and triumphant possession."

But for me, as an Italian American person, the most unnerving example of such feelings is the xenophobia that was induced in me, myself, by attitudes toward Italians that intensified my childish dread of identification with Mussolini. The more we can learn about such attitudes and the disturbing history they have engendered, the more likely we may be to avoid similar problems in the future. For instructing me so dramatically on this history of which I was unaware, even though it made a not-so-subtle mark on my childhood, I am deeply grateful to Lawrence DiStasi and all the other writers who have contributed to his unveiling of *Una Storia Segreta.*

Sandra M. Gilbert
March 2001

Introduction
One Voice at a Time

In a letter written from his place of internment at Fort George Meade, Maryland, in January 1943, Louis Berizzi tried to clarify an apparently damaging response he had given at his first hearing the previous year:

> When I testified on an occasion before the hearing board, I was
> asked whether I wanted this country to win the war. I replied that
> I believed in democratic principles and did not believe in Fascism,
> but naturally I did not like the idea of having my mother bombed.
> This was construed as meaning that I did not want Italy bombed,
> and that I referred to Italy as my mother country, or the land of
> my preference. Whether the acoustics of the room was bad, or
> whatever other reason, the stenographer committed error [sic] and
> also the hearers. My wife and brother, who were present, under-
> stood what I really meant. And I hereby state unequivocally that I
> prefer this country to Italy and wish it well. And I nevertheless
> still say that I regard with horror the thought that someday
> American planes will bomb the city where my mother is living
> and that she might come to harm by reason thereof.[1]

Like almost all those of Italian descent who were interned during World War II, Berizzi was an immigrant to America who had lived and worked in the United States for years. Yet, without U.S. citizenship (as a raw-silk importer, Berizzi believed he had to retain his Italian citizenship to facilitate his business), he was branded as an enemy alien during the war and arrested right after Pearl Harbor. At the hearing, where he was presumed guilty unless he could "prove" his innocence, his remark about not wanting his mother bombed apparently weighed against him, and he was interned.

The remark deserves our attention not only because it seems so harmless now. It turns out that several other Italian immigrants arrested in those days expressed their dual status in similar terms. Joe Cervetto, for example, when asked which he liked better, Italy or the United States, responded, "You have a mother, and you have a wife. You love both of them, different love. You cannot go in bed with your mother, but you love your mother, and you love your wife. You can't say I want one to love or the other. It's the same thing like your country. I said I would never go against the United States. Because the U.S. is my country." Nonetheless, Cervetto was detained for several months in 1942 before being released on probation. Nereo Francesconi of San Francisco reportedly used the same mother/wife analogy, adding, "and don't forget, you *choose* your wife [i.e. America]." The authorities were apparently not impressed, for he too was interned as a danger "to the public safety of the United States."

What this suggests is that mother love, even when used as a metaphor to express sentiment for the country of one's birth, carried a powerful charge for American authorities during World War II, especially when the country in question had become the enemy. Any reference to maternal allegiance made authorities suspicious. It also tapped into a more general notion that has operated from the very beginning of the republic: the insecurity felt by an America which, even as late as 1942, still did not fully trust those born elsewhere. It is as if America has looked upon herself as Lady Liberty, willing and eager to be courted by the immigrant lover, but always fearful that the one who has immigrated does so not out of love but out of necessity: "You don't really want me; you simply need what I have. And when you are no longer in need, you will leave me, or betray me."

To allay such fears, the immigrant has always faced the imperative to choose between two nations, with the choice framed as Americanization: become American in your speech, your habits, your dress, or you will be viewed with suspicion. After Japanese aircraft attacked Pearl Harbor on December 7, 1941, and after the United States declared war on Japan, Germany, and Italy,[2] this imperative grew far more urgent. "If you have not yet become a citizen," the government seemed to say, "it must mean that your loyalty is at best divided, at worst primarily directed towards that mother country." Hence you must be considered an "enemy alien." And even if you have gone through the motions of citizenship, it may well be that the primary attraction of the mother still operates, especially if you live in one of the Italian American neighborhoods known as Little Italy. There, reminders of that maternal origin are everywhere—in the language, the food, the clothing, the smells, the ways of walking, the allegiances—and, as dangers, need to be neutralized and ultimately forsaken.

Such ideas were not just implied. They were given voice in a colloquy that took place at the Joint Fact-Finding Committee on Un-American Activities in California, the so-called Tenney Committee hearings, held in San Francisco in May 1942 to investigate the alleged Fascist influence in San Francisco. There, Gilbert Tuoni, a committee witness not yet a citizen himself, and committee member Kellems explicitly stated that the only way for San

Francisco to be secure from the wartime threat of disloyalty would be for its Italian-born residents—including those naturalized citizens specifically under investigation—to abandon their traditional ways:

> TUONI: As I was saying to you before, gentlemen of this committee, the best thing is to close the papers, close the Italian broadcasting, reorganize or close the Italian organizations, they are poison—this is the time that the Italians should come into the American family and to breathe finally the free atmosphere of this country. If you do not do that, they will still persist in a campaign which finally the result will be you will have the Italians away from the American family, and maybe tomorrow the situation will be as to the war effort right here in San Francisco.
>
> DR. KELLEMS: It is your opinion—or rather, I should say conviction—that there are a special group of people whose culture and background is so different from ours, and I think we do admit it is radically different—
>
> TUONI: (Interrupting) Yes.
>
> DR. KELLEMS: (Continuing)—and it will only be possible for them to forget that only if they will enter the American way of life—
>
> TUONI: (Interrupting) They will.
>
> DR. KELLEMS: (Continuing)—and I believe they will. Is it not your feeling that instead of persisting generation after generation teaching these things, creating a Little Italy here, that they will only find their own happiness and strength by forgetting...?[3]

Thus did the Tenney Committee put into words what the federal government had already put into action: Italian Americans had to prove their loyalty. The way to do that was to *forget*—forget what they knew, forget who they were. To become American, that is, to be trusted as loyal Americans in the crisis at hand, a kind of cultural amnesia was required. The old ways, never quite adequate to the new world in any case, had become fatally corrupted by their association with the Fascist government with whom the United States was now at war.

Like Japanese Americans, for whom the equation bore an even more pernicious meaning—i.e. that even American birth did not erase Japanese ways, for those ways were racial, genetic, indelible—Italian Americans had already gotten the message. They got it right after Pearl Harbor when the older immigrants among them without citizenship—600,000 of them nationwide—were branded enemy aliens. They got it when all 600,000 were required to register and carry pink booklets identifying them as such. They got it when all 600,000 had to turn in "contraband," such as radios with a shortwave band. They got it when untold numbers had their homes entered and searched to make sure they were not harboring those radios or other contraband in secret, a crime for which they could be arrested. They got it when some 10,000 in California were forced to move from their homes in prohibited zones and another 52,000 were subjected to a dusk-to-dawn curfew. And they got it when hundreds like Louis Berizzi, usually the publishers and writers of Italian newspapers, or teachers in Italian-language schools, or Italian veterans of World War I, or those maintaining suspiciously close ties to their mother country, suddenly disappeared from the community, whisked away to places of internment that remained secret to all but their families (and for a time, even to them) for the duration of the war.

Italian Americans got the message and they felt shamed. For that is what happens. People who have done nothing wrong and are targeted as enemies feel shame. They feel, that is, that if the penalty they have incurred is not for something they have done, then it must be due to *what they are*. "Something is wrong with who I am"—that is the basis of shaming, and that is what reached its climax during the war. "We are Italian, and Italy has become the enemy, so to the extent that we are that, we are the enemy; inimical to America and the American way"—to counter which accusation one must suppress, keep hidden, keep secret, forget, and, to the degree that it is possible, change.

It is for these reasons—secreting and forgetting, aided and abetted by a healthy dose of government suppression of the facts—that fifty years after these wartime events took place, they remained unknown not just to the vast majority of Americans, but to the majority of Italian Americans themselves. And it was for the same reasons that we in the American Italian Historical Association's western chapter put together an exhibit about these events in 1994 and called it *Una Storia Segreta*.

Una Storia Segreta. The words in Italian mean both "a secret story" and "a secret history": both the secret shame of those who suffered the wartime restrictions, and the dirty little secret of those who imposed them.

Like the exhibit itself, this volume is intended to inform those who have been told repeatedly that these events did not happen that, in fact, *they did*. It is also meant to help those who suffered the events realize that they were not alone, and to place their experience in a broader historical context—one, indeed, that includes the more widespread and egregious violations suffered by Japanese Americans at the same time. Not least is it meant to remind those who have denied these events that the secret is uncovered, it has developed a life of its own, and cannot be re-secreted in the back room of nonhistory, ever.[4]

For we now know what Rose Scherini has been doggedly uncovering over a period of more than twenty years: FBI files indicate that many, if not most internees from San Francisco were incarcerated on suspicions that would be laughable were they not so painful for the families involved. This and much more about the general shape and tenor of the government measures imposed on Italian Americans are included in her essay "When Italian Americans Were 'Enemy Aliens.'" Scherini's second piece, "Letters to 3024 Pierce," fills in this general picture with the specifics of one internee's experience, as told through his correspondence with his wife and six-year-old daughter.

We also know what Stephen Fox was the first to report in 1988: that a large-scale "Relocation of Italian Americans in California during World War II" did in fact take place in February of 1942; and that an even larger relocation was pursued by government officials and by Lieutenant General John DeWitt of the Western Defense Command for several months afterwards, until it was laid to rest by a president concerned primarily about the economic and political damage that would result from so large a movement of people.[5]

Geoffrey Dunn pursues this same story from the vantage point of how it played in the Santa Cruz area. In *"Mala Notte"*—a name coined by his grandmother for the "bad night" of February 24, 1942, when she had to leave her home in a prohibited zone—Dunn describes how the wartime restrictions rocked the largely Italian fishing community of Santa Cruz. Along the way he points up the contradiction felt by some of his own family members, who came home on leave from the navy to find a boarded-up house and their mother evacuated they knew not where.

Gloria Ricci Lothrop does the same for Southern California. In "Unwelcome in Freedom's Land: The Impact of World War II on Italian Aliens in Southern California," Lothrop draws on her own family's experience and on current research to demonstrate that the restrictions were implemented far differently, if not haphazardly, in various areas of California and the United States.

Guido Tintori returns us to the fight between the Justice and War Departments over enemy-alien policy in "New Discoveries, Old Prejudices: The Internment of Italian Americans during World War II," along the way making several signal discoveries. First, he points out that the much-heralded removal of enemy-alien status from Italian Americans on Columbus Day in 1942 derived not from within the Justice Department itself, as previously thought, nor even through the influence of *prominenti* like labor leader Luigi

Antonini, but via a series of position papers emanating from the Office of War Intelligence, papers which eventually reached the Oval Office through the sympathetic hands of Eleanor Roosevelt. Tintori's second major discovery has to do with the Provost Marshal General's Office. Searching the National Archives, he was able to uncover, after more than fifty years, documents that provide information on every internee of Italian descent. The importance of this discovery cannot be overestimated, for it has provided us with the name and disposition of each internee—information heretofore unavailable except in some dozen cases on the West Coast.

That information forms the underpinning of several articles I have been able to write for this volume. The War Department's internee files contain not only the Basic Personnel Record for each internee, but also copies of internee letters, transcripts of conversations with visitors, parole orders, and various other documents. The death certificate of Giuseppe Protto in his file confirmed what his friend Prospero Cecconi wrote about that same death in his notebook, featured in "Morto il Camerata." Deletions from censored letters inform the essay on "Let's Keep Smiling: Conditions in Internment Camps." Information on internee families adds depth and variety to the essay about Italian Americans and the military, "War Within War." And letters from two internees who were not aliens but naturalized citizens—a situation no one suspected before these files came to light—were indispensable to the essay "A Tale of Two Citizens." In short, the ability to locate and search through internee files has added immeasurably to the depth and breadth of the knowledge now available about the internment of Italian resident aliens during World War II.

To be sure, the knowledge we have accumulated over the past few years, especially where the presence of the exhibit *Una Storia Segreta* has stimulated survivors in a community to remember their own stories, cannot be overlooked. It is that knowledge which led directly to my essay "A Fish Story," an account of the way the wartime restrictions devastated Italian fishing communities, such as Pittsburg and Monterey in California and Boston on the East Coast. Likewise, from our work with the exhibit have come the excerpts also printed here: Remo Bosia's account of his endless battle with Lieutenant General DeWitt, as told in "The General and I"; Jerre Mangione's chapter about his 1943 inspection tour of the internment camps, "Concentration Camps— American Style," as it appears in his memoir, *An Ethnic at Large*; and Sal Colletto's unique, originally handwritten narrative about his adventures fishing the Pacific during the war, "A Sardine Fisherman."

Last but by no means least, all of these circumstances together made possible the collection of personal memoirs and letters that enliven these pages. In that regard, *Una Storia Segreta* has been a double-edged sword. On the one hand, the very name has attached to these events their singular mark, their logo, their power as secret, in the public mind. The story remains *segreta*, even where it becomes well known. On the other hand, the very fact of its secrecy has induced those who witnessed these events to remember them, impelled them to tell what they saw and heard and felt. Something powerful is released when such a secret can be brought to light, something contagious that wants to tell more, for the secret itself is always a demand to reveal it. Thus, a vital part of this volume is the secrets told, the secrets brought—however reluctantly or painfully—to light; and though I cannot mention them all here, I can express my admiration for the courage it has taken to voice them, as well as my gratitude for having been allowed to witness that voicing—one voice at a time.

For in the end, in this age of mass humanity and mass movements, when only what happens to masses, in massive numbers, can pierce the cacophony of voices competing for our attention, that is what *Una Storia Segreta* amounts to. A story of our time. A story of orders and restrictions and humiliations imposed, quietly, one person at a time. Of men in suits coming to search, suddenly, one home at a time. Of families bereft of parent or husband or father, one day at a time. Of estrangement and suspicion and return, one parole at a time. Of days and days thereafter repeating the one phrase each time: "Don't talk about it."

Until one day, one voice says yes. It did. It was. It was *Two Men in Suits with Orders to Take Him Away*. It was *My Uncle Augusto, Sundays in Colma*. *A Tragic Episode, Wrong Side of the Highway, A Market Off Limits* it was; and *Pippo l'Americano, Alien in Texas, You Can Go Home Now, Rejected First Generation, Exclusion* it was. That's what it was. What it was was a *four-letter word*.

A secret mother of a story. One voice. At a time.

Lawrence DiStasi
March 2001

Endnotes:
1. Copy of undated letter from Louis Berizzi to hearing board in possession of Lucetta Berizzi Drypolcher.
2. Actually, the United States did not declare war on Italy until December 11. Nonetheless, on December 8 the president signed Proclamation 2527, which stated that "an invasion or predatory incursion is threatened upon the territory of the United States by Italy" and that therefore all Italian-born noncitizens were henceforth "alien enemies" of the United States, subject to arrest and internment—though even before this proclamation, some enemy aliens, like Filippo Molinari, had already been arrested.
3. Joint Fact-Finding Committee on Un-American Activities in California, transcript, pp. 3667–68.

4. This is all the more true now that the Wartime Violation of Italian American Civil Liberties Act has been signed into law. H.R. 2442 was introduced in the House by Representatives Rick Lazio and Eliot Engel of New York, and its companion bill, S. 1909, was introduced in the Senate by Senator Robert Torricelli of New Jersey. The legislation, which includes provisions for a comprehensive study, release of records, public education, and funding and recommends a formal acknowledgment of these wartime events by the president, became Public Law 106–451 on November 7, 2000.

5. Stephen Fox's first article on these events, "General DeWitt and the Proposed Internment of German and Italian Aliens during World War II," appeared in the *Pacific Historical Review* in 1988. His book on the subject, *The Unknown Internment*, was published by Twayne Publishers in 1990.

Morto il Camerata

by Lawrence DiStasi

In a notebook kept by Prospero Cecconi during his internment as an allegedly dangerous enemy alien during World War II and only recently found by his daughter Doris Giuliotti, we find this terse comment recorded for July 7, 1942:

> July 7. *Morto il camerata Protto.*[1]

"My comrade Protto has died." Nothing more. The notebook contains no further references to internee Protto or to his death in camp, notwithstanding the fact that he was one of only a very few internees of Italian descent who died while imprisoned, or that the journal entries in the little ring-bound notebook Cecconi titled "Via Crucis" continue for another three years. Just the cryptic comment about the death of a friend.

It is a comment all the more moving for that austere matter-of-factness because, in its way, it perfectly encapsulates what Italian Americans endured on the home front during World War II and the way they responded to it.

To understand this, it will be helpful to know something about the Italians who emigrated to the United States in the first part of the twentieth century in such huge numbers that, by 1940, they comprised the largest foreign-born group in America.

To begin with, though Italian emigration was a long and complex phenomenon, one generalization can be made: the average person who left his village rarely did so except under severe economic duress. This is because roots run deep in Italy, and a person's identity within a specific region, and within that region a specific village, and within that village a specific familial house and plot of land, is virtually unshakeable. The result was that most villagers who left Italy planned to return some day and buy the house or plot of land that would allow them and their families to survive and perhaps even thrive in a known place and in a known way.[2] This dream of return figured as strong or stronger than the dream of succeeding in America itself. With it went a longing for the soil and scent and social life of the Italian village that survived every degradation and disappointment met in the cities of America. No matter that

Italian immigrants were treated in America as the lowest of the low; no matter that they were exploited and lynched and vilified for everything from their foods to their religious practices to their language; in the colonies they created to mimic, however crudely, the villages they had left, they could find others who shared their lot, and places and organizations by means of which they could keep their dream of return alive, even as they saw its realization growing dimmer with each new Americanism—hairstyle, dress, language, schooling—adopted and brought home by their children.

It was there, in those Italian colonies present in every major city of America, that the Fascist government which took power in Italy in 1922 found its most receptive audience. For Benito Mussolini had the insight to recognize that Italian immigrants did indeed long for Italy, and longed for it increasingly in proportion to the Americanization they saw seeping into and around them. Accordingly, his government orchestrated programs—such as Italian-language schools offered free to children of immigrants—designed to exploit that longing, increase it, and turn it to support for his grandiose plans to make Italy a major world power. All this was expressed in a simple declaration: once an Italian, always an Italian. No matter where in the world you may settle, you can never lose your *Italianità*—your Italianness. No matter how long you have been away, or how far you have roamed, you and your descendants will always be able to share in Italian greatness. Such a message played perfectly into hearts and minds that had been wrenched from their true place and which were constantly under assault from a society which seemed to have nothing but scorn for that place. Though the original longing of most had focused not on the nation but on a specific village or region, Mussolini's moves and message were intended to inexorably focus that longing on the national entity now called *Italia*. And what increased its cachet was that it had become an entity which steadily appeared to be garnering from the American public the admiration and respect it and its impoverished migrants in America had for so long lacked.

Increasingly, then, throughout the 1930s, Italian American newspapers and radio programs celebrated the apparent triumphs of Mussolini and his Fascist government. Both domestic and foreign policy seemed to be racking up one success after another, and the immigrants, so long forced into a humiliating silence in the face of their suppression by the Anglo-American majority, became gradually more vocal in their support for their homeland, its culture, and the increasingly pivotal position it seemed to be assuming on the world stage.

This new visibility would come back to haunt those who indulged in it, for beginning in 1939, the FBI began keeping track of all who voiced such opinions. Consulting ethnic newspapers, organizations, and a host of informants, it began preparing a list of Americans with roots in Germany, Italy, and Japan whom the FBI thought might be dangerous to national security in the event of war. That many appeared on this list who were harmless, or even opposed to the enemy governments in question, did not deter those who prepared it. The result was that when Pearl Harbor was attacked on the night of December 7, 1941, the attorney general activated this "Custodial Detention List." Federal agents in every part of the United States began what the *Los Angeles Times* called a "great manhunt" to take the noncitizens on the list into custody. In the Italian community, upwards of 1,500 resident aliens were eventually arrested and given hearings meant to determine how dangerous they were. Some 257 of those deemed most dangerous were then interned for the duration of the war. Until recently, almost no one knew who or even how many they were, exactly, or what they had gone through.

Prospero Cecconi as he appeared in 1936. Courtesy of Doris Giuliotti

Prospero Cecconi was one of those 257 interned, though he was not among the first ones arrested in December. For some reason it took the FBI until February 21, 1942, to decide he was dangerous. This seems to have been a banner day for arrests, particularly in and around San Francisco, due, perhaps, to the promulgation two days before of Executive Order 9066, which authorized the U.S. government to intern not just enemy aliens, but anyone, including citizens. At 5 p.m. that day, agents picked Cecconi up at his place of work—he was a pasta maker at the Roma macaroni factory in North Beach—and took him to the detention center which the Immigration and Naturalization Service (INS) had set up at a former Bible college on Silver Avenue in San Francisco. There he was interrogated and, on March 10, given his official hearing, a procedure at which the detainee was considered guilty unless he could prove his innocence before a three-man hearing board. Like many others denied a lawyer or any knowledge of the charges, and lacking a thorough command of English, Cecconi failed to convince the board of his innocence and was ordered interned. That began a series of travels from internment camp to internment camp which was typical for Italian American internees.

Cecconi recorded his travels in his notebook. On March 30, he wrote that he had been transferred to the quonset huts which formed the hastily constructed INS detention center at Sharp Park, a little town on the coast just below San Francisco (now part of Pacifica). He remained there until April 21, when he recorded another transfer, this time to the army-controlled Fort McDowell on Angel Island, in the middle of San Francisco Bay. It was on that day that his photo and fingerprints were recorded for War Department files: both the official PMGO Form 2 and Cecconi's notebook testify to this, though the notebook is more vivid. It says, "We arrived at 7 o'clock and truth was quietly fear. Pitcher, finger print, and searching our clothes."* The army recorded that internee ISN-19-4-I-24-CI had $125 in defense bonds on his person and $13.87 in cash. Cecconi's next move came on May 20, when his notebook says he left Fort McDowell and in three days reached Fort Sam Houston, Texas, his first out-of-state internment camp.

Giuseppe Protto was arrested on the same day, February 21, as Cecconi. Unaccountably, he was kept at Sharp Park until June 2, when he was taken to Angel Island's Fort McDowell to be formally recorded as interned, and then, after two days, sent off to Fort Sam Houston to rejoin his comrade Prospero Cecconi.

As to the central question—why these two men were deemed too dangerous to remain at liberty—it is not easily answered. During the war, no person of Italian extraction was ever charged with, much less convicted of, espionage or sabotage or any other hostile action. Virtually all were interned for what authorities thought they *might* do, based on their past sentiments or writings or associations. Many of those initially arrested were thought to be community leaders— Italian newspaper writers and editors, radio broadcasters, or heads of organizations with some link, however tenuous, to the Italian government.

Cecconi and his friend Protto, contrarily, were simply workers. Cecconi had, it is true, served in the Italian army in World War I and been captured by the Austrians (a postcard he wrote from his prison camp is extant), but in that war, America and Italy were allies. His problem probably arose from the fact that, as a World War I Italian veteran, he had joined a veteran's group known as the *Ex Combattenti*, a kind of Italian Veterans of Foreign Wars. This was a

---

*Cecconi's original spelling has been retained in this and the following quotations.

group the FBI had targeted as "highly dangerous," ostensibly because of its role in collecting money and gold rings in America to be sent to Italian war widows and orphans. The group was duly registered and legal, it had suspended its fundraising activities in May 1941 when its permit was rescinded by the State Department, and it had disbanded two days after war with Italy was declared on December 11, 1941, but these facts did not seem to affect the FBI's assessment. Membership in the *Ex Combattenti* was an almost certain ticket to an internment camp.

Another problem for Cecconi was the fact that his family—a wife and two daughters—had lived in Italy since 1936. Though Cecconi had immigrated to America in 1924, to be joined by his wife, his daughter Rita, and his sister Elvisa in 1926, he had returned to Italy with his family (which by then included seven-year-old Doris) in 1936. According to Doris,[3] Cecconi longed for his hometown of Crespiano, where his mother still lived

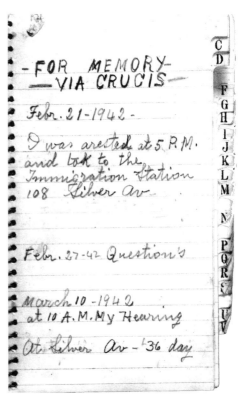

A page from "Via Crucis," the notebook Prospero Cecconi kept during his internment. Courtesy of Doris Giuliotti.

and where the family owned a house. To clear up affairs from the sale of his wife's cleaning business, however, Cecconi decided to return to San Francisco around 1939, to dispose of furniture and perhaps make a little more money for his family. It was an unfortunate decision. The outbreak of war on December 7, 1941, caught him still in San Francisco, and so the man who had been a prisoner of the Austrians in World War I became likewise a prisoner, of the opposite side this time, in World War II.

As for Giuseppe Protto, all we know is that he was listed as a "junk man" by the War Department.[4] Whether this meant he worked with the garbage collectors, then mostly Italian, is not clear. He claimed no wife or family in the United States or elsewhere, and only one contact, a friend named Pete Montobios. Like Cecconi, Protto had been born in Argentina. Perhaps this, and the fact that both had been arrested on the same day, in the same city, and gone the same route through detention centers and internment camps drew them together when Protto arrived at Fort Sam Houston in early June of 1942 and rejoined Cecconi.

Of that reunion we know almost nothing. We do not know if it was joyous. We do not know if the two internees compared notes about their experiences. Nor do we know whether Protto was ill by then, or if he was feeling depressed because of his internment. All we know is what is recorded in Prospero Cecconi's little notebook. On May 23, it tells us that Cecconi arrived at Fort Sam Houston and "was received with cortesy" and "found the fine tend [tents in which internees often lived while interned] and plenty of innabitant." On May 28, "I received prisoner clothing." On May 31 it was "heavy raining," which rains continued through June 15. On June 17, "I left Fort Sam Houston San Antonio Texas, and have 32 hours on the train and arrived here in Camp Forest Tenn." On June 19 is added this bit of ironic observation about his arrival in Tennessee, in Italian: *"ed accolti dal publico e dai soldati (col massimo rispeto) fischi ed insulti d'aqui genere"* [and received from the public and the soldiers (with maximum respect), whistles and insults typical of their kind].

Protto's War Department record confirms Cecconi's account, noting that he too arrived at Camp Forrest, Tennessee, on June 19, no doubt on the same train, sitting beside his friend Cecconi, perhaps responding with the same irony to the derisive greeting they received.

Then comes the fatal entry in Cecconi's journal on July 7:

Morto il camerata Protto.

"My comrade Protto has died." Stoic, almost Homeric in its brevity, the report tops the page alone, surrounded by white silence.

And therein lies the essence of the story we are considering. Though we are eager to find out what happened, what caused what the army hospital called in its report "a cerebral embolus"—a sudden clot or blockage in a blood vessel—we are left imagining. Had Giuseppe Protto exhibited a history of heart disease before? Atrial fibrillation perhaps, which, if left untreated, can sometimes release a blood clot from the heart? Did the camp doctors know about it? Did they care?

We do not know.

And from Prospero Cecconi, the sole recorded witness to his comrade's death, only *"Morto il camerata."* Does this mean there had been no illness leading up to the final one? Would Cecconi not have noted that in his journal? All we know is that he did not. Nothing is noted about the events in Camp Forrest from June 19 till July 7, when Giuseppe Protto suddenly died.

But why, we want to ask. Why nothing more? Surely Cecconi cared. Called Protto his "comrade": comrade in misfortune, comrade in arms, traveling companion from internment camp to internment camp, fellow Argentine, fellow Italian, fellow worker with his hands, fellow prisoner dwelling in camp tents in the rain, cleaning latrines, growing flowers, laughing at the food, joking dryly at the greetings they received, smoking into the night discussing their fate, the world, life in San Francisco compared to the Italy they had left, perhaps the Argentina they remembered—the two seared in friendship by their similar stories, their similar fears and pains and grievances against their adopted country, which had branded them enemies and imprisoned them.

"My comrade is dead." Nothing more. Nothing about how it hit him, laid him low. Nothing about the funeral service. Were Cecconi and the others allowed to attend? We don't know—all we have are the cold, confirmatory facts

The front of the Basic Personnel Record (PMGO Form 2) for Cecconi's comrade, Giuseppe Protto. Courtesy of National Archives and Records Administration, College Park, Md.

typed in the space for remarks at the bottom of Giuseppe Protto's record: "Died, cerebral embolus, 11:05 A.M., July 7, 1942. Buried Grave #31, Maplewood Cemetery, Tullahoma, Tennessee, July 10, 1942. Catholic services rendered."[5]

The rest is silence.

Which it remained evermore, apparently. Cecconi's daughter Doris Giuliotti maintains that she never heard her father say a word about Protto—which she did not find all that surprising. He was a taciturn man, her father. Very religious. Speaking only when he had something important to say. A quiet man who responded to the death of his friend as he did to all else: with silence.

And that says it all. The entire wartime ordeal for Italian Americans was blanketed in silence. It is a response testified to by many, many others: we didn't speak about it. Weren't allowed to even raise the question. Too painful, perhaps. Too shameful. Which could never be mentioned either—how it hurt. Only after many, many years could it be even referred to, with a bitter laugh perhaps: such is the way of the world. What is the good of complaining?

Even in that notebook, upon the death of a friend, there is no complaint, no sign of pain.

And yet. There is the notebook's title, "Via Crucis."[6] Prospero Cecconi likened his wartime journey to the way of Christ dragging his cross, in agony, to Calvary. Only that *that* way, *that* agony, were said to heal the sins of the world.

What had Prospero Cecconi's journey healed? Or the death of his friend? Whom had they served?[7]

We have only a few hints. "He was bitter," says his daughter Doris. "He had done nothing, and it cost him two years of his life." And when he was finally paroled in October 1943, the stomach ulcers for which he was first hospitalized in the internment camp at Missoula, Montana, brought him close to death. He landed in the hospital in San Francisco with peritonitis and no family to care for him, only the social worker at the Italian Welfare Agency, his parole sponsor and steadfast friend Rina Bocci, to look in on him from time to time and coax him back to health.[8] It was she, as well, who intervened when he applied for citizenship in 1945 and was turned down. She it was who got him a top lawyer to work pro bono, with the result that finally, on November 25, 1945, Prospero Cecconi, former internee of war, received his U.S. *carta di cittadinanza*, whose number he carefully recorded in his little notebook: "No. 6690034, Petition No. 79873." Like a talisman.

But though his daughters returned to resettle in California after the war, and though his wife would have come back too, Prospero Cecconi had been wounded once too often. In 1951, he departed from the United States for good, to live out his days with his wife and mother in his home town of Crespiano, province of Massa Carrara, Italy. It was a place where, when he got depressed, as he often did, he could pack a sandwich and a little wine and walk in the nearby mountains he loved, to eat his lunch and drink his wine and sip water from a spring he knew there, which, alone of all the places he had been in his life, was able to restore him.

Endnotes

1. Prospero Cecconi, journal entry, unpaginated manuscript, personal holdings of Doris Giuliotti.

2. See Dino Cinel, *From Italy to San Francisco: The Immigrant Experience* (Stanford: Stanford University Press, 1982) p. 65. As one peasant in the province of Cosenza said about the value of land in his native village, "This is the only true land. We can live somewhere else for a while. But we can buy land only here."

3. All information on Prospero Cecconi's personal life derives from personal interviews with Doris Giuliotti.

4. PMGO Form 2 from Giuseppe Protto file, RG 389, Records Relating to Italian Civilian Internees During WWII, 1941–46, Boxes 2–20, Provost Marshal General's Office, National Archives and Records Administration, College Park, Md.

5. Ibid.

6. The title of Cecconi's notebook would seem to be an appropriate rejoinder to Tom Brokaw's comment in *The Greatest Generation* (New York: Random House, 1998, p. 216), that wartime for Italian Americans amounted to little more than "some uncomfortable moments." So should the fact, only recently uncovered in War Department files, that Protto was not the only internee who died while interned. Three other Italian American internees are now known to have died while they were interned: Ben Gasparini (McAlester), Emil Theodori (Missoula), and a woman, Claudia Hoppe (Seagoville). These deaths and the five suicides we know about among Italian resident aliens who were despondent over their ignominious fate should end, once and for all, comments that trivialize the impact of the wartime measures, or those Italian Americans who suffered them.

7. This question forms the basis of much of the recent response to the story now known as *Una Storia Segreta*. Who was served by the arrests, searches and seizures, evacuations, and exiles? Consider these words from the records of the Justice Department and its head at the time, Attorney General Francis E. Biddle. On July 16, 1943, he wrote a memo to Assistant Attorney General Hugh Cox and FBI chief J. Edgar Hoover which said, in part, "The department fulfills its proper functions by investigating the activities of persons who may have violated the law. It is not aided in this work by classifying persons as to dangerousness…it is now clear to me that this classification system is inherently unreliable. The evidence used for the purpose of making the classifications was inadequate; the standards applied to the evidence for the purpose of making the classifications were defective; and finally, the notion that it is possible to make a valid determination as to how dangerous a person is in the abstract and without reference to time, environment, and other relevant circumstances is impractical, unwise, and dangerous."

   For this and other reasons, Congressmen Eliot Engel and Rick Lazio of New York introduced H.R. 2442, the Wartime Violation of Italian American Civil Liberties Act, in August of 1997. That act was passed by the House of Representatives on November 10, 1999. A Senate version of the bill, S. 1909, was introduced by Senator Robert Torricelli of New Jersey. The legislation passed the Senate on October 19, 2000, and was signed by President Clinton on election day, November 7, 2000. Now Public Law 106–451, it at last ends the official silence and denial of the United States government about these events.

8. Rina Bocci also aided Cecconi in being fully released from parole, which he considered a continuing humiliation. Here is part of what she is reported to have told the immigration inspector: "He feels grateful that he was released from internment; however, the parole is also caus-

When Italian Americans Were "Enemy Aliens"

by Rose D. Scherini

Rose Scherini is the daughter of Italian immigrants who settled in the San Francisco Bay Area in 1921. She has a doctorate in educational anthropology from the University of California, Berkeley, and was, until 1986, on the staff of the Office of Student Research at that university. For over twenty years she has been investigating the World War II experiences of Italian Americans in California, authoring *The Italian American Community of San Francisco* (Arno Press, 1980) and several articles, including "Executive Order 9066 and Italian Americans: The San Francisco Story" in *California History* (Winter 1991–92) and "The Fascist/Anti-Fascist Struggle in San Francisco" in *New Explorations in Italian American Studies* (Richard N. and Sandra P. Juliani, eds.; American Italian Historical Assocation, 1994). She is the curator of the exhibit *Una Storia Segreta: When Italian Americans Were "Enemy Aliens,"* which opened at San Francisco's Museo ItaloAmericano in 1994 and has traveled throughout the United States for the last six years. She is the vice president of the American Italian Historical Association's western chapter.

Nineteen forty-two, the first full year of World War II for the United States, was devastating for many Italian families, who were part of the largest immigrant group in the nation. For all "enemy aliens"—Japanese, Germans, and Italians—this was a time of fear and uncertainty. New regulations required the 600,000 Italian "resident aliens" to carry photo-identity cards, restricted their freedom of movement, and forced an estimated 10,000 Italians along the West Coast to relocate. Local police searched many homes to enforce prohibitions against aliens' possession of guns, cameras, and shortwave radios; within six months, 1,500 Italians were arrested for curfew, travel, and contraband violations; and some 250 Italians were sent to military camps for up to two years. Even some

This article was first published in *Enemies Within: Italian and Other Internees in Canada and Abroad* (Franca Iacovetta, Roberto Perin, and Angelo Principe, eds.; Toronto: University of Toronto Press, 2000). It is reprinted here with permission of the publisher.

naturalized citizens had to leave their homes and businesses because the military decided that they were too "dangerous" to remain in strategic areas.[1] Only on Columbus Day in October 1942 did the situation begin to improve.

By 1941, there had been Italians in the United States for more than a hundred years. Peak immigration took place between 1900 and 1920, slowing after the Immigration Law of 1924, which cut back quotas for Italy and other southern European nations. However, by that time, Italians and Germans were the two largest immigrant groups in the country, and in 1940, Italians were the largest foreign-born group.

At first, Italians were viewed with suspicion and distrust as outsiders from a very different culture who did not even speak English. Many were uneducated and worked at the most menial jobs, but a well-educated minority soon became successful in business and professional careers. When the war came, the mayors of two major cities on the Atlantic and Pacific coasts were of Italian descent: Fiorello La Guardia in New York City and Angelo Rossi in San Francisco.

After Britain and France had declared war on Germany in early September 1939, the United States had declared itself a neutral nation, and President Franklin D. Roosevelt proclaimed a state of "limited national emergency." Privately, the president had requested the Federal Bureau of Investigation (FBI) to prepare, in conjunction with the army and navy intelligence units, a list of "potentially dangerous" persons to be detained in case of national conflict. This came to be known as the Custodial Detention List. Then, in June 1940, Congress passed the Smith Act, requiring all aliens to register and report any change of residence or employment. That same month, Italy entered the war on the side of the Axis and joined in the attack on France. Within months, Congress passed the Selective Service Act, requiring men between twenty-one and thirty-five years of age to undergo one year of military training. The following March, the Lend-Lease Act authorized "all possible aid to Britain." The president authorized the FBI to wiretap "persons suspected of subversive activities," with emphasis on aliens. In June, a German submarine sank an American merchant ship, and Roosevelt declared a state of "unlimited national emergency." That same month, the United States closed Italian and German consulates in the country and repatriated the diplomatic staff. Thus were events set in motion that eventually led to Italian resident aliens becoming enemy aliens for most of 1942.[2]

Internment of "Dangerous" Aliens

Arrests of enemy aliens began the night of December 7, 1941. Early that morning, Japanese airplanes had attacked ships of the U.S. naval fleet at Pearl

Harbor, Hawaii. After the news reached President Roosevelt just before 2:00 P.M. Washington time, he conferred with key government officials during the afternoon and evening and planned emergency procedures went into effect. The office of the attorney general prepared arrest warrants for certain Japanese, German, and Italian aliens, and that evening and over the next several weeks the FBI detained 1,540 Japanese Americans, 1,260 German Americans, and 231 Italian Americans.[3]

Many of those arrested and later interned were longtime residents and, while not naturalized citizens, had American-born children or wives who were U.S. citizens. Although the authorities never informed these individuals of the reasons for their detention, it is apparent from their FBI records that nearly all fell into one or more of these three categories: members of the Federation of Italian War Veterans, or IWV (veterans of the First World War in Italy known as *Ex Combattenti* in the Italian community); editor/writers for Italian-language newspapers and announcers on Italian-language radio; and instructors in Italian-language schools sponsored by an Italian consulate.

The FBI had identified these organizations as profascist and had placed the names of members and staffs on the Custodial Detention List. Although the Italian veterans in the United States had fought with the Allies against Germany in the "Great War," the IWV, with headquarters in Rome, was then associated with Mussolini's government. Branches in major U.S. cities had raised funds for Italian war widows and orphans under a permit issued by the U.S. State Department. When that permit was rescinded in May 1941, the organization ceased its fund-raising. Nonetheless, all noncitizen members were interned, and even naturalized citizens were later ordered to relocate from areas that the military designated off limits for individuals on the Custodial Detention List. According to an August 1942 Department of Justice document, there was a "lack of evidence of any subversive activities" on the part of the IWV; and although there had been a "technical violation" of the Foreign Agent Registration Act, the consular agents considered that all "the leaders of the organization" had been repatriated to Italy prior to December 1941. And so the Department of Justice saw no point in prosecuting the organization as subversive. Indeed, the group had actually disbanded two days after the United States declared war on Italy. Perhaps this decision was unknown to the War Department, which continued to take action against it, ordering the exclusion a month later of a dozen or more IWV members, even though they were naturalized citizens. All noncitizen members had already been interned for several months.[4]

In the case of Italian-language newspapers, only a handful of key staff on major western papers were interned or, in cases of naturalized citizens, later excluded from the prohibited areas. On the West Coast, San Francisco's *L'Italia*, Los Angeles's *La Parola*, and Sacramento's *La Capitale* lost their editors and other staff, and some papers simply closed. Yet the authorities never touched Generoso Pope, the editor/publisher of New York's *Il Progresso Italo-Americano*, the profascist paper with the largest circulation. That was perhaps because Pope was a powerful man with contacts at the highest levels of the government. By contrast, Ettore Patrizi, editor/publisher of San Francisco's *L'Italia*, was ordered excluded from the area of the Western Defense Command (WDC), even though he was seventy-six and in ill health.[5]

There was almost no publicity about this internment of Americans, and the public, even most Italian Americans, knew nothing about it then or later, partly because the explicit government policy was to keep it confidential. The exact number and names of internees remain unknown, and various sources report the number as 228, 250, or 277. Some names have become known to researchers, who have located and interviewed their families. Unfortunately, no internee himself has been interviewed, as all died before contact was made with the families. Like the Japanese American story, it has taken a new generation to reopen this history.[6]

When the FBI arrived to arrest an alien, it told him and his family only that there was a presidential warrant for the arrest. Individuals were held in a detention facility of the Immigration and Naturalization Service (INS) and later transported to a military camp in an inland state, still not knowing the reasons for the arrest or what to expect.

Filippo Molinari, sales representative for *L'Italia* in San Jose and an IWV member, described his arrest on December 7, 1941, in a letter to a relative many years later: "I was the first one arrested in San Jose the night of the attack on Pearl Harbor. At 11 P.M. three policemen came to the front door and two at the back. They told me that, by order of President Roosevelt, I must go with them. They didn't even give me time to go to my room and put on my shoes. I was wearing slippers. They took me to prison...and finally to Missoula, Montana, on the train, over the snow, still with slippers on my feet, the temperature at seventeen below and no coat or heavy clothes!"[7]

FBI agents arrested Carmelo Ilacqua at his San Francisco home one evening the week before Christmas 1941, searched his desk, found no "incriminating" papers, and yet detained him at the local INS facility. His family learned of his whereabouts only several days later, when he telephoned to say he was leaving for "parts unknown." He and some other Italian and Japanese Americans were transported in a train with armed guards to Fort Missoula, Montana. The army had refurbished this old fort in the spring of 1941 to house Italian nationals who were merchant sailors from several luxury liners quarantined in U.S. ports at war's outbreak. Ilacqua, forty-six, had emigrated to the United States in 1924 and resided in San Francisco since 1928. As a "local employee" at the Italian consulate, he provided liaison with immigrants and their organizations and was contact person for visiting Italian ships, having been a merchant marine officer in Italy. Married to a naturalized citizen, he was the father of a six-year-old daughter when the FBI arrested him. At the time, the FBI knew little about him except that he had held the position of "chancellor" at the consulate until it was closed in June, and that he was a member and former officer of the *Ex Combattenti* and an admitted past member of the Italian Fascist Party—a requirement of employment at the consulate in the 1930s. Another requirement was Italian citizenship, and Ilacqua had applied for U.S. citizenship within days of the consulate's closure.

The first FBI report about Ilacqua is dated January 10, 1942, when he was already interned in Fort Missoula. His FBI file consists primarily of apparently unimportant or unverified bits of information: that he was the "dominating figure" and "most active member in the San Francisco section of the *[Ex] Combattenti*"; that search of his residence "failed to reveal any pertinent evidence"; that he "apparently directed the...collection campaign" of the IWV; and that he was "observed to leave the *Tatu Maru*" on March 20, 1941. (In fact, he was on the Japanese ship to pick up Italian diplomatic mail then being routed through Japan because of the submarine war in the Atlantic.) The FBI file also contains twelve pages that appear to be a record of phone taps on the consulate's telephone lines from February through June 1941; the notes on Ilacqua's conversations reveal only normal contacts with local Italian American organizations.[8]

The army censored all mail to and from internees, who could write only two short letters and one postcard per week.[9] Bruna Ilacqua saved the letters that her husband wrote during his two-year detention, and this correspondence serves as the basis for much of the information available on life in these internment camps.* Ilacqua and some other San Francisco internees were moved to a new camp every three or four months and were in four camps, in Montana, Oklahoma, Tennessee, and Texas. The reason for these moves is not clear; perhaps it was partly wartime chaos, space needs for the increasing numbers of incoming prisoners of war, or fear that these "dangerous" persons might revolt and attempt to escape.

When internees arrived at their first internment camp, a hearing was held before an "enemy alien hearing board" with two army officers and two citizens, usually attorneys or professors. The accused was not informed of the charges against him or allowed representation by legal counsel. Individuals

---

*See "Letters to 3024 Pierce," p. 223, for more about the Ilacqua family's wartime correspondence.

were usually far from home, often without resources, so their own testimony was their only defense. There is no known record that anyone was released at a first hearing. A former member of one such board at Missoula reported that the board had no written reports about the internees, did not know how the individuals had been selected for internment, and heard only testimony from the military, which they did not question.

Word soon spread that family members could request a rehearing, at which letters attesting to the internee's trustworthiness could be presented. Rehearings were scheduled many months after a request and resulted in exoneration for many. Carmelo Ilacqua was released in September 1943, three months after his rehearing reached this conclusion: "The board is thoroughly impressed with the alien's loyalty to the U.S. and his truthfulness when he stated he 'believed that Italy would be better off if the Allies won the war as he had always been opposed to the Axis.' He stated he fought against the Germans once and would fight them again, and the board's conclusion was that 'this man is very loyal to the U.S.'"[10]

The U.S. Department of Justice made the final decision in these cases, and when the FBI objected to Ilacqua's parole on the basis of its so-called information about him, the attorney general overruled its objection, approving the internee's release on September 4, 1943, twenty-one months after his arrest. After his return home, the U.S. Army hired Ilacqua to teach Italian to servicemen in the Specialist Training Program at Stanford University. At least one other former internee, Angelo Baccocina, also went to teach there, later that year. These two formerly "dangerous" men were now helping with army plans for the occupation of Italy! By November 1943, Italy was no longer an enemy but an ally, and all Italian American internees were released on parole by December.[11]

Even some antifascist aliens had been interned. Guido Trento, an actor who wrote for *L'Italia* on theater and special events, and Giovanni Falasca, editor of Los Angeles's *La Parola,* were two such internees, who, though members of the *Ex Combattenti,* considered themselves antifascists. The hearing board that reviewed Trento's internment in June 1943 concluded that he had been interested in the theater and not at all in politics, and that his membership in the IWV was indeed, as the man had claimed, inactive. When Trento's release was approved in October 1943, the hearing board noted that he had been "erroneously regarded as a Fascist."[12]

Besides interning some Italian American resident aliens and Italian nationals, the U.S. government also negotiated the internment of some 2,000 enemy aliens from Latin America. The purpose was to exchange them for U.S. citizens detained abroad, including the 3,300 Americans in China interned by the Japanese. The United States and Panama had discussed such a plan as early as October 1941. South American leaders wanted to rid themselves of enemy aliens, especially Peru, where a long-established colony of Japanese emigrés owned thriving businesses in spite of anti-Asian prejudice. Along with the Japanese, some Germans and a smaller number of Italians were arrested in eleven Latin American countries—the majority in Peru—and transported to the United States beginning in spring 1942. The FBI had helped to identify these aliens in Latin America, where it had been authorized to conduct operations since the autumn of 1939.

The process consisted of arresting and placing these aliens on ships bound for the United States. Aboardship, they were asked to surrender their passports, and when they landed in the United States, authorities arrested and detained them as illegal immigrants! By August 1942, the United States had exchanged 737 Japanese Latin Americans for an equivalent number of American citizens held by the Japanese. The remaining Latin Americans were held in military camps in Texas until the end of the war; most were deported to their or their parents' country of origin, but some 200 Japanese Peruvians fought in the courts against deportation and were eventually allowed to remain. It is believed that the Italian Latin Americans were probably deported to Italy, but the full story remains unknown.[13]

Enemy Alien Registration and Restrictions

This program affected all 600,000 Italian aliens and their families, so that many Italian Americans experienced the stigma of being an "enemy alien" in spite of having long-term residence in the country and native-born children. Several weeks after the declaration of war, local officials posted notices for the 1.1 million Italian, German, and Japanese noncitizen residents to register at local post offices. Each alien was required to bring a passport-sized photograph, be fingerprinted, and then carry this photo-identity card, entitled "alien registration certificate" at all times. Regulations set out a curfew between 8 P.M. and 6 A.M.; restriction on travel more than five miles from home; prohibition against possession of guns, ammunition, shortwave radios, cameras, and signalling devices; and a requirement to report any change of residence or employment to local police. The curfew and travel restrictions hurt the livelihood of many Italians working in restaurants, fishing, garbage collection, janitorial work, or other employment requiring either hours or travel proscribed by the regulations.[14]

By June 1942, the number of Italians who had been arrested for such reasons as contraband, curfew, or travel violation reached 1,500; the largest numbers were in the New York City area, California, and Louisiana; many were released within days, but some were held for several months. Aristide Bertolini, a truck farmer near Santa Rosa, was arrested while returning home between 8:30 and 9:00 P.M. after delivering a rush order of tomatoes to one of his clients. He was detained for over two months in Sharp Park, a camp of quonset huts hastily constructed by the INS in early 1942. Joseph L. Cervetto,* a new immigrant working as a window washer, was also arrested for curfew violation and held for two weeks on San Francisco Bay's Angel Island, where FBI agents questioned him every day about whether he had emigrated to San Francisco to "blow up the bridges." Cervetto's reply, every day, was, "I came to San Francisco to wash windows." Marie Ferrario of Marin County remembers a Sunday drive with her parents (naturalized citizens) and her aunt (an alien) when a policeman stopped them and inquired if all were citizens; her mother responded that they were. Her aunt was so frightened by this encounter

UNITED STATES DEPARTMENT OF JUSTICE

NOTICE TO ALIENS OF ENEMY NATIONALITIES

★ The United States Government requires all aliens of German, Italian, or Japanese nationality to apply at post offices nearest to their place of residence for a Certificate of Identification. Applications must be filed between the period February 2 through February 7, 1942. Go to your postmaster today for printed directions.

FRANCIS BIDDLE,
Attorney General.

EARL G. HARRISON,
Special Assistant to the Attorney General.

AVVISO

Il Governo degli Stati Uniti ordina a tutti gli stranieri di nazionalità Tedesca, Italiana e Giapponese di fare richiesta all' Ufficio Postale più prossimo al loro luogo di residenza per ottenere un Certificato d'Identità. Le richieste devono essere fatte entro il periodo che decorre tra il 2 Febbraio e il 7 Febbraio 1942.

Andate oggi dal vostro Capo d'Ufficio Postale (Postmaster) per ricevere le istruzioni scritte.

BEKANNTMACHUNG

Die Regierung der Vereinigten Staaten von Amerika fordert alle Auslaender deutscher, italienischer und japanischer Staatsangehoerigkeit auf, sich auf das ihrem Wohnorte naheliegende Postamt zu begeben, um einen Personalausweis zu beantragen. Das Gesuch muss zwischen dem 2. und 7. Februar 1942 eingereicht werden.

Gehen Sie noch heute zu Ihrem Postmeister und verschaffen Sie sich die gedruckten Vorschriften.

Post This Side in States of
Arizona, California, Idaho, Montana, Nevada, Oregon, Utah, Washington

Several weeks after the declaration of war, officials posted registration requirements at local post offices. Courtesy of Japanese American Library

that she did not go out again until the restrictions were lifted in late October 1942. One Italian immigrant cogently expressed the frustration and dissonance felt by many at being classified as enemy aliens: "Don't those imbeciles in Washington understand that to have American-born children is to become an American for the rest of your life?"[15]

Chaos in Government Agencies

The myriad government agencies assigned to administer the enemy-alien regulations were new at the task, even though this U.S. policy had precedents in earlier wars and the internment procedures were patterned after Britain's in this

---

*See "Impersonizing Columbus," page 266, for more on Joseph Cervetto.

war. The resulting confusion, overlapping functions, and conflicts lead one to wonder whether control of enemy aliens could have been more poorly administered. Similar to conflicts between the Home and Foreign Offices in London, Washington's Departments of War and Justice engaged in a running battle over jurisdiction and individuals' civil rights. The War Department had established three military commands for the nation's defense—Western, Eastern, and Southern—each headed by a general with authority for designating areas in which restrictions, evacuation, and exclusion would be imposed on enemy aliens and some naturalized citizens; for promulgating the regulations and restrictions on all enemy aliens; and for guarding the Italian and German internment camps and, later, the Japanese relocation centers as well. The military issued over one hundred separate orders affecting enemy aliens during the war. Lieutenant General John L. DeWitt, commanding general of the Western Defense Command, became the best known because of the perceived greater threat of invasion on the West Coast, as well as what were seen later as his racism and paranoia concerning enemy aliens.[16]

Units in the Department of Justice, headed by Attorney General Francis E. Biddle, had responsibility for most other functions regarding enemy aliens: the FBI for designating dangerous aliens, for arresting aliens in violation of regulations, and for supervising those naturalized citizens who received exclusion orders from the army; the Enemy Alien Unit for coordinating the legal aspects of regulations and other actions affecting enemy aliens through the regional offices of U.S. attorneys; and the INS for administering the internment camps. Interagency clashes occurred most often between Attorney General Biddle and Secretary of War Henry Stimson. Frequently, such conflicts arose from DeWitt's actions and would have to be resolved at the cabinet level, sometimes involving the president himself.[17]

Although Congress did not openly debate internment of enemy aliens, the House of Representatives set up the Tolan Committee to investigate "national defense migration," covering, among other things, the restrictions on aliens' freedom of movement. While the committee was holding hearings in March 1942 and concluding that each enemy alien should be evaluated as an individual, with loyal aliens exempted from restrictions and relocation, the Western Defense Command had already ordered all enemy aliens out of zones along the Pacific coast that the military had designated as "prohibited."[18]

Areas Prohibited to Enemy Aliens

It was the designation of prohibited areas that imposed hardships on the largest number of Italian Americans—an estimated 10,000 in California alone. The authority for this action came from Executive Order 9066, signed by the president on February 19, 1942, and enforced by congressional passage of Public Law 503, which authorized the military to designate areas from which they could exclude any person. Intended primarily to facilitate wholesale relocation of the Japanese on the West Coast—two-thirds of whom were American-born and thus U.S. citizens—but naming no specific groups, this document became the basis for ordering all enemy aliens from coastal areas and other strategic areas adjacent to military bases or war production plants. This evacuation took place only along the Pacific because of the fear of Japanese invasion, not on the Atlantic, which was the scene of more submarine activity and closer to the enemy in occupied France. It was on the Atlantic coast that in early 1942 two German submarines landed eight men whose mission was to sabotage wartime facilities; they were, however, captured before they could engage in any such acts. The Japanese did invade the Aleutian Islands of Alaska, then a U.S. territory, only six hundred miles from the Japanese Kurile Islands and within bombing distance of Seattle. However, the differential treatment of aliens on the West Coast had more to do with previously existing anti-Japanese attitudes that then spilled over onto Italians and Germans in the early days of the war.[19]

The military was seeking scapegoats for the attack on Pearl Harbor, and the immigrants—often the targets of fear and hatred—were thrust again into that role. These attitudes formed the basis of policies in the Western Defense Command. DeWitt himself promoted a notion that Japanese Americans had been providing information to the enemy, claiming as evidence unidentified radio signals from offshore; government archives confirm that even he knew these allegations to be false. The FBI and the Federal Communications Commission had investigated and identified all radio signals as having originated from U.S. sources.

An estimated 10,000 Italian aliens had to move from prohibited areas in California during February and March 1942. Many were older women with little English, living in extended family households, who had not applied for final citizenship papers for various reasons: fear of the English-language examination, distance from the INS office, or simply not understanding the significance of naturalization. The aliens had to find other places to live at a time when housing was extremely scarce because of the migration to the West Coast caused by wartime job opportunities. A committee from the town of Pittsburg, California, traveled by train to Washington, D.C., to protest the removal of its Italian aliens—a large part of this community—but the relocation proceeded on schedule.

Some Italians moved into available but substandard migrant-labor housing; some found housing just a block away from their homes, while others went some distance. Rosa Viscuso left her Pittsburg home and family, taking only her twelve-year-old daughter; they joined other evacuated relatives in renting a house twenty miles away in Concord. Mr. Viscuso and the four older children remained in their home; a citizen, he was employed in building warships, and two sons worked at Columbia Steel, also in war production. Even people bedridden and those in wheelchairs had to relocate: Placido Abono, eighty-nine years of age, was carried out of his Pittsburg home on a stretcher. Several Italian men in the San Francisco area and one in Stockton committed suicide rather than suffer the indignity of giving up their homes and businesses. This evacuation created considerable emotional and economic turmoil in thousands of families; then, inexplicably, within five months, the order was lifted, and enemy aliens could return home! Government records suggest that, because the "dangerous" aliens were by then interned, the others could safely return; however, the Italians on the dangerous list were already in detention several weeks before the posting of the evacuation order.[20]

Italian fishing families along the California coast—where they account-ed for eighty percent of the fishing fleet—suffered most from the relocation. Alien fishermen were not allowed to fish in coastal waters; the Coast Guard confiscated boats owned by aliens as well as by naturalized citizens and used them to patrol the coast looking for submarines. Most fishing families resided in prohibited areas, so they also had to relocate. Although the Coast Guard paid monthly compensation for use of the fishing boats, the fishermen had lost their livelihood as well as their homes. Ironically, within a short time, the U.S. Department of Agriculture issued a series of posters urging greater food pro-duction for the war effort; the caption on one poster read: "Fish Is a Fighting Food: We Need More."

Vitina Spadaro of Monterey described her family's situation: when she was thirteen, her father could no longer fish because his boat was confiscated, and then the six of them had to move inland because her mother was not a cit-izen. When they arrived at a house in Salinas that they had arranged to rent, the landlord barred their entry because he had discovered that they were enemy aliens. He was unresponsive to their claims that they, except for the mother, were all citizens, so they left in the rain to look for another place to live. Rosina Trovato had to move from her home in Monterey even though her son in the U.S. Navy had been killed during the Japanese attack on Pearl Harbor. Celestina Loero, member of a Santa Cruz fishing family with two sons and two grandsons serving in the armed forces, had to leave the only home she had known for fifty years; many years later, she would still break into tears whenever she recalled the evil night—*la mala notte,* she called it—when she was ordered to leave. Even on the East Coast, where enemy aliens were not relocated, Italian fishermen were forbidden to ply their trade in coastal waters: in Boston, 200 Italian fishermen were affected by that restriction.[21]

Columbus Day, 1942

In October 1942, after all the restrictions and relocation endured by thousands of Italian American families, the government removed Italians from the category of enemy aliens. Attorney General Biddle made the announcement on Columbus Day, the U.S. holiday that is uniquely Italian American, noting that members of this ethnic group had shown themselves to be responsible citizens. Government records suggest, however, that the impetus for this change had more to do with two other factors: congressional elections in the following month and army plans to invade Italy in the spring. As the largest immigrant group in the country and the largest ethnic voting bloc, Italian Americans' goodwill suddenly became an overriding issue. Moreover, a large proportion of the armed forces was made up of the sons of Italian immigrants—according to some reports, 300,000—and it was crucial to ensure their unqualified support in the Italian campaign. There were reports that men in the armed forces who had enemy alien parents were angry enough to revolt. Another consideration was that this move might help to soften resistance in Italy to the Allied invasion.

No longer technically enemy aliens, the several hundred Italian fishermen barred from coastal waters were allowed to resume fishing by the end of 1942. Still subject to some restrictions, an Italian alien could work only on a boat where the captain or fifty per cent of the crew were citizens; port captains issued an identity card to any alien who met this requirement. The fact that Italians were no longer enemy aliens made no difference, however, for those "dangerous" Italians who had been interned or excluded: they remained exiled or imprisoned until the end of 1943.[22]

The Individual Exclusion Program

The Custodial Detention List included some naturalized citizens among the potentially dangerous. Although their U.S. citizenship had forestalled internment, they were still not in the clear, as the War Department, especially DeWitt, alleged that they were as dangerous as aliens. When the administration did not support the removal of all enemy aliens and naturalized citizens from the Western Defense Command, DeWitt proposed the exclusion, at a minimum, of those on the Custodial Detention List, on the basis of Executive Order 9066, which authorized the military to remove any person from strategic areas. So in

August 1942 the exclusion process began on the West Coast, and it was later applied in the eastern and southern commands, resulting in the removal of only 30 Italians (out of a total of 244 exclusions). They resided primarily in San Francisco and Los Angeles, the two largest centers of Italians in the West. These Italians, after receiving exclusion orders, chose to move to inland cities such as Reno, Las Vegas, Denver, and Chicago. Although only men had been interned in the earlier action, some women—two Italians in San Francisco—now received exclusion orders: one a teacher in an Italian-language school, and one a member of the Ladies' Auxiliary of the IWV.

Two additional forces supported the exiling of these Italians: the West Coast's small contingent of antifascists and the California legislature's Joint Fact-Finding Committee on Un-American Activities (the Tenney Committee). What role did the antifascist community play in the exclusion? It had, for some years prior to the war, tried to counter the pro-Mussolini bias that was prevalent in the U.S. press before Mussolini's invasion of Ethiopia and in most Italian-language newspapers until December 7, 1941. The antifascists—most of them political exiles from Italy—had received little support from the U.S. government, with Congress and the FBI continuing to focus on Communists as the major threat to the nation. In fact, the antifascists—who had supported the loyalists in the Spanish Civil War of 1936—were then categorized in FBI reports as "Communist" and later as "prematurely antifascist." (Carmelo Zito, editor of San Francisco's socialist newspaper, *Il Corriere del Popolo,* and leading spokesman of antifascists on the West Coast, appeared on the Custodial Detention List and was described in his FBI file as prematurely antifascist.)

When the Tenney Committee held hearings in San Francisco in 1941 and 1942, the antifascists' frustrations of many years burst forth—they finally found someone to listen to their complaints about the Fascists—and thus contributed to devastating consequences for their *paesani,* both profascist and antifascist, in ways that they could not have predicted. Prior to the outbreak of war in Europe, the committee had been concerned primarily with identifying Communist groups and individuals; later, it gave more attention to Nazi groups. Not until late 1941 did it investigate Fascists, holding hearings in San Francisco and Los Angeles and concluding that three men in San Francisco's Italian community were the "leaders of the Fascist movement in California." The three were Sylvester Andriano, an attorney active in the Italian community and in city government; Ettore Patrizi, editor-publisher of *L'Italia,* the leading Italian-language newspaper in the West; and Renzo Turco, another attorney and community leader. The committee heard testimony for five days in December and three days in May, testimony based largely on hearsay, newspaper reports, and unverified allegations of events occurring long before the war.

Within four months, these three men, all naturalized citizens and residents for twenty years or more, received individual exclusion orders.[23]

While *L'Italia* had supported Mussolini prior to Pearl Harbor, when there was considerable support for his Fascist government among San Francisco's Italian community, the Tenney Committee heard no testimony that these three men (or any others) had engaged in any subversive actions either before or after the declaration of war. Considerable evidence of their loyalty to the United States could have been found, had anyone cared to look. All three became naturalized citizens within several years of arrival in the United States. (Seven years of residence was then a requirement for citizenship.) Just prior to his exclusion, Andriano was chair of a draft board—these bodies made decisions on exemptions from service in the armed forces—and earlier had served as elected member of the city's board of supervisors and appointed member of its police commission. He was also director of the Dopo Scuola, an Italian-language school, and board member of the Italian Chamber of Commerce—two organizations on the FBI's list of suspect groups. A respected citizen in both the Italian and the wider civic communities, he had graduated from St. Mary's College and Hastings College of Law. Twenty years after his exclusion, St. Mary's honored him as alumnus of the year for his many civic contributions.

Patrizi was a patron of the arts and sponsor of Italian opera in San Francisco. A U.S. resident since 1898 and a citizen for thirty years, Patrizi was seventy-six years old and in the hospital when he was served with an exclusion order. A. P. Giannini, founder of the Bank of Italy (later Bank of America) and an officer in the American Legion, asked that Patrizi be exempted from the exclusion because of age and infirmity, but the only concession that the army made was to allow him ten additional days to leave the area, or twenty-four hours after his discharge from the hospital. On his release from the hospital, he moved to Reno, Nevada, where several other San Francisco excludees had resettled. In October 1943, Patrizi was allowed to return home because of failing health; he died within a year.

Turco closed his law office and disposed of his home furnishings within the ten days allowed by the exclusion order; he and his wife moved to Chicago. Required to report weekly to the FBI office and to inform prospective employers of his status, he was unable to find work until he presented a letter of recommendation from a San Francisco judge; with that, and assistance from the FBI's Chicago office, he obtained a position as tax auditor for the U.S. Internal Revenue Service. The War Manpower Administration was responsible for assisting excludees to find employment and found it difficult to convince employers to consider an applicant banned as dangerous and required to report weekly to the FBI.

Andriano, the third "Fascist leader," also moved to Chicago. Although he had suggested that Patrizi appeal his exclusion order, Andriano did not appeal on his own behalf. Others began a petition drive for a presidential exemption for Andriano, and San Francisco's Catholic archbishop appealed in person to Assistant Secretary of War John J. McCloy in Washington, but to no avail. Andriano did resist some exclusion procedures by refusing to sign the exclusion order and by declining to inform the army of his destination. Moreover, he returned to visit his mother in California in April 1943, and when the Western Defense Command learned of this violation, it asked the Department of Justice to prosecute him; he had already violated his exclusion by traveling to Washington, D.C., another prohibited area. Because of Attorney General Biddle's refusal to prosecute, the War Department took Andriano's case to the attention of the president. Roosevelt referred it back to Biddle with a request to try to iron it out with Secretary of War Stimson. Biddle believed the individual exclusion orders to be unconstitutional, and the issue became moot when Andriano moved to Reno. (Several German American excludees also violated their exclusion orders, and the Justice Department refused to prosecute any of these cases.)[24]

No Italian American brought a suit against the U.S. government over the exclusions (or the internments). Most who were affected wanted to forget the experience; they did not even consider court action. Angelo de Guttadauro, son of an excluded man, testified many years later to the federal commission investigating these wartime events.* When asked if his father had sought relief through the courts he replied, "My father did not....He was an old-fashioned man. He was not the type of man to ask redress from anyone. He would never ask for anything, the very nature of the man...he was brought up in a very closed society....It was not like people of his background to ask redress from a government." Several German Americans did file lawsuits appealing their exclusions, and the decision in most of these cases was that, despite finding no evidence of dangerousness, the court did not wish to supersede the military's judgment. In some other instances of resistance to exclusion orders in the Los Angeles area, the military took enforcement into its own hands, forcing entrance through locked doors and escorting violators to Las Vegas.[25]

Remo Bosia's exclusion was perhaps unique: he is the only known native-born American of Italian descent who received an exclusion order.† Born in Madera, California, of immigrant parents, Bosia moved to Italy at the age of six, when his family decided to return there. Then in 1923, when he was eighteen, he

---

*See "Exclusion Is a Four-Letter Word," page 156, for excerpts from de Guttadauro's testimony.
†See "The General and I," page 290, for more on Remo Bosia.

returned alone to live in San Francisco. After several short-term jobs, he found employment in 1928 as a translator with *L'Italia*, eventually becoming its managing editor....He received an exclusion order on September 9, 1942—apparently because of his fourteen-year employment with the profascist *L'Italia*....[26]

Eventually, across the country, 254 citizens received exclusion orders: 174 in the Western Defense Command, including only 25 Italians; the majority of excludees were German Americans, plus a small number of "American" Fascists. Even though the exclusion and internment procedures were meant to be confidential, some names appeared in local newspapers, creating the impression that these persons were indeed dangerous. Exclusions began in the autumn of 1942, just before Italian Americans were removed from the enemy-alien category, but this change did not affect those who had been excluded. Most excludees, like internees, were not allowed to return home until the end of 1943, having been exiled for fifteen months.

Sadly, government records indicate that, although most internees and excludees had been indicted on the basis of membership in an organization, there was no information on these organizations available to the hearing boards, the army, its intelligence division, or the commanding generals of the defense commands who made the final decisions on exclusion. Apparently, the decisions on both internments and exclusions were made solely on the basis of

Arriving at the Missoula, Montana, internment camp, ca. 1941. Courtesy of the Mike and Maureen Mansfield Library, University of Montana.

the FBI's list, unaccompanied by supporting evidence. According to the army's own report, information on the organizations was available to it only "many months after war started."

Moreover, Eugene Rostow, a noted law professor, has written that the courts have made it clear that exclusion can be sustained only on a showing of "clear and present danger" of an imminent threat to public safety, or of aid to the enemy. He also noted that international law permits controls on enemy aliens solely to prevent them from aiding the enemy. No evidence of such threat or aid was demonstrated in the Italian American cases.

In fact, Attorney General Biddle himself prepared a memo to FBI Director J. Edgar Hoover in July 1943 in which he declared that there was no justification for the Custodial Detention List; that the list was invalid; that the evidence used was inadequate; and that determination as to how dangerous a person is cannot be made in the abstract but "must be based on investigation of activities of persons who may have violated the law." Biddle directed that a copy of this memo be placed in the FBI file for each person whose name had been on the list and that each document classifying that person as dangerous was to be stamped: "This classification is unreliable. It is hereby canceled, and should not be used as a determination of dangerousness or of any other fact."

Although the Department of Justice had instituted denaturalization proceedings in all cases of exclusion, it appears that no Italian lost his or her citizenship. To carry out denaturalization, officials must present evidence of either fraud in the citizenship process or disloyal actions after the declaration of war. There was no such evidence. Sadly, none of the agencies involved, except perhaps that of the attorney general, paid much attention to evidence, nor did they understand the difference between being pro-Italy and being subversive.[27]

Remembering and Forgetting

Not until many years after the war ended did the story of the civilian internments come to public attention, and then only after Japanese Americans in California waged a campaign to submit a request for redress to Congress. Their efforts resulted in the establishment of a Commission on Wartime Relocation and Internment of Civilians (CWRIC) in 1980. The commission held hearings on both coasts and issued its report and recommendations in 1982. The report included a chapter on German Americans, wherein there is one mention of interned Italian Americans. Only one Italian American, Colonel Angelo de Guttadauro, U.S. Army, appeared before the commission to describe the effects of his father's exclusion on his family. While the commission's files indicate that some efforts were made to locate persons who could testify on the experiences of the Italians and Germans, those efforts were minimal, and no German American gave testimony, even though thousands had been interned and hundreds excluded.

In December 1982, CWRIC published its recommendations that Congress acknowledge that a grave injustice had been done to Japanese Americans; offer the nation's apologies for the acts of exclusion, removal, and detention; and pay redress to those who had been excluded. The recommendations for redress made no reference to any other group except the Alaska Aleuts, who, though not enemy aliens, had been relocated because of an expected Japanese attack. While the omission of the other two groups is understandable because the wholesale relocation of Japanese Americans—the majority, 70,000, being American-born—was the more egregious violation, it is nonetheless unfortunate that the affront to Italians and Germans has not yet been acknowledged. When Congress implemented the CWRIC's recommendations in the Civil Rights Act of 1988, one of the law's purposes was "to discourage the occurrence of similar injustices and violations of civil liberties in the future." Unless the numbers of Italians and others who also suffered are considered, that purpose will not be fulfilled.[28]

In contrast to Japanese Americans, the Italian community has not made a coordinated effort even to seek acknowledgment and apology from the government. One of the primary barriers to such action has been widespread ignorance that Italians and Germans were also interned, excluded, and evacuated. Another obstacle has been that the selective internment and individual exclusion provisions that applied to the Italians were not publicized either by the authorities or by the victims, who felt stigmatized by being selected for banishment. Even today, some in the Italian American community feel that the story should be not publicized, but rather forgotten, because they consider it a blot on their history. The stories of the fishermen and others who had to move from their homes are known primarily in their own close-knit communities, where most families shared that experience.

Recently, a few scholars have begun to write about these events, and some preliminary steps are being taken towards informing the public and, it is hoped, the appropriate authorities. Most of the activity has taken place in California, where the largest number of Italians were affected. In 1992, the Sons of Italy's Social Justice Commission wrote President George Bush, requesting acknowledgment of and apology for the wartime treatment of Italian Americans. The annual convention of the Grand Lodge passed a resolution requesting "full public disclosure of the injustices suffered by Italo Americans during World War II and that an apology be made not only to Americans of Italian ancestry, but to the nation as a whole." The Department of Justice's response was that since just a relatively small group of ethnic Germans and Italians received exclusion orders, no further action was necessary. Such a statement is not only unresponsive but also reflects ignorance of the actual events of 1942.

A second effort to publicize the wartime story has at least informed more Italian Americans around the nation. In early 1994, the western chapter of the American Italian Historical Association presented an exhibit, *Una Storia Segreta: When Italian Americans Were "Enemy Aliens,"* which has traveled under the sponsorship of numerous Italian American organizations within California and on the East Coast, receiving good media coverage.[29]

The historical experience of immigrants has taught them to avoid drawing attention to themselves, because this has often elicited negative reactions to the entire ethnic group. Nonetheless, historians and many whose families suffered these indignities want very much to see this story told, so that public knowledge may create pressure to prevent it from happening to others. The recent past does not offer much hope, as whenever conflict occurs between the United States and another nation, there are media stories of possible detention of yet another immigrant group.[30]

Conclusion

Prior to the Second World War, resident aliens generally had the same legal rights as citizens, except for voting, serving on a jury, holding a government job, or obtaining a business or professional license. Aliens were also required to serve in the armed forces during both world wars, but this principle was not generally accepted in international law. Most important, aliens are covered by the Fourteenth Amendment to the Constitution, which forbids any state to deny to any person within its jurisdiction the equal protection of its laws. This protection includes a right to due process of law and protection from unreasonable search and seizure, both rights that were violated during the war.

According to some legal scholars, the U.S. Supreme Court, final arbiter of individual rights in the United States, has not satisfactorily answered questions about alien rights in wartime. Most cases of wartime exclusion brought before appeal courts resulted in decisions upholding the military's authority to override constitutional protections in wartime. Still, congressional action in ordering reparations for the Japanese relocation, in specifying that there was no military necessity for it, effectively denied the claim of military prerogative. And, if there was no need for the Japanese relocation, surely there was no necessity for the relocation, exclusion, and internment of Italian Americans. The Second World War experiences of civilian internees around the world cry out for preventive measures in both national and international law.[31]

Endnotes

1. Much of the information in this chapter is derived from documents found in the National Archives, Washington, D.C., whose records are classified by record group (RG), and in the Franklin D. Roosevelt Library (FDR Library), Hyde Park, N.Y.; from records obtained under the Freedom of Information Act (FOIA) from the Federal Bureau of Investigation (FBI), the Immigration and Naturalization Service (INS), and the Criminal Division of the Department of Justice; from papers collected by the Commission on Wartime Relocation and Internment (CWRIC) on microfilm at the Green Library, Stanford University, Palo Alto, Calif.; and from records of the Japanese American Evacuation and Resettlement Study (JERS), Bancroft Library, University of California, Berkeley. I obtained data in interviews with participants in these experiences and with their family members. Statements of some were collected at forums in California and in the New York City area at showings in 1994 to 1996 of the exhibit *Una Storia Segreta: When Italian Americans Were "Enemy Aliens,"* sponsored by the Western Regional Chapter of the American Italian Historical Association; see the catalog of the same name edited by Rose Scherini and Lawrence DiStasi with Adele Negro (San Francisco, 1994).

2. On immigration and population, see Graziano Battistella, ed., *Italian Americans in the '80s: A Sociodemographic Profile* (Staten Island, N.Y.: Center for Migration Studies, 1989), and *U.S. Census of Population, Characteristics of Population* (Washington, D.C.: Government Printing Office, 1940) vol. 11, Table VII, "Foreign-Born White by Country of Birth for the U.S.: 1940." On events after 1939, see Roger Daniels, "Bad News from the Good War: Democracy at Home during World War II," in Kenneth O'Brien and Lynn H. Parsons, eds., *Home-Front War: World War II and American Society* (Westport, Conn.: Greenwood Press, 1995), 157–72. The Custodial Detention List of Italian Americans is on CWRIC microfilm, reel 24: 25780–5. On similarities with Britain, see Peter and Leni Gillman, *"Collar the Lot": How Britain Interned and Expelled Its Wartime Refugees* (London: Quartet Books, 1978), 8–10, 42–4.

3. Until April 1942, these actions applied to Germans and Japanese as well as Italians. Then, all Japanese Americans in the West were "relocated," i.e., interned. For that story, see Roger Daniels, Sandra C. Taylor, and Harry H. L. Kitano, eds., *Japanese Americans from Relocation to Redress* (Salt Lake City: University of Utah Press, 1986).

4. I have FBI files of nine Italians who were either interned or excluded, which I obtained through an FOIA request accompanied by written proof of the subjects' death; Department of Justice, Criminal Division, Caldwell to Berge, 8-15-42, 146.6–18, section 05; "Report on Organizations"/General Sedition Section, Box 15, RG 60.

5. FDR Library, PPF 4617: Generoso Pope; Individual Exclusion Case Files: Ettore Patrizi, Box 10, RG 210.

6. On numbers of Italians interned, see War Relocation Authority, *San Francisco Daily Press Review*, no. 1715, 8 Oct. 1942; Jerre Mangione, *An Ethnic at Large: A Memoir of America in the Thirties and Forties* (New York: Putnam, 1978), 343; and 3 May 1942, Department of Justice Press Release, Fiorello La Guardia Papers, Box 425, New York Municipal Archives.

7. Filippo Molinari to Carlotta [surname unknown], Arcadia, Calif., 25 July 1985; personal collection of Andrew M. Canepa, San Francisco.

8. The Ilacqua story is based in part on my interviews with Costanza Ilacqua Foran, Sacramento, Calif., 27 May 1988, 14 July 1989, and 2 July 1993, and correspondence and telephone conversations over those years; World War II Detention Centers: Missoula, boxes 68–70, RG 85; FBI Headquarters file 100–5929: Carmelo Ilacqua.

9. Carmelo Ilacqua's letters are in the personal collection of Costanza Ilacqua Foran, Sacramento, Calif.

10. "Instructions to U.S. Attorneys re: Alien Enemies," A 7.03, JERS; Alfonso Zirpoli, "Faith in Justice: Alfonso Zirpoli and the U.S. District Court for the Northern District," 5862 (1984), Regional Oral History Office, Bancroft Library, University of California, Berkeley; my interview with Thomas Barclay (former hearing board member), 4 Aug. 1989, Palo Alto, Calif.; Department of Justice file 146-13-2-61-23, "Rehearing Memo for Chief of Review Section," 18 Aug. 1944, in author's collection.

11. FBI file on Ilacqua; interviews with Costanza Ilacqua Foran; Mussolini was deposed in July 1943, and the new Italian government soon joined the Allies; see Dennis Mack Smith, *History of Italy* (Ann Arbor: University of Michigan Press, 1975).

12. FBI Headquarters file 100-61677: Guido Trento; interview with Gloria Ricci Lothrop (re her stepfather, Giovanni Falasca), Sacramento, Calif., 6 Aug. 1996; on wartime experiences of Los Angeles Italians, see Gloria Ricci Lothrop, "The Untold Story: The Effect of the Second World War on California Italians," *Journal of the West* 35, no. 1 (1996), 6–14.

13. C. Harvey Gardiner, *Pawns in a Triangle of Hate: The Peruvian Japanese and the United States* (Seattle: University of Washington Press, 1981); Japanese Peruvian Oral History Project, "The Japanese Latin Americans and World War II," National Japanese American Historical Society, n.d.; INS Annual Report (1947), 29.

14. INS, Report on Alien Registration (Washington, D.C.: Government Printing Office, n.d.), D.203, JERS; U.S. Army, Western Defense Command and Fourth Army, "Civilian Exclusion and Restriction Orders and Collected Documents," 1942–43n, CWRIC Reel 25: 26376–8.

15. FBI Custodial Detention files, "1521 Italian Aliens Taken into Custody by FBI," 30 June 1942; on Aristide Bertolini, see *Santa Rosa Press Democrat*, 3 June 1994, "Gaye LeBaron's Notebook"; Joseph L. Cervetto Sr., telephone conversation with author, San Rafael, Calif., 11 March 1991; and Lawrence DiStasi, "Impersonizing Columbus," *Before Columbus Review* 3, no. 2 (1992), 6–11; Marie Ferrario, public statement at meeting of Gruppo Lonatese, 30 July 1995, Corte Madera, Calif.; Mangione, *An Ethnic at Large*, 343.

16. P. and L. Gillman, "*Collar the Lot,*" 7–9; Stephen C. Fox, "General DeWitt and the Proposed Internment of German and Italian Aliens during World War II," *Pacific Historical Review* 57 (1988), 407–38; Peter Irons, *Justice at War: The Story of the Japanese American Internment Cases* (New York: Oxford University Press, 1983), 2–47; and Dale Minami, "Coram Nobis and Redress," in Daniels et al., *Japanese Americans*, 81–5.

17. Irons, *Justice at War*, 32–48; FDR Library: OF 4805, Military Areas 1942–43, Biddle to President, 9 April 1942; James Rowe Papers, Box 37, Loyalty Boards, Rowe to Clark, 22 April 1942; PSF, Box 10, War Department, Jan.–Aug., 1942, President to Secretary of War, 5 May 1942; Biddle Papers: FDR, Box 2, Biddle to President, 27 Jan. 1943.

18. Stephen Fox, *The Unknown Internment: An Oral History of the Relocation of Italian Americans during World War II* (Boston: Twayne Publishers, 1990), 126–34; House Select Committee Investigating National Defense Migration, 77th Congress, 2nd session, Fourth Interim Report, "Findings and Recommendations on Evacuation of Enemy Aliens and Others from Prohibited Military Zones," May 1942.

19. Executive Order 9066 is in Federal Regulations 7, No. 140 (1942), 2199; "Instructions to U.S. Attorneys re Alien Enemies," A 7.03, JERS. On German saboteurs, see Irons, *Justice at War*, 23, and FDR Library, PSF, Box 57, Justice, President to Attorney General, 30 June 1942; on anti-Japanese attitudes, see Morton Grodzins, *Americans Betrayed* (Chicago: University of Chicago Press, 1949), and Roger Daniels, *The Politics of Prejudice* (Berkeley: University of California Press, 1962).

20. Fox, *The Unknown Internment*, 145; written statement of Rose Viscuso Scudero re February 24, 1942, in *Una Storia Segreta*, Pittsburg Historical Society (June 1994); Fox, *The Unknown Internment*, 1, 65; "Individual Exclusion Program of Non-Japanese," Supplemental Report on Civilian Controls Exercised by the Western Defense Command, Part III (Jan. 1947).

21. Fox, *The Unknown Internment*, 72, 83–6; Scherini and DiStasi, eds., *Una Storia Segreta*, 20; Geoffrey Dunn, "Mala Notte: Santa Cruz Italian Relocation and Restriction during World War II," *Santa Cruz County Historical Journal* (1994), 83–8; Pasquale Verdicchio, "Little Italy," *Journal of San Diego History* 27, no. 4 (1981), 220; *Boston Globe*, 18 Oct. and 20 Nov. 1942.

22. Francis Biddle, *In Brief Authority* (New York: Doubleday, 1962), 229–31; *San Francisco Call-Bulletin*, 3 Nov. 1942; Wartime Civilian Control Administration, press release, 23 Nov. 1942.

23. Supplemental Report, 836–8, 842–52; Scherini, "The Fascist/Anti-Fascist Struggle." Richard N. Juliani and Sandra P. Juliani, eds., *New Explorations in Italian American Studies*, American Italian Historical Association (1994), 63–71; War Relocation Authority, *The Evacuated People: A Quantitative Description* (1946), 180, 185; interviews with author: Renzo Turco, 11

Nov. 1973, San Francisco; Remo Bosia, 10 Sept. 1987, San Carlos; and Josephine de Guttadauro (daughter of Nino de Guttadauro, excluded), 16 May 1988, Palo Alto; Scherini, "Fascist/Anti-Fascist Struggle," 68–70.

24. Calif. Legislature, Report of the Joint Fact-Finding Committee on Un-American Activities in California (1943), 309–14; Scherini, "Executive Order 9066 and Italian Americans," *California History* 70, no. 4 (1992), 372–4; Scherini, "Fascist /Anti-Fascist Struggle," 63–71; Supplementary Report, 856; Individual Exclusion case files: Sylvester Andriano, Ettore Patrizi, Renzo Turco, Box 10, RG 210; FBI Headquarters file 100–6471, Lorenzo Palmiro Turco.

25. Transcript of Angelo de Guttadauro's testimony, CWRIC: Washington hearings, 23 Nov. 1981, in personal collection of de Guttadauro, San Antonio, Tex.; U.S. Army, "Individual Exclusion Program," typed government report, 1947, 912–32.

26. Remo Bosia, *The General and I* (New York: Phaedra, 1971); *U.S. Army v. Remo Bosia,* transcript of Court Martial Proceedings, 23–4 Dec. 1942, Italian American Collection, San Francisco Public Library; Fox, *The Unknown Internment,* 171; Remo Bosia, interview with author, 10 Sept. 1987, San Carlos.

27. Peter Sheridan, "The Internment of German and Italian Aliens Compared with Internment of Japanese Aliens in the United States during World War II: A Brief History and Analysis," typed report for U.S. Congress, 24 Nov. 1980, 9, Congressional Research Service, Library of Congress; *San Francisco Call-Bulletin,* 12 Oct. 1942, "Andriano Leaves: 39 Cases Pending," and *New York Times,* 19 Oct. 1942; Supplemental Report, 856–9; Eugene Rostow, "The Japanese American Cases: A Disaster," *Yale Law Journal* 3, no. 54 (1945), 489–533 (see especially note 13, 495–56); Attorney General to FBI Director, 16 July 1943, FBI file 100-5901: Nino de Guttadauro. On denaturalization, see "Miscellaneous Bulletins," 4 Oct. 1942, D 2.03, JERS, and "FBI General Intelligence Survey" (June 1943), 19, RG 59.

Much has been written about the inadequacies of FBI investigations. For example, see Athan Theoharis, *Spying on Americans* (Philadelphia: Temple University Press, 1978), and Wesley Swearingen, *FBI Secrets: An Agent's Exposé* (Boston: South End Press, 1995), wherein a former FBI agent alleges that agents sometimes created "paper informers" providing fictitious information about suspects.

28. The CWRIC report was published as *Personal Justice Denied* (1982), and *Part 2: Recommendations* (Washington, D.C.: Government Printing Office, 1983. On Aleuts, see Part 2, 10–12.

29. News articles about the internments appeared in the *New York Times,* 12 Jan. and 5 Feb. 1942; *San Francisco Call-Bulletin,* 18 Dec. 1941; and *San Francisco Examiner,* 21 Feb. 1942. Richard Armento to President George Bush, 10 April 1992; "External Resolution" of Sons of Italy in California, 26 June 1992; John Dunne, Department of Justice, to Armento, 25 June 1992 (this correspondence is in the files of the Social Justice Commission, Sons of Italy, San Francisco); Scherini and DiStasi, eds., *Una Storia Segreta,* 30.

30. CWRIC witness files: Washington hearings, John J. McCloy, 1982; Gulf War news accounts in *New York Times,* 8 Jan. 1991, and *San Francisco Chronicle,* 21 Feb. 1991.

31. Ernest Puttkamer, ed., *War and the Law* (Chicago: University of Chicago Press, 1944), 48–9; also see Jacobus ten Broek, "Wartime Power of the Military over Citizen Civilians within the Country," *California Law Review* 41, no. 2 (1953), 168–208.

A Market Off Limits

by Velio Alberto Bronzini

> Unlike Japanese Americans, whose loss of businesses represented a major element of their ordeal, business losses in the Italian American community seem to have been more the exception than the rule. As Al Bronzini indicates here, however, such losses were not unknown. Moreover, the loss of his father's business led to even more serious health losses in the Bronzini family.
>
> As a teenager, Bronzini felt these losses keenly; he buried the painful details for many years. With the appearance of *Una Storia Segreta,* he remembered and wrote down what he increasingly recalled as a time when "the American dream was about to end."

After being discharged from the Italian army in 1923, my father, Guido Bronzini, came to America, being sponsored by his older brother, who had come nine years prior. He worked at many different jobs, primarily agricultural. He worked for five years in America, saving up enough money and, as promised, he returned to Italy to marry his childhood sweetheart, my mother, Clara Filippi. He used to tell me…[when I was] a child that when he returned to Italy to marry he would say to his family, *"Io trovata l'America,"* I've found America. America was all that he had dreamed it would be.

They returned to America a year later, arriving in Oakland, California, in mid-July, and I was born in December of that same year. My father had found the land of opportunity. My father and mother applied for their citizenship papers, but probably due to the language barrier, having a fifth-grade Italian education, and adjusting to a new land, they never completed the process.

My father started selling fruit and vegetables on street corners of various neighborhoods in Oakland, off of the back of a Model T Ford truck that he bought for twenty-five dollars and one dozen chickens. From that humble beginning he eventually opened a produce market in the Fruitvale district of east Oakland. In the late 1930s we moved from a rental house to our own home on East 12th Street in the Melrose district of Oakland. My father bought our first refrigerator and a new gas stove, he put in a hot water heater, and in 1939 he purchased a brand-new Pontiac automobile. In 1940 he added a new Philco console radio that could pick up opera music and news from Italy. I remember there being so much static that he would have a hard time getting a clear station. We had one of the first telephones in the neighborhood. Even during the Great Depression, we had a good life. I guess you could say that we were living the American dream.

My father was a smart businessman, and this country had given him the opportunity that he used to dream about. My mother was a beautiful blonde woman. She handled the family finances, and they used to joke that she could squeeze a dollar so tightly that George Washington would yell for help. My mother and father were the traditional Italian couple; there was no limit to how much they could do for each other.

One evening in early 1942—it could have been January or February— while we were all at the dinner table, there was a knock on the front door. Nobody knew it then, but the American dream was about to end. My mother answered, and she came back into the kitchen and told my father that there were two policemen that wanted to talk to him. I remember my father inviting them into the house—he knew many of them as customers of his market.

They told him, "John, we have to take your radio, the one with the short-wave band on it." (My father's name was Guido, but he preferred the American version of it, John.) My father offered no resistance, but my mother pleaded with the policemen to not take the radio. I remember her crying hysterically, pulling on his uniform sleeve as they were taking it out of the house.

My parents were classified as "enemy aliens" and, like so many others in our neighborhood, were put on certain restrictions. They couldn't travel more than five miles from their home without special permission, we could not be out of the house after eight o'clock at night. I recall that we used to walk to the library Friday evenings, to have their alien registration book stamped.

Shortly thereafter, my father was informed that his produce market was off limits to him. It was declared to be in the restricted zone, or the military sensitive zone, and he would not be able to go to his place of business. All businesses on the west side of the center line on East 12th Street in that part of Oakland were off limits to enemy aliens. Had his market been across the street, he would not have been affected—in his case, he was fifteen feet from being able to go to his place of business. The market ended up being closed. This led to some terrible arguments in the basement of our house between my father and his two associates, of which one was his older brother. The closing of the market created hard feelings between them that lasted a lifetime.

I remember going to the police station and to the courthouse with my father. He felt that perhaps there had been some mistake made, but he was told

Shortly before the United States entered the war, the Bronzinis pose with their new 1939 Pontiac (left to right: Clara, Al, Guido; front: Lorenzo). Courtesy of Velio A. Bronzini

that there was nothing that could be done about the situation; the restriction order came from the federal government. I remember my mother always crying; she and the ladies of the neighborhood already had sons in the military, and they would huddle together and cry constantly.

My mother used to repeat, over and over, "Why is this happening to us? *Non abbiamo fatto niente a nessuno,* we have done nothing to no one, we have done no wrong. *Non e giustizza,* this is not justice." My father became quite ill over these events and ended up being bedridden for weeks with a severe case of the shingles. I remember him sitting at the kitchen table with his head resting on his crossed arms, lamenting to my mother the closing of his market. My mother suffered the most; she got into such a state of depression that she had a total mental collapse, and eventually had to be admitted to a mental hospital in Livermore, California.

I remember that we used to visit her on Sundays. One Sunday when we went to visit her we found her in her bed in a straitjacket, and I remember being scared. My father got upset and started swearing at the doctor and made him take it off; my father was Toscano and had a pretty good vocabulary of swear words. They said that they had to restrain her to give the electric shock treatments. How ironic: she was the one whose basic civil rights were being violated, and she ends up in a straitjacket. My mother was not crazy by any means; maybe she had flashbacks of her teenage years in Italy when the black-shirted police used to kick their door down because my grandfather refused to display the Fascist flag.

The gossip in the neighborhood was that Clara had been taken to a hospital for crazy people. At that time, the Livermore hospital was like the Napa hospital today; if you had what was considered to be a mental problem, that is where they would take you. I am sure that hearing that kind of gossip must have been painful for my father, because they were proud people. In the summer of 1943 my father moved the family to Castro Valley, a farming community about fifteen miles south of Oakland. I believe he wanted to get away from the gossip, *la vergogna*, the shame of all that was happening.

During the restrictions, my father had difficulty finding work, and took whatever he could get. He got a job at an electrical manufacturing company in Oakland, but when his alien status was discovered, he was asked to leave. He took a job with a poultry producing company, and he was regularly reminded by the owner that were it not for this job, he would be in a bread line. My father was a man of principle and, especially after having been in business for many years, was not going to subject himself to that kind of degradation. He took a job building water towers for farmers. At five feet, six inches and weighing a hundred and fifty pounds, he hardly had the physical attributes for heavy construction work.

It was time to get serious about becoming citizens, so they enrolled in classes at Lockwood Junior High School. I used to go to the classes with them and used to help them with their homework. A lady from the neighborhood used to tutor a lot of the Italians that were studying for their tests. They used to hold classes in the basement of our house; some of them would come walking down the street carrying their own chairs. I remember the men sampling the wine from the barrels as she was teaching class.

Shortly after the restrictions were lifted they all prepared for the big day, the citizenship examination. A group of them went to the courthouse in Oakland, and they all passed on the first try. I remember the rejoicing in the neighborhood, my mother and her friends this time crying tears of joy while congratulating each other. They were saying, *"Ora siamo Americani,"* now we are Americans. One of the neighbors played the accordion, there was dancing in our yard, and I think my father opened every barrel of wine in the basement.

My father was able to go back and reopen the produce market, which grew to include a bar and restaurant, a liquor store and a fish market. My parents never held any hard feelings against this country. They always felt like they were responsible for what happened. My father often said that the biggest mistake they ever made was not becoming citizens before the war.

After it was over, it was not talked about much in the Italian community. Until I became aware of the project *Una Storia Segreta,* I had actually put it out of my mind as well. My father and mother didn't marinate themselves in self-pity, or in ethnic pity. It was time to get on with the challenge of fulfilling the American dream. They went on to become good Americans. My mother used to say that her favorite song was our national anthem, and my father used to hold his hat over his heart whenever there was a parade and the colors would march by. They were proud to say that they were Americans.

They were well respected; they had integrity; they believed in God and they loved their family, they were now proud Italian Americans. I am still saddened that they and so many others had to endure such pain. The basic civil rights which are afforded to us under our Constitution should never again be taken from any immigrant from any land.

Sundays in Colma

by Floyd Gonella

Floyd Gonella, currently the elected San Mateo County superintendent of schools, lived during the war with his parents in the town of Colma, just south of San Francisco, where his father was a truck farmer. Gonella recalls some of the more ironic aspects of wartime, among them the fact that Italian prisoners of war, while incarcerated in California, enjoyed more latitude for travel and recreation than did the resident enemy aliens during their restriction.

We lived in Colma, just south of San Francisco, with many other Italian American truck farmers, most of whom had originally come from the area around Genoa. The specialty crops in Colma were cabbage and cauliflower. Five different varieties of cabbages were grown and were reputed to be the largest cabbage heads in the nation. There were many photographs taken by the famous photographer Gino Sbrana of Colma truck farmers. One portrayed a group of thirteen men beside a truck loaded with thousands of heads of cabbage. The cabbages were meticulously piled level upon level, all woven together with their leaves. My father, Amedeo Fiorino Gonella, is in one of those photographs. He was also well known for playing his accordion at local Italian functions.

During the war, the activities of my mother (Margherita "Tina" Gonella) were restricted, like those of many others in our area. By law, she had to register as an enemy alien, and we had to turn in our radio, which had a shortwave band, as well as my father's hunting rifle, even though he was an American citizen.

After the war, my mother went through the process of obtaining her citizenship papers, and when she appeared before a judge in San Francisco, he said, "What are you doing here? You are already a citizen." It turned out she had come to the United States a few days before her twenty-first birthday, and her father, an American citizen, was already here. She automatically became a citizen when she entered the United States. Because she did not realize this, she was compelled to register as an enemy alien, in compliance with the Smith Act of 1940, which required the annual registration and fingerprinting of aliens. In addition to these requirements, aliens were subject to curfews which restricted them to their houses after a certain hour. My mother was highly distressed by this governmental "house arrest" and used to talk about the troubles with neighbors. There was a Mrs. Matteucci, whose husband, Nello, was detained or interned—I'm not sure which.* I heard a story about his son and someone else's daughter both visiting their fathers in the internment camp, meeting, and getting married.

Perhaps one of the greatest ironies involved the Italian prisoners of war being held at the San Francisco Presidio during the war. They were allowed to come to Colma on weekends. The Italian families would go to the Presidio, pick them up, and bring them home for Sunday dinner. Often they would go to the Monte Cristo Club in San Francisco to hear my father and his little Italian band. My parents would sometimes go into San Francisco and pick up an Italian prisoner of war who came from somewhere near my father's or mother's hometown and bring him home for a Sunday meal. Again, it was ironic that the Italian prisoners of war had greater flexibility during their visits to the community than my mother, who, when under restriction as an "enemy alien," had to comply with specific curfews. This simply did not make much sense to the Italian families in Colma, but I suppose there was a great deal that did not make sense during the war. Fortunately, the restrictions were lifted after a period of time, and families could return to a normal life. I was very young then, but I clearly remember the good and bad times of those years as if they occurred yesterday.

---

*Records indicate that Nello Matteucci, a plasterer from Colma, was indeed interned for approximately a year.

The Relocation of Italian Americans in California during World War II

by Stephen Fox

Stephen Fox, a navy veteran, received his Ph.D. from the University of Cincinnati, after which he taught U.S. history at a Northern California university for thirty years. His other published works on Italian Americans include: "General John DeWitt and the Proposed Internment of German and Italian Aliens during World War II" (*Pacific Historical Review*, 1988), for which he received the annual Louis Knott Koontz Memorial Award for Best Article; *The Unknown Internment: An Oral History of the Relocation of Italian Americans during World War II* (Boston: Twayne Publishers, 1990), which was honored twice, as a 1991 outstanding book by the Gustavus Myers Center for the Study of Human Rights in the United States and with an American Book Award from the Before Columbus Foundation in 1992. *The Unknown Internment* is now republished as *UnCivil Liberties: Italian Americans Under Siege during World War II* (Upublish.com, 2000). Fox has recently turned his attention to German Americans and published "The Deportation of Latin American Germans, 1941–47: Fresh Legs for Mr. Monroe's Doctrine," in the *Yearbook of German-American Studies* (Society for German-American Studies, 1997), and *America's Invisible Gulag: A Biography of German American Internment and Exclusion—Memory and History* (Peter Lang Publishing, 2000).

The locomotive engineer never saw the object that lay ahead of him on the tracks that cold night in February 1942, nor could he have guessed why it was there. The next morning's newspaper gave only a brief account of the incident: Martini Battistessa, age 65, unable to complete his naturalization before his adopted country classified him an enemy alien and expelled him from his home of twenty years, went to a bar and offered a friend $50 to shoot himin the head.

Stephen Fox's article is based in part on his book *The Unknown Internment: An Oral History of the Relocation of Italian Americans during World War II* (Boston: Twayne Publishers, 1990).

The friend laughed, and Battistessa left. A short time later he threw himself in front of the southbound passenger train as it passed through Richmond, California.[1]

When authorities told Giuseppe Micheli that he could not live in his Vallejo home after February 24, the 57-year-old fisherman cut his throat with a butcher knife. And before 65-year-old Stefano Terranova leaped to his death from a building, having refused to leave his home as ordered by the Justice Department, he left a note that read in part, "I believe myself to be good, but find myself deceived. I don't know why....It is my fault for blaming others. My brain is no good." Near Stockton, Giovanni Sanguenetti, aged 62 and unable to live with the stigma of being called an enemy alien, hanged himself.[2]

Probably few readers of the morning newspapers around San Francisco Bay paid much attention to the two or three lines reporting each of these last desperate acts, dwarfed as they were by news from the global war fronts. But these four aliens' deaths, incidental as they might have seemed in the rush of world events in 1942, were nonetheless important pieces in a larger mosaic of human tragedy.

Hindsight makes it deceptively easy to dismiss the threat that native Americans perceived in domestic Fascists and Nazis and their sympathizers before Pearl Harbor. While there may have been no militant fifth column, the existence of ethnic ghettoes and the reluctance of Italian Americans to denounce Mussolini and Fascism until Il Duce made his bargain with Hitler and Italy allied itself with Germany heightened these suspicions. Thus, spurred by the popular press, ignorant of the Italians' conflict between nationalism and their sentimental ties to Italy, and duped by the Fascists' propaganda, U.S. politicians and the military began to treat the threat of so-called enemy aliens as genuine.

To any Californian who read the newspapers during those first desperate days of the war, it was obvious that the United States was not winning. Thus the political pressure that drove alien policy at home paralleled the bad news from the Pacific war front that climaxed with the surrender of Bataan and Corregidor in April 1942. In the ensuing confusion, desperation, and panic, the public extended the politicians an unlimited mandate to act. The demand to remove all enemy aliens came not only from the public and the media, but from every level of local, state, and national government. Resolutions from citizens, city councils, chambers of commerce, boards of supervisors, Congress, and law enforcement officials urging swift action poured in to the president and other responsible officials.[3]

Lieutenant General John L. DeWitt, commanding general of the Fourth Army and Western Defense Command in San Francisco, believed passionately

that communities of enemy aliens in the United States harbored fifth columnists waiting to strike on orders from Rome, Berlin, or Tokyo. Just before the
federal government promulgated its enemy alien policy in mid-February,
California Attorney General Earl Warren, fearful of what the aliens might do,
telegraphed a critical question to city police chiefs, county sheriffs, and district
attorneys: "Can we assure the public of their safety by treating all enemy aliens
alike, regardless of nationality, or do you believe that we should differentiate
among them as to nationality?" Nearly half of the respondents—fifty-four—
identified the Japanese as the most dangerous; only four believed that either the
Italians or Germans posed a greater threat. But close to twenty-five percent,
regardless of whether they thought the Japanese more dangerous, believed that
authorities should treat all three groups alike.[4]

In Washington, officials far removed from the pressures of a panicky public struggled to find a way to match concerns expressed on the West Coast with
their own requirements for national security. Assistant Secretary of War John
McCloy told DeWitt that he feared the economic dislocation that would
accompany mass relocation.[5] Most of California's congressional delegation did
not endorse the cry for mass expulsion of Italians and Germans. California
Attorney General Earl Warren told the California Joint Immigration
Committee that it would disrupt "national unity" to expel Italian and German
aliens, for, despite their governments at home, they were just like "everybody
else"—that is, they were not Japanese. U.S. Attorney General Francis Biddle,
knowing Franklin Roosevelt's political instincts, told the president that the
hysteria on the West Coast had begun to affect Italian and German morale in
New York and Boston. And he also warned Secretary of War Henry Stimson
that "the evacuation of all enemy aliens from [these areas] would…present a
problem of very great magnitude." Biddle's reluctance to back Lieutenant
General DeWitt's plan to relocate the bulk of the enemy aliens also received
the approval of a trio of respected lawyers who, at the attorney general's request,
issued an advisory recommendation later accepted by the War Department that
isolated the Japanese Americans from the other enemy nationalities and fore-
shadowed future policy:

> Persons of Japanese descent constitute the smallest definable class
> upon which those with the military responsibility for defense
> would reasonably determine to impose restrictions.…Similar dan-
> gers of disloyal activities by citizens of other racial stocks can-
> not…be handled in the same way. It would…present an insupera-
> ble problem of administration, not to mention the consequent

disruption of defense production, to bar the millions of persons of German and Italian stock from either seacoast area...⁶

By February 11, Stimson had decided to recommend to the president that authorities not expel Italians and Germans right away. This shifted the government's attention to the Japanese Americans. But despite Attorney General Biddle's and other officials' belief that the exclusion order of February 19 affected only the Japanese, a postwar investigation conducted by the War Department concluded that when the president signed Executive Order 9066, some military officers believed it applied to the Italians and Germans as well. Certainly California governor Culbert Olson believed so, and as a result many Italian and German aliens feared that they still faced eventual relocation.⁷

Ironically, there was no hurry to rid California of its enemy aliens immediately after Pearl Harbor, when the United States was most vulnerable to attack. Not until the hastily convened Roberts Commission (named after Supreme Court Justice Owen J. Roberts) released its report nearly two months later, alleging that Japanese Americans on Oahu had aided Japan's air assault, did the hue and cry to do something about Axis aliens on the mainland commence in earnest.⁸

In the first days and weeks after Pearl Harbor, the authorities treated enemy aliens in California more as a nuisance than a threat. The Justice Department had warned enemy aliens in mid-December that they must give up their firearms or face internment.⁹ Two weeks later the government added cameras and radios. These new regulations swamped local officials, who had received no advance warning. In San Francisco alone, aliens surrendered nearly five thousand radios and cameras the first day. The deluge soon included ammunition, explosives, maps, photographs of the exteriors and interiors of defense plants, signaling devices, codes or ciphers, and papers, documents, or books that might conceal invisible writing.¹⁰

Implementation of the new policy was arbitrary. Sometimes the military was overzealous, as when the commander of the Northern California Defense Sector told the mayor of Monterey that unregulated "vice resorts" (bars run by aliens) might impair military efficiency and become nests of treasonous activities. Sometimes implementation was ridiculous, as when an Oakland car dealer and civic leader, who also happened to be an Italian alien who had lived in the United States since the age of six, was told that he could not collect the $3,500 owed him on five cars the county had purchased four days after Pearl Harbor, because payment by Alameda County would constitute "trading with the enemy." A ban on travel further than five miles from home or work as well as an 8 P.M. to 6 A.M. curfew caused additional inconvenience, and applicants seeking permits flooded the offices of local authorities.

The most stunning blow was, however, the government's successive announcements in late January, after release of the Roberts Commission report, that it had created eighty-six prohibited and restricted zones on the West Coast forbidden to aliens for their own "protection." Army officials predicted the evacuation and internment of between 200,000 and 226,000 enemy aliens and their children by the end of February, including 100,000 alien Italians and 71,000 Germans.

Hardest hit by this decree were the Italian fishermen who dominated the industry along the California coast. Economic life for them stopped for the remainder of 1942 when, in late February, the Coast Guard barred all enemy-alien fishing in bay and coastal waters for the remainder of the war. The restrictions idled seventy-five percent of Monterey Bay's small boat fleet.[11]

> [My dad] had a fishing boat when the war started, and he kept it docked at Fisherman's Wharf. He would go down there and, with my older brother, just take a look at it during the day to make sure that it wasn't being mistreated. Nobody objected to his being there. Guards patrolled the wharf continuously—twenty-four hours a day—because they wanted to make sure the Italian fishermen were not abusing the law, and that they didn't go out in their boats. (Joseph Maniscalco, San Francisco)

Soon the army and navy began to requisition the fishermen's boats and industry-related property. Appeals made to the Justice Department were unsuccessful as Biddle's staff deferred to the War Department.

> The government took our fishing boats. We had to earn a living, so some of the other fishermen and I went up to Seattle to charter boats. With those, we were able to call out our crews again and resume fishing.
>
> The government kept my boat for about two years. But when they returned it, it was in very bad shape. I spent a lot of money to repair it so I could fish again, but it was no use. I had to moor it to Wharf No. 2 and continue to fish with the rented boat. (Giuseppe Spadaro, Monterey)

In Monterey alone, which was within a restricted zone, between 2,500 and 3,000 Italian aliens had to move. Most scattered to new homes in seventy-five towns throughout the state; 300 others remained within a fifty-mile radius.

> We packed our belongings, very cheerfully, and everything was put into a moving van. The house next door was vacated too. Moving vans were moving the people out. Most of them that had husbands that were citizens were moved to Salinas so that the husbands could come in and fish. We established our residency there, and we were there from February to May. I don't remember too many details, but it was a very sad thing. I had just started Catholic school, and I remember how hard it was for me to leave. (Anita Ferrante, Monterey)

Opponents of the policy initially had difficulty organizing their protest, because no one knew precisely who would have to move. Justice Department officials, including Attorney General Biddle, had first ruled out any exceptions. Then they allowed that some adjustments were possible where "compelling reasons" existed and following a "suitable investigation." But initially, no one received favors from the government, not even religious and political refugees, the aged and infirm, or aliens living with naturalized sons or daughters.[12]

As the Italians prepared to move, a congressional committee, sympathetic to the plight of European aliens, began West Coast public hearings on relocation and internment. It issued periodic reports and recommendations and met frequently with Stimson's closest associate in the War Department, John McCloy. The Tolan Committee, so-called after its chairman, John H. Tolan of Oakland, hoped to exert a calming influence by publicizing the effect of the relocation program on the economy and social fabric of the West Coast.[13] In the end, the committee proved to be the salvation of the Italian and German aliens.

While the Tolan Committee fully supported the administration's decision to remove the Japanese, it believed little time remained to save Italian and German aliens or refugees. To the witnesses gathered before the committee shortly after the commencement of the hearings, Tolan vouched for the loyalty of Oakland's Italians and insisted that the witnesses adopt his view. Witness Edward Corsi, an expert on Italian Americans, estimated that in 1942 there were 400,000 young men of Italian parentage in the armed forces, and thousands of Italian defense workers. The family of popular baseball player Joe DiMaggio was used as an example of the problems the removal of Italians would cause:

CHAIRMAN JOHN TOLAN: Tell us about the DiMaggios. Tell us about the DiMaggios' father.

ATTORNEY CHAUNCEY TRAMUTOLO: Neither of the DiMaggio seniors is a citizen. They have reared nine children, five boys and four girls, eight of whom were born in the United States, and the other one is a naturalized citizen. Three of the boys are outstanding persons in the sports world. Joe, who is with the Yankees, was the leading hitter for both the American and National Leagues during the years 1939 and 1940. His younger brother, Dominic, is with the Boston Red Sox, and his older brother Vincent is with the Pittsburgh team of the National League....To evacuate the senior DiMaggios would, in view of the splendid family they have reared and their unquestioned loyalty, present, I am sure you will agree with me, a serious situation.

The committee also attempted to determine whether extenuating circumstances existed in the cases of alien families threatened with disruption, which, if not addressed skillfully, might arouse resentment that would carry over into the postwar period.[14]

The Tolan Committee's witnesses addressed four central issues on which the committee built its case for alien relief: hardship and exemptions were two, the others being whether Japanese, Germans, and Italians should be treated alike, and lastly whether the army or local authorities should handle relocation. Many witnesses presented the argument that Italians and Germans posed more danger than the Japanese because their racial characteristics made them hard to distinguish from other Americans. But this reasoning was overridden by Governor Olson and others who held that Caucasian authorities could not distinguish between loyal and disloyal Japanese as well as they could between Italians and Germans, because the Japanese "all look alike." On this basis alone, the committee concluded that the three groups should not be treated in the same way.[15]

Without exception, the witnesses agreed that the final relocation decision rested with the army and the one person who had ultimate responsibility for coastal defense: Lieutenant General DeWitt.[16] Thus the Tolan Committee faced exactly the same dilemma that had earlier proved so vexing to Attorney General Biddle and his staff: the nation needed protection, but the committee, having no plan of its own, could not hold out against the army, which did.

Now Stimson, who heretofore had listened halfheartedly to the aliens' passionate advocates and was uneasy about the political, economic, and morale aspects of the relocation program, gathered his civilian staff in the War Department to plan how to rein in Lieutenant General DeWitt. For his part, DeWitt, although contemptuous, was not entirely insensitive to pressure from above. His private assurance to the Tolan Committee that no mass relocation would take place, with the exception of "necessary" and "humane" removals carried out step by step, was the first hint that the War Department had decided to scale back the expulsion program temporarily. On February 20, Stimson had instructed the general to develop plans for relocating German aliens, but to ignore the Italians for the moment because they were more numerous and posed less danger.[17]

As a result, DeWitt's first "Public Proclamation" in early March divided all Italian, German, and Japanese nationals, as well as Japanese American citizens, into five classes. It put Japanese aliens, persons of Japanese ancestry, and "dangerous enemy aliens" in greatest jeopardy. At the same time, DeWitt hinted that all Italians and Germans might eventually have to go. This veiled threat forced the War Department to face head-on the implications of a mass relocation. McCloy again impressed on DeWitt the need to forget about the Italians and Germans, since the Japanese problem already threatened to overwhelm the army's limited logistical resources.[18]

DeWitt's ambiguous statements also alarmed the Tolan Committee, and in questioning Tom Clark [coordinator of the Alien Enemy Control Program for the Western Defense Command] soon thereafter, one member warned Clark:

> We are reluctant to see policies created here concerning Germans
> and Italians which may stand as precedents for subsequent action
> in other parts of the country where the size and scope of the prob-
> lem are of such enormous magnitude as to jeopardize the very war
> effort....It is unthinkable that we should treat this matter lightly.[19]

Clark, evidently not yet in harmony with the War Department, assured the committee that DeWitt thought of removing Italians and Germans only from Military Area No. 1, where approximately 86,000 of them lived. If one subtracted the exemptions, he guessed that only a fraction of that number would have to relocate—provided they behaved themselves. Some committee members, weary of Clark's cavalier and hard-nosed attitude, worried about national public reaction to Italian and German relocation. Thus, just two days after Clark gave his vague commitments, three members of the committee met with McCloy in San Francisco, after which a joint communiqué proclaimed the conferees in "thorough agreement on steps which have been taken and which remain to be taken."[20]

Despite this apparent top-level accord, documents unavailable to Tolan show that DeWitt and the provost marshal general's office remained wedded to a course of mass relocation of Italians and Germans. For example, the Senate Committee on Military Affairs, looking into relocation on its own in Washington, tried to learn the total number of aliens from the provost marshal general, as well as how many the army wanted to remove, so that the committee could estimate the effect nationwide. The committee had reluctantly concluded, based on the witnesses' testimony, that "the same thing is going to have to be done on the East Coast." The provost marshal's aide replied that authorities had marked about 100,000 people for relocation to concentration camps, sixty percent of them Japanese and the remainder divided equally between the two European enemy alien groups.[21]

In its preliminary report, released on March 19, the committee expressed its fear at the proposed size of the expulsion in unambiguous terms: the government, it pointed out, had not removed the Japanese from Hawaii, despite the obvious threat to American security there, because the Japanese made up thirty-seven percent of Hawaii's population. On the other hand, the Japanese constituted only one percent of the population in the Pacific states. Moreover, Italians and Germans on the mainland had built different kinds of communities than the Japanese, and where the Japanese had only one economic base, agriculture, the Italians and German pursued a variety of occupations. Thus, the committee concluded:

> The numbers involved in the Japanese evacuation are large, but they are by no means as large, for the whole country, as those who will be involved if we generalize the current treatment of the Japanese to apply to all Axis aliens and their immediate families....Any such proposal is out of the question if we intend to win this war.[22]

By early April, with Japanese Americans on their way to Manzanar and other relocation camps as far east as Arkansas, the Italians and Germans who remained in California continued to be restricted. Failure to register as enemy aliens, possession of a shortwave radio or camera, and not observing the curfew and travel restrictions made them liable for imprisonment.

Lacking confidence in his own bureaucracy, particularly in DeWitt, Stimson hired Alfred Jaretski Jr., a New York City corporate lawyer with recent refugee relief experience in Europe, to work for McCloy. Soon thereafter,

Jaretski wrote Stimson about the approximately 80,000 Italian and German enemy aliens on the West Coast subject to possible relocation whose disloyalty should not be assumed. Their removal would be unjust, he emphasized, "but of more importance in this period of national emergency would be the undoubted national repercussions of such a movement....It would inevitably lead to incessant demands for [relocation] from other areas," i.e. New York. "If public apprehension is unnecessarily aroused in respect [to] these alien groups, public clamor for protection will greatly impede the war effort."[23] Other behind-the-scenes attempts to influence DeWitt's superiors in Washington continued. Among them, a conference of U.S. district attorneys informed the provost marshal general of its conclusion that "to attempt to [relocate] all the million-and-a-quarter alien enemies would mean serious economic disruption involving about fifteen million people directly," greatly handicapping war production.[24]

Then, astonishingly, considering the weighty lobbying effort against the army, the reach of the removal threatened to escape all reasonable bounds: Biddle wrote Roosevelt that he feared the army planned to evacuate enemy aliens from the East as well as the West Coast. Stimson, who saw the attorney general's letter, sought to ease the president's mind: "It was a foolish matter without any foundation...and Biddle ought to have been ashamed of himself." No "mass" relocation of the East Coast would occur; the army would do it "very carefully with very small numbers."[25]

Having said this, Stimson no doubt believed that the problem on the East Coast had been laid to rest, but he still had to sell a limited expulsion to his officers on the West Coast, where DeWitt continued to oppose the suggestion that individual loyalty examinations might provide a way to sort through the aliens, and Karl Bendetsen, DeWitt's chief of staff, remained convinced that there were "a lot of dangerous" Italians and Germans who had to go. Jaretski patiently explained to Bendetsen that any mass expulsion of Italians and Germans would mean more relocation camps:

> Any sizable evacuation from the West Coast [is] going to inflame
> public opinion....It's going to mean a sizable evacuation from
> other areas. Therefore, we are loathe to go into any wholesale
> program of this kind, unless where defense is necessary....There's a
> lot of difference whether you're talking about moving twenty
> thousand people, or moving two or three thousand.[26]

But Stimson's thoughts on this subject, on which his assurance to the president rested, had not yet filtered down through the War Department's chain of command. In fact, Lieutenant General Hugh A. Drum, commanding general of the Eastern Defense Command, had publicly announced his intention to establish prohibited and restricted areas covering the entire Atlantic seaboard and inland—some sixteen states and 52 million people, fulfilling the Tolan Committee's worst fears.[27]

The same day that Jaretski issued his warning to Bendetsen and General Drum announced his exclusion plans, Tom Clark, who was supposed to be working for Attorney General Biddle, again rekindled doubts when he wrote to James H. Rowe Jr., a Biddle assistant, that "anyone who had the idea that General DeWitt is going to delay the evacuation of German and Italian aliens is in error. He has consistently said publicly and otherwise that he intends to evacuate these groups as soon as his program with reference to the Japanese is completed." Rowe, who passed Clark's letter along to Edward Ennis, also a member of the anti–War Department clique in the Justice Department, wrote cynically in the margin, "I think you had better talk to McCloy [?] about this. We will soon see who is the boss. I'm betting on DeWitt."[28]

But Lieutenant General DeWitt was not "the boss." Electoral strategy mattered most at the highest level of decision making, and the vote counters vetoed General DeWitt's grandiose plans. For Franklin Roosevelt and his electoral strategists, one sobering trend had appeared in the otherwise satisfying victory over Wendell Willkie in November 1940: Italian American voters had drifted away from the Democratic Party in the large urban centers of the East. Thus the changed attitude in the White House emanated from an electoral sensitivity that public opinion and events—even Pearl Harbor—never completely eroded. In time, FDR made sure that the downward spiral of Italian American support for the Democrats did not continue, even if it meant refusing to allow the military to dictate the terms of the relationship between the aliens and their adopted homeland.

By early May, the president had become thoroughly alarmed by the repeated warnings from the Justice Department and complaints from Capitol Hill and New York, and he swung into action. He ordered Stimson to take no action against Italian or German aliens on the East Coast without first consulting him. Alien control, he said, except for the Japanese, remained a civilian matter, and all the talk about evacuations lowered civilian morale. Ever the politician, he assured New York governor Herbert Lehman that the federal government contemplated no mass evacuation of Italians or Germans. But Stimson, mindful of his responsibility to protect the country against dangerous individual aliens, thought the Justice Department had unduly panicked the president, and he argued successfully against compromising the War Department's prerogative to remove dangerous aliens.[29]

Meanwhile, the indefatigable DeWitt pressed on; he now threatened to put 6,000 to 10,000 aliens in "relocation centers in a manner similar to that employed in the case of persons of Japanese ancestry." Bendetsen warned McCloy of DeWitt's seriousness. The general, he emphasized, believed that the probability of German retaliatory raids grew stronger as each month passed, and he proposed to justify removal of all other enemy aliens, not then exempted, as "an essential war measure." Carefully separating his views from those of DeWitt, Bendetsen recommended to McCloy that authorities not move the Italians by groups, but merely continue the Justice Department's individual internment policy. But Bendetsen insisted that if the Justice Department failed to act more diligently, the War Department would take action under Executive Order 9066 "similar to that taken in the evacuation of the Japanese"[30]

Following two quick conferences with the more contrite Bendetsen (in Washington to press his and DeWitt's proposals on the War Department in person), McCloy at last found a compromise solution. He told Stimson that the country could expect little danger from the Italians, although more so from the Germans; that DeWitt and Drum needed the authority to remove, but not to detain, dangerous individuals; that the commanding generals use this power sparingly; and that they should make weekly reports of the numbers involved to the assistant secretary. It would help, he added, in deference to Bendetsen, if the FBI stepped up its investigations and detentions. When DeWitt learned that McCloy and Stimson did not agree with his proposed mass evacuation of Italians and Germans, he demanded written instructions exonerating him from all the consequences of such blatant disregard.[31]

When the War Department conducted a series of internal conferences in mid-May to prepare Stimson for a cabinet meeting, it had in hand the Tolan Committee's latest report, which continued to hammer home the logic of its earlier paper: the size of the Italian and German communities, more diverse and ten times larger than the Japanese, presented "problems more vast and far reaching than the Japanese....Emergency measures must not be permitted to alter permanently those fundamental principles upon which this Nation was built." It now appeared to the committee, as it had not in February, that Japanese relocation might "serve as an incident sufficiently disturbing to lower seriously the morale of vast groups of foreign-born among our people," meaning that Italians and Germans would not have to go.

Clearly, the public conclusions and recommendations of the Tolan Committee had affected attitudes in the War Department; Stimson recommended to the president that the government not evacuate Italians and Germans in the same manner as the Japanese. Roosevelt immediately approved

Stimson's recommendation, expressing relief that the secretary had, as Roosevelt put it, "laid a ghost."[32]

It remained to deal with Lieutenant General DeWitt. McCloy wrote the general that FDR and Stimson had approved Executive Order 9066 "with the expectation that the exclusion would not reach such numbers [as proposed by DeWitt]....We want, if at all possible, to avoid the necessity of establishing additional relocation settlements." DeWitt did not get the accompanying waiver of responsibility he had insisted on.[33]

Between May and October, the wheels of government ground inexorably toward a total relaxation of restrictions. By the end of June, with the Japanese gone, Lieutenant General DeWitt abolished the six-month-old prohibited and restricted zones (except in certain sensitive areas); only the curfew, a change-of-residence requirement, and travel restrictions remained.[34] On Columbus Day, a day of special significance for Italian Americans, Attorney General Biddle announced that the government would no longer classify Italian aliens as enemies. As Biddle remembered it twenty years later, Roosevelt wished that he had thought of reclassification himself, and immediately gave the idea his blessing, calling it "a masterly stroke of international statesmanship and good politics."[35]

The discomfort and anxiety of the aliens and their families had ended; they could resume nearly normal lives. Justice Department officials, civilians in the War Department, and strategic members of Congress finally realized that it was neither feasible nor necessary to remove Italian and German aliens. Little likelihood existed of Germany, or certainly of Italy, attacking the Pacific Coast. Because investigators had more information relative to dangerous individual Italians and Germans, the government believed that it could handle them more efficiently than it had the Japanese. But the principal consideration in taking this decision proved to be that relocation would create a logistical nightmare. Alfred Jaretski summarized this conclusion in June 1942: "Any action with respect to the Italians and Germans on the West Coast would have serious repercussions in other parts of the country where the alien populations were much greater." In dealing with the problem of internal security, he posed three issues to bear in mind:

> One, the...impossibility of moving en masse approximately one
> million aliens of Italian and German nationality, or any very sub-
> stantial number of them; two, the terrific cost involved in any
> such action, including the dislocation of our economy and the
> effect on public morale; and three, the fact that the vast majority
> of this group are believed to be loyal or harmless.[36]

Because the racial explanation for internment policy has been so pervasive in recent years, historians have overlooked the government's pragmatic response to the alien crisis, particularly its having chosen to distinguish between the Italian and German influence in the country in contrast to the Japanese. But no one who reads Secretary Stimson's reply to a request from House Speaker John McCormack (D-Mass.), which asked that he look into the Japanese threat on Hawaii, can fail to notice that in his answer Stimson applied the same principle to the Italian and German population on the mainland that he outlined to McCormack regarding Hawaii: "Our greatest difficulty in dealing with [the Japanese] problem," the secretary wrote, is the economic aspect. "The Japanese population is so interwoven into the economic fabric of the Islands that if we attempted to evacuate all Japanese aliens and citizens, all business, including that concerned with the building up of our defenses, would practically stop."[37] Colonel Bendetsen told the Commission on the Wartime Relocation and Internment of Civilians that most of the Japanese on the West Coast had "concentrated themselves into readily identifiable clusters." Thus, he implied, they remained more vulnerable to relocation than the vastly larger and more scattered Italian and German communities.[38] Indeed, the millions of Italians and Germans diffused across the country made the logic of Hawaii imperative from California to New York.

Economics, politics, and morale rather than Californians' prejudices drove U.S. internment policy during World War II, with race as a reinforcing element. Authorities ultimately judged that the withdrawal of perhaps millions of Italians and Germans from civilian production jobs, many in heavy industry—or even the shutdown of commercial fishing in California waters—was too high a price to pay to thwart potential sabotage.

Endnotes

1. *Los Angeles Times*, February 17, 1942, p. 6; *San Francisco Chronicle*, February 22, 1942, pp. 4–5.
2. *San Francisco Chronicle*, February 12, 1942, p. 9, and February 17, 1942, p. 6; *Humboldt Times*, February 21, 1942, p. 1.
3. Local governments acted almost immediately. Seventeen counties, along with the statewide County Supervisors Association, urged alien evacuation in formal resolutions. Reportedly, "aroused" organizations in Southern California planned reprisals against all enemy aliens (Morton Grodzins, *Americans Betrayed: Politics and the Japanese Evacuation*, Chicago: University of Chicago Press, 1949:113). The Los Angeles Council of California Women's Clubs adopted a resolution petitioning Lieutenant General DeWitt to place all enemy aliens in concentration camps immediately, and the Young Democratic Club of Los Angeles went a step further, passing a resolution that demanded the removal even of American-born Italians and Germans from the Pacific Coast. "Resolutions of County Boards of Supervisors in Re-control Measures over Alien Enemies, Japanese, Etc.," February 3 and 20, 1942, Bancroft Library, file 67/14, folder A 15.12; "Resolutions of City Governments in Re-control Measures over Enemy Aliens, Japanese, Etc.," February 9, 1942, Bancroft Library file 67/14, folder A 15.13; U.S. Congress, *Hearings of the Select Committee Investigating National Defense Migration,*

77th Congress, 2nd session, pts. 29–31 (Washington, D.C.: Government Printing Office, 1942), 29:11238 (hereafter cited as Tolan Committee *Hearings)*; and *San Francisco Chronicle*, February 13, 1942, p. 13.

4. Historian Morton Grodzins's analysis of Warren's questionnaire to district attorneys, sheriffs, etc. *(Americans Betrayed*, 1949). The original replies may be found in the Bancroft Library, University of California, Berkeley. U.S. Commission on Wartime Relocation and Internment of Civilians, Papers, microfilm editions ed. by Ralph Boehm, reel 9, frames 757–758 (hereafter cited as CWRIC followed by reel and frame numbers).

5. Telephone conversation, McCloy and DeWitt, February 3, 1942, CWRIC 5:809, 1:139.

6. Karl R. Bendetsen to Major General Allen W. Gullion, Provost Marshal General, February 4, 1942, CWRIC 5:588–592; Grodzins, 1949:96; memo of luncheon meeting, Biddle and Roosevelt, February 7, 1942, Biddle to Stimson, February 9, 1942, CWRIC 5:419, 12:264–265; Stephen Conn, Rose C. Engleman and Byron Farichild, *Guarding the United States and its Outposts* (Washington, D.C: Office of the Chief of Military History, Department of the Army, 1964)30–31; Benjamin V. Cohen, Archibald Cox, and Joseph L. Raid to Biddle, ca. February 10, 1942, CWRIC 11:587–588.

7. Biddle to Roosevelt, February 17, 1942, CWRIC 5:423–424; Earl Warren Oral History Project, 1976:31; Peter Irons, *Justice at War: The Story of the Japanese American Internment Cases* (New York: Oxford University Press, 1983): 62; Grodzins, 1949: 271–272; Edward J. Ennis, "Government Control of Alien Enemies," *State Government* 15 (May 1942):112; Stimson diary, February 18, 1942, CWRIC 17:238–239; Biddle to Roosevelt, April 17, 1943, CWRIC 1:349; "Supplemental Report on Civilian Controls Exercised by the WDC," January 1947, CWRIC 24:120–122; Bendetsen to McCloy, May 11, 1942, CWRIC 1:287–289; CWRIC, 1982:285; McCloy diary, February 16, 1942, and interview with John McCloy, CWRIC 4:268; and George C. Warren, "The Refugee and War," *Annals of the American Academy of Political and Social Science* 223 (September 1942):95.

8. U.S. Congress, House, *Report of Select Committee Investigating National Defense Migration*, 77th Congress, 2nd session, H.R. 1911, March 19, 1942, 2, (hereafter cited as Tolan Committee, *Preliminary Report)*.

9. Grodzins, 1949:113; "Resolutions of County Boards...," February 3 and 20, 1942; "Resolutions of City Governments...," February 9, 1942; Tolan Committee, 1942:11238; and *San Francisco Chronicle*, February 13, 1942, p. 13.

10. *San Francisco Chronicle*, December 29, 1941, p. 1; December 30, 1941, p. 8; January 1, 1942, p. 8; and January 7, 1942, p. 10.

11. *Monterey Peninsula Herald*, February 27, 1942, p. 15; and *San Francisco Chronicle*, February 27, 1942, p. 6.

12. *Pittsburg* [California] *Post-Dispatch*, February 4, 1942, pp. 1, 3; and U.S. Congress, House, *Fourth Interim Report of the Select Committee Investigating National Defense Migration*, 77th Cong., 2d sess., H.R. 2124, 19 May 1942 (hereafter Tolan Committee, *Fourth Interim Report):*1, 6.

13. Telegram from Tolan to his son, San Francisco, February 18, 1942, Bancroft Library, file 67/14, folder A 12.052.

14. Tolan Committee, Hearings, 29:10966–67, 11 10l–2; Tolan Committee, *Preliminary Report*, 15–16; Edward Corsi, "Italian Immigrants and Their Children," *Annals of the American Academy of Political and Social Science* 223 (September 1942):105; *San Francisco Chronicle*, February 21, 1942, p. 1, 6.

15. Tolan Committee, *Hearings*, 31:11631, 11634–36.

16. Ibid., 29:11095–96, 11103, 11106–7, 11115–17.

17. Stimson to DeWitt, February 20, 1942, Stimson diary, February 20, 1942, CWRIC 4:381–82, 17:243; Western Defense Command and Fourth Army, *Final Report: Japanese Evacuation from the West Coast*, 1942 (Washington, D.C.: Government Printing Office, 1943):25–29.

18. *Federal Register* 2320; Tolan Committee, *Preliminary Report; Fourth Interim Report*, p. 163; *San Francisco Chronicle*, March 4, 1942, pp. 1, 10. Officials in Los Angeles told a Tolan Committee staff member that they did not fear the Germans and Italians as groups. Interview

of Robert K. Lamb with Los Angeles County Defense Council, March 2, 1942, CWRIC 10:644; Stimson diary, February 26–27, 1942; Biddle, notes on cabinet meeting of February 27, 1942, CWRIC 17:262, 311, 3:764.

19. Tolan Committee, *Hearings*, 31:11629, 11784.
20. CWRIC 10:644; Tolan Committee, *Hearings*, 31:11781–82, 11784, *Preliminary Report*, p. 4; and *San Francisco Chronicle*, March 9, 1942, p. 1, 10 and March 1952, p. 9.
21. Western Defense Command, 1943:58–59; Tolan Committee, *Fourth Interim Report*, p. 3; U.S. Congress, Senate, Committee on Military Affairs, Report of Proceedings, 77th Congress, 2d session, S. 2352, March 13, 1942, (not printed); and CWRIC 10:283–285, 291.
22. Tolan Committee, *Preliminary Report*, note, 2, 21–22, 24.
23. "Status of Alfred Jaretski, Jr.," Office of Assistant Secretary of War, March 26, 1943, CWRIC 2:83. Jaretski served as advisor to the U.S. delegation at the International Refugee Conference at Evian, France, in 1938 and made four trips that year to Vienna to help Jews and other refugees after the Anschluss. *New York Times*, August 24, 1976, 32; Bruce Allen Murphy, *The Brandeis/Frankfurter Connection* (New York: Oxford University Press):202–204, 206, 217, 240, 298, 302; Jaretski to Stimson, March 31, 1942, CWRIC 1:59–69.
24. Biddle to Roosevelt, April 9, 1942, cited in Conn et al., *Guarding the United States*:145; John Burling, Edward Ennis, and Bernard Guffler, State Department, February 20, 1942, Bendetsen and Guffler, February 21, 1942, CWRIC 3:3637; Rowe: 23–24; notes taken in conference of U.S. district attorneys, Washington, D.C., April 9, 1942, CWRIC 12:572–574.
25. Stimson diary, April 15, 1942, Dwight Eisenhower to the adjutant general, April 24, 1942, CWRIC 17:330–31, 5:561.
26. Bendetsen to Jaretski, April 27, 1942, CWRIC 4:907–913.
27. Tolan Committee, *Fourth Interim Report*, 2, 21–22, 36.
28. Clark to Rowe, April 27, 1942, CWRIC 25:573.
29. FDR to Stimson, May 5, 1942, CWRIC 1:193; McCloy diary, May 7, 1942, CWRIC 28:618; James MacGregor Burns, *Roosevelt: The Soldier of Freedom* (New York: Harcourt Brace Jovanovich, 1970):268, 653; *San Francisco Chronicle*, May 10, 1942, p. 8; Jaretski to McCloy, May 2, 1942, CWRIC 1:215–217.
30. Bendetsen to McCloy, May 10–12, 1942, CWRIC.
31. McCloy diary/log, May 11–12, 1942, CWRIC 28:619; McCloy to Stimson, May 14, 1942, CWRIC 1:19520–1; and Conn, et al. 1964:146.
32. McCloy diary, May 15, 1942, CWRIC 28:620; McCloy and DeWitt, May 15,1942, CWRIC 25:445; Stimson to FDR, May 14, 1942, CWRIC 1:194; McCloy to Stimson, May 15, 1942, 1:190–192; Stimson diary, May 15, 1942, CWRIC 1:285; Bendetsen to McCloy, May 15, 1942, CWRIC 1:366–367; McCloy to Drum, July 15, 1942, CWRIC 17:335; McCloy to Major General A. D. Surles, July 24, 1942, CWRIC 3:763; and Surles to Bryon Price, July 25, 1942, CWRIC 5:354.
33. McCloy to DeWitt, May 20, 1942, CWRIC 24:816–817; Major General J. A. Ulio to DeWitt, May 22, 1942, CWRIC 4:885; Jacobus ten Broek, Edward Barnhart, and Floyd Matson, *Prejudice, War and the Constitution* (Berkeley and Los Angeles: University of California Press, 1954):113.
34. "J. A" [Ulio] to Bendetsen, July 7, 1942, CWRIC 1:271; Bendetsen to DeWitt July 14, 1942, CWRIC 1:273; and DeWitt to McCloy, August 14, 1942, CWRIC 1:267.
35. McCloy diary, October 15, 1942, CWRIC 28:641; 7 *Federal Register* 8455; and Francis Biddle, *In Brief Authority* (New York: Doubleday, 1962):229.
36. "Supplemental Report," January 1947, CWRIC 24:120–122; and Jaretski to Colonel Ralph H. Tate, June 4, 1942, CWRIC 6:242–294.
37. Charles F. Ayer to McCormack, June 6, 1942, CWRIC 1:533–534; and Stimson to McCormack, July 8, 1942, CWRIC 1:529.
38. Bendetsen to the Commission, June 22, 1981, CWRIC 4:167–168.

Pittsburg Stories

Rose Viscuso Scudero was twelve years old when her mother was forced to move from her family's home in Pittsburg, California, to a temporary residence out of the prohibited zone. Pittsburg is an old fishing town on the Sacramento–San Joaquin Delta, northeast of San Francisco. During the war, the entire town was off limits to enemy aliens. The Viscuso family's evacuation took place in February 1942. Rose has often spoken in public about her ordeal, including an appearance at the House Judiciary Committee Hearings on H.R. 2442, the Wartime Violation of Italian American Civil Liberties Act. The following account of her evacuation with her enemy alien mother refers to her time in exile and includes testimony about her brother's family, similarly affected.

Angelina Bruno and Frances Cardinale add their accounts of what it felt like to separate from one's family because of the evacuation order that forced nearly 2,000 noncitizen residents of Pittsburg and their minor children to leave town.

You Can Go Home Now

by Rose Viscuso Scudero

The year was 1942 and I was twelve and a half years old. My mother received a letter from the U.S. government stating that because she had not become a U.S. citizen, she would have to move to a specified area in the county we lived in, because our house was too close to the Columbia Steel Company and other vital industries and the San Joaquin River.

Because we were at war with Germany and Italy, it didn't matter that my father (a U.S. citizen) was employed at Kaiser Shipyards in Richmond, California, building the liberty ships for the Defense Department, and my two brothers worked at Columbia Steel Company. My three sisters worked in downtown Pittsburg establishments. Since I was a minor, I had to accompany my mother.

I was attending junior high school, and I felt bad about leaving all of my childhood friends. I thought it would be forever, so I gave away my collection of fancy pins that I wore on my sweaters to my classmates. My favorite was a phonograph record with two jitterbugs hanging from it.

I believe it was February or March of 1942 when we went to live in a rented house on West Street and Clayton Road in the outskirts of Concord, California, about nineteen miles from our home in Pittsburg. Mount Diablo was nearby. The view from our front porch was spectacular. Across the street was an abandoned, small crop-duster airport and hangar next to acres of strawberry fields that had to be abandoned by a Japanese family that were sent to concentration camps. I can remember sitting in the strawberry patch and eating strawberries until I became ill. We had strawberries for breakfast, lunch, and dinner!

We shared the house with my aunt Sara and uncle Filippo Nicolosi and my aunt Mary Viscuso and her two children, Salvatore and Johnny. My uncle Filippo was a U.S. citizen, but he stayed with us so that we had a man in the house.

I can remember my mother, Rosa, crying herself to sleep at night, missing her family. Other Pittsburg families settled in houses about a mile or so away and we would walk in the evenings to visit them. It was all country fields with a scattering of farmhouses.

I attended Clayton Valley School and the bus would pick us up first in the morning and drop us off last after school, so we had a ride all over the countryside. There were three classrooms in that school and each class had three grade levels. Maybe six pupils in one level and five in the next and three in the next and so forth. The teacher would give reading assignments to one group and oral work to the other. I found it very much to my advantage because I learned much of what the upper class was being taught.

My family, brothers Dante and Salvatore, my sisters Josephine, Gena, and Marie, and my father, Giuseppe Viscuso, would come to visit us on weekends. It was like a party when they came but sad when they had to leave.

When school was out in June, we moved to downtown Concord because my aunt Sara and uncle Filippo were one of the first families to be able to go back home to Pittsburg. My mother and Aunt Mary felt it would be safer to be in town, since we didn't have a man in the house. We lived upstairs from Pix Patio, a very

Rose Viscuso Scudero with her parents, Giuseppe and Rosa Viscuso, two years before Rose and her mother were forced to evacuate from their home in Pittsburg. Courtesy of Rose Viscuso Scudero popular bar and grill at that time. The city park was across the street, and at that time, Concord had only a few stores. It was a small country town with houses scattered several blocks apart.

I remember one day in June or July when my mother put me on a Greyhound bus and sent me to Pittsburg to find out if any news on when they could return home was available. When I arrived in Pittsburg, the news was good, so they sent me back to Concord to alert everyone. I can remember the joy and the tears when I told my mother and aunt. Momma sent me on to alert the others in a one-mile radius, blocks apart from one another. I can remember knocking on doors and shouting "You can go home now!" and the excitement of it all....Paul Revere rides again!

What Good Was That?
by Angelina Bruno

I don't remember all the details; it was so terrible I wanted to put it out of my mind. We weren't sure what they were going to do next. Everybody was saying so many different things. We had just bought this house [in Pittsburg], and then we had to move to Concord. The house stayed empty for a while, and we later rented it.

What burned me up was this: I came here at age ten, went to school here. I had three children, my husband was an American citizen, and still I had to move out. When I got married I thought I automatically became a citizen. But when the war came, they said I wasn't. So my husband and three children went with me. Why should I be taken out of my home when I hadn't done anything wrong?

It was mostly women who were shipped out, and old men, the ones who weren't fishing any more. Even some women who had sons in combat were shipped out. My husband's grandmother moved to Oakland, looking over the shipyards. What good was that?

It Looked Like a Funeral
by Frances Cardinale

My parents were Caterina and Vincenzo. With Vincenzo's sister and his sister-in-law, they all had to move from Pittsburg to Centerville, which is near Fremont. With the family we had in Monterey, it was halfway between.

My brother and I stayed in Pittsburg, so we had to keep two households going. I worked at the cannery; my brother worked at the steel mill. We divided the things, they had to bring everything. They had no idea how long they were going to stay.

The worst part was, I had to be operated on, for appendix, in April. So they took me to be operated on at St. Francis Hospital in San Francisco, but my mother and father couldn't come to San Francisco. They had to get permits to travel, so they didn't get there till the next day.

My father was a fisherman, but he couldn't fish. He paced all day long. What could he do? And the curfew—inside at eight o'clock. After, whenever my father heard the eight o'clock factory whistle, he would get scared and go to bed.

I remember the day we moved out, it looked like a funeral. We were all dead. We couldn't part. We never were separated before.

Photos taken of these "enemy aliens" from Pittsburg, most of them longtime residents, were run in the local newspaper during early February of 1942. Courtesy of the Pittsburg Historical Society

A Tragic Episode

by Sergio Ottino

> Like many others whose parents immigrated from Italy, Sergio Ottino remembers not only the wartime moment when his mother had to move from the family home to live outside the exclusion zone, but the residual effects this had on him. It not only removed the caregiver from the house when she was most needed, but resulted in suspicion directed toward Ottino himself when he joined the navy to serve his country. Such suspicions, he makes clear, were not and could not be limited only to those who were so-called enemy aliens. Of necessity, they crossed the generations, leaving their scars on those who were American-born, a fact which testifies, once again, to the pernicious and persistent effects such measures can have.

My mother, Amalia Querio, and my father, Giacomo Ottino, both emigrated, separately, to California in 1921. Both of them left behind cousins, aunts, and uncles. They were both from Piedmont, *Piemontesi,* so they were thrown together by a mutual language, [and by] customs and social gatherings customary at that time among immigrant groups in the United States.

They were married in 1921, and shortly thereafter my father filed an application to become an American citizen. I very recently (two weeks ago) discovered a similar application by my mother [from] about the same time. My father received his citizenship, but my mother apparently never followed through with her application.

We lived in Berkeley. My father was a partner with my maternal grandfather, my mother's brother, and a brother-in-law. They ran a successful business of two grocery outlets and a salami factory in west Berkeley. The main store was the Franklin Market. The entire "clan" lived in the one building, with living quarters upstairs and the grocery downstairs. They were well known in the community and very well respected by the citizens and all the authorities, and very active in Italian circles like the Order Sons of Italy in America and the Fratellanza club. I recall attending conventions in Weed and Santa Barbara where members from all over the state attended. These gatherings were openly cultivated by politicians for electoral support. Berkeley city officials came to our stores seeking votes and support during electoral campaigns.

While I was in high school, my mother supported a *dopo scuola* (after-school) project which encouraged young people of Italian ancestry to learn the Italian language. I believe that this project was sponsored and supported by the Italian consulate in San Francisco. Practically all of the first generation Italian Americans enrolled in this project at one time or another. I do recall one incident when the secretary to the consul came to a class and talked about the glory and grandeur of Italy under the guidance of Mussolini and the Fascists. He offered to instruct all of us in the use of the saber or foil in the art of fencing (there were no takers). There was also then a young persons' offshoot of the Sons of Italy called the *Loggia Giovanile*. Again, my mother and other like-minded parents sponsored our membership and participation in our lodge called the *Loggia Giovanile Savoia* No. 6. I have cited all this "history" only to call attention to the fact that my mother and many, many others were very visible in our communities as supporters of things Italian.

When World War II broke out, I was a student at St. Mary's College High School. I recall being on debating teams and always taking an antiwar stance in all of our debates. Upon graduation, I matriculated at UC Berkeley, seeking a degree in mechanical engineering.

Then in 1941, when the United States entered the world conflict, I was still at UC Berkeley. Almost immediately, I saw all my Japanese friends moved out of their homes and taken away, former classmates and childhood friends. My first reaction was one of disbelief. My friends couldn't be disloyal, but then, at age eighteen, I didn't question the motives behind this act. Shortly afterwards we Italian Americans became aware of the fact that the Italians and Germans were to be similarly treated because they were part of the Tripartite Alliance, the Berlin-Rome-Tokyo axis. We learned that noncitizens (like my mother) were to be rounded up. The commanding general, John DeWitt, we discovered later, made this suggestion to our president, Franklin D. Roosevelt, who gave his approval for this action. There was a popular story circulating in the East Bay at that time about the lack of internment of the Italians. I believe the mayor of San Francisco was one Angelo J. Rossi, who had nominated FDR for the office of president at the Democratic Party convention in 1928. Al Smith won the nomination, but Rossi had nominated FDR and was well known and respected in the Democratic Party. On the weekend preceding the "roundup," Rossi allegedly contacted the White House and asked FDR, "Mr. President, what are you going to tell the American people Monday morning when they learn that Joe DiMaggio's mother is in a concentration camp?"

There was no "roundup." Instead, those noncitizens, my mother among them, were forced to move from their homes to other designated areas, but not to detention centers. About this time I applied for work and was accepted at the Mare Island Naval Shipyard in Vallejo.

We were then living at 1207 Francisco Street in Berkeley, in the prohibited zone. My mother and a close friend in similar circumstances, "Ninin" Ponsetto, moved from our home and shared an apartment together at 2234 San Pablo Avenue, six blocks away, but across University Avenue and below the horizon of San Francisco Bay (presumably so that no signals could be sent to ships at sea). They resided there for some time, until I contracted a severe case of measles (for the third time) and my father had no one to care for me. He then called the Berkeley Police Department and talked with Inspector Charles Ipsen and Captain Johnson, who was acting chief at that time, and informed him of our predicament. He told Captain Johnson that his son was sick and needed care, so he was going to get his wife and bring her home. He said, "Tell the police to arrest me if they want to, but I am going to get my wife now and bring her home to care for our son." Captain Johnson replied, as closely as I can recall, "Get her, put her on the floor of the car in the back seat, cover her with a blanket, and take her home, and tell her to stay inside!" My father did that, and nothing happened. Our "clan" was well known and respected by the Berkeley police force and many city office holders, many of whom offered their apologies for this relocation of my mother and others.

By then I had been drafted into the United States Navy. My first assignment was to San Diego. I recall my wife and mother calling me on the phone. My mother would speak to me in English, and I would respond in *Piemonteis* or Italian. When I asked her why she didn't speak in "our" language, she replied that she didn't want to cause me any trouble, since I was in the navy. I remember replying that she could speak in English if she wanted to, but that I would continue to speak to her in our own language. She told me years later how much she appreciated my reply. She apparently was concerned that she had jeopardized my security and my future by association with an "enemy alien" mother.

This was a tragic episode in my life. I carry no scars or grudges. It probably has made me more understanding and tolerant of the plight of others who I believe may be unjustly accused. But I will never forget what we endured. While I was in the navy as a member of the SRU, Ship Repair Unit, there were two occasions when I was reminded that my mother was "not a citizen." For the first few weeks I got a lower priority than others. And for a while I was kept apart, with no access to certain areas. Then, while in training at Farragut, Idaho, I took a placement test. When the results came in, I was told that another candidate and I had achieved the highest scores ever recorded there, and would

With restrictions off, Sergio Ottino's mother, Amalia, was able to visit him, with his wife, Ernestine, at the base in San Diego, ca. 1945. Courtesy of Sergio Ottino.

be receiving orders for preflight school as officer candidates. Within weeks, the other man did receive his orders, but I did not. When I finally asked about it, I was called into my commander's office. After some small talk about my name, the officer asked about my mother. "Amalia..." he remarked. "She's not a citizen?" I looked at him and he looked at me. There was a long awkward silence between us. No other explanation was needed. After asking me how I felt, he told me to return to my barracks, and that I would get over it later on. But I took it pretty hard.

Of course, many injustices occurred, and certainly we were never subjected to the indignities and travails of our Japanese friends, but this does not lessen the pain. Is it any wonder that so many Italian immigrants and first generation American-born became Republicans after the war? We blamed the government! Our resentments may have been misplaced, but all we remember is what happened, when it happened, where it happened—but why, we still don't understand. A fault of leadership, paranoia, lack of knowledge, misjudgment?

I've tried to determine what I would have done at the time, had I been Lieutenant General DeWitt or even FDR. Perhaps, caught up in the confusion and fear of a possible invasion, I might have taken the same action. Now, however, realizing that grave errors were committed, it is time for Italian Americans living in the USA, citizens or not, to have a public apology delivered to them for the unlawful actions taken at that time.

Editor's note: Public Law 106-451, the "Wartime Violations of Italian Americans Civil Liberties Act," enacted November 7, 2000, directs the attorney general to prepare a report on civil rights violations, provides for funding for public education programs, and suggests that, when the report is completed, the president should acknowledge that "these events during World War II represented a fundamental injustice against Italian Americans."

A Fish Story

by Lawrence DiStasi

The Japanese attack on Pearl Harbor on December 7, 1941, established a fundamental pattern for the American home front during World War II. Americans would not be forced, like many nations in Europe and Asia, to defend themselves against an assault by ground forces. Rather, America would feel vulnerable mainly along its 12,383 miles of seacoast.[1] The Japanese navy had already exploited this weakness when its attack on Pearl Harbor not only left America's Pacific Fleet in tatters, but left the West Coast's 7,623 miles of seacoast (5,580 of them in Alaska) virtually unprotected. In the days after Pearl Harbor, rumors abounded that the Japanese were already planning their next move—sending a fleet northward along the Bering Sea, which would then swoop down to invade Alaska and British Columbia and possibly even occupy the Pacific Northwest. Though this turned out to be a feint intended to distract American naval planners away from Midway, the early rumors caused no little amount of anxiety. And though it elicited less panic among the population, the situation on the East Coast was worse. Submarine wolf packs from Germany sank hundreds of merchant ships in the early days of the war. Moreover, in February 1942, the SS *Normandie*, one of the largest ships then afloat, was nearly destroyed in a fire widely viewed as sabotage.[2]

For these reasons, much of the American military strategy in the early days of the war focused on protecting the American coastline, particularly in the West. Naturally enough, those who bore the brunt of this strategy were those who worked the ports and harbors and offshore waters: the fishermen. And since large numbers of fishermen on both coasts were immigrants from the then-enemy nation of Italy (the majority of them from Sicily), they found themselves in the direct line of a barrage of measures designed to protect the nation from the threat of sabotage and possible invasion.

Recall, first, the situation of the West Coast fishery on the eve of war. It was (and still is) one of the richest fisheries in the world. From tuna in San Diego, to squid in San Pedro, to sardines in Monterey and San Francisco, to salmon from Santa Cruz north to Alaska, to a host of other species including herring, halibut, rockfish, and crab, the Pacific fishery had become, in the days leading up to the war, a world leader in new technology and in the wealth and size of its fleet. Key to its growth had been Italian immigrants, beginning with fishermen from Genoa whose sail-powered feluccas first roamed the waters around San Francisco in the 1850s and continuing with immigrants from Sicily, who settled in San Francisco and in smaller ports, from Pittsburg on the Sacramento–San Joaquin Delta to Santa Cruz and Monterey on the central coast to San Pedro and San Diego in the south. Building their settlements through chain migration, these Sicilians by 1940 manned a large percentage of all boats fishing the West Coast, including the purse seiners—huge diesel-powered vessels eighty or ninety feet long that could store up to one hundred and fifty tons of sardines in their holds, with another fifty tons on deck. Indeed, this sardine fleet was exploiting a boom of epic proportions, hauling in stagger-ing tonnages of the sardine schools that honed in on Monterey Bay and its environs each year from August to February and selling them to the canneries and fish reduction plants whose appetite for tinned sardines and/or fertilizer seemed inexhaustible.

It was at the height of this sardine-based gold rush that Pearl Harbor stunned and then panicked the West Coast, overnight making the situation for fishermen very dicey indeed. Beginning on the night of Pearl Harbor, the port of San Francisco, home to more than 1,500 fishermen of Italian origin, was put under heavy guard. Construction crews in the headlands around San Francisco had been working for over a year, building artillery emplacements on strategic points both inside and outside the Golden Gate. Now, mine-laying crews quickly implemented their plan of laying mines in a huge semicircle across the outer shoals of the Golden Gate. And, most disastrously for fishermen, the fear of submarine attack had prompted naval authorities to begin preparing, start-ing in July 1941, a huge submarine net to stretch across the inner entrance to San Francisco Bay, just inside the Golden Gate. A monumental undertaking, the sub net would have to withstand the powerful flood tide washing out of San Francisco Bay along a distance of over three miles, from the St. Francis Yacht Club on the south side of the inner bay entrance to Point Sausalito on the north, including the central channel where maximum depth reached 392 feet. To accomplish this, ten-ton concrete anchors held the net in place. And though on the surface the net appeared to be only a row of steel buoys, just beneath the surface loomed a huge curtain of steel wire joined by clamps, vary-ing from a height of 30 feet near shore to 150 feet in the center of the channel. To allow the tremendous wartime traffic to pass, a thousand-yard movable sec-tion was set up a quarter mile off the San Francisco side. Two net tenders were moored at each end, each attached to the sea floor by huge anchors, controlling this gate within a gate by activating powerful winches, two to pull the huge movable section open, two to pull it closed.[3]

Though the net was designed not so much to trap entering submarines as to discourage their even attempting to enter the bay, its "net" effect, as it were, fell more heavily upon San Francisco's fishermen than on the enemy. As a Monterey newspaper put it in retrospect, "Anti-submarine precautions at San Francisco killed sardine fishing, for all practical purposes, on the first day of the war."[4] The reporter who made this comment was making a point in favor of the local sardine fleet, of course, pointing out that since Monterey Bay, with its huge mouth and canyon-like depth, could not be blocked in the same way, the sardine bonanza could remain very much alive there.

But local boosterism aside, neither in Monterey nor in any other port along the West Coast would fishing remain as before. That is because the military authorities were extremely concerned about the national origins of so many of the nation's fishermen and their tendency to isolate themselves from all but relatives and friends in the fishery. This was owing not just to the general Italian immigrant variant of *campanilismo*, wherein migrants from the old country always clustered in the same neighborhoods as those who had left the village before them. It was due as well to the nature of fishing as a more or less ingrown, almost genetic way of life. Son followed father to the sea. Boat crews were related, if possible, to reduce friction and enhance the cooperation needed. In Monterey, indeed, many of the terms used to impel purse seine crews into action had remained Sicilian[5]—the same as they had been for generations.

The corollary to this world and its still-Italian ways was that hundreds, if not thousands, of America's fishermen on the eve of the war still lacked American citizenship. After all, what was the need? Their work was carried on with *paesani*, often relatives, who spoke the same language, ate the same foods, married the same women, retained the same values, and virtually thought the same thoughts. At the other extreme, citizenship required the ability to use English, not to mention the memorization of whole sections of documents with unpronounceable names like "declaration," the articulation of which would only make a man look as silly and weak as a child.

The result was that right after Pearl Harbor, word spread through shops and homes along the wharf that those without citizenship were now the target of government edicts that each week grew more detailed and restrictive. Especially for fishermen. It was not just that one's loyalty to America was questioned, though that was bad enough. It was also that the waterfront everywhere, the whole Pacific coast—indeed, the whole U.S. coast—had become a zone of suspicion. Though in some places a fisherman with proper identification might still approach the docks to check on his boat, if he were an enemy alien he certainly could not go out in it. As Captain Stanley Parker, the senior Coast Guard officer and captain of the Port of San Francisco, put it in a January 27, 1942, letter to Dominick Strazulo of Monterey's Market Fishermen's Corporation (Strazulo had thought perhaps Monterey's Italian fishermen might be given a little slack since there was no clear border, no Golden Gate between Monterey's bay and the open sea):

> The movement of aliens is controlled by paragraph 10 of the President's proclamation of December 7, 1941. This forbids movement except in compliance with the regulations issued by the attorney general....The movement from the waters of a port or bay to the high seas is across a coastal frontier and is, in my opinion, of much greater significance than movement from home to office or church. I have taken the position that alien enemies may not pass this frontier casually, but only in compliance with the attorney general's regulations. Until they are issued, I assume that such movement is not permitted.[6]

In short, if you were an alien who lived by fishing offshore waters, you could forget about it. And if you were a fisherman in San Francisco, alien or not, you were in trouble. That port, in 1941 considered the most vital on the Pacific Coast and therefore the most vulnerable target for the enemy, was closed to commercial traffic completely. This meant that no fishing or merchant or pleasure boats, no matter their size or the composition of their crews, were allowed to pass into the open Pacific. Period.[7]

But, the Sardine Fishermen's Association wanted to know, what about the sardine season? What about the billions of sardines waiting to be caught, if only this enormous fleet of purse seiners could finish what had promised to be a record season? What about the fact that sardines were a crucial industry, key to the production not only of canned foods vital to U.S. forces, but also, as they wrote to Captain Parker, "of certain oils which are controlled by Government National Defense Priorities Agencies?" What about the fact that the sardine fleet in San Pedro—the 11th Naval District—had been allowed to go out? Captain Parker, in turn, explained the situation in a memo to the Chief of Staff, 12th Naval District, asking for his opinion:

> 1. The Captain of the Port has insisted upon keeping commercial vessels, including fishermen and also including yachts, within the harbors of the 12th Naval District until the situation clarifies itself.

2. Representatives of the Sardine Fishermen's Association have called twice upon the Captain of the Port to plead their case for relaxation in their favor of this restriction of operation at sea…

3. The operators of fifty-five of these boats are intensely anxious to take advantage of favorable conditions now existing and have reported that under an arrangement with the Captain of the Port at San Pedro similar vessels are now permitted to proceed to sea. The Association's representatives agree to eliminate from their crews all but native-born individuals and naturalized citizens other than Japanese and Italians. In other words, Japanese and Italians, even though naturalized, are to be eliminated from the crews, and the Captain of the Port would be supplied with a list of the vessels concerned, the names of the masters, and cards containing the names of the crew members of each vessel.[8]

In short, knowing they were in a hot zone, the fishermen agreed to do just about anything to salvage the season, including purging themselves of anyone with even a hint of Italy about him. But it wasn't good enough. Though the Coast Guard commander was sympathetic and "desired to cooperate," he knew that the situation was delicate, because "a release at this port, which would seem to be desirable, would also raise the question as to like treatment with respect to vessels at Monterey and Humboldt Bay,"[9] and he had to know what the chief of staff of the 12th Naval District opined. And we can infer, from the *Monterey Herald's* report that anti-submarine precautions at San Francisco killed sardine fishing there, that the chief didn't budge, at least not for San Francisco.

Still, hope dies hard. After all, the center of the sardine industry had never been San Francisco. It had always been, from the 1930s on, Monterey. And no submarine net could even be contemplated across that stretch of water. Nor could mines be laid very easily, for the depth of the canyon underlying that bay was staggering—more than a mile in places. Sooner or later, they were going to have to listen to reason and let the fishermen go out and fish. The problem was the crews. Unless someone could get the government to let up on the noncitizen Italians—who made up the majority of the manpower on the 12th District purse seiners[10]—who was going to man them?

Unfortunately, every new regulation that came out seemed to make things worse for those who had been branded "enemy aliens." First, no fishing. Then no movement without permission. Then no weapons of any kind, or cameras or shortwave radios or flags, or even flashlights—which led to periodic raids by the FBI on homes where aliens were suspected of living and perhaps harboring such "contraband." Newspaper reports of such raids made employers more than a little reluctant to hire out-of-work Italians. This meant that even the old Italians who couldn't fish still came to the wharf out of habit, to mend nets or play cards or just sniff the air, for what else could they do?

"Take a man off the water after he's fished thirty or forty years and give him a laborer's job ashore," said Benny Palazzalo, president of the Fishermen's Association of Boston, "and he's dead."[11] Though not literally true, this sentiment came close, for with all the surveillance at every wharf, and the boats just sitting in the water like empty buoys, and the old gents constantly looking over their shoulders before they made even the slightest move, it was like a morgue—or maybe a funeral home just before the undertaker comes in to take the body.

Then in early February of 1942, when those regulations from the attorney general became really specific—every enemy alien had to obtain a photograph and report to the post office, there to be questioned again and get one of the little pink booklets that every enemy alien was required to carry in his pocket at all times—the real effect of all those increasingly hostile regulations suddenly became crystal clear: if you were one of the ones who had to carry a booklet, you were not going to be allowed. Whether it was Boston, where over 200 Italian-born fishermen were grounded[12] or Gloucester or Philadelphia or New Orleans, if you were Italian-born, you weren't going to be fishing for a while.

And if you lived on the West Coast, if you usually fished out of Eureka or San Francisco or Monterey or Santa Cruz or San Diego, you weren't even going to be able to think about it. For on January 30, the order the attorney general had been preparing for weeks rolled in like a pent-up storm: from that day on, if you were an Italian without citizenship, not only could you not take your boat out, you could not even come to within blocks of the place where it was sitting idle. For on every fishing wharf, and in San Francisco along the entire waterfront from China Basin to the Presidio, there were armed guards who examined every person approaching. And if they got even a whiff of an Italian way of walking, much less that pink booklet, they immediately tightened their grip on the weapon that made them, more than any captain on any fishing boat, the lord of your destiny.

Thus was it reported that not even the father of the great Joe DiMaggio could get within blocks of Fisherman's Wharf, not even to look in on his son's San Francisco restaurant. He was an enemy alien. The same was true of hundreds of fishermen, all of whom knew each other, many of whom were related, with names like Aiello and Mercurio and Maniscalco, fishing out of ports from Seattle to San Pedro, from the Delta towns of Pittsburg and Martinez to the barranca at Santa Cruz. Go near the wharf at any of those places and you were sure to be questioned and inspected, and maybe jailed. Maybe you would even be sent to the internment camps like both Maioranas, the Sercias, one of the Billantes, an Aliotti—all of them fishermen in San Francisco until one day they and several others were gone, and no one knew where, or what for, or how many more were about to join them.

Nor were things about to get better. Word was, the West Coast generals had been huddling with the admirals and the Justice Department lawyers, and they had decided that not only were enemy aliens prohibited from going onto the wharves, they were, in late February, going to be prohibited from being anywhere near the water at all. This was going to be a mess, for where else would a fisherman live but as close to his work as possible? Too bad. Come February 24, everyone with a pink booklet was going to have to move away from the coast entirely, and the worst of it was that no one could quite agree on how far. In Eureka it might be only a few feet, to the east side of Highway 101. In Pittsburg you had to get out of town completely. It was the same in Monterey, though again, no one could agree how far: some said moving the few miles to Salinas would do it; some said you had to go all the way to San Jose— which many did.

For most, it didn't matter much at that point, for already, in December and on into January and February, what was no doubt the worst blow of all had already struck, focused this time not just on the aliens, but on the boat own-ers—American citizens they were, owners of the most aristocratic and expen-sive boats on the whole coast. The navy needed their purse seiners. And there was no arguing.

The deal had already been cut.

———

In fact, the United States Navy had been preparing since at least the mid-1930s for a war with Japan, and for the emergency measures it would have to take. Naval documents refer to such a conflict as an ORANGE[13] war, and though they do not anticipate an attack as devastating as Pearl Harbor turned out to be, they do make clear that the United States Navy anticipated surprise hostile action against American coastal defenses. The above-mentioned submarine net and artillery emplacements at the Golden Gate made up one phase of prepara-tions. The other, most relevant to fishermen and their boats, concerned the possible planting of enemy mines in American harbors. A November 1938 memo from the commandant of the 12th Naval District in San Francisco to the chief of naval operations in Washington, D.C., lays out the problem:

1. The Planning section of the Twelfth Naval District has been much concerned with the problem of achieving security of San Francisco Harbor and its approaches immediately before and during the period of Fleet concentration preparatory to an ORANGE war. No minesweepers are habitually stationed in this area. Only three XAMs [minesweepers] are listed for this District, and their availability or even presence at the time of a sudden emergency is problematical.

2. It is envisioned that the outbreak of an ORANGE war may be not only undeclared, but sudden, and disclosed by an incident on the Pacific Coast of the United States, such as the planting of mines by submarines or a submarine campaign against merchant or naval vessels. If such an incident were to occur, instant defense measures would be required for San Francisco Harbor, and this would require, with little or no notice, such vessels as might be available and suitable for minesweeping. Little or no time would be available for alterations. The only class of such vessels probably available in considerable numbers is the purse seiner class, discussed in references (c) and (d)."[14]

The memo goes on to describe purse seiners and their capacity to serve as minesweepers with little or no need for retrofitting. Of no little significance is the fact that the navy envisioned not simply using such vessels, but using them along with their crews—of mainly Italian fishermen:

Personnel of the fishing boats are being investigated and it is believed that an adequate number of boats will be found available with crews already aboard suitable for this work. Future correspondence will cover the advisability of inducting an appropriate number of these men into the Naval Reserve.[15]

The memo ends by recommending, as a consultant, Lieutenant Commander Grant Stephenson, then a resident of Monterey, who was familiar with both the purse seiners and with the use of a converted fishing trawler, the *Douglas*, as a minesweeper during World War I. It is signed "W. R. Gherardi," then acting commandant in place of Admiral Hepburn of the 12th Naval District.

Thus we have the impetus for what was to transpire, indeed what had already transpired, in the 12th Naval District almost immediately following Pearl Harbor: the emergency seizure of fishing vessels, many owned by Italian

Americans, for use by an American navy not yet equipped to fight a major war. In its early stages, this program involved countless technical and organizational details. On the technical side, the navy would have to determine how well the purse seiners could serve not only as minesweepers, but also as submarine chasers and other types of patrol craft it needed. Were they fast enough? Powerful enough? Most were about eighty feet long and equipped with diesel engines of about 250 horsepower that could run them at about ten knots, though some of the newer ones were bigger and faster. That would seem to be enough. But what would have to be done to convert the seiners into a general class fit to serve in possibly hostile conditions? How quickly could it be done? All this would have to be worked out, both as a general set of instructions, and in individual cases. Surveys would have to be taken to determine which vessels were fit for a career as minesweepers and which were not. Negotiations with owners and with the Maritime Commission would have to take place, stipulating how the commission, acting for the navy, could either buy the vessels outright or charter them for a monthly fee, and what to do if the boat owners proved resistant. And finally, perhaps the touchiest question: could the existing crews be drafted into service as a naval reserve unit that could respond to the navy's needs?

There was much discussion about all these matters, particularly the last one—for there was the foreign question. This was not just a question of loyalty; it was a question of reactions and capabilities as well. Most of these vessels were owned and operated by fishermen with origins in foreign countries— "Slavonians," Scandinavians, Japanese, Italians—and the navy wanted to know how they would respond: how they would react to the seizure of their boats, how they would fit into naval ranks, and so on. To answer such questions, the navy embarked on a large-scale but quiet program designed to fill in all the blanks, not just for the purse seiners, not just for their use in minesweeping duty, but for other fishing craft and other duties as well. And though it may not rank in importance with the building of victory ships or the Battle of Midway, this program was approached with the same degree of urgency, and in the early days with perhaps more ugency, than those more global operations.

To begin with, it is important to note that the conversion of fishing boats was not limited to West Coast ports. Evidence indicates that, based on the experience of England and Canada, which had already in 1940 implemented their emergency plans to draft fishing boats along with their crews into a naval reserve, the 1st naval district in Boston had also begun experiments converting East Coast fishing trawlers into minesweepers. A memo to this effect was sent from the Bureau of Ships, U.S. Navy, to the commandants of the sixteen other naval districts on July 6, 1940. Its subject: "Arrangement of Vessels Converted to Naval Auxiliaries (XAM) Mine Sweepers." An attachment, "Specifications for Emergency Conversion for Naval Use of Fish Trawlers Built by the Bethlehem Shipbuilding Co. Ltd., Quincy, Mass.," recommended several general moves. Most important for the purse seiners would be:

> Install two 50 cal. A.A. machine guns in the following locations:
> 1) on top of the After Deck House, the gun to be located on the centerline of ship about 12" aft of frame #6; (2) on the Forecastle Deck, the gun to be located on the centerline of ship at about frame #44.
> Provide a circulating water cooling system for each of the 50 cal. A.A. machine guns...
> Install magazine in Hold...
> Remove the fish hoist and foundation for same located on the Forecastle Deck...[16]

There is quite a bit more about reinforcing the structure of the boat to support the new equipment, but the template for the purse seiner conversions—both the sardine seiners in use in the Pacific and the mackerel seiners in use in eastern ports like Boston and Gloucester—is here.

By this date in 1940, of course, the navy had already received specifics about purse seiners from those on the scene. Indeed, letters about the need for minesweepers and the possible use of fishing boats for such duty had been circulating in the 12th Naval District since 1936 and earlier.[17] Most relevant is a memo of February 1939 written by Admiral Hepburn, commandant, 12th Naval District, to the chief of naval operations in Washington. Its subject is "Fishing Vessels Suitable for XAM(c)," i.e. minesweeping duties, and it includes already at this date an enclosure with a "List of Owners and Captains of Purse Seiners Recommended for Naval Service."[18]

The memo opens by noting that "approximately 100 vessels" have been "discreetly" inspected and their personnel characteristics estimated by a list of people also noted, among them the assistant chief of the California Fish & Game Bureau, an admiralty lawyer, a marine surveyor, a manager of a fish-packing company in Monterey, and so on. Then it describes the physical characteristics of purse seiners, their structure, living quarters, equipment, hold capacity, engine specs, radio-telephone equipment, and methods of navigation (very few carried sextants), ending with the note that the "ships are extremely sturdy, generally well powered, and are adapted to naval use except for the following particulars." The defects were, in the main, no place to mount guns except on top of the deck house, not enough living quarters, inadequate sanitary facilities, and need for about twenty tons of ballast (for when they leave the harbor "light," i.e. with no fish in the holds, and run into rough weather, the ships "are so unstable that captains will not risk returning to port.") These defects seem not to have been considered fatal, for a memo the next year, on August 20, 1940, from the Bureau of Ships in Washington to the commandant of the 13th Naval District (centered in Seattle) briefly describes that the conversion of purse seiners to coastal minesweepers could proceed according to the general plan.[19]

Finally, after a description of the ownership pattern—which often involved partnerships, with crewmen getting shares—and the fact that the current bonanza in the sardine industry had led to so much profit that some owners controlled several boats, the last five pages of the eleven-page memo are devoted to the most sensitive part of the matter—*the personnel.*

Recall that the navy, based on the prior experience of Canada and England, anticipated that in an emergency it would want to induct not just boats, but whole crews along with them. Yet it was nervous about this, as the memo's discussion of personnel vividly indicates. First, it notes that though the fishing captains were permanent in their assignments, the crews were "in general, highly transitory." Next it evaluates the worth of each of the major groups of fishermen then operating, "Slavonians, Italians, Scandinavians, Japanese, and a few Spaniards and Greeks." Were there a textbook for the type of stereotyping and racism then operating in the United States, what follows would be a pre-eminent example. After a short paragraph on Scandinavians, most of them from Puget Sound, most of them Norwegians, who are said to be "good seamen, good fishermen, good navigators, and intelligent good citizens," the text moves to the Italians. It is worth quoting at length:

> *Italians.* The Italians are sprung from the south of Italy and Sicily. Many of them are second-generation Americans. They are fundamentally paternalistic and have a tight family organization with great authority vested in the head of the family. They are volatile in nature and are therefore not completely reliable. Those who came from Italy are Italian in loyalty, although perhaps naturalized United States citizens, which would largely be for the purpose of avoiding payment of "light money"—more special taxes on foreign-owned vessels. Their American-born sons are loyal citizens, except that they are accustomed to doing as their fathers tell them, and their loyalty to Italy, if opposed to the United States, is probable....

The majority of the Italians are not good seamen, good fisher-men, nor good navigators. They are not over-intelligent, do not know the Rules of the Road, and, in general, appear to have the characteristics of big overgrown children. However, among the captains, 15% to 20% may be selected who are considerably above the average in intelligence and leadership, and are, in gen-eral, reliable men....

Many of the boats are owned by packing companies or one or two individuals who are in effect absentee owners. The captains of these vessels have been chosen by the owners because they have made for themselves a reputation as natural leaders and are generally able and forceful men. In the cases where vessels are owned by groups of six or eight men, the captain is likely to hold that position because he is an uncle of the majority of the owners and so has paternalistic authority rather than ability.

The packers are of the opinion that the Italians, in addition to being volatile and excitable, are not energetic, would rather tie up to the dock than fish, and, as a rule, do not have the courage to prosecute an energetic naval task independently.

...The above remarks apply more generally to the crews than to the captains and the majority of the crews can be made into competent deckhands who will obey orders with moderate intelli-gence, but are incapable of much more.[20]

Though most of this is too blatant to warrant commentary, the explanation about why some of the Italian boat owners have become citizens—to avoid pay-ing special taxes—is particularly noxious, for it casts doubt on the loyalty of even those who have become naturalized. By contrast, the report goes on to describe the "Slavonians" as feeling "little loyalty to Yugoslavia, in that the state and government are strange to them, and are, in general, extemely loyal to the country to which they have come....The Slavonians appear to be loyal, fairly intelligent, and fearless. Their most valuable characteristic is their phleg-matic, unexcitable nature...." From this it proceeds to describe the animosity towards Italians by the Slavonians, partly stemming from "traditional racial antagonisms," partly from their conflict in World War I and the Italian seizure of Zara, and partly because of their membership in opposing unions: Italians with the older American Federation of Labor (AFL), the Slavonians newly affiliated with the Congress of Industrial Organizations (CIO). The result is a continuing low-level war, in which Italians are cast as villains who "damage nets and jam the radio waves with endless petty conversation to prevent the

Slavonians from using their radio phones with news as to location of fish and other matters."

Another memo, a draft handwritten in July of 1940 from the port director at San Francisco to the director of the naval reserve, reinforces some of the racial stereotypes seen above, but also provides some factual demurrers, such as, "These fishing crews will be proficient in tending sweeping gear. The tests recently made by Commander Buchanan bear this out."[21] The writer therefore recommends a special reserve designation, V-8 rather than V-6, and a trial induction of fishermen for about six months so as not to frighten them with the threat of long, "regular service." This is because "they are inclined to be timid and feel something of an inferior complex [sic]." With this, the memo moves into the area of racial stereotyping like its predecessor. It mentions the success that both the British and the Canadians have been having with their naval reserves, but notes that those crews are largely British, and, "in the case of the Canadian patrol in the Pacific, the patrol crews are largely Scandinavian." Then comes the cautionary "but":

> But in the West C[oast] of the United States the racial situation
> is different. From Eureka, California, north the fishing fleet is
> American, Jugo Slav, and Scandinavian generally, with all other
> aliens represented in a small degree. From Eureka to Monterey,
> the Italian racial element predominates, with some Jugo Slav and
> others. There is only one Japanese purse seiner in this area....The
> American-born of these races of fishermen are loyal and look
> upon themselves as Americans, but the foreign-born vary. Many
> are naturalized and are as good Americans as any aliens born.
> Many of the foreign-born are not citizens, and some expect even-
> tually to return to the land of their birth. However, the latter are
> in a small minority. These people as a general rule are inclined to
> be clannish and mix little with the communities. This is especial-
> ly true of Japanese and Italians. Each group has its leaders and the
> mass do as these leaders wish. Though not always.

Finally, in the last paragraph, the writer recommends the formation of a minesweeping patrol using the fishermen, but feels obliged to add, "These men, being of Latin blood, require special treatment. They must have something different that is their own. If done properly, the navy will have an excellent sweeper fleet. The remarks apply to Italians alone."

Several points are worth noting here. First is the common idea, held even as late as 1940, that Italians comprise a separate "race," with such inherent defects as clannishness, volatility, unreliability, timidity, paternalism, not being energetic, lacking courage, and that devastating catch-all, being like "big, overgrown children." This last comment really gets to the core of the racist appraisal at work here, for the essence of racism, as David A. J. Richards has recently argued,[22] is really a judgment that a group is developmentally inferior, and even genetically incomplete. This means its members are judged as lacking in the full mental and moral development that would make them truly human. We see this demonstrated in the first memo. Italians are said to be "overgrown children" who can perhaps be "made into competent deckhands who will obey orders with moderate intelligence, but are incapable of much more." That is to say, Italians in general cannot take on the full responsibilities assumed by British or Canadians or Scandinavians, because as a racial group they are simply not far enough advanced.

The assessment of the purse seiners and their captains which is attached to this 1939 memo, while generally more favorable, contains remnants of the same attitude. Thus, we have a comment about one captain from Mr. Burnett, manager of the Richmond Fisheries Company: "For an Italian he is pretty good." This same Burnett says of another captain, "A good fisherman, but an agitator."[23]

With these expectations, it is perhaps not surprising to learn that, in the end, the navy decided against drafting the fishing crews along with their purse seiners. A July 16, 1940, memo from the commandant, 12th Naval District, to the chief of the Bureau of Navigation lists some of the anticipated problems. First it cites the reluctance of fishermen to sign a four-year contract of enlistment in the naval reserve. Then it cites the fishermen's need of assurance that they would serve on their own boats, with their own crews, something which would force the navy to accept men with "physical disabilities and other disqualifications," here unnamed. Then it notes that petty officer ratings would be required for captains, and most would not be qualified "for that rating on a man-of-war." And finally,

> American citizens may be obtained but the advisability of taking
> into the naval service large groups of men of hyphenated loyalty
> is open to question.[24]

The conclusion is obvious: "the enlistment of West Coast fishermen on a large scale in the naval reserve is undesirable and is impracticable now." It remained undesirable and impracticable for the duration of the war.[25]

This wasn't the end of it for the fishermen, however. For the navy found it both desirable and practicable to commandeer the purse seiners that had always comprised the core of the whole initiative, and commandeer them in numbers so large as to, in the words of the navy's own 12th Naval District administrative history, "cripple the canning and reduction industries in Monterey and San Franicsco."[26]

Tom Cutino described it this way:

> My brother John had registered for the draft and had a prewar deferment for fishing. Then they took my father's boat. We were, I guess, desperate—there were all kinds of fears at the time, like would the block warden chastise you for having your lights on, and there was a big fear of going fishing. You were not even allowed on the wharf; there were armed guards there, and I still have my plastic I.D. card from the Coast Guard which later allowed me to go out and fish.
>
> So these navy plainclothes guys came to our house, it was right after Pearl Harbor, a knock on the door, and they're telling my father, "Mr. Cutino, we need your boat." He was so fearful, he just said, "Go ahead, take it." No questions asked. As it turned out, in a few months they paid him for it, no depreciation.
>
> At that point, he just wanted them to take it, but they said, "We want you to bring the boat to Treasure Island." My uncle Orazio was one of the owners, but he was not naturalized. So he was afraid, my brother John didn't want to go, nobody wanted to go out there with the boat to San Francisco. But the navy pleaded

Tom Cutino's port pass, which he needed to enter Fisherman's Wharf in Monterey during the war. Courtesy of Tom Cutino, Sr.

with my father, gave him some patriotic talk, it's war, you know, and so finally my father and my Uncle Orazio and my brother all ran the boat up to San Francisco. And they were so fearful, of submarines and who knew what, that they nearly burned out the engine, which was pouring black smoke—they were going so fast. They finally got it to Treasure Island and left it and came back by the Del Monte Express, the train that used to run from San Francisco to Monterey in those days.[27]

Tom Cutino remembers that December night in 1941 vividly, mainly in connection with the fear that then prevailed. He also remembers that his father was lucky: his boat was paid for outright, at its original cost. His brother John, having signed up for the navy, and having gotten his call and traveled to San Francisco for processing, ran into another piece of good fortune. Waiting for an assignment at Treasure Island, he came upon a fleet of requisitioned purse seiners, including his father's. A team of navy men were trying to remove its skiff, a twenty-foot auxiliary which purse seiners carried to spread their enormous nets. Heavy, unwieldy, the skiff was refusing to be muscled over the side when John Cutino, in civilian clothes, shouted, "Hey, that's my father's boat. I can do that." Since the navy crew were meeting with little success, they agreed to let him try:

> And he says, "First thing, get everybody off the boat." The officer in charge couldn't believe it: "You mean you're going to get the skiff off by yourself?" John nods, "That's exactly what I'm going to do." They were pretty skeptical, how was one guy going to do what they couldn't? They wanted to see this.
>
> John uses the boom. He grabs hold of the skiff with the boom, and he maneuvers it not to the side but to the back, and lowers it over the stern, which is what you're supposed to do, and drops it gently into the water.
>
> After that, they loved him, especially when he proved he knew how to start up all the different kinds of purse seiner engines. They made him a second-class machinist's mate, no tests or anything, offered him whatever he wanted. So he asked to be put on his father's boat, and he was.[28]

Not long after, John Cutino, on his father's now-converted purse seiner, took part in tests to see if the seiners could be used as submarine chasers. But in trying to drop depth charges, the seiners proved so slow they could not get out

The Cutino family's purse seiner, *Cutino Brothers*, requisitioned by the navy during World War II. Courtesy of Tom Cutino, Sr.

of the way of their own explosives. When the mount for the .75 caliber cannon proved shaky as well, the attempt to turn the fishing boats into sub-chasers was abandoned, and John Cutino requested that his boat be assigned to Monterey. It was to be employed there on patrol and for towing targets for naval aircraft. Tom Cutino recalls that his father could now see his old boat, painted navy gray and with a number on it, nearby—but in truth very far out of his reach.

The Cutinos were not alone. Within a week after Pearl Harbor, no less than sixteen purse seiners from Monterey had been commandeered. They included the *El Cortez*, the *Belvedere*, the *Western Star*, the *Santa Rosa*, the *New Hope*, the *San Jose*, the *Belle Haven*, the *Redeemer*, the *San Giovanni*, the *Ardito*, the *Stella Maris*, the *Dante Alighieri*, the *St. James*, the *Twin Brothers*, and the *Joe DiMaggio*. The next week saw two more, the *Exposition King* and the *Aurora*, disappear from San Francisco. Five others had already been taken from Berkeley and Oakland.

Even with several other boats taken from different ports, this might have left something of the sardine industry still breathing. As the 12th Naval District's administrative history puts it, however, two more calls were received for additional vessels: "the first for fifteen vessels for outer patrol, and one vessel

The *Cutino Brothers* after it was outfitted as a naval patrol boat. Courtesy of Tom Cutino, Sr.

for army and mine planting." This took "the best of the Monterey and San Francisco purse seiners," probably on or about February 15, 1942. The second call was for "seventeen 'tuna clippers' and thirty-three purse seiners for use in the 15th Naval District," and came the next week, around the 23rd of February. Use in the 15th Naval District, which included Hawaii, meant the boats would travel very far afield indeed. Some, like the *Phyllis*, saw action in the Canal Zone. Some were deployed as far away as Saipan and the Philippines, where one Monterey native, Rocco Costanza, saw them serving as supply boats. These were the seizures which crippled the canning and reduction industries in Monterey and San Francisco.[29]

We know some of the Monterey boats taken in this breathtaking second call: the *Little Flower*, the *El Rey*, the *California Star*, the *Juanita*, the *El Capitan*, the *Phyllis*, the *Sea Lion*, the *New St. Joseph*, the *Anna B*, the *Sea Star*, the *San Vito*, the *Mineo Brothers*, the *Virginia II*, the *Santa Lucia*, the *Sherman Rose*, the *California Rose*, the *New Rex*, the *Sea Maid*, the *Diana*, the *New Roma*, the *Star of Monterey*, the *Marettimo* and the *St. Anthony*.[30] While most of the first group mentioned seems, like the Cutino vessel, to have been "requisition-purchased," most of this second group were "requisition-bareboat chartered," i.e. leased to the navy for a monthly fee. This added up to no less than forty-five purse seiners removed from the Monterey fleet, which indeed crippled it.

Anthony Bruno remembers the taking of his father's boat, the *St. Anthony*. Gus "Cosimo" Bruno was the only Pittsburg fisherman who owned a purse seiner. Each year he and his family would travel to their rented house in Monterey and stay there for the sardine season, from August to February and a little later. Sometime in February 1942, Anthony remembers his family getting a letter from the government saying they wanted his father's boat:

> The boat was brand-new, built in San Francisco by Anderson and Cristofani, probably around 1938. Most other boats were gray or black, but my father wanted it white. It was about 175 hp, 78 feet long. They just notified him in the mail that they were going to take his boat and to deliver it to San Francisco. It was terrible, because, hell, he was making good money and they took his livelihood away. You know, he was a boat owner and the owner got three or four shares. I remember once taking money to the bank, one month, $14,000 in one envelope and $7,000 in the other. I remembered that much money.[31]

If one took the navy's assessment at face value, it would appear that Italian fishermen were irresponsible in the extreme—overgrown children capable only of obeying simple orders from a father figure. The reality suggests something quite different, a kind of cooperative industry in which everyone had a stake. Purse-seine crewmen didn't work for wages; they each had shares, with a total of some twenty shares divided among the boat owner, the captain, and the crew. Anyone who had extra responsibility, or more of an investment, such as the boat owner or the net owner, got extra shares. An owner might get five shares, the net owner three shares, each crew member one share, the captain an extra share or two. If a given run for sardines netted one hundred tons of fish, at the wartime rate of $21 a ton, the cannery paid $2100 to be distributed as shares. Even one-twentieth of $2100 amounted to a rather tidy sum in 1940 for a night's work (sardine fishing must be done at night, with little moonlight, so that the phosphorescent glow of the sardine schools can be detected). And if the boat netted more fish, there would be more to distribute—a keen incentive to hard work.

The naval assessment of Italian personnel, it would appear, was based on a fundamental misunderstanding grounded in deep prejudice. This also makes one wonder if, in fact, its willingness to plunder the mostly Italian fishing fleets of Monterey and San Francisco stemmed in part from this prejudice, and the related feeling that the rights of these "volatile and childish" fishermen, who derived from a country that was now an enemy, could be dismissed with impunity.

Certainly some of the Monterey fishermen felt unduly targeted. Vitina Spadaro recalled the situation when her father, Giuseppe, learned that his vessel was to be taken:

> His boat, the *Marettimo,* was a purse seiner. There was a fishing
> fleet in Monterey, all owned by Italians. Then I remember my
> father saying there was someone from the government who wanted
> our fishing boats. "What can we do," he said, "the government
> needs our boats." So he had to deliver his boat to San Francisco,
> to the navy. There must have been fifty boats from Monterey
> taken; it was a deal made by the boat owners' association. Being
> good Italians, they wanted to help the government, so they were
> willing to let the boats go. But up north they had a fishing fleet,
> mostly Scandinavians, and down south they also had a fishing
> fleet, mostly Slavonians. I feel the reason they wanted the
> Monterey boats was because they were Italians. They had to char-
> ter boats from up north and bring them down here to fish, to sup-
> port their families. Why not take the boats up north?[32]

No one ever got an answer to this question. What was known was that like many other boat owners in Monterey, the Spadaros not only had to give up their boat, but because Giuseppe Spadaro's wife had not quite completed her citizenship process, had to give up their Monterey home as well. As Vitina remembers it:

> When orders came for my mother to leave Monterey, I went with
> my parents to look for a house in Salinas. When we would ask for a
> place to live, they would ask why we had to move. We told them,
> and they said, "Italians from Monterey? You're aliens. We're not
> renting to you." I felt devastated. I would say, "I'm an American cit-
> izen, my father is an American citizen." My father would say, "Keep
> quiet." But how could they hurt my mother like this? She was cry-
> ing all the time. When we were getting ready to move to Salinas,
> there were moving vans all over the neighborhood, and all the
> women were crying. After we found a place, my father would go
> back and forth to Monterey, check the house there.[33]

To make ends meet, Giuseppe Spadaro chartered a boat from Seattle for the next seasons until his own boat, the *Marettimo,* was decommissioned. But when it was returned, he found it in very poor shape. In addition to the damage from the gun mounts, the skiff was missing and the navy told him it had been destroyed. When he said he needed money to get the boat back into fishing shape, the navy offered him $3,000. He knew $3,000 would be required to replace the skiff alone, and when he checked further, he found the other repairs would probably cost $15,000. According to Vitina Spadaro, when her father reported this to the navy, they told him, "Either you accept what we give you, or we keep your boat." After consultation with his wife, Giuseppe Spadaro agreed to accept the $3,000 and bring the boat home at a loss.

> So here he was with a boat in poor condition, no skiff, and he
> had already chartered a boat for the season. So he had to tie the
> *Marettimo* at anchor. A terrific storm came in December. The
> Coast Guard called to say the boat was in danger. My father was
> anchored in a cove, unable to come in. I said to the Coast Guard,
> "Please see what you can do to save the boat." They refused, and
> the boat was wrecked. The insurance covered very little; most
> went to try to salvage the boat. Eventually my father sold the
> *Marettimo* to a boat builder for next to nothing. Then he had to
> get a loan, from the Bank of America, to get a new boat. Many
> other fishermen in Monterey had to do the same thing to repair
> their boats.[34]

John Russo had a similar experience. His purse seiner, the *Star of Monterey*, which he had just purchased in 1940, was taken by the navy in the big requisition in February of 1942. He, too, had to deliver it to San Francisco, after hearing the bad news from Peter Ferrante of the boat owners' association. And though the navy took possession of his boat on February 23, 1942, neither that fact, nor the fact that his brother had earlier been drafted into the navy helped his parents, both of whom had to evacuate from Monterey by February 24—the next day.

Like Giuseppe Spadaro and others, Russo chartered a boat from Seattle to make what money he could while his own boat was gone, but it was not easy:

> It's a loss. They took my boat, they took my job. You charter a
> boat, you right away have to give four shares to the boat owner.
> There's only eight shares for the boat and the net to begin with,
> so you've got four shares left. But four shares just about cover
> expenses. At that time we didn't have nylon nets, they were cot-
> ton, so we had to tan them, and every year we had to replace half
> the net. There goes the four shares. So essentially, I just made my
> own share [i.e. one of twelve crew shares]. And also, the capacity

of the boat I chartered was only half of my boat, it packed only 80 tons where mine packed 145 tons, so what we make is cut in half to begin with.[35]

When his boat was returned in 1943, Russo found that the boat "wasn't in too bad shape," perhaps because it had been used in the San Francisco area. But he would have to do much of the restoration work himself:

> The navy took the turntables out, and all that. There were mounts in the stern for depth charges. They took care of the dry-dock work, but the rigging we had to take care of ourselves. It took a while, but we did it. I had kept the skiff, so that was okay. We were able to fish the next season. After the war, I got the last deckload of sardines caught in Monterey. There's a newspaper story about it. I put 180 tons in the boat that day.[36]

That "last deckload of sardines" refers to the other aspect of the decimation of the sardine fleet: World War II began for the United States right in the middle of the great sardine bonanza. Many of the purse seiners taken by the navy had been newly built to take advantage of the apparently infinite schools of sardines waiting to be hauled in. But the sardines were not to last. And not only did the navy deprive fishermen of their boats when they needed them most, but its wartime orders for ships overwhelmed the shipyards where boat owners might have replaced the ones taken by the navy. This turned out to be precisely the plight of Salvatore Colletto.*

Colletto's boat, the *Dante Alighieri,* had been one of the very first taken, purchased by the navy in December 1941. As he described it in a manuscript he wrote in 1960, Colletto had just decided, in the boom year of 1939, to go into business for himself, and had contracted to build a top-of-the-line purse seiner with a shipyard in Tacoma, Washington. To his astonishment, he was contacted two weeks later and questioned about the planned boat:

> A week after I signed the contract for the construction of the vessel with E. Martinolich Shipyards [in] Tacoma, Washington, the keel was laid out. Two weeks later I get a telephone call at my home from a retired rear admiral from the San Carlos Hotel in Monterey. He said he would like to see me. We made an appoint-

---

*See the next selection, "A Sardine Fisherman during the War," for more of Salvatore Colletto's memoirs.

ment for 2 P.M. to meet him at his room. When I got there that afternoon, he told me that I was building an 82-foot vessel, 22 feet beam and 400 horsepower, Fairbanks Morse heavy-duty engine for $44,000....I asked him where he got that information. He said, "From the shipyard." He wanted to know from me if I would give the vessel to the government. I told him, "Why don't the government build its own boats?" "Well," he said, "I am asking you in case of a national emergency." In that circumstance, [I said], "I will be glad to turn it over to the government." At that time there were rumors we get involved in a war. But no one took it seriously...[37]

This "admiral" seems to have been Lieutenant Commander McCord, the man officially in charge of inspecting Monterey's purse-seine fleet. Oddly enough, in that early assessment, Colletto's boat was apparently judged inadequate for use as a minesweeper. Nonetheless, it was purchased by the navy and used in coastal patrol duty and then for patrol duty in Panama.

In his memoir, Colletto describes the convoy of seven Monterey purse seiners in which he took the *Dante Alighieri* to San Francisco, to be met by a destroyer outside the Golden Gate so the purse seiners could be guided past the mine defenses, through the gate and the submarine net, and into the bay to Treasure Island. He also describes what it was like to be obliged to charter boats each year to continue fishing. The first season, he managed to charter the *Robert B.* The next two seasons, he chartered other vessels, but like other captains whose own boats were requisitioned, Colletto found most of his profit going to pay for the charters. In two seasons, he writes, he paid a total of $60,000 to the boat owners from whom he had chartered. According to his son, Sal Colletto Jr., he felt aggrieved:

> He was paying out large fees to charter a boat each season, losing money. He was catching a lot of fish, but paying most of it to charter. He had sold his own boat as a patriotic duty, and these other guys who had refused and kept their boats were now making big money leasing them to him. He felt it was unfair.[38]

Nor was that all. It was becoming harder to charter boats. In his third season without a boat, Colletto contracted with a fishing company in Seattle, but the vessel was "still in the herring fisheries in Southeast Alaska" when the Monterey sardine season began on August 1. Other boats were already out catching fish, and he was idle. It was infuriating, and he was becoming desperate to get a boat.

That only added to his frustration, for the shipyards had become impossible for a small fisherman to deal with. Finally, on September 3, 1943, still without a boat, Colletto wrote a long letter to the Secretary of the Interior, Harold Ickes. He began by describing himself, his long experience, his reputation as a fisherman, and the boat he had just had built and which he had been happy to give up to the navy because of the national emergency. Then he got to the real problem, which involved government-issued "priorities" for boat and ship building. When the United States first entered the war, only military ships could be built. Later, when these were in sufficient supply, the government would occasionally authorize the construction of private vessels:

> I went to Tacoma, Washington, on the 9th of August with the purpose of building a vessel for next season. And I contacted the Petrich Boat Builders and the Pacific Boat Builders....They told me they had priorities to build six fishing vessels apiece. The Petrich Boat Builder told me that he could not give me a price on the vessel, that it would have to be on a time and material [basis]. I went to the Pacific Boat Builders...and told them that I was willing to pay $65,000 for a boat that cost $45,000 in 1939. They would not talk to me for that price. They told me that it would cost nearer to $1,000 a foot, which I figured would cost $82,000. In the experience I have had in the fisheries, I can't see how I can make out in the payments of the vessel at that price. If the price of fish should drop next season, it's impossible to make payments...
>
> I personally think the shipyards take advantage of the priorities and charge more than they should for the construction of a fishing vessel. At any rate it's worth investigating the priorities of the shipbuilders. I recommend that the priorities to build fishing vessels should be issued to experienced fishermen, not the shipyard. When the shipyard gets the priority, they build the boats for the big fishing companies. The yards don't even consider a bona fide fisherman, because they have difficulties in financing.[39]

Colletto ends his letter by asking if, since he cannot buy a boat, the secretary could prevail upon the navy to release his requisitioned boat, the *Dante Alighieri,* for next season. As it turned out, the navy either could not, or would not do that. But Colletto's letter had struck a nerve. After all, the navy had made fishing a top national priority; fishermen were given deferments, and sardines were needed not just for food but for their oil, which was used in an antirust paint that was critical to naval operations. And yet, the navy had deprived scores of sardine fishermen of their boats—which was essentially what Sal Colletto had said in his letter. Someone must have recognized this contra-diction, for shortly thereafter, the government did issue higher priorities to Colletto and about a dozen other fishermen, whereupon Sal Colletto contracted for a new boat, which he named the *U.S. Liberator*. An 85-footer with a 400 hp engine, it cost him about $75,000.

Tom Cutino's father also got a new boat at about this time, but on a slightly different basis. Government representatives had visited Gaetano Cutino once more, some two years after taking his boat, and urged him to fish again. The nation needed sardines, they said. Gaetano Cutino replied, "What do you want from me? You've got our boats. You want fish, give us back the boats." This might have seemed a simple solution to the fisherman, but the navy found it impossible to implement. Accordingly, it provided Gaetano Cutino with one of the new priorities, and he got a new boat, from Pacific Boat

Tom, John, and Gaetano Cutino aboard the *Pacific Raider,* the purse seiner they leased during the war. Courtesy of Tom Cutino, Sr.

Builders, named the *Pacific Raider*. Gaetano Cutino did not buy his boat, however, but operated it on a charter basis, earning one of the five owner shares for running the boat. The official owner was Pacific Boat Builders. Whether this was a front organization for a navy that had decided that, since it could not yet return the original boats it had purchased, it should commission boats for use by those fishermen who could not afford to buy them is not yet clear. But Tom Cutino remembers that at the end of the war, his father could have purchased the *Pacific Raider* for "peanuts," as government salvage. Instead, he repurchased the boat for which he still had an abiding affection, the *Cutino Brothers*, on the same basis, paying $25,000 for the boat itself, and $25,000 to have it restored to its fishing condition.

The coda to all this is that by the 1944–45 sardine season, most sardine fishermen in Monterey either had new boats or had their old boats back and were eager to redeploy those boats in a sardine fishery that still seemed healthy. It was not. In the first season after the war, 1946–47, the sardine catch in Monterey suddenly plummeted: from averaging around 200,000 tons in prior years, the 1946–47 catch totaled a meager 31,000 tons. San Francisco was hit even harder, recording only 2,869 tons that year. It was the beginning of the end. Something—overfishing, natural cycles, or both, or something else—was decimating the Pacific sardine stock.[40] Though it would take a few years more for the full effect to hit more southern waters, the sardine bonanza was coming to an end. And what no one knew at the time, but what is now apparent, was how critically abundant had been the years during which the sardine industry had been bent, and almost broken, by the navy's needs.

––––––––––

Though the records for the fishing boats requisitioned by the navy are most complete at this writing for the Pacific purse-seine fleet, that does not mean these boats comprise the full story. A combination of anecdotal and official evidence suggests that many additional boats were requisitioned from Italian fishermen in San Francisco, Boston, and no doubt countless other ports on the Atlantic seaboard.

To begin with San Francisco, the navy initially "estimated that 477 small vessels would be needed to fill district requirements."[41] This included a host of crafts of all types, from tugs to river freighters to tuna clippers, but also included the smaller crab boats. In *Artillery at the Golden Gate*, Brian Chin writes that a Lieutenant Colonel Usis requisitioned at least sixteen of these crab boats for use by the Harbor Defense Corps.[42] Chin points out that these crabbers served another function besides their official one. Given that enemy aliens were prohibited from the wharf and that, according to the *San Francisco Chronicle*, the government "would rout approximately 1,400 Italians from the 2,000 men employed in San Francisco's $500,000-a-year fishing industry," closing the city's commercial crabbing industry, the same Colonel Usis who had commandeered sixteen crab boats was left without one of this favorite foods. According to Chin,

> Usis put the Mine Flotilla to work as a private crab fleet for the gastronomic benefit of the Harbor Defenses. The Mine Groupment commander equipped his mine yawls with crab pots obtained from the Coast Guard. Several recruits in the Mine Battalion had been crab fishermen in civilian life and they were now utilized by the command to do the same work in the army. When the yawls went out in the morning to service the mines, the crews set out crab pots in the water. After the workday, mine crews hauled in the pots and headed back to the mine base at Fort Baker with their crab bounty.[43]

The ironic footnote to this episode is that while most of San Francisco's crab fishermen were grounded and their boats taken for the national emergency, Lieutenant Colonel Usis's crab fleet was feasting on the abundant crab left in their absence and also distributing it to "higher-ups of the Western Defense Command at the Presidio," probably including the rigidly authoritarian commander responsible for many of the harshest restrictions against those crab fishermen, Lieutenant General John DeWitt.

Tony D'Amato remembers some of this. D'Amato's family had been fishing in San Francisco since before the turn of the century, when his grandfather, Giuseppe Crivello, arrived from Sicily. By the time war broke out, D'Amato's family on both sides owned no less than four boats: the *Anna B*, a purse seiner owned by Salvatore Billante, Tony's uncle through marriage; the *Virginia*, his grandfather's crab boat; the *Rose*, a Monterey-type boat belonging to his Uncle Joe; and the *Josephine*, also a Monterey-type boat, belonging to his father. With the war, half the family's boats were requisitoned by the navy. The first to go was the *Virginia*. According to naval records, the *Virginia* was acquired on December 11, 1941, for use by the Coast Artillery, which strongly suggests it must have been one of the sixteen (the record says seventeen) boats mentioned above.[44] According to Carlo Crivello, the navy offered him $750 for the *Virginia*. A bit taken aback, he refused the money. Instead, he told the navy, "Don't give me any money. I just want my boat back." He apparently thought that he had a better chance of getting his boat back if he didn't sell it outright. Though the *Virginia* was indeed returned, he would live to regret that move.

On February 15, 1942, the navy made its next requisition of purse seiners, and the *Anna B* was included in that second seizure. An eighty-foot purse seiner, it had been built just two years earlier to take advantage of the sardine bonanza. The navy purchased the boat outright, and with the proceeds, Salvatore Billante and his brother decided to acquire a smaller, all-purpose boat, capable of fishing for sardines during that season, and for salmon, herring, and crab during the off-season. Fortunately for the D'Amato family, their other two boats were not touched, and were able to continue fishing once clearance was given to fish outside the Golden Gate.[45]

Thus, in addition to the forty-seven purse seiners taken from Italian American fishermen in Monterey, approximately thirty other seiners were taken from San Francisco, including the *Anna B*. And in addition to the sixteen crab boats turned over to the Coast Artillery, the *Virginia* among them, we know of at least one other crab boat, the *Twin Sisters,* which the navy records as being decommissioned in 1945.[46] Another record of acquisitions, "Vessels Acquired for the Coast Guard," includes fifty-four vessels acquired between early December 1941 and February 1942.

While the records for the 1st Naval District have not been searched at this writing, it is clear that something similar happened to the fishermen of Boston. Recall that it was the 1st Naval District in Boston which produced the initial template for the conversion of fishing yawls to minesweepers. According to Frank Firicano, a longtime Boston fisherman and at one time secretary of his union, there were many other parallels between the situation in Boston and that in San Francisco. To begin with, Boston and Gloucester fishermen also employed eighty to hundred-foot seiners when fishing for mackerel. Firicano knows of at least two seiners taken by the navy and converted for patrol duty. He also remembers that two were sunk by German submarines. When told that an October 1942 *Boston Globe* article estimated that 200 Boston fishermen of Italian origin had been grounded during the restrictions, Firicano thought that the figure was probably more like 300, a figure that included his father, his grandfather, and several uncles. Firicano also remembers that, just as in San Francisco,

> They had a sub net in Boston harbor too. Because there's the Boston Navy Yard, and there were convoys leaving night and day from Boston. Eventually, they let us go fishing. We had to have a password each day, go to the Customs House to get clearance, a pass, and then on the way out, stop at a barge off Deer Island manned by the Coast Guard, and they would check out the boat to see we weren't taking provisions to the Germans. We were allowed provisions for seven, which was our crew. There was the

steel gate—it opened, but no one could get out after 5 P.M. We had radio silence too; we had locks on the radios. Only in an emergency could you use it. We had to stop at the lightship, give them the password. When we returned, it was the same thing. We had to stop at the lightship, get the password of the day, and give it to the Coast Guard at the barge going in.[47]

Sal Patania, now retired from fishing, remembers the Boston requisitions as well:

> The government in those days took a lot of the boats. The guy I went fishing with after the war, he had a sixty-five-footer and the government took it. There were a lot more. They took a lot of other boats; they used them for minesweepers.[48]

Sal's wife, Josie, also recalls what it was like within her family when her mother, her father, and her brothers were all affected by the wartime restrictions:

> During the war, they took my father off the fishing boat. So he went to work in the spinach plant, washing the spinach. My brothers Carmelo, Angelo, and Vincent were all in the service at this time. Carmelo and Vincent weren't even citizens. They swore them in before they went, Vincent to Normandy and Carmelo to the Philippines.
>
> My father had worked on a boat. He wasn't a citizen but he had a lot of children who were citizens. I went to work at age fourteen, to work in the 5 & 10, to bring some money in because they took my brothers.
>
> I remember filling up an alien card every year for my mother and father. We were witnesses. Then we made my mother go for citizenship. We taught her how to write her name and to say George Washington and Abraham Lincoln. If she saw Mussolini, we said to shoot him. They actually asked her that question. She said "Me boom-boom."
>
> She had had to leave her son, fifteen years old, in Italy, so he was drafted into the Italian service. That's why my brothers told them if they have a choice they'd rather not go to Italy. One said he wanted to go to Germany, one to the Philippines.
>
> And I remember when they took the boats. They used them to send them to war.[49]

Though many details are still lacking about the true extent of what happened in Boston and other ports along the Atlantic seaboard, it seems fair to say that the United States Navy requisitioned the boats of fishermen from many of those ports, and that a goodly number of those boats belonged to Italian American fishermen.

The navy's business with the fishermen was not finished until the navy was finished with their boats. Then it would have to decommission the hundreds of boats it had requisitioned and either sell or give them back to the previous owners.[50] In the case of the *Cutino Brothers*, the boat was sold back for about $25,000, took another $25,000 in repairs, and ended up with the Cutinos in the black. Anthony Bruno remembers that his father's boat, the *St. Anthony*, was returned very well refurbished. In fact, he worked at the shipyards that did much of the restoring, and in the case of the *St. Anthony*, the government essentially signed a blank check, commissioning the work that Gus Bruno wanted:

> Actually, it was in better shape than when they got it. It had a
> poop deck—a rear deck raised about a foot—so the boat could
> hold more fish. We found out it had been in Panama because we
> found the log and read it.[51]

It seems that the terms of requisition made by the Maritime Commission with individual boat owners on the navy's behalf varied widely, as did the use to which the boats were put, the time of their return, and the condition in which they were returned. Some boats were purchased outright; some were chartered with equipment, some without. The navy could do whatever it wished, for if boat owners got stubborn, a legal provision allowed the navy to simply set its own price and pay seventy-five percent of that, thereafter letting the owner sue for the rest in court—a prospect that few boat owners could have relished.[52] The same tactics could be used in returning boats.

The story of Giuseppe Spadaro's *Marettimo*, already mentioned, is a case in point. Giuseppe Crivello's crab boat, the *Virginia*, provides another. Recall that Carlo Crivello, when the navy offered $750 to purchase the *Virginia*, told them to keep the money; he simply wanted his boat back. The navy complied. But according to Crivello, "what we got back was a boat that was basically run into the ground. We got the shell of the boat, and an engine, and that was it." Furthermore, the navy demanded a payment of $1,000 for a boat they had been given free of charge and had then proceeded to "run into the ground." But having lost two boats to the navy and borne the stigma of enemy-alien status, the Crivellos bowed to the inevitable. They accepted the deal, never complained, and spent a good deal of money to have the *Virginia* restored.[53]

If there is a common thread running through such stories, it is surely this: most fishermen whose boats were seized sustained losses. While some did better than others, it is not easy to determine whether such varied treatment depended on when a boat was taken, or when it was returned, or whether it had been requisition-purchased or requisition-chartered. Some fishermen maintain that the first boats returned were beautifully restored, but after that, the navy simply made a flat offer—take it or leave it—and returned the boats in miserable shape. It could also be the case that the condition of the boats, as well as their time of return, depended upon where they had been put into service. Some boats, including a half dozen from Monterey, were decommissioned as early as the spring of 1943. Others, for example, the *Phyllis* and the *Dante Alighieri*, were not released from service until the spring of 1945. Whether this was due to the distant places the latter had served is not clear, for as usual the record is mixed. A naval speedletter informs the 12th Naval District that the *Phyllis* was scheduled to depart from Panama for San Francisco on March 21, 1945,[54] but a naval speedletter about the *Dante Alighieri*, reportedly used for coastal duty near Monterey, simply says it was "delivered to war shipping administration and simultaneously returned to owner fourteen March nineteen hundred forty-five."[55] Nor does duty in Panama seem to be the deciding factor, for as was seen earlier, Gus Bruno's *St. Anthony* also did duty in Panama, and records indicate its "placed-out-of-service" date as May 12, 1943.[56]

Lacking a complete survey of the records on every vessel that was seized, one must attribute the varying experiences to chance, or luck, or some as-yet-unknown level of influence, or prejudice, or some combination of these factors. Or perhaps to none at all. For what is apparent is that in the heat of the emergency sounded by Pearl Harbor, the navy operated sometimes rigidly, sometimes wildly, sometimes chaotically, and even comically. It was the fishermen who were left to figure out what had happened, and why. Many of them would have concluded what Giuseppe Spadaro did when his teenage daughter Vitina asked, "Why, why are they doing this to us?"

"There's a war going on," he said. "People in command don't know what they're doing."[57]

Endnotes

1. If we were to define the shoreline to include places like Connecticut's Long Island Sound, the figure would be 88,033 miles.

2. Rodney Campbell, *The Luciano Project* (New York: McGraw-Hill, 1977). It is interesting that, as Campbell points out, the serious danger to shipping on the East Coast prompted the military, through its Office of Naval Intelligence, to seek a deal with Lucky Luciano and the mob to secure the waterfront. On the West Coast, the far milder threat led the authorities to intern community leaders and clear approximately 10,000 enemy aliens, many of them elderly women, from coastal areas.

3. See Brian B. Chin, *Artillery at the Golden Gate: The Harbor Defenses of San Francisco in World War II* (Missoula, Mont.: Pictorial Histories Publishing Co. Inc., 1994), pp. 41–42.

4. *Monterey Peninsula Herald*, February 27, 1942, p. 11.

5. As one example, to release the skiff and begin the process of encircling a sardine school with the net, the word "Mola!" was used, meaning "Let her go!" Sal Colletto Jr., "Growing up in a Monterey Fishing Family," in The J. B. Phillips Historical Fisheries Report, vol. 1, no. 1, Spring 2000

6. Letter, Stanley Parker to Dominick Strazulo, RG 181, Records of Naval Districts and Shore Establishments, 12th Naval District (hereafter NDSE), Box 0294, National Archives and Records Administration, San Bruno, (hereafter NARA SB).

7. At some point in early January, Elios Anderlini, the lawyer for the Crab Fishermen's Association, prevailed upon Earl Warren, California's attorney general, to arrange a meeting with the military authorities. Finally, they agreed on a plan: "If the fishermen would assemble, the navy would convoy them out, en masse, early in the morning to fish for the day. They would then assemble at a certain time before dark to be convoyed back in." (personal interview, Elios Anderlini.)

8. Memo, December 9, 1941, Stanley Parker to Chief of Staff, 12th Naval District, RG 181, 12th Naval District Commandant's Office, General Correspondence, Accession 58–3224, NARA SB.

9. Ibid.

10. A February 24, 1942, report in the *San Francisco Chronicle* estimated that 1,400 of the city's 2,000 fishermen were enemy aliens banned from wharf.

11. Quoted in Louis Lyons, *Boston Globe*, "Italians of Boston Lift Heads Again; 'Enemy' Ban Is Off," October 18, 1942, p. 27.

12. Ibid.

13. ORANGE was the code which referred to a possible war with Japan.

14. Memo, November 30, 1938, "Minesweeping by District Forces," RG 181, NDSE, Box S–432, NARA SB.

15. Ibid.

16. Memo, July 6, 1940, Bureau of Ships to Naval Districts, "Arrangement of Vessels Converted to Naval Auxiliaries (XAM) Mine Sweepers," RG 181, NDSE, Box S–432, NARA SB.

17. A 1936 letter from the Fisherman's Cooperative Association to the Los Angeles meeting of the American Legion announces a three-part program to combat a potential national emergency: first, eliminate all alien owners of boats in the California fishing fleet; second, eliminate all aliens from the fishing fleet in general; and third, pledge the fishing boats, especially of San Pedro, to a naval reserve. Not to be outdone, Peter Ferrante of Monterey wrote a letter in March 1939 on behalf of Monterey Sardine Industries, Inc., a boat-owners' group, complaining that only a few boat owners in Monterey had been asked to join a naval reserve when many more wished to do so. "Some of these men who have asked me to write to you are American-born boys of Italian descent and they feel as though they have been slighted when naturalized citizens have been asked to join the naval reserve and they have not." As it turned out, they needn't have worried. (Memo and letter, RG 181, NDSE, Box S–432, NARA SB.)

18. Memo, February 6, 1939, "Fishing Vessels Suitable for XAM(c)," RG 181, NDSE, Box S–432, NARA SB.

19. Memo, August 20, 1940, "Conversion of Purse Seiners to Coastal Mine Sweepers (XAMc)," RG 181, NDSE, Box S–432, NARA SB.

20. Memo February 6, 1939, "Fishing Vessels..."

21. Memo, July 1940, "Fishermen's Reserve," RG 181, NDSE, Box S–432, NARA SB.

22. David A. J. Richards, *Italian American: The Racializing of an Ethnic Group* (New York: New York University Press, 1999).
23. Attachment to Memo, February 6, 1939, "List of Owners and Captains of Purse Seiners Recommended for Naval Service: San Francisco–Monterey Area," RG 181, NDSE, Box S–432, NARA SB.
24. Memo, July 16, 1940, "Enrollment of Fishermen in Class V-6, USNR, for Service in Their Own Vessels as Minesweepers," RG 181, NDSE, Box S–432, NARA SB.
25. It is worth noting that the U.S. Army had no such reticence, having already by this time drafted noncitizen Italian Americans when it could. Of course, it did question them closely about their willingness to fight in Italy, in some cases segregating even citizens of Italian descent who expressed reservations about such combat.
26. *United States Naval Administration in World War II*, 12th Naval District, 1939–1945, vol. III, p. 52, RG 181, NDSE, Box 1, NARA SB.
27. Tom Cutino, personal interview, July 12, 2000.
28. Ibid.
29. *U.S. Naval Administration in WWII*, p. 52.
30. "List of Newly Acquired Vessels," RG 181, 12th Naval District Commandant's Office, General Correspondence, Accession 58–3224, NARA SB.
31. Anthony Bruno, personal interview, July 12, 2000.
32. Vitina Spadaro, personal interview, October 2, 1999.
33. Ibid.
34. Ibid.
35. John Russo, personal interview, July 19, 2000.
36. Ibid.
37. "A Sardine Fisherman," by Salvatore Colletto, manuscript, Monterey Maritime Museum, p. 192.
38. Sal Colletto Jr., personal interview, July 23, 2000.
39. "A Sardine Fisherman," p. 239.
40. Some Monterey fishermen maintain that the War Production Board's insistence on removing the limits on what an individual boat could catch (as a way of making up for the decrease in catches the navy's requisitions had instigated?) aggravated the problem. The state-instituted limits had led to conservation: if a boat netted more fish than its limit, it would usually call another boat and take the time to share its catch rather than discard hundreds of tons of dead fish. Fishing without limits, by contrast, gave fishermen the incentive to race in to the cannery to unload their catch, simply discarding the excess fish. Then, since there were no limits, they could race out and catch another load the same night, again discarding the excess. The result was that, without limits, far more fish were discarded after being caught, fish that were thus destroyed to no purpose, except to help decimate the stock. For a discussion, see *A History of Steinbeck's Cannery Row*, by Tom Mangelsdorf (Santa Cruz, Calif.: Western Tanager Press, 1986), pp. 145ff. (I am indebted to Tom Cutino for this discussion, and for directing me to the Mangelsdorf history.)
41. *U.S. Naval Administration in WWII*, p. 34.
42. Chin, *Artillery at the Golden Gate*, p. 82.
43. Ibid, pp. 83–84.
44. "List of Newly Acquired Vessels," p. 15.
45. Tony D'Amato, personal interview, August 9, 2000.
46. Memo, February 6, 1945, "Small Vessels—Laying up and Disposal of," RG 181, Box S–434, NARA SB.
47. Frank Firicano, personal interview, July 26, 2000.
48. Sal Patania, personal interview, July 25, 2000.
49. Josie Patania, personal interview, July 25, 2000.
50. The 12th Naval District administrative history previously cited (note 26) estimated that "477 small vessels would be needed to fill district requirements," including: "pleasure launches, Coast Guard vessels, pilot boats, tugs, lighters, harbor tankers, gasoline barges, river freighters, crab boats, tuna clippers, and lighthouse tenders," p.34.

51. Bruno interview, July 12, 2000.

52. The terms cited by the U. S Maritime Commission in a memo it sent to its district managers include the following: "By an act approved August 7, 1939, Congress amended Section 9092, Merchant Marine Act, 1936, and as so amended that section now reads as follows: Sec. 902 (a) Whenever the President shall proclaim that the security of the national defense makes it advisable or during any national emergency declared by proclamation of the President, it shall be lawful for the Commission to requisition or purchase any vessel or other watercraft owned by citizens of the United States, or under construction within the United States, or for any period during such emergency, to requisition or charter the use of any such property.... (d) In all cases, the just compensation authorized by this section shall be determined and paid by the Commission as soon as practicable, but if the amount of just compensation determined by the Commission is unsatisfactory to the person entitled thereto, such person shall be paid 75 per centum of the amount so determined and shall be entitled to sue the United States to recover such further sum as, added to said 75 per centum, will make up such amount as will be just compensation therefor, in the manner approved of by section 24, paragraph 20, and section 145 of the Judicial Code (U.S.C. 1934 edition, title 28, sections. 41, 250). RG 181, Box S–434, NARA SB.

53. D'Amato interview, August 9, 2000.

54. Naval speedletter, March 21, 1945, "YP 305, ex-Phyllis," RG 181, Box S–434, NARA SB.

55. Naval speedletter, March 19, 1945, "YP 370, ex-Dante Alighieri," RG 181, Box S–434, NARA SB.

56. Memo, May 24, 1943, "Vessels Under 100' Length Over-all–Placed out of Service," RG 181, 12th Naval District Commandant's Office, General Correspondence, Accession 58–3224, NARA SB.

57. Spadaro interview, October 1999.

A Sardine Fisherman during the War

by Salvatore Colletto

Salvatore Colletto was born in Pittsburg, California, and resettled in Monterey with his fisherman father in 1910, when he was six years old. He fished with his father until he made it apparent that he had an unusual aptitude for fishing, at which point, still a teenager, he began captaining his father's boat. After purchasing his own boat in his late twenties, he fished in Monterey, primarily for sardines, until he retired and began writing his memoirs—three volumes of hand-written pages detailing his experiences. These excerpts derive from that manuscript, now in the Maritime Museum of Monterey. The first takes place around the time when the United States first entered the war, in December 1941; the second occurs towards the end of the war, in January 1945, when, in heavy fog off Point Montara, he gambled that he could haul in a load of sardines before daybreak would put him and his crew in danger. The fisherman's life is built on such gambles, but usually they do not involve heavy artillery.

On the day of the Pearl Harbor catastrophe, the fishermen were congregating on the wharf....Fish were running in the Half Moon Bay area, and we were to leave port for the fishing grounds about 10 A.M. We heard the news that morning, and there was lots of excitement on the wharf. The FBI were looking for some Japanese fishermen. A couple were supposed to be Japanese naval officers. And the rumor was that they were picked up by a Japanese submarine which had been laying on the bottom off of Watsonville. We had seen a submarine heading east into the bay a week before, but we did not think of a Japanese sub. We were coming in from Half Moon Bay with a load of fish. There was a ground swell running....We were about six miles from Point Pinos—it was getting daybreak—when we seen a gray silhouette of the conning tower in the trough of the sea, crossing our bow, heading towards Moss Landing. We thought it was one of our submarines. No one went fishing that day....

My boat [the *Dante Alighieri*] was one of the first fishing boats they [the U.S. Navy] took: a week later I took it to Treasure Island in San Francisco. There were three officers aboard my boat and we had a convoy of seven purse seines, the first group of boats to leave the bay. We were ordered to run in the dark and make rendezvous with a destroyer that was waiting outside the Golden Gate. All city lights and lighthouses were darkened. We met the destroyer about 10 A.M., and it escorted us in through the channel. Both sides of the channel, they told us, were mined. We delivered the boats to Treasure Island. Later, ninety percent of the boats from Monterey were requisitioned by the navy. Superstructures and living quarters were built on the boats. And they were used for coastal patrol duty. A couple years later, a fair price was paid for most of the boats. Some boats were on charter basis, and they were the first to be released by the navy to their owners…[1]

After the navy requisitioned the *Dante Alighieri*, I managed to finish that season by chartering the vessel *Robert B.* The boat was owned by a Seattle fisherman and it was chartered by a Japanese fisherman. When the Japanese were evacuated inland, I took over the *Robert B,* on the 20th of December 1941, the day the fishermen that had boats resumed fishing. There were only about one-third of our fleet that went fishing; the other two-thirds of the purse seines were taken over by the government.[2] All fishing was done in the dark. The cities were blacked out. There was a Japanese submarine off Santa Cruz that fired on an oil tanker. It did not do any damage.

Every day we had to report to the port captain the vicinity we were to fish in that evening, so he could notify the coastal batteries of the fishing fleet's location. The first night fishing we went south below Pt. Pfeiffer; lots of fish were reported. We were about ten miles below Pt. Pfeiffer; there we seen an enormous school of sardines. We went into a set and caught about 200 tons of sardines. The fish hold of the *Robert B.* carried 95 tons of fish. We were [trying] to put some fish on deck, but we had to discontinue because the fish-hold pumps were giving us trouble. We lost lots of time loading the fish hold, caus-ing us to be one of the last boats to unload at the cannery. It was 7 P.M. before we finished unloading our catch.

It was too late to go south, because it was a five-hour run down. So we tried scouting in Monterey Bay. We left without notifying the port captain that we were [going] to try fishing in Monterey Bay. There had been no signs of fish in the bay. We headed towards the cement plants, and when we were abreast of the cement plants I seen a large phosphorescent glow, thought it was a school of fish from our position. I told the crew to get ready while I steered for the glow. It was pitch dark that night. Upon getting close to the glow, I noticed it was a large ship running in the dark. The bow of the ship pushing the water made that glow that appeared to be a school of fish. I swung our steering wheel hard over to starboard to get out of the way.

From the cement plant we scouted towards Santa Cruz. Abreast of the city we seen a large school of sardines. I kept track of our position, running by dead reckoning. The time spent and courses of the compass gave me my exact position. When we went into a set there was a light westerly wind, and the fish were traveling west, causing us to drift into the net as we were pursing. When we got the leads aboard, part of the stern net got caught into the propeller. We had to turn on our deck lights to free the portion of net caught. In freeing the net we ripped a portion and lots of fish escaped from the torn net. But there still was enough fish to fill the hold.

When we got all our net aboard and had started brailing,[3] we heard the noise of a high-speed motor coming towards us. It was a speedboat with a dozen soldiers armed with machine guns. They came close to us and asked, "Who goes there?" We said, "A fishing boat from Monterey." They said, "We have a report from the port captain that the fleet is fishing south." We said, "It's true, but we got through unloading late, and I thought I would try the bay, and I forgot to notify him."

They told us we were lucky they came out to check, because there were a lot of itchy fingers ready to shoot the coastal batteries at us...

———————

It was 2 A.M. and we were nearing the firing area that had been closed to fishing. Antiaircraft firing practice was conducted every day; the danger area was to about twelve miles offshore from Montara, and all craft were to stay clear of that area.

It was 2:15 A.M. when we saw our first sardine school that evening. It was a school of sardines of approximately 50 tons. It wasn't worth laying our net. Five minutes later we encountered a large school. But we were in the danger area, and I was debating with myself whether to go into a set. I decided to go into a set, thinking that we would be out of the area when firing commenced.

We put ourselves in position to go into a set in the fog. Orders were given to lay out the net in a circle. The skiff with one end of the net had two men in it, which was customary. One man held a flashlight, which he flickered off and on to keep us informed of their position. The fog was very thick and we barely could see the light on the skiff. We completed the circle of the net, corralling the whole school, and starting pursing. The submarine light was set out about twenty fathoms deep. And with a switch controlled from the deck, the light flickered off and on, scaring the fish into the net.

As we were pursing, we kept feeling the two purse cables; that practice was used by all skippers. The object of that was to observe if the cables were clear from the rocks. Everything seemed to be going nicely. The net was now pursed in, the rings of the bottom of the net were lifted aboard. And as the rings were being hoisted aboard by block and tackle and by winch, several sardines were falling on deck, an indication that it was a good catch. We laid the leads aboard, and tied our rings secure with chains that were tied secure on the opposite side of the boat. The...sardines were so thick in the net that they were jumping all over the net. I estimated there were approximately 300 tons; orders were given to pull the zipper in the middle of the net. The idea of that was to separate the fish, one half to go in the stern section of the net, and the other half in the bow. Lines were tied secure from the vessel to the corks on the bow half of the net; that was done to prevent the net from sinking. In that manner the fish could not escape. The only way for the sardines to escape was from the net tearing. There was little possibility of that, because the net was fairly new.

When we had the net secure, the skiff tied itself on the stern half of the corks. And we commenced hauling in the net. There were lots of sardines coming up, tangled in the net, a sure indication that there were lots of fish.

It was 4 A.M. before we brailed our first scoop full of fish into the fish hold of the vessel. By 7 A.M. we had our fish hold full of 160 tons of sardines. We made the hatches secure, pumping out water and fish blood continuously from our hatch. We still had about 50 tons of dead sardines in the stern half of the net, and about 150 tons in the bow half....It took us approximately one hour before we pulled in the stern half of the net. The bow portion was still in the water with fish in it, most of the fish dead.

It was now 8 A.M. and we heard a rumble of coastal batteries, firing from the direction of Point Montara. It was still foggy, visibility was about one-fifth of a mile. We at first did not mind the shooting. But when two shells landed within two hundred feet, we were very much concerned and scared. We could not very well get out of the firing area, because half of our net was still in the water.

I immediately got on the radio phone and called the Monterey Coast Guard station and explained our predicament to them. And I advised the Coast Guard to get in touch with the Montara coastal batteries [and tell them] to cease firing until we were out of the danger area. The Coast Guard got in touch by phone, and in ten minutes we no longer heard the coastal batteries.

Tom Lucido of the boat *Rose Marie* got in touch with us by radio phone and wanted to know what was wrong, and if they could help. I told him a couple of shells landed near us, and that I got in touch with the Monterey Coast Guard, and that everything seemed under control. I told Lucido that it will be a couple of hours before we get our net hauled in from the water. He said he would keep in touch with me. About half an hour later, he was calling us by radio phone. I went to answer the call, but something happened to the radio set. We could hear everything that was said, but no one could hear us. I tried to answer, but we were not getting on the air. I could hear Lucido talking to other boats, telling them that he was talking to me and that he could no longer raise me.

He was saying, "I don't know, a couple of shells landed near the *U.S. Liberator*, now I can't talk to them." In the meantime the fog was still thick, and we could hear planes flying overhead. The Coast Guard had dispatched planes to try to locate us, but they could not spot us through the fog.

It was 12:30 P.M. before we got all our net hauled on the vessel. The fog had lifted, [improving] visibility…but it was not sufficient to spot us from the air.

Sal Colletto mending nets in Monterey before the war. Courtesy of the Captain Sal Colletto Collection, Maritime Museum of Monterey

We were underway for Monterey at 12:35 P.M. with a full load of 160 tons. We could continuously hear the boats, talking to one another;...they were concerned about our outcome. At Monterey, our families were worried about us, and they kept calling the Coast Guard station by telephone, hoping that they could get some good news.

From our position, the run to Monterey was eight hours at full speed. In the meantime, my brother-in-law, who had two years of college in the electrical field, worked continuously on our set. It was 7 P.M. when he got the set working. We talked to the Coast Guard and told them what had happened to our set, and [asked them] to inform our families that we will be in at 8:30 P.M. That news relieved the anxiety of our families.

The fog cleared about 7:30 P.M. We were outside Moss Landing, steering a course of southeast by east. The lights of the peninsula became visible from our position, they appeared like jewels glittering in the stillness of the night. The sea was calm in the bay, the fog bank was laying to the west of us. All the lights in the bay were visible to us. The lighthouse at Pt. Pinos kept giving its signal as usual.

When we arrived at the cannery, we commenced unloading. By 11 P.M. we were through unloading and underway again for Half Moon Bay...

Endnotes:
1. A later part of the manuscript reads as follows: In May 1945 I received a letter from the Secretary of the Navy, [which read]: Dear Mr. Colletto: Soon after hostilities, and at a time when the menace to National defense and vital interest was most critical, your vessel *Dante Alighieri* was made available to the navy and became a contributing factor towards the furtherance of the war effort. The *Dante Alighieri* has now been returned to you and it will no doubt be a matter of great pride and interest to you to know that the *Dante Alighieri* gave valuable and excellent service in the important duties assigned to her. In recognition of the war service rendered by the *Dante Alighieri*, you are authorized to place on the stack or in the vicinity of the bridge four chevrons, or one for each six months' service with the Navy. The Navy Department takes this opportunity to express its sincere appreciation and grateful thanks for your patriotic and generous contribution in the hour of the country's most urgent need. [signed by James Forrestal]
2. According to naval records, the requisitions that depleted the Monterey fleet by two-thirds took place in late February. Colletto seems to be conflating several events here, including the mass Japanese American evacuation, which began two months later. Perhaps the Japanese fisherman referred to here was interned as a "dangerous" alien; many of them were arrested in December.
3. Brailing is a process of using a large scoop to take sardines from the net, still in the water, and into the hold.

Mala Notte
The Relocation Story in Santa Cruz

by Geoffrey Dunn

> Geoffrey Dunn is a fourth-generation Italian American from Santa
> Cruz. An award-wining journalist, filmmaker, and historian, Dunn is
> the author of *Santa Cruz Is in the Heart* and the director of several
> documentary films, including *Dollar a Day, Ten Cents a Dance,*
> *Miss…or Myth?*, and *Chinese Gold*. He currently serves as a lecturer
> in community studies at the University of California, Santa Cruz, and
> as executive director of Community Television of Santa Cruz County.

On a quiet evening in late February of 1942, Celestina Stagnaro Loero, my
great-grandmother, was greeted at the doorstep of her clapboard home at 17
Laguna Street, in the coastal community of Santa Cruz, by two agents of the
Department of Justice. A native of Riva Trigoso in northern Italy and seventy-
six years of age at the time, she spoke little English, while the federal agents
spoke no Italian, much less the Genoese dialect that was the common tongue
of the Santa Cruz Italian fishing colony. A granddaughter who lived next door
was summoned to serve as a translator.

As a so-called enemy alien living in what had recently been declared a
restricted area by the Western Defense Command of the United States Army,
my great-grandmother was told that she was in violation of recently passed federal law. The agents informed her that she had forty-eight hours to move herself and her belongings inland of Highway 1 (Mission Street, in Santa Cruz), or
she would be subject to immediate arrest.

A few weeks earlier, my great-grandmother had registered with the Alien
Registration Division of the federal government. Standing all of four feet, ten
inches tall and weighing 140 pounds, my great-grandmother could hardly have
been a threat to the U.S. war effort against the Axis powers. Two of her sons
and two of her grandsons, not to mention several nephews and cousins, had
recently enlisted in the U.S. Navy. She had lived on the same plot of land for
a little more than forty-one years and rarely ventured more than a few blocks

away. But move she did, to a room on the inland side of Highway 1, where she was to live for the remainder of the year.

My great-grandmother was in her nineties when I was a small child, but I have vivid memories of her strong, busy hands, always seeming to be at work in her vegetable garden or in her kitchen. She had an ever present smile, she enjoyed an afternoon glass of red wine, and she loved to hold me and my young cousins in her lap and play games with our hands. Occasionally she would break out into tears, and when she did, she would mumble something about *"la mala notte"* (the bad night), about which we children knew nothing—and would know nothing for years and years to come.[1]

It was nearly a quarter century later, long after she had died, that I happened across news of my great-grandmother's forced relocation while researching some World War II history in the pages of the local paper, the *Santa Cruz Sentinel*.[2] For the first time, I understood the meaning of *"la mala notte,"* the sad, unforgotten night she had been forced to move from the safety and comfort of her home.

As I read through the microfilm, I also discovered that she had not been alone. Scores of other Santa Cruz Italians also were relocated in the first months of the war, and as I would come to realize over the years, so too were tens of thousands of other Italian immigrants along the West Coast, including thousands in Monterey, just across the bay. Many others throughout the country were arrested on dubious charges and sent to prison or to inland internment centers run by the Immigration and Naturalization Service. Throughout the United States, I discovered, more than 600,000 Italian Americans were subjected to strict travel restrictions and seizure of their personal property.[3]

I also came to realize the historical misconception that Executive Order 9066, issued by President Franklin Delano Roosevelt on February 19, 1942, applied only to Japanese (and Japanese Americans) living in the western states. Such was not the case. The order authorized the secretary of war "to designate military areas from which any or all persons may be excluded"—including my great-grandmother.[4]

All of this had come as something of a shock to me. As historian Stephen Fox has pointed out, in the early months of the war, Lieutenant General John L. DeWitt, commanding general of the Fourth Army and Western Defense Command in San Francisco, interpreted the order to include all enemy aliens—Italians and Germans, along with the Japanese. Indeed, DeWitt, paranoid about so-called fifth-column activities (spying by enemy nationals) pushed for the forced relocation of all enemy aliens. It was only in the ensuing months, for reasons that are far more complex than simple racism, that the treatment of the Japanese would become more heinous than that of their Italian and German counterparts.[5]

The author's uncles and great-uncles, with long-line basket, on Santa Cruz wharf ca. 1944. Joe Stagnaro (top/center, grandson of Celestina Loero) was home on leave from the U.S. Navy. Courtesy of Geoffrey Dunn

The Japanese bombs that destroyed Pearl Harbor and President Franklin Roosevelt's subsequent declaration of war in December 1941 rocked immigrant communities along the West Coast out of their political slumber. Until then, the gloomy events in Europe and Asia had appeared vague and distant, particularly to those engaged in agricultural and commercial fishing activities throughout the largely rural West. Santa Cruz County, located on the northern sweep of Monterey Bay in central California, was no exception.

The events of December 7, 1941, changed all that. Almost immediately, Santa Cruz residents of Japanese descent, previously ambivalent about the Asian-Pacific conflict, declared their allegiance to the U.S. war effort. At a dinner given at the St. George Hotel in downtown Santa Cruz on December 8 by the Japanese Association of Santa Cruz, the organization's president, Tommy Kadotani, told local officials in attendance, "We are yours to command in this emergency."[6]

Across the country in Washington, that same evening, President Roosevelt ordered the arrest of all Italian, Japanese, and German aliens whom the FBI and other federal agencies deemed "dangerous to American security." Thousands were arrested. Less than two weeks later, Lieutenant General

DeWitt was recommending that all enemy aliens fourteen years of age and older be removed to the interior.[7] For a short time, the Justice Department resisted the pressures mounting from DeWitt and the War Department and proposed a more moderate alien policy. By mid-January, however, with the war effort deteriorating in the Pacific, the moderate voices at Justice caved in and the War Department announced that it was constructing internment camps for "all classes of enemy aliens." In late January, DeWitt submitted an extensive list of "restricted zones" which were prohibited to all enemy aliens—German, Italian, and Japanese alike.[8]

With its large populations of farmers and fishermen of Japanese and Italian descent, the Monterey Bay area was of particular concern to DeWitt and the War Department. By January 25, 1942, all areas west (or ocean side) of Highway 1 in Santa Cruz and Monterey counties were declared restricted to all enemy aliens (with curfew, travel, and residence restrictions enforced). Local German, Italian, and Japanese immigrants who had not yet declared American citizenship were forced to move out of the restricted areas by February 24, after which time they would also be subjected to a 9 P.M. curfew and permitted to travel only between their homes and places of employment. Signs were placed throughout the county boldly announcing: "ENEMY ALIENS PROHIBITED AREA NO. 28. The United States Government requires all aliens of German, Italian, or Japanese nationality to vacate this area." It was estimated that 1,500 local residents would be affected by the decree.

The *Santa Cruz Sentinel,* a longtime conservative Republican paper run by the McPherson family for the better part of a century, quickly jumped on the relocation bandwagon. In an editorial dated February 3, the local daily reasoned, "The United States can take no chances by trying to pick for exclusion only those aliens who are known enemies. All aliens originating from countries with which we are at war [should] be banned from the defined areas."

For Italian fishermen working at the Santa Cruz Municipal Wharf, restrictions on their activities were enforced immediately after the Pearl Harbor bombing. The day following FDR's declaration of war, a dozen Italian nationals were no longer allowed to take their boats out to sea. The restricted fishermen included Stefano Ghio, Giovanni Olivieri, Marco Carniglia, Batista and Frank Bregante, Serafino Canepa, Niccolo Bassano, Giacomo Stagnaro, Agostino Olivieri, Fortunado Zolezzi, Johnnie Stellato, and Johnnie Cecchini. Their plight became well publicized. In a front-page article with banner headlines, the *Sentinel* declared: "Fishermen With 23 Sons in Army and Navy Are Bound to Wharf While Boats Lie Idle and Sea Food Is Needed."

The article, more than likely written by the *Sentinel's* legendary waterfront reporter, Ernest Otto,[9] was sympathetic towards the fishermen and also noted the confusion and inequities of the government's relocation efforts: "With its problem of separating fifth columnists from peaceful and worthy residents of foreign birth, the Department of Justice has had no time to work out formulae which will safeguard the nation and at the same time allow such men as Santa Cruz's fishermen to earn a living for their families and add to the country's food supply."

Local Italian activists Mary Carniglia, whose fisherman husband had been restricted from earning a living, and my great-uncle Malio Stagnaro, a longtime political activist who had enlisted in the navy at the age of forty-one as a chief boatswain, joined with Santa Cruz Judge James J. Scoppetone of the Marconi Civic Service Club in writing letters to government officials on behalf of the restricted fishermen, many of whom were their relatives and all of whom lived either in the Italian neighborhoods overlooking the Santa Cruz waterfront or in the flats east of Neary Lagoon. Local congressmember John Anderson responded to these early pleas with typical political aplomb: "I am doing everything I can to bring the [fishermen's] trustworthiness to the attention of proper authorities, and I earnestly hope that a policy will be adopted which will permit your people to return to their normal way of living."

One of the local fishermen prevented from going to sea was Stefano ("Stevie") Ghio, father of veteran Santa Cruz fisherman Victor Ghio. "Here I was in the navy," Victor Ghio would later recall. "I had another brother in the navy and another brother in the army, and they do this to my father? It was a bunch of b.s., a lot of b.s. I talked to my superiors about it, but hell, there was nothing they could do. They told me to do my duty and that was it. It's too bad, that's all. My dad and some of the rest lost some good fishing seasons, I'll tell you that."

Victor's older brother, Steve ("Ghighi") Ghio, recalled coming home from leave during the spring of 1942 and not being able to find his parents, who had been forced to relocate inland. "I came home to the Barranca (the Italian neighborhood)," he remembered, "and I couldn't find my folks or my aunts and uncles. All the houses were boarded up shut. I couldn't find anybody. Finally, I went down to the police station and they told me what had happened. I was still in my navy uniform. They looked through some records and found out where they were. So one of the officers drives me up to where my folks had been moved. They were all so happy to see me, and my mother says, 'I was worried you wouldn't find us,' and she started to cry. It was pretty upsetting. They'd lived here thirty, forty years, and to have this happen to them—well, it just wasn't right, but there wasn't much we could say."[10]

In one of his daily "Waterfront" columns, Otto noted the locations where many of the Italian fishing families had moved: "Serafino Canepa and family to Market Street, Marco Carniglia to Berkshire Avenue, Agostino Olivieri to

Pacheco Avenue. In that vicinity are also families of John Stellato, John Cecchini, and Salvatore Ferrante. Mr. and Mrs. Steve Canepa of Monterey Avenue moved to Berkshire, the mother of John Loero to High Street, Giacomo Stagnaro and family to Olive Street."

Italian artichoke and brussels sprouts farmers on the north coast of the county were also hit hard by the early restrictions. "The growers are definitely facing a labor shortage," declared Luis Poletti, head of the Davenport Producers Association. "It hits pretty hard. I don't know how we're going to replace them in the fields, but we'll have to."

The relatively small German community in Santa Cruz also felt the impact of the restrictions and impending relocation. As depicted by John Steinbeck in his novel *East of Eden*, anti-German sentiment was particularly virulent along the central coast during World War I, and it was rekindled once again by events in Europe. On February 13, the body of German national George M. Heckel was found on a beach near Woodrow Avenue. Despondent over his impending relocation and not wanting to suffer through hostilities like those twenty years earlier, the seventy-three-year-old native of Germany walked out into the surf and committed suicide. At least four similar suicides, by both Italians and Germans, took place in the San Francisco Bay Area in the early weeks of February.[11]

The periodic announcements coming from the Justice and War Departments, many of them contradictory, had the effect of putting the local Japanese, Italian, and German communities on edge. No one here knew what exactly was going on—and in reality, no one in Washington knew what was going on, either. Various departments and competing bureaucracies established policy one day, only to have it overruled and contradicted by another the next. Looking back on them from the vantage point of fifty years, the daily reports of those activities read like a Kafkaesque novel. At the time, they must have been a living nightmare.

On February 1, for instance, a *Sentinel* headline declared: "No Zones Barred to Enemy Aliens in This County." A few day later, another headline declared: "New Alien Rules Are Outlined," with the accompanying article affirming that "no enemy aliens may live, work, or visit" the restricted areas in the county. The following day, headlines reported: "No Exceptions for Santa Cruz Aliens: Confusion [Here] after First Order." The article went on to read:

> Italian, Japanese, and German aliens in Santa Cruz who may have
> harbored a hope that some disposition would come to exclude
> them from the evacuation order had those hopes completely

quashed Tuesday in a Justice Department announcement that "no exceptions" would be made.

There will be no relaxation of regulations to permit the aged and infirm, or those Axis aliens living with citizen sons and daughters, to remain in the area.

A few weeks later, all of Santa Cruz County was declared prohibited to Italian, Japanese, and German nationals, and vast areas inland extending throughout the Central Valley were deemed restricted. Meanwhile, headline after headline emphasized the urgency of the enemy-alien issue.

Local Italians did not take the restrictions lightly. Many violated them flagrantly, while others vowed to have them overturned. In an interview conducted in 1975, Malio Stagnaro recalled a trip he took to San Francisco to confront Lieutenant General DeWitt about the hardships his policies were creating. Stagnaro, then serving as a chief boatswain on Mare Island, characterized DeWitt as a "damn fool…a complete nut, in my opinion."

"I went up to DeWitt to try to talk to him," Stagnaro recalled, "and he wouldn't listen to any reason whatsoever, to nothing. Everybody to him was an enemy that wasn't an American citizen. I said, 'General, these are the greatest people in the world.' 'Well!' he says, 'Why didn't they become citizens?' I said, 'General, they never had the opportunity, never had an opportunity to learn. They raised big families, and they stayed at home.'" DeWitt was unmoved.[12]

Another vocal opponent of the alien restrictions was Mary Carniglia, whose husband, Marco, was facing relocation, while her eldest son, John, was serving in the navy. "The kids are asking their parents, 'What are they going to do to you?' The smaller children can't understand," Carniglia declared in a lengthy interview with the *Sentinel*. "The adult Italians have such faith in the government, they say it's all paper talk. But it hurts. My people have lived here in the same houses for three generations, and I'm going into a fourth generation. I'm a citizen, but my husband is not.

"My people are proud to be in America. Their coming here gave them a taste of paradise. They aren't disloyal. If the government can show disloyalty, then they should be punished. I wouldn't fight for them if I thought they weren't loyal. But I know they are."

Carniglia battled to have the local fishermen allowed to return to their livelihoods. She also fought against "racketeering" by local landlords who she felt were taking advantage of the relocation controversy. She charged that in some cases landlords were hiking rents, while others were refusing to rent to families with children. She also charged that deposits were being stolen. "If we're all helping toward the aim of victory," she queried local realtors, "why

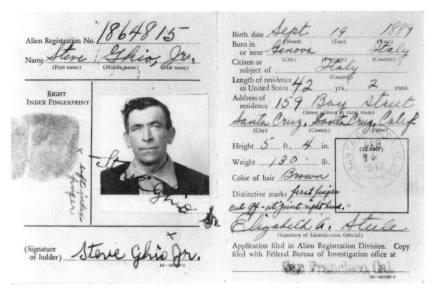

Steve Ghio's Alien Registration Card. His son returned from the army to find his home boarded up. Courtesy of Geoffrey Dunn

should these [landlords] throw the monkey wrench in at this time? Why crush these unfortunate people with further blows?"

Santa Cruz realtor Joseph Jacoby defended his profession against Carniglia's charges. Local landlords, he declared, were merely charging what the "market will bear." He also suggested that "Italians were taking advantage of the situation....One Italian paid a five-dollar deposit, then came back to say he didn't want the house—with renting days having passed—and received his money back. This happened in two instances. In still another, the Italians made an appointment to view the house, then never showed up because the rent was too high."

Carniglia, however, would have none of Jacoby's explanation. She called for an emergency rent-control measure to protect the dislocated residents. "People should have more love and wisdom," she declared. "These narrow-minded people are taking advantage of these unfortunates." No rent-control measure was ever adopted, and the racketeering crisis eventually passed.

For Japanese residents, citizens and noncitizens alike, their crisis was just beginning. As the February 24 relocation deadline neared, it was becoming more and more apparent that the Japanese were being singled out by government activities, both in Washington and on the West Coast. On February 9, *Sentinel* headlines read, "FBI Arrests 20 Japs in Monterey Bay Territory." Most of those arrests took place in Monterey and Salinas, but federal agents also swept nearby Watsonville, where Ben Torigoe, owner of a sporting-goods store, was picked up for being in possession of a dozen shotguns, a camera, an alleged "illegal radio," and so-called subversive literature that had been published in Japan. Three Buddhist priests were also arrested in the raids.

On February 21, two days following the signing of Executive Order 9066, nearly 200 aliens—119 Japanese, 54 Italians, and 9 Germans—were arrested throughout California. In Santa Cruz County, arrests were limited to two Japanese residents, Tommy Kadotani and Tsumoru Kai, both active members of the Santa Cruz Japanese Association. Kadotani, a native of Santa Cruz who, ironically, had grown up on the fringes of the Italian fishing colony on Bay Street, was a widely respected florist and gardener. Both he and Kai were charged with raising moneys that "eventually found their way to the Japanese Imperial army," charges that were never substantiated and which Kadotani denied.[13] Kadotani and Kai were shipped to San Francisco for questioning by the FBI and didn't return to Santa Cruz until the end of the war.

That weekend, FBI agents arrested ten more Japanese residents in Watsonville, including grocer Keijuro Sugiyama, apple driers Charles and Frank Huira, and farmer Saikichi Yamamoto. At the same time, sixteen Italians were arrested in Salinas.

The following Monday, an event that helped codify anti-Japanese feelings took place down the coast in Goleta, near Santa Barbara, where a Japanese submarine fired twenty-five shells at an oil refinery just off the coast. Damage was minimal, but the boldness of the attack created a panic along the West Coast. That shelling, combined with lingering animosity from the Pearl Harbor bombing and long-standing anti-Asian prejudices dating back to the nineteenth century, led to stepped-up calls for the removal of all Japanese from the western halves of California, Oregon, and Washington. The local chapter of the Native Sons of the Golden West, headed by president Tom Kelley, passed a resolution calling for the ouster of all residents of Japanese descent, while in Washington, D.C., Congressmember Anderson demanded "immediate evacuation of all persons of Japanese lineage."

California Attorney General Earl Warren, later to become both governor of California and chief justice of the U.S. Supreme Court, was a vociferous proponent of Japanese relocation. "When we are dealing with the Caucasian race we have methods that will test the loyalty of them," Warren opined. "But when we deal with the Japanese, we are on an entirely different field."

In addition to such overtly racist sentiments, there were political factors preventing Italian (and German) relocation. Mounting pressures from Democratic politicians in East Coast cities, particularly New York, Philadelphia, and Boston—all with large Italian populations—had a powerful effect in swaying the president and his staff against mass Italian internment on the West Coast. There were no such Japanese strongholds in the East; in Hawaii, however, where there were 140,000 Japanese nationals (constituting thirty-seven percent of the population), the Japanese were neither relocated nor interned (although individual Japanese, along with Germans and Italians, were arrested.) Even though such actions would have appeared even more congruent with strategic concerns, the political and economic implications of such a move would have been overwhelming. The Japanese were politically vulnerable only on the mainland.[14]

Thus, by late March, the idea of evacuating Italian and German residents out of the state was losing support, while the movement to relocate all Japanese residents gained momentum. In the ensuing five months, more than 100,000 Japanese—seventy percent of them U.S. citizens—were forcibly removed to inland concentration camps, beginning one of the greatest political and social atrocities in American history. (While they were interned, the all-Japanese 442nd Regimental Combat Team, drafted out of the internment camps and Hawaii, became the most decorated unit of World War II.)[15]

As the spring of 1942 turned into summer, Lieutenant General DeWitt's promise to follow the Japanese evacuation with the evacuation of the estimated 114,000 Italian and 97,000 German aliens in the western states never materialized. Slowly and gradually, life returned to normal for the Italian fishing colony in Santa Cruz—although certain travel, work, and residency restrictions in the coastal zones continued for the duration of the war.

Well into the summer of 1942, Lido Gemignani and Louis Aluffi, both Italian citizens who had come to Santa Cruz as children, were arrested for dancing at the Coconut Grove Beach Ballroom past the 9 P.M. curfew in a restricted zone. Aluffi, who had already enlisted in the army and would eventually participate in the invasion of Germany, and Gemignani were immediately sent to the federal prison in San Francisco and then to Sharp Park detention center, near Pacifica, where they were held for more than two weeks.[16]

On October 12, 1942, Columbus Day, in a move designed purely to generate political support, FDR had his attorney general, Francis Biddle, announce that Italian nationals in the United States would no longer be classified as "enemies." Back in California, Lieutenant General DeWitt reluctantly lifted all military restrictions on Italians. (He lifted them for Germans the following January.)

In Santa Cruz, the majority of Italian nationals forced to move from their Italian neighborhoods in the coastal zone were allowed to return to their homes. My great-grandmother was among them. Her *mala notte* was over.

Little of what the Italians suffered through compares to what their Japanese neighbors were forced to endure, nor does it in any way diminish the

Japanese experience. At the same time, it was painful, and as historian Lawrence DiStasi has pointed out, the government measures taken during the war had long-term consequences on the Italian American community and on Italian American culture.

"A powerful message was sent and received. Italian language and culture, and those who represented either or both, represented a danger to America," DiStasi notes. "After the war, people were afraid to be too Italian. To this day, large numbers of Italian Americans remain in an ethnic shadow. Most feel stigmatized without knowing why."[17]

In Santa Cruz, there have been lasting effects. Prior to the war, children born into the Italian fishing community had learned Genoese as their first language. None of my cousins born after the war would be allowed to

Celestina Stagnaro Loero, ca. 1938. Four years later she would be forced to leave her home. Courtesy of Geoffrey Dunn

speak it. Many of the families moved far away from the waterfront, as far away as they could from the stigmas and the stains of the war. Some anglicized their names and still others did whatever they could to abandon Italian practices and traditions. In a sense, there was a cultural genocide in Italian communities across the country.

More than a half century later, I can still hear my great-grandmother weeping over her *mala notte*. It was to become her children's, and her grandchildren's, *mala notte* as well.

Endnotes

1. The reminiscences about my great-grandmother come from personal memory and discussions with my aunt, Gilda Stagnaro, and my uncle, Robert Stagnaro. I have also recently found, torn and discarded in an attic, the remnants of my great-grandmother's enemy alien registration card, dated February 3, 1942, and signed by John A. Ulrich of the Alien Registration Division.

2. Ernest Otto, "Waterfront News Notes," *Santa Cruz Sentinel,* February 25, 1942.
3. There is a growing literature on sanctions against Italian Americans during the war. See Stephen C. Fox, "General John DeWitt and the Proposed Internment of German and Italian Aliens During World War II," *Pacific Historical Review* 57, November 1988:407–438; Stephen C. Fox, *Unknown Internment: An Oral History of the Relocation of Italian Americans during World War II* (Boston: Twayne Publishers, 1990); Rose Scherini, "Executive Order 9066 and Italian Americans: The San Francisco Story," *California History* 71, Winter 1991–92:366–77, 422–24; Rose Scherini, "The Other Internment: When Italian Americans Were 'Enemy Aliens',", *Ambassador,* Fall 1993:11–14; Geoffrey Dunn, "Una Storia Segreta: The Secret Story of Italian Internment and Relocation During World War II," *Metro San Jose,* July 7, 1994:18–21. Earlier versions of this article appeared in *Santa Cruz Magazine,* February 1992:16–21, and in the *Santa Cruz County History Journal* 1, 1994:82–91.
4. Executive Order 9066 is in 7 *Federal Register* 140 (1942), 2199. Cited in Scherini, 1991/92:422.
5. Fox, 1990:41–57. See also Arthur D. Jacobs and William J. Hopwood, "Letters," *The Nation,* April 1, 1991, p. 398.
6. Unless otherwise noted, all subsequent references to Santa Cruz Italians, Germans, and Japanese during the war are taken from the *Santa Cruz Sentinel,* December 7, 1941, to June 30, 1942.
7. See Fox, 1988:407–29.
8. Ibid.
9. For a discussion of Otto and his sensitivities to various ethnic groups, see Geoffrey Dunn, *Santa Cruz Is in the Heart* (Capitola, Calif.: Capitola Book Company, 1989), 38–50.
10. Interviews with the Ghio brothers were conducted in December 1991.
11. Suicides are referenced in a press release for *Una Storia Segreta,* the traveling exhibit about World War II measures taken against Italian Americans, sponsored by the Italian American Heritage Foundation, 1994:5.
12. Elizabeth Calciano, Malio Stagnaro: "The Santa Cruz Genovese," University of California, Santa Cruz Regional History project, 1975:422–24.
13. Years later, when Kadotani and I were fishing on his boat *Sake* one afternoon, I gently tried to broach the topic of his arrest. Kadotani politely, though sternly, informed me that there was nothing to talk about, save fishing. See also *San Jose Mercury Herald,* February 22, 1942:1–2.
14. Ronald Takaki, *A Different Mirror: A History of Multicultural America* (Boston: Little, Brown, 1993), pp. 378–85.
15. For a lengthier discussion of Japanese American internment see Ronald Takaki, *Strangers from a Different Shore* (Boston: Little, Brown, 1989), pp. 379–405.
16. Denise Franklin, "Forgotten Aliens," *Santa Cruz Sentinel,* April 12, 1987, pp. E1–3.
17. Lawrence DiStasi, cited in press release, *Una Storia Segreta,* 1994, p. 6.

Wrong Side of the Highway

by Ivano Comelli

Job losses among Italian resident aliens evacuated from coastal areas, though not routine, did occur, as this account by Ivano Comelli indicates. Comelli also gives us a child's-eye view of what it was like to have the soldiers and guard dogs patrolling his home ground.

During World War II, my father, Gervasio Comelli, born in Nimis, Italy, in 1900, lost his job because he was classified as an enemy alien.

He was a farmer in the county of Santa Cruz, California. Our house was located on the east side of Highway 1. The majority of the farm was located on the west side, or ocean side, of the road. Because of restrictions during the war, he was not permitted to cross the roadway to work that portion of the farm that was located on the west side of the road. I presume that it was because of the Pacific Ocean, which was located on that side. Unable to work the farm, he was forced to find a job with a tannery located in Santa Cruz.

The farm, or rancho, as the Italians called it, was located about five miles north of Santa Cruz. My father was in partnership with about five other Italians at the time. He sold his partnership in 1953 or 1954. The farm is still there and is called the Gulch Ranch. I think the state of California now owns the land, and Mario Rodoni is currently leasing the property. Mario used to be my play-mate when I was growing up. The funny thing is that his father was Italian, but had Swiss citizenship. Although their house was located on the west side of the highway, the restrictions did not apply to them. They were free to come and go as they wanted.

Unfortunately, I do not have any documentation for that period of time. I do not know how my father was advised that he could not cross to the west side of Highway 1. We were fortunate that we did not have to move from our house, and I don't know of anyone else that did....My older brother, who was seven or eight at the time, seems to remember that the restrictions on my father were lifted prior to Italy's surrender. My father did get his job back and he did not lose the farm.

Another thing, there were military personnel stationed to guard the oceanfront. I remember that every evening, at dusk, a truck carrying Coast Guard personnel would come and drop off two uniformed persons and one german shepherd dog. The two Coast Guardsmen, armed with rifles, and their dog would march down to the oceanfront, where they had a small one-room shack located on the bluff. These shacks (lookout houses, as we kids used to call them) were placed at different locations along the coast. As one man slept, the other would keep watch over the beach and ocean. The beach was definitely off limits to my father and mother. I believe that the guardsmen would have taken some sort of action if they had caught my father on the wrong side of the road, especially after curfew. As an aside, I remember these young men being very friendly toward us, especially during the latter stages of the war. I distinctly remember one time, seeing the two guardsmen eating at the ranch-house boarding table. I think that they even drank some wine. I'm sorry I don't have any documentation on this matter, just the memories of a five-year-old boy.

Concentration Camps—
American Style

by Jerre Mangione

> Jerre Mangione's book about his life in the Sicilian section of
> Rochester, New York, became so successful that its title, *Mount
> Allegro*, was officially applied to the neighborhood about twenty years
> after its publication in 1942. Following that, Mangione wrote a num-
> ber of other books, including his account of his work with the Federal
> Writer's Project, *The Dream and the Deal* (Little, Brown, 1972), *A
> Passion for Sicilians: The World Around Danilo Dolci* (W. Morrow,
> 1968), and *La Storia: Five Centuries of the Italian American Experience*
> (HarperCollins Publishers, 1992), a history he co-wrote with Ben
> Morreale. His memoir, *An Ethnic at Large: Memoirs of America in the
> Thirties and Forties*, provided an insider's look at the wartime intern-
> ment camps run by the Immigration and Naturalization Service
> (INS), for whom he worked. Mangione became an English professor
> at the University of Pennsylvania in 1961, where he remained until
> his retirement in 1978. He died in August 1998 at the age of 89.

The mass internment of 110,000 West Coast Japanese in February 1942 gave
no comfort to the thousands of anti-Nazi refugees in the country who found
themselves categorized by the United States government, their supposed pro-
tector, as "alien enemies." Although the Department of Justice had announced
that it would intern only those aliens of enemy nationality whom it had reason
to believe might be disposed to endanger the national security, the refugees
were afraid that what had happened to the Japanese would happen to them.

As the attorney general discovered on the first day we were at war with
Germany and Italy, their fear was not groundless. Biddle tells about it in his
memoir, *In Brief Authority*. Arriving at the White House with some proclamations that required the president's signature, the attorney general found

"Concentration Camps—American Style" is excerpted from Jerre Mangione's *An Ethnic at Large:
A Memoir of America in the Thirties and Forties* (New York: Putnam, 1978).

Roosevelt with his physician, Admiral Ross T. McIntyre, who was busy swabbing out the chief executive's sinus-infected nose. While the president was signing the proclamations, he asked Biddle how many German nationals there were in the country.

"Oh, about six hundred thousand," replied Biddle. (Actually there were half that number; Biddle had apparently confused their number with that of the Italians.)

"And you're going to intern all of them," said the president in a tone that suggested he approved of the idea.

"Well, not quite," replied Biddle.

"I don't care so much about the Italians," continued Roosevelt. "They are a lot of opera singers, but the Germans are different; they may be dangerous...."

Biddle, who was determined that German and Austrian nationals be spared the fate of the West Coast Japanese, became apprehensive as to what the president would say next.[1] Inadvertently, Dr. McIntyre, who was having difficulty working on the chief executive's nose, came to his rescue. "Please, Mr. President," he pleaded, and Biddle promptly used that as an excuse to withdraw, unwilling to hear the president make any further statements about wholesale internment.

I never learned what made the president go along with Biddle's policy of selective internment, but he was undoubtedly influenced in part by the mail the White House was receiving from scores of anti-Nazi refugees, among them Thomas Mann, Albert Einstein, and Bruno Frank, who emphasized the ironical fact that many of those categorized by the American government as "alien enemies" were among the first and the most farsighted adversaries of the governments against which the United States was presently at war.[2] In any case, there was no mass internment of them.

As a result of the Department of Justice's selective internment policy, less than one percent of the more than 1,000,000 aliens of enemy nationality in the country were interned during the course of the war—some 10,000 altogether. Of that number approximately 5,000 were German, 5,000 Japanese, and 250 Italian. In addition to those aliens who had been individually arrested as "potentially dangerous," there were interned several hundred German and Italian seamen who had been seized, along with their ships, as soon as we went to war with the Axis countries.

Actually, the Department of Justice's selective internment policy was not nearly as selective as it might have been. As I discovered in my two-month tour of the enemy alien camps, many of their occupants represented no threat to the national security; had they been accorded due process of law, they would probably never have been interned.[3] Some had been arrested because of their close ties with their native countries; some because they were members of pro-Axis organizations, such as the German-American Bund, which they had joined for purely social reasons; some because they had not understood the enemy-alien regulations and had in their possession radios or weapons forbidden to them. Others were interned because they were known to have opposed American intervention in the war. I encountered one Italian who had been arrested on the day we went to war with Italy because he had written the White House a few months before Pearl Harbor, begging the president not to go to war with Italy, "since Italy is my mother and the United States my father and I don't want to see my parents fighting."

For me, one of the most curious aspects of the internment program was the presence in the camps of several thousand men and women (with their children) from Latin American countries who, at the request of our State Department, had been seized by their own governments as potentially dangerous enemy aliens and handed over to American authorities. Compounding the bizarreness of the program was the Machiavellian device that was contrived to legalize their detention by the Immigration and Naturalization Service. This consisted of escorting the Latin Americans over our borders, then charging them with illegal entry into the country. As an INS camp commander told me, "Only in wartime could we get away with such fancy skullduggery."

The rationale for this international form of kidnapping was that by immobilizing influential German and Japanese nationals who might aid and abet the Axis war effort in the Latin American countries where they lived, the United States was preventing the spread of Nazism throughout the hemisphere and thereby strengthening its own security. However, the project turned out to be something of a farce, for as the internment camp commanders became better acquainted with their Latin American charges, they learned that a number of them were not the "potentially dangerous" Germans and Japanese originally arrested, but impoverished peasants who had been paid to act as substitutes for them.[4]

The media knew nothing of the Latin American phase of the internment program, but even if they had known it is unlikely they would have revealed it. At the outset of the war, in the interests of national security, the media had cheerfully acceded to the Department of Justice's request that as little as possible be said about the arrest and detention of enemy aliens, since any publicity given to the subject might seriously interfere with the government's observance of the Geneva Convention of 1929. Based on the concept of reciprocity, the pact provided the government with its only means of assuring the safety and humane treatment of Americans who became prisoners in enemy countries. It protected all interned men and women from acts of violence as well as from insults and public curiosity and, unlike previous agreements of its kind, made it possible for its signatories to determine whether or not the enemy nations were abiding by its provisions.[5]

To drive home the significance of the Geneva Convention in our operation of the internment camps, I sometimes shared with members of the press an off-the-record report of an explosive situation that developed in Santa Fe in the spring of 1942, after a local newspaper had published an account of the disastrous defeat the Americans suffered in the Philippines, which reported that among those killed were several members of the New Mexico National Guard. In a spirit of vengeance, a mob of angry New Mexicans armed with a variety of weapons ranging from hatchets to shotguns marched on the Santa Fe internment camp with the intent of murdering all of its 2,000 Japanese occupants.

The mob would have had its way had it not been for the camp's quick-witted camp commander, Ivan Williams, who, realizing that his small contingent of guards was no match for it, confronted the men alone and talked to them about the consequences of killing or injuring any of the Japanese. Williams emphasized the reciprocal features of the Geneva Convention, pointing out that any action they took against his charges might result in the death of their sons, brothers, and friends who were prisoners of the Japanese. After he had spoken for about an hour, the ringleaders were persuaded he was right and ordered their followers to disperse.

Unfortunately, not all newspapers in the country were aware that the Department of Justice was anxious to avoid having its internment program publicized. From time to time a newspaper published near one of the internment camps would print an angry editorial to the effect that the aliens in the camp were eating better than most Americans. Usually, the writer of the editorial received a visit from one of the camp officials, who would explain that the Geneva Convention stipulated that as part of the "humane treatment" guaranteed to interned aliens, the food they were served had to be "equal in quantity and quality" to that of the United States troops at base camps. The official would also point out that food costs for internees averaged less than fifty cents per person per day and that much of the food consumed they raised themselves at a cost to the government of only ten cents an hour for their labor.

This would often end the matter, but the readers of the angry editorial were not likely to forget it. When casualties of American soldiers were headlined, their antagonism toward the interned aliens was liable to ignite to a perilous degree. In Bismarck, North Dakota, where the service [INS] operated a large internment camp for Germans and Japanese, the hostility of neighboring Americans became so intense that when one of the German aliens escaped from the camp, they formed a posse and went hunting for him, eager to kill him. Fortunately, the service's border patrolmen were able to get to him first and return him to the camp unharmed.

I began my tour of the major camps by interviewing Willard F. Kelly, a colleague in the Philadelphia office who was directly in charge of the internment program. At the outbreak of the war, Kelly had headed the service's border patrol, whose primary function was to prevent the smuggling of aliens and goods into the country by patrolling more than eight thousand miles of American land and coastal boundaries. Then one day Major Schofield told him that he wanted the border patrol to establish and operate an internment camp in Texas for a group of German seamen who had been apprehended by the service at the outset of the war. Kelly argued strongly and, he thought, convincingly that the border patrol should stick to its primary function, but the major was not convinced. "Get going," he told him. And Kelly, the most diligent of men, got going with such speed and efficiency that from then on he bore the burden of the service's internment program.

The success of the border patrol in doing their new assignment well was largely due to the deep respect that Kelly engendered among the patrolmen. A decent man who was long on wisdom and short on formal education, he was an instinctive leader of men and a good judge of them. Although he had not gone beyond high school, he expressed himself with a clarity and succinctness that persons with far more education might well envy. I could not be in his presence without thinking of the strong men with few words that became my Hollywood heroes in the Saturday afternoons of my youth....

———————

My last stop in Texas was a former federal minimum-security reformatory known as Seagoville, on the outskirts of Dallas. The new and attractive $1.8 million facility, which occupied only a small segment of its 830-acre tract, resembled a prosperous college campus. At the outbreak of the war, after it had been a reformatory for barely a year, the facility was transferred to the Immigration Service, staff and all, for the internment of aliens who would be repatriated at the close of the war. The first group of prisoners arriving there were families from Latin American countries. After their transfer to Crystal City, Seagoville was used mostly for female aliens, but within a couple of days after my arrival the service's new policy of permitting husbands and wives to be interned together went into effect, and the population of the facility almost doubled. The single women remained in the comfortable dormitories of the facility, the couples were ensconced in some sixty prefabricated one-room, eighteen-foot-square living quarters sold by the manufacturer as "Victory Huts."

I was lucky enough to be present on the morning when the spouses were first reunited. It began with the arrival of several busloads of German aliens from other internment camps. Their wives waited for them, lined up about fifty yards away from the buses. As soon as the buses were unloaded, the couples rushed toward one another, hugging and kissing, crying with the joy of being together again. Then, still holding on to each other tightly, they proceeded to the mess hall to lunch together.

When the Japanese husbands arrived a little later, I witnessed a totally different scene. There was no show of emotion; the encounter was sedate, ritualistic. On leaving the buses, the men lined up opposite the line formed by their wives and the two groups solemnly bowed to one another. Then the men turned their backs on the women and marched toward the Japanese mess hall, while their wives, still maintaining a respectful distance, followed. Unlike the Germans, they did not dine together. The men sat at the tables waiting to be served; the wives crowded into the open kitchen at one end of the mess hall, preparing the meal and giggling like children as they identified their husbands for one another. Only after their men had been served and left the mess hall did the women sit down to their own lunch. And only in the privacy of their own quarters did the spouses finally come together.

None of this surprised Dr. Amy N. Stannard, the officer in charge of Seagoville, who had been observing the differences between Occidentals and Orientals for more than a year. The arrival of the German and Japanese husbands would accentuate the differences and complicate the station's administrative problems, she thought, but it would do a great deal for the morale of the women. A psychiatrist by training, she believed that internment was a greater ordeal for women than it was for men, but she admired the women for their strong community spirit, particularly for their concern in trying to help those who found internment especially hard to take. Seagoville was equipped with various facilities to ease the strain of confinement—an auditorium with a stage where the women performed ballet and theatricals, an extensive library with books in Spanish, English, Japanese, and German, a weaving room where prisoners could learn to make drapes and rugs, and a completely equipped garment factory where they could learn, teach, or engage in dressmaking. Most of the women made the best of their internment, but for some, as Dr. Stannard observed, the trauma of having been plucked from their families and imprisoned in a distant place had inflicted a wound that would not heal.

As the former warden of Seagoville when it was a women's reformatory, Dr. Stannard was a more experienced administrator than the other camp commanders I was to encounter. Working closely with her assistants, she was able to keep a close check on what was happening in the camp day to day. Part of her information came from the staff censors who read all letters written or received by the prisoners. The more revealing of the letters were by the prisoners who had been uprooted from their native habitat in Latin America and brought here for internment. Many of them had been living in poverty under primitive conditions, and expressed enthusiasm for the good food and housing they now received, which was far superior to what they had known before internment. Some of the letters expressed considerable fondness for their American keepers, whom they described as "considerate" and "gentle." Occasionally there were amusing misinterpretations. Writing to a Peruvian relative in Spanish, one woman said: "The ladies are so kind they even put out food at night for the *cucarachas*" (cockroaches), apparently unaware that the "food" was poison. Yet for all the comforts available to them at Seagoville, most of the letters dealt with the anguish of being parted from loved ones.

Among the letters Dr. Stannard received was one from a recently paroled German woman who had spent a year at Seagoville and was now living in San Diego. The letter thanked her for "all your kind words and deeds, for the smile you had for each of us," and described being interviewed by her San Diego parole officer. "The man must have expected me to resent the past year because he seemed so very much relieved to get my report on Seagoville," she wrote. "I told him I never had it so good in all my life—no work unless we wanted to, no worry about food—it's good and served regularly three times a day."

Unlike all the other internment camps I visited, the Seagoville staff included a trained dietitian, a beautiful blonde named Marian Brooks, who made certain that the food served to the approximately 700 German and Japanese internees (in separate mess halls with separate menus) conformed to their ethnic tastes and contained enough vitamins to maintain their health. "Miss Brooks is one of the main reasons why no one ever thinks of escaping from this place," one of her colleagues told me.

Because of Miss Brooks, with whom I went dancing at a Dallas nightclub, I too had no desire to leave Seagoville, but one morning there was a telephone call from the camp commander at Santa Fe, my next stop, urging me to get there as soon as possible, explaining that through the grapevine the Japanese aliens there had learned of my forthcoming visit and were anxious to talk with me about urgent problems. I left Seagoville the next day.

After I had been in the Santa Fe compound for less than an hour, Seagoville, by comparison, seemed like a relaxed and convivial country club. I had barely arrived when a three-member committee representing the 2,000 Japanese in the all-male camp presented Lloyd H. Jensen, the camp commander, with a petition asking that the barbed-wire fence surrounding the compound be made at least a foot taller. The petition was motivated by the fear that the residents in the surrounding area might become incited by recent reports of heavy American casualties in the Pacific and try again to storm the camp, as they had the year before.

The internee committee spokesman then turned to me and, explaining that there were a number of Japanese in the camp with pressing problems that only I could handle, asked that I meet with each of them. I pointed out that they were crediting me with powers that even the head of the Immigration Service did not have, and Jensen vouched for the fact that I had no judicial authority whatsoever. But the spokesman and his associates kept addressing me as "Honorable Commissioner" and politely but unrelentingly kept requesting that I listen to the petition of their "clients." We finally reached an understanding: if they would explain to their "clients" that I lacked the authority to solve their problems, I would agree to listen to them and pass on their petitions to the proper authorities.

While two of the committee members went about the camp rounding up the men who wanted a hearing, the spokesman produced an empty crate and a chair which were to serve as courtroom props and now began addressing me as "Honorable Judge." Planting the two props in the middle of a street, he flicked away some imaginary dust from the chair with a grandiose gesture of his handkerchief and invited me to be seated. "The court is in session," he shouted and clapped his hands like a character in an Alice-in-Wonderland scene.

In a matter of minutes some 25 Japanese, young and old, were lined up in front of me. With my self-appointed tipstaff sometimes acting as interpreter, I listened to each of their stories. Nearly all of them evolved around the tribulations of families who had been cruelly separated by the petitioners' internment. Their wives and children were suffering. When could they be reunited? It had been many months since they had applied for admission to the family camp at Crystal City, and still no word from Washington. Meanwhile, they were alarmed to hear that the family camp was rapidly filling up and would soon reach capacity. One man was too filled with emotion to talk. He wept as he showed me the copy of a letter his wife had written the attorney general: "My husband is still detained. I am not in good health and have two children, eight and ten, to look after. My sisters are in different camps and my brother is in the American army. I do not know why my husband is detained there, but could you please tell me if it is possible for him to be with us?"

Many of the men were fishermen who had been arrested at the outset of the war because they fished off the California coast in radio-equipped boats. A paranoiac United States attorney in California was able to convince the attorney general's office that the fishermen could conceivably communicate with and assist any Japanese submarines which might be operating in those waters.

On the basis of such flimsy conjecture, 545 Japanese fishermen were ordered interned as "potentially dangerous to the national security."[6]...

————————

From Santa Fe I traveled north to the INS internment camp at Missoula, Montana, which quartered an equal number of Italians, Germans, and Japanese. Most of the Italians were seamen who had been captured in American ports on the first day of the war; only some 250 were civilian aliens, residents of the United States who had been arrested because they had been profascist journalists or active members of profascist organizations in the United States, or simply because there was some reason to suspect that their loyalty to Fascist Italy might be stronger than their loyalty to the American government. Among the latter were fathers of sons fighting in the American armed forces.

The Italian civilians I spoke with were invariably bitter about their internment. "Six hundred thousand Italian aliens in this country get the attorney general's blessings for being good Americans—and they had to pick on me," one of them lamented. "So what if I did write in a newspaper that I thought Mussolini was doing a good job? Does that make me a Fascist? I was finished with that son of a bitch as soon as he teamed up with that other son of a bitch in Germany, but I can't get that through the skulls of those people in the attorney general's office."

I had come upon him while he was painting a landscape at an improvised outdoor easel. The prickly quality of his remarks was at odds with the soft blend of colors on his canvas. "I see you're an artist as well as a journalist," I said.

He laughed but there was no mirth in his laughter. "I never painted a goddamn thing in my life until I got to this place. It was the fucking FBI that made an artist out of me."

I was attracted to one of the prisoners because he looked so much like my father. I thought he must be a Sicilian, but his birthplace turned out to be Venice. When I asked him in Italian what he was doing in an internment camp, he shook his head dolefully. "I'm here because I'm unlucky. I've always been unlucky. I'm even unlucky about my children." He showed me a letter he had recently received from a daughter in Detroit named Gladys. "Dear Dad," it read, "I was sorry to hear of your detention. I wouldn't worry about it though. You being an Italian and unnaturalized has put you in an enemy classification. But there is no need to worry as long as you have done nothing. There is great satisfaction in knowing that Uncle Sam is on the job, isn't there? I'm just tickled pink they aren't letting anything slip past them. I do hope you will soon be out though."

"She takes after her mother," he grumbled. "A woman with the brain of a *cretina*. What can you do to get me out of here?"

I told him I had no authority and no influence with the attorney general's office.

"That figures," he replied. "If you had, you wouldn't bother talking with me."

Later, when I examined his file, I learned he had so antagonized the civilian hearing board that handled his case that the board characterized him "as dangerous an alien enemy as could be found in the United States." Yet the most serious charge they could point to was that government agents had found two contraband articles in his possession: a radio equipped with a shortwave band and a Graflex camera. The only other charge against him was that, according to "a confidential source," he had been heard to make some anti-American remarks, one to the effect that Hitler would one day conquer the United States.

An assistant U.S. attorney disagreed with the civilian hearing board; he did not consider their charges substantial enough for interning the man, especially as he had never belonged to a profascist organization. Swayed by the civilian hearing board's strong indictment of the Italian, the attorney general's office overruled him and ordered the man interned until a careful investigation could be made of the case. As a result of the investigation, he was released from the camp shortly after my encounter with him. [7]

The most cheerful of the Italian internees were the seamen. It was not that they liked being confined—some of them complained that being deprived of women was a definite breach of the Geneva Convention, which protected war prisoners from "cruel and inhuman treatment." Nor were they happy with the camp's heavy reliance on canned foods, which they regarded as potentially poisonous, for a time refusing to eat them. Yet none questioned the American government's right to intern them for the duration of the war—an attitude which enabled them to accept their detention with far more grace than the civilian Italians. Some were openly pro-American. One seaman told me he was grateful to the American government for interning him, for otherwise he would be risking his life in the war for a philosophy of government he despised. He and several others wanted to know what steps they could take to become permanent American residents after the war.

The camp's favorite Italian was a gentle elderly ship captain, the official spokesman of the seamen, who served as their father away from home. From his numerous trips to the States in the course of a long career, he had acquired a fluent command of English and a host of American friends who, on learning of his internment, kept bombarding him with gifts of clothes and cash. The clothes he passed on to the seamen who could fit into them. The money embarrassed him; he would try to return it but more often than not it came back. When that happened, he would accept it as a gift for his dog, who, as he wrote his friends, was addicted to desserts. This was no mere whim on his part. Every day he and his dog, inseparable companions, would visit the camp PX, where the captain would order a single-scoop ice cream cone for himself and a double-scoop one for the dog, while explaining to the clerk that it was the dog who was treating.

The captain's engaging personality undoubtedly influenced the camp commander's opinion that of the three nationality groups in the camp, he preferred the Italians, despite their occasional indulgence in temperament, because he considered them "the most human." Yet, like all the other camp commanders, he found the Japanese the easiest to deal with; no other prisoners were as willingly cooperative and as democratic. He noted that while some of the Italians and Germans considered it demeaning to their social rank to do such menial chores as washing dishes or scrubbing floors and toilets and would pay compatriots of inferior social rank to do the work for them, the Japanese took no notice of social rank. The millionaire businessman and the poorest fisherman uncomplainingly worked side by side at whatever menial work was assigned to them.

The camp commander marveled at the efficiency of the Japanese in organizing themselves as a community. "The Germans have the reputation for being good organizers, but they can't compare with the Japanese." At his suggestion I tried to interview the man whom the Japanese had elected as their mayor but was told by one of his assistants that the mayor was on vacation. "And how is he spending his vacation?" I asked, certain that he must be joking. But the assistant was perfectly serious; the mayor, he explained, was spending most of it on the miniature golf course the Japanese had built in the camp. The assistant was willing to take me to his chief but requested I desist from discussing camp business with him, since he had been working hard for many months and deserved a complete rest from his duties. When we reached the golf course the assistant pointed him out to me and offered to introduce us, but the mayor seemed so immersed in the game that I decided not to disturb his concentration and postponed my meeting with him until he had returned from his vacation.

The longer I remained at Missoula, the more aware I became of the lack of love between the Japanese, Germans, and Italians. The Japanese, who had their own mess hall, behaved as though the other two groups did not exist. The Germans and Italians, on the other hand, expressed open contempt for the Japanese, whom they regarded as an inferior people, but they also had a low opinion of one another. They were compelled to share the same mess hall, but since they could not agree on a common menu, they maintained separate cuisines, with the Italians turning up their noses at sauerkraut and the Germans disdaining spaghetti. Their general incompatibility sometimes resulted in fisticuffs, at which time their leaders would feel obliged to remind the men that they were allies, not enemies. All in all, the relationship between the three groups hardly augured well for the solidarity of the Axis alliance. "If, God forbid, the Axis powers should win the war," an Italian seaman told me, "there would soon be another war between the winners."…

The last internment camp on my itinerary was Fort Lincoln at Bismarck, North Dakota. After the vivacious atmosphere of Missoula, the camp seemed dreary and listless. The general gloom was accentuated by the flatness of the surrounding landscape and, to some degree, by the tight-lipped personality of the camp commander, who appeared to derive little satisfaction from his job. Yet for all of his grimness, his staff members described him as a fair-minded commander with a compassionate heart. I was told that shortly before my arrival his attention was drawn to a German prisoner who was walking up and down the length of the barbed-wire fence like a caged tiger. When he asked the German what was wrong, the prisoner showed him a letter he had received that day which indicated that his grandmother was ill and without help. Since she spoke no English and lived alone, he worried that no one was likely to come to her assistance. Promising to do what he could, the commander made a long-distance call to a social-service agency in the town where the grandmother lived. Within a few hours the old woman was getting the help she needed, and a report about her condition was on its way to the camp.

After I had been there for a few days and met the camp commander's family, I realized how much his personal problems may have contributed to his sense of gloom. After being a widower for several years he had recently acquired a second wife who could be a substitute mother for his two young sons. She was a handsome woman in her late thirties with dark flashing eyes and a voluptuous figure. St. Louis had been her home from the time she was born and now, as she told me, she felt as if she were in Siberian exile, cut off from all her friends and from all the cultural diversions she enjoyed in the city. Her stepchildren had not warmed up to her and it was apparent to me, as it must have been to her husband, that unless he were soon transferred to a post in a more urban area, their relationship would be in serious trouble.

Adding to the camp commander's difficulties was the ornery behavior of some of his German charges, who systematically created as many problems as possible for their American keepers. Internees who became troublemakers in the other camps often wound up at the Fort Lincoln camp. One of them, who had arrived in the States in 1935 as a propagandist for the German Travel Bureau, had been in three other internment camps before being transferred to Fort Lincoln. His record indicated he had been "a source of trouble" ever since his arrival there, spreading false rumors among the internees and "instigating unreasonable demands on the camp administration." While in the hospital malingering, "he complained unduly about hospital food and opened windows to discomfort other patients." On one occasion he painted an obscene picture on a wall, then refused to remove it. The writer of his report described his attitude as "arrogant and overbearing." Yet the report was careful to point out that he was probably not a Nazi, that his unfavorable record was a result of his personality, not of his political beliefs. He was judged to be a "product of Imperial Germany," which he had served as a navy captain in World War I. There was little about his camp behavior that escaped the attention of the guards. "At Christmastime," one sentence of the report read, "he burned candles on Christmas trees, though he knew full well that it was against fire regulations."

A constant complainer in the camp was a former chemist who had committed the terms of the Geneva Convention to memory, so that he could make certain the Americans were living up to their obligations. Attorney General Biddle, who had met him while visiting the camp the year before, described him as "a herr professor type." Biddle reported that the chemist had only one complaint, but one which he pressed obstinately: they did not get enough butter. Biddle asked him how much they got, then told him that it was substantially more than he received under rationing. The chemist's rejoinder was "wonderfully Teutonic." "But that's not the point, Mr. Attorney General. Under the Geneva Convention we are entitled to as much butter as the American troops—and we are not getting it!"

Among the most disgruntled prisoners in the camp was a group of Germans who had been seized a few days after the United States declared war on Nazi Germany and hustled off to Fort Lincoln without a hearing. Twenty-five of them addressed a strongly worded petition to the president and the attorney general demanding their immediate and unconditional release "unless warrants charging specific law violations can be sworn to against any or all of us." Although the writer of the letter did not know or pretended ignorance of the Alien Enemy Act of 1789, which empowered the president to arrest and confine aliens of enemy nationality without regard to the Bill of Rights, it was an admirably articulate statement of the questions and objections which must have occurred to the hundreds of aliens who were confined without proper explanation within a few days after Pearl Harbor. One of its most forceful paragraphs read:

From a letter written by the Hon. J. Edgar Hoover we are led to
assume that we will "be accorded every opportunity" to establish
our "loyalty to the United States." Who accuses us of disloyalty?
What is the evidence of disloyal acts on our part? We insist upon
the elementary right to be confronted with our accusers, to examine the evidence against us, and thereafter prepare our defense
and refutations accordingly. We believe that our imprisonment,
the seizure of our papers and effects, the freezing of such funds as
are necessary to the maintenance of our families, the refusal to
grant us the elementary right of legal counsel, the imposition of
strict censorship upon letters addressed to us, the failure to inform
us of specific charges against us, all to be wholly without the sanction of any law applicable to us as permanent residents of this
country and an abrogation of the fundamental guarantees of our
Constitution and the lawful acts promulgated thereunder.

All of the signers shortly thereafter received hearings before civilian hearing
boards, but for those who were not ordered released the hearings only served to
illustrate the government's abrogation of constitutional guarantees, since the
aliens were not permitted legal counsel nor the opportunity to face their accusers. In the interests of national security, we had suspended these and other
rights which, presumably, we had gone to war to preserve. No one at Fort
Lincoln, or at any of the other camps, with whom I could discuss this crude
irony could tell me to what extent it may have influenced the pro-Nazi attitudes of the internees, but no one could dispute the bitterness it must have
engendered.

The signers of the petition, along with the German seamen who had
been confined since 1939, constituted the most militantly pro-Nazi group in
the camp. They were eager for Germany to win the war and enthusiastically
looked forward to their repatriation. Meanwhile, their chief project was to
make the lot of the camp administrators as difficult as possible. The camp
commander told me that every time the news of a German victory was reported
on radio, the group would invariably present his staff with a fresh set of
demands which exceeded the bounds of the Geneva Convention.

"It's their way of fighting the Americans," the camp commander
explained. "We don't mind, because we know we are living up to the provisions
of the Convention. We also know from experience that when the Swedish representative hears what their demands are on his next trip here, he'll tell them
they're unreasonable, and that will put an end to it—that is, for a while." He

kicked away a stone in his path. "I guess that if I were in an American internment camp over in Germany I'd be raising the same kind of hell."

I was glad to leave Fort Lincoln. Of all the camps I visited and would be
visiting in the months to come, it was the grimmest reminder that we were
engaged in a war of hopelessly conflicting wills. It was also one more reminder
that the war had thrust us into the shameful position of locking up people for
their beliefs.

Endnotes

1. Editor's note: Mangione is conflating events here; at the time of Biddle's and Roosevelt's conversation (the first day the United States was at war with Italy and Germany, December 11,
1941), Biddle would not have known of the "fate of the West Coast Japanese." No one raised
the issue of mass internment of all Japanese, including citizens, until well into January 1942.

2. The attorney general's selective internment policy was derived from the experience of the
British government with its own aliens of enemy nationality. In the panic that seized the
British when the Low Countries and France collapsed, the government mass-interned almost
85,000 German and Austrian refugees, many of them avowed enemies of Hitler who had fled
to England for safety. After a few months the public came to its senses and began condemn-
ing the government's wholesale internment policy. In turn, the government admitted it had
victimized "some of the bitterest and most active enemies of the Nazi regime" and returned to
its initial policy of selective internment.

3. The Department of Justice's policy of reexamining regularly the cases of interned aliens led to
the parole or outright release of many aliens before the war was over.

4. Although there is ample documentation regarding the internment of men and women from
Latin American countries in the official records of the Immigration Service, I could find no
recorded information about the presence of proxies in the internment camps. Presumably, the
subject was too embarrassing to receive official recognition.

5. This was accomplished by delegating neutral powers to inspect the camps regularly in behalf
of the warring nations they represented. In the United States, representatives of the Spanish
government acted in behalf of the Japanese, the Swiss government represented the interests
of the Germans, and the Swedish government looked after the interests of Italy and the rest
of the nations at war with us.

6. Eventually, after the fear of Japanese submarines on the Pacific coast had subsided, most of the
arrested fishermen were permitted to join their families at the Crystal City camp or in War
Relocation centers.

7. By 1944 about half of the interned Italian civilians were either paroled or released unconditionally. (One man was released a few hours after it was learned that his American soldier son
had been killed in action during the invasion of Sicily.) The rest of the civilians, about one
hundred hard-core admirers of the Fascist regime, remained in internment until the end of
the war. Nearly all of them, willingly or not, were then deported to Italy.

My Uncle Augusto

by Dr. Nicholas A. Sceusa

> Augusto Mauro's internment conforms to an all too familiar pattern:
> he had for years written a social and cultural column for several
> Italian American newspapers. As a presumed community leader, and
> grandson of the last installed marchese of Pavia and Volterra, he was
> arrested right after Pearl Harbor and interned for several years.
>   Nick Sceusa came to know Mauro through his wife, Lilli.
> Childless, she "adopted" Sceusa after having taught him in grammar
> school. Over the years, Nick Sceusa learned about his "uncle"
> Augusto's internment, his "aunt" Lilli's outrage about it, and her way
> of getting back at the government for what she considered the injus-
> tice of Mauro's treatment.

I would like to recount the story of my adoptive uncle, Mr. Augusto Mauro, and
of his wife, Mrs. Lillian Leppe-Mauro, Aunt Lilli.

Don Augusto was interned in Montana with many other Italian American
notables, such as Angelo Gloria, the Sicilian comedian. While he met the cream
of Italian American society there, he returned home a broken man in ill health,
plagued by the arthritis he developed in Montana. He said he was well treated,
but was unjustly imprisoned. He was never compensated for this.

I have Angelo Gloria's portrait of the camp hanging in my dining room.[1]
Angelo Gloria did many comic sketches over the radio for the Italian community. I never heard them, but my older friends remember them as very, very funny.
He collaborated with Augusto on many radio plays, sponsored by several manu-
facturers. Ronzoni and LaRosa[2] were among them. The most lauded of these radio
plays was "L'Asino in Tribunale." It was about a young couple eloping and how
they wound up in court with their donkey. Augusto also produced another serial,
"Il Cavaliere della Giustizia," for LaRosa. To me, it was like the Lone Ranger
translated into Italian, and I wouldn't be surprised if it was, but I remember
people coming to their house asking how episodes were going to end, and "How
was he gonna get out of this one?" There was also a sort of Dick Tracy flavor to
the serial, which ended I think around 1952. The entire collection of these plays

Augusto Mauro at his home on East 87th Street in Brooklyn shortly after the war. Courtesy of Dr. Nicholas A. Sceusa

was donated to the New York Public Library and resides in the Museum of Radio and Television at Lincoln Center, where they are available to the public. I would like to see that Augusto's work is rediscovered and translated.

Augusto's only crime was being a journalist and having written for *Il Progresso* and other Italian American newspapers here in New York. He was never a "foreign correspondent," but had the society, social, and cultural pages. He was also the Sunday editor for *Corriere d'America*. He did the social and cultural pages and also the lonely-hearts columns. Lillian also used to pitch in on the advice to the lovelorn. He tried many times to generalize his writing, but the optic of the American public was more expository than poetic, and the usage of metaphor and simile, common to Italian, was missing in the American language of the time. His writing was viewed as too sentimental, though he was accepted finally by *National Geographic* magazine in October 1956.

Augusto's "enemy status" may have also stemmed from his boyhood friendship with Michael Mussolini, the son of the "Duce." Augusto had the poor fortune to have attended the University of Rome and shared a few music and poetry classes with him.

Mussolini actually looked pretty good from 1920 to 1939. He did do a lot, and he healed the rift between the Roman church and the Italian state and, for a time, stabilized the Italian currency. The huge inflation of the previous period was one of the factors in the last wave of Italian emigration. He was fairly tough and got rid of the Mafia and the Camorra, which we liberated as we fought our way through Italy. He would have kept his seat—if he had had the good sense to remain seated. When Adolf came into the room, Benito was not another Franco. Mauro was aware of this, and to the extent that Italy's condition benefited, he agreed. His correspondence with Michael Mussolini may have contained comments which landed him in the camps. Although he was prudent enough to stop writing as soon as the war began, it doomed him to be interned.

When the FBI took him away and tried to get his photographic equipment, my aunt Lilli, a retiring school teacher of Neopolitan extraction, literally swept them out of the house with her broom. They did manage to get Augusto, but they certainly never got the photo equipment! I am certain they remembered the many knocks on the head they got too! However, to their credit, they were gentlemen enough not to charge her for assaulting them.

Although a loyal American, born in Uniontown, Pennsylvania, in 1905, and one who vainly lied about her age, Lilli never forgave the United States government for the four years Augusto was interned.[3] She swore she'd get it back, and she did, pretty much. She became a tax expert and took it out on the IRS, and "gypped 'em" every chance she got. Augusto often pleaded with her

Lillian Mauro at age thirty-two, ca. 1937.
Courtesy of Dr. Nicholas A. Sceusa

to relent, fearing further involvement with the government, but she was a determined and forceful woman. Augusto, the youngest grandson of the last installed marquis of Pavia and Volterra, passed away in 1956, and Aunt Lilli "bought the box," as she often said she would, in 1993.

I often heard Lilli mention Generoso Pope.[4] She didn't like him much, and she suspected that, although he was a friend of Roosevelt, he was playing a double game. This did not stop Lilli from talking her way out of a moving violation based on her acquaintance with Mr. Pope. Augusto's grandfather the marquis knew Teddy Roosevelt and often hunted with him in Africa. Unfortunately, Teddy was out of the picture by the time World War II rolled around.

Before her death, Lilli, who was a very private person, systematically destroyed all her papers. She was particularly careful to destroy those love letters Augusto had written to her from the concentration camps. I shared one or two of the hundreds he wrote. He wrote almost daily. They were full of hope and tenderness, almost maudlin by American standards. My wife helped to burn them so that they would remain private. There was almost no mention of the camp life. Augusto did mention that he was well treated, that he often went into town to buy cigarettes, that he ate well but

Lillian Mauro, at about age forty-five, serving homemade Italian cheesecake to actress Arlene Dahl. Courtesy of Dr. Nicholas A. Sceusa

missed real cooking, and that he enjoyed very good company. He said he was having such a good time that any thought of escape never occurred. He was being positive. He returned home a broken man, in ill health.

What is really ironic is that after being accused of rabid fascism in the forties, poor Augusto was hunted up again as a communist in the fifties! He almost met Senator McCarthy and the House Un-American Activities Committee. It was for this reason that he wanted to repatriate to Europe as the bureau chief of *National Geographic* magazine in Rome. The source of the accusation? The portrait bust of his grandfather the marquis by the well-known sculptor Tripisciano that he kept in his living room looked, to many, too much like Joseph Stalin! What brilliant luck!

Augusto had a sweet and dreamy temperament. He was a quiet man who was given to riding the subway in search of his characters. He liked to garden and also kept cats, which he named after operatic characters. I remember Mustafa and Azucena, the gypsy.

Augusto and Lilli had no children, but she was my schoolteacher in the fourth grade. She recognized my learning disability, and I suppose I filled a void in her life. She was my friend and mentor for over forty years, and I owe to her my learning. I started out in life the son of a fishmonger, which is still something to begin with, but I now run my own biotechnical consulting firm in Manhattan. I still can't spell worth a damn in English, but she sure could!

She used to say, "The Italians found America, named it, and built it!"

Endnotes

1. Like many of the internees arrested in New York City, Augusto Mauro was taken first to Ellis Island, then to the internment section at Fort George Meade, Md., from thence to the camp at McAlester, Okla., and finally to the INS internment camp at Missoula, Montana.

2. The preferred spaghetti manufacturing companies of Italian Americans of that time. Ronzoni still exists.

3. According to his PMGO file, Mauro was picked up late, on July 17, 1942, and paroled in November of 1943. Mauro file, RG 389, Records Relating to Italian Civilian Internees During WWII, 1941–46, Boxes 2–20, PMGO, National Archives and Records Administration, College Park, Md.

4. Generoso Pope published the largest Italian American newspaper in the country, *Il Progresso.* A power in the Italian American community, and in Tammany Hall, he had access to political figures up to and including President Roosevelt. His prewar sympathy for Mussolini's Fascist government doomed him as a political power, but by disavowing this position after war was declared, he managed to both avoid the internment that befell many of his writers and retain some influence in the postwar Italian American community. See Philip Cannistraro, "Generoso Pope and the Rise of Italian American Politics, 1925–1936," in *Italian Americans: New Perspectives in Italian Immigration and Ethnicity*, Lydio Tomasi, ed. (New York: Center for Migrationi Studies, 1983).

A Tale of Two Citizens

by Lawrence DiStasi

Like many others of Italian birth, Pasquale DeCicco must have had some anxious moments when he heard on December 11, 1941, that the United States had declared war on Italy. He would, to be sure, have known that war was imminent, would have been dreading it since the day in June 1941 when the New Haven consular offices in which he had worked for over thirty years had been closed, along with all other Italian consulates, by order of President Roosevelt. But the reality was something else again. So was the series of announcements tightening the restrictions on his fellow immigrants—all those Italians in America without citizenship who were now to carry the stigma of enemy-alien status—which initially meant that they would have to request permission to travel more than five miles, notify authorities if they moved, and be subject to search and seizure of any items designated contraband, but which in February meant that they would have to re-register as enemy aliens (700,000 nationwide had just registered in 1940 to comply with the Smith Act) and carry at all times their little pink booklets bearing an identifying photo and fingerprints. Again and again in those early days right after Pearl Harbor, as he read about the "dangerous" resident aliens being rounded up and sent to internment camps, as he heard rumors of a wholesale evacuation of the noncitizens in California that might soon hit his home state of Connecticut as well, DeCicco must have given thanks to God that he had seen fit from the very first to become a United States citizen; that he had finally got his papers in 1909, seven years after immigrating; and that he had forced and cajoled every one of the seven brothers and sisters he had brought to America to do the same, so that now, humiliating as it was to have an Italian name, neither they nor he would have to really worry. The citizen in the United States was *protected*.

At least that is what he must have thought. Must have thought it even on the morning of April 24, 1942, when the knock had come on his door, and stiff men in suits had entered and asked without ceremony if he was Pasquale DeCicco, and when he had answered in the affirmative had ordered him to come with them, he was under arrest by order of the president of the United States. Must have thought it even as he kept trying to lay his hands on his citizenship papers, which surely would convince them or those in charge that there had been a terrible mistake; he was a *citizen, a citizen of* the United States since 1909 who knew his rights.

He must have kept thinking it, repeating it like a mantra even when they were transporting him to the Immigration and Naturalization Service detention center in Hartford for his initial interrogation. At which interrogation he must have begun to get some sense of what they were thinking—some nonsense about his service in the Italian army in World War I, when the United States and Italy were allies, did they not know that?—and which they kept up when he was transferred to the detention center in east Boston, and on July 14 to the one on Ellis Island to await his hearing—the hearing which, he was sure, would surely exonerate him, *he was an American citizen.*

After which hearing he must have thought it with considerably less certainty. For his next stop was the internment camp at Fort George Meade in Maryland—where, on July 31, 1942, Pasquale DeCicco, naturalized U.S. citizen, was formally registered and interned as an enemy alien of the United States for the duration of the war.

———

Still, though Pasquale DeCicco's internment at Fort Meade may have shaken his faith in the protection afforded him by U.S. citizenship, it did not destroy it. He kept fighting. For his case was by no means usual. Indeed, to date it seems to be only one of two cases where an American citizen of Italian descent was interned by the U.S. government during World War II. This is not to say that the government lacked the power to intern citizens. As the forcible relocation to remote camps of about seventy thousand native-born Japanese Americans grimly testifies, the presidential proclamation known as Executive Order 9066 gave the president of the United States, from February 19 onward, the power to intern anyone, citizen or alien alike, for the duration of the war. But until now, historians have maintained that the Japanese American case was unique. Where Italian Americans were concerned, only the resident aliens—those lacking U.S. citizenship—were known to have been specifically targeted by the restrictions. Thus, those whom J. Edgar Hoover had termed his "bad boys" and interned as dangerous, those whose homes were open to search and seizure, those who were subject to the West Coast curfew and the evacuation from prohibited zones in California, were invariably noncitizens. The only known exceptions were citizen children under fourteen who had to evacuate prohibited zones with their noncitizen parent(s) and, in some cases, American-born or naturalized citizens whose homes were violated because an Italian-born

parent lived there with them. The other major exception involved the exclusion of a group of mainly naturalized citizens who were targeted for their alleged
Fascist inclinations and, in the fall of 1942, forced to leave coastal military
zones—such as the huge zone that encompassed most of the western states.
Nearly two hundred of these naturalized citizens, including dozens of Italian
Americans, were so exiled. Yet though their lives were seriously disrupted and
in some cases ruined, as American citizens they were apparently considered by
the authorities to be immune from internment.[1]

Pasquale DeCicco's case was thus unusual. And he seems to have known
it. From his internment quarters at both Fort Meade and later at Fort
McAlester in Oklahoma, he never stopped petitioning the Justice Department
for a reconsideration of his case. He even took his case to federal court.[2] The
record of some of his thinking and writing is on file at the National Archives
and forms the basis for most of what follows.

Like many internees, Pasquale DeCicco had been prominent in his
Italian American community of New Haven, Connecticut. Though it might at
first appear to have been an advantage, this fact weighed against him, for it was
primarily the leaders of Italian American communities nationwide whom the
government targeted as dangerous. So it was for DeCicco. His work as acting
vice consul in the Italian consular offices in New Haven appears to have
doomed him—even though it was a job which he described as helping Italian
immigrants in the state of Connecticut adapt to the American legal system,
such as when they had to liquidate estates or deal with damages for deaths or
injuries deriving from accidents at work. As he says in a January 16, 1943, letter he wrote to Attorney General Biddle from his internment quarters at Ft.
McAlester, Oklahoma:

> My concern had always been the maintenance of cordial relations
> and friendship between the United States and Italy, and to this
> task I earnestly devoted my modest efforts, by continually and
> consistently explaining to Americans and Italians the life, the
> customs, the habits and traditions of the two countries, their long
> traditional and uninterrupted friendship, their almost similar
> struggle for their independence and freedom, their lofty ideals.[3]

DeCicco goes on to tell of the thousands of talks he gave over thirty-six years
of service, talks which he describes as "practically preaching Americanism,"
including the virtue of American citizenship. In this arena in particular,
DeCicco considered himself a practitioner of what he preached: only a year
after immigrating to New York in 1903 to escape the dead-end job he then had

with the Provinicial Engineering Office in Potenza, Italy, he had declared his intention to become an American citizen, and in May 1909 "took my oath as a full-fledged American citizen."

By then he was married and on his way to fathering three children, two boys and a girl, the boys to become Yale graduates. Also part of his extended family were the seven brothers and sisters he brought to America, orphaned when their father died in Italy. Helping all to get on their feet in the new country, he was not only "father, mother, and supporter" to them all, but also apostle of citizenship: of the forty-two members of the DeCicco family in 1942, all, proclaims DeCicco, were U.S. citizens, several of them serving in the U.S. armed forces.

Had it not been for the world wars, DeCicco's story seems likely to have continued in this line of unbroken American success. Unfortunately for him, war engulfed Europe in 1914, and when it did, Pasquale DeCicco, like thousands of other Americans volunteering to fight with England or France or Italy while America debated about whether or not to enter, decided to join his native country's war effort. Leaving his job at the Italian consular agency in New Haven, and his wife and three children in the care of in-laws, DeCicco sailed to Italy in November 1915 and began active service in the Italian army. It was a move that would later be used against him, though at the time he was more concerned about the loss of hearing he soon sustained in his right ear, a loss which, by making him unfit for active duty, caused him to be shifted to office work. He was attached to the War Office in Rome, then to the Italian Military Mission in London, and finally to the newly organized Italian High Commission in Washington, D.C. During all this service, DeCicco maintained, and in fact carried the certificate of his American citizenship, and refused, he says, to take an oath of allegiance to the Italian government.

When World War I was over, DeCicco returned to America and resumed his duties at the consular agency in New Haven, which was upgraded in 1923 to a vice consulate. There he remained until the day it was closed by order of the president on June 28, 1941, this time because of the century's second world war. During all that time, which coincided with Mussolini's rise to power in Italy, DeCicco states that "although believing that it [Fascism] had been a salvation for Italy...considering the unhappy circumstances in which the country was at the time, I did not think that we had any use here for its philosophy or principles." His behavior upon the closing of all Italian consulates in the United States in 1941 seems consistent with this statement: according to DeCicco, when asked by his boss, the Italian consul general in New York, whether he intended to return to Italy should all consular personnel be repatriated (as most, in fact, were), he "answered in the negative, giving my reasons for my decision, most important the fact that, being an American citizen, I had no business in Italy." As to why he had remained at the consular offices as long as he had, DeCicco attributes this to economic factors, specifically the Italian law which promised him a substantial bonus:

> All civil employees…were entitled in case of dismissal for reduc-
> tion of personnel, or the closing of the plant or the office, to a
> bonus equal to one half of their monthly salary for each year of
> service. If I had left right then, of my free will, without going back
> to Italy, I would have lost my chance to the above liquidation
> which, considering my thirty-six years of service, would have
> reached quite a considerable figure.[4]

As it turned out, the bonus for which DeCicco held on to his job kept being delayed because of lack of instructions from Rome, and "in the end, I did not receive one penny."

Pasquale DeCicco's decision to remain in America after June of 1941 thus cost him dearly. Without his consular job, he was unable to pay either the tax or the mortgage payments on his home. He managed to make an arrangement with the bank to give him time to pay, counting always on the bonus he still expected for his thirty-six years of service to the Italian government, but when that did not materialize, he called on some friends for help. This last measure might have worked but for one thing: on April 24, 1942, the FBI called on Pasquale DeCicco and arrested him. As DeCicco writes from the McAlester camp:

> The arrest eliminated all chances of redeeming my home, and I
> lost it. My sacrifices, my savings of twenty years, my resources
> went to naught. Our home was to us all very dear, I had built it in
> 1923, it cost me a good deal of money, and someone else got it for
> a song. It was heartbreaking, my wife and my daughter had to
> leave it and go to one of my sons in Hartford, Conn. And myself,
> at the 63rd year of my life, broken in health by the humiliating
> life of this camp—have already lost 32 pounds of my weight—
> burdened by an undeserved and unjust stigma, I am afraid I am
> heading toward a nervous breakdown.[5]

Pasquale DeCicco did not break down. He wrote letter after letter pleading for reconsideration. He had lawyer friends take his case to federal court in what became the central dispute of his internment: whether or not he was an American citizen. Apparently, in the eyes of the Justice Department, his decision in 1915 to join the Italian army—to fight for his mother country in a war in which that country was an ally of the United States—had not only jeopardized but nullified his citizenship. As DeCicco puts it, "The Hartford Immigration Office attempted to put on trial some intentions that they claim were into my head some twenty-five years ago, when I went back to Italy in 1915, basing its allegations on an arbitrary interpretation of an old Italian law, of which I did not even know the existence." Yet for that same twenty-five years, DeCicco says, he had voted in every American election, and "no one ever did challenge my right to vote." This was because, DeCicco maintains, he remained always an American citizen, living in New Haven with three American-born children, and even when in the Italian army and working for the consular office, never taking "an oath of allegiance" to the Italian government. Therefore, he insists, he remained always an American, not an Italian citizen. The most telling proof of this, he writes, was his refusal to repatriate to Italy when the consular offices were closed in June of 1941.

DeCicco offers further proof in another letter,[6] pointing out that his:

> …position as consular agent first and acting vice consul after, at New Haven, Conn., cannot be considered in the light claimed by the Department of Justice, because these positions abroad [i.e. in the United States] were, by law, open also to non-Italians and to citizens of the country where these offices were located. As a matter of fact, the same regulation exists in the case of the U.S. consulates abroad. I had been accredited with the U.S. Department of State as the Italian representative in New Haven, Conn., and the fact that I was an American citizen had been stated also.

Moreover, DeCicco adds, retaining his American citizenship during all that time cost him still more, for by doing so, he forfeited his chance for promotion or pension, and "a substantial increase in my salary of over $1500 a year."

All of this detailed argument appears to have fallen upon deaf ears, for Pasquale DeCicco was not released from internment by the attorney general until December 10, 1943 (Italy had surrendered and joined the Allies three months earlier, in September), having been paroled, like many of his co-internees, earlier that year. This meant that he had been forced to spend at least a year in internment, beginning at Hartford and ending at the McAlester Internment Camp in Oklahoma. For a man the bulk of whose life had been spent in the United States, whose children were American-born, and who had himself become an American citizen in 1909, this must have been hard time indeed. It also means that the Justice Department considered Pasquale DeCicco an enemy alien because his World War I service for Italy or his work in the consular office had invalidated his citizenship, or that Justice Department officials felt they had a perfect right to intern a U.S. citizen of Italian descent with the enemy aliens they considered dangerous. Whatever its rationale, it would appear that the United States government, at the very least, has the obligation to explain its actions in the case of Pasquale DeCicco.

———

One would have to say the same thing about the actions of the United States government, at about the same time, with respect to Mario Valdastri of Hawaii.*

As he explains in a memo to the American Civil Liberties Union (ACLU)[7] written while he was interned, Valdastri came to America penniless from his home town of Sassuolo, near Bologna, Italy. He was thirteen. By the age of eighteen, he had joined the U.S. Army in World War I, serving mainly in France, and been honorably discharged in 1919 as an American citizen. He had lived in the United States continuously since then, first in New Jersey, then in California, and finally settling in Hawaii. He had attended the Cooper Union in Manhattan to study sculpture, got married in 1920 to an American citizen of Italian origin, and fathered two children, a boy and a girl. In California, he had worked as a sculptor and a plasterer on San Simeon—the ornate estate built for newspaper magnate William Randolph Hearst—which work brought him to the notice of the Bank of Hawaii, then planning a new building. According to his son Mario Jr., Valdastri agreed to go to Hawaii to work on the new bank and, liking what he found, stayed.[8] Quickly recognized for his skill and artistry, he built a prosperous contracting business—doing plain and ornamental plastering—and became known as the best concrete and acoustics man in Hawaii, inventing and patenting a new method of plaster acoustics for auditoriums. Among the buildings with his signature sculpture and acoustics work is the city hall in Honolulu. During all this time, he asserts in his memo, he remained a model citizen, never condemned for or accused of any offense whatever.

Notwithstanding all this, and in spite of the fact that at age forty-five he had been under medical care since 1939, Valdastri received what he called the worst shock of his life when, on December 8, 1941, the day after Pearl Harbor, federal agents came to his home and arrested him. He was detained under what he called "very inhuman conditions" at the Honolulu immigration station and then transferred to the INS detention facility at Sand Island, T.H. (Territory of

———

*See "Two Men in Suits," page 153, for more on Mario Valdastri.

Hawaii; Hawaii did not become a state until 1959.) While under detention in Hawaii, he was never allowed to see his family, nor to learn the charges against him, even at the hearing which would determine if he would be released on parole or interned.

In late February 1942, Valdastri learned the result of that hearing. Not only was he not released, he was shocked even more profoundly to find himself again transported, this time over three thousand miles of ocean under what he called "conditions of unbelievable discomfort" to the continental United States. He landed first at the prisoner-of-war enclosure at Fort McDowell, on Angel Island in San Francisco Bay. There, on March 2, according to his Basic Personnel Record, he was photographed, fingerprinted, given the internment serial number ISN HI-252-CI, and prepared to begin his formal term as a civilian internee under the jurisdiction of the War Department. On March 6 this resulted in yet another journey, this time to the internee facility at Camp

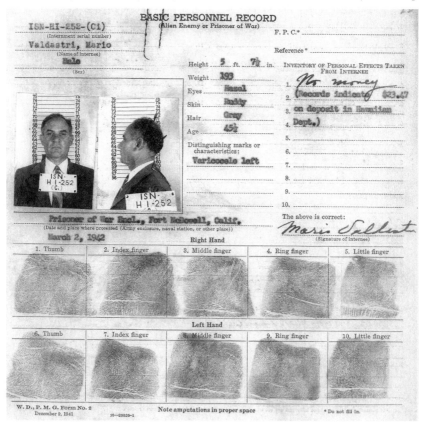

The front side of Mario Valdastri's Basic Personnel Record (PMGO Form 2). Courtesy of National Archives and Records Administration, College Park, Md.

McCoy in Wisconsin.[9] The change from the mild climate of Hawaii to the hard winter of Wisconsin was, he wrote, "very hard to bear." He was now five thousand miles from the family he had never once, since his arrest, been allowed to see. Like other internees, including the Japanese American internees he had traveled with from Hawaii, he had never been allowed to consult with a lawyer.

Valdastri then began a campaign of writing letters to the relevant authorities, demanding some explanation of his internment. He was an American citizen. He had never been faced with any formal accusation: "No facts for which I, an American citizen of good and honorable standing, should have been subjected to such a harsh treatment and punishment have ever been brought to my knowledge." If such facts should exist, he adds, "Although I cannot imagine what they could be—I should at least be given an opportunity of having my case brought before a regular court and of assuring my defense."

Clearly, Mario Valdastri had not been brought up to date about the power of a government at war to do whatever it wished with those it considered dangerous. For the truth was, the United States government owed no explanations, and certainly no regular court proceeding, to those it chose to intern. Its power to intern, vested in the Alien and Sedition Acts and Title 50 of the U.S. Code, reduced its attitude to one of benign simplicity: The hearings which we provide for resident aliens with origins in enemy nations are not required by law; we provide them at our discretion, our pleasure, and to indicate that we are doing all we can to uphold legal, democratic, and fair standards for all Americans. Of course, Mario Valdastri was not an alien; he was a citizen. But citizenship in a territory under martial law seemed to matter little. Further, since the promulgation of Executive Order 9066 on February 19, 1942, the United States government could do whatever it wished to whomever it wished, including native-born American citizens. Indeed, to "protect" itself or its territories during the war in which it had become engaged, it could and would intern tens of thousands of Japanese American citizens in camps in remote deserts.

Still, Mario Valdastri was outraged. This, after all, was not Nazi Germany nor Fascist Italy nor Imperial Japan. This was America, a nation which had organizations like the ACLU to protect citizens' rights, and in his letter to the ACLU Valdastri concludes:

> It seems outrageous that in a country like ours an American citizen should be treated as I have been, that he should be torn away from his wife and children, deprived of his liberty without accusation, trial, or defense, and thrown into an internment camp with enemy alien nationals whose ideas and ideologies are violently opposed to his own.

But that was exactly what had happened. And his letters and appeals to the Justice and War Departments, he said, had so far received no answer.

Valdastri's War Department file does not indicate whether the ACLU replied or not. What it does indicate is that Valdastri kept writing. First, he wrote to the president of the United States after he had listened to the "I Am an American" radio broadcast and found Franklin Delano Roosevelt's words too hypocritical to bear. The letter, dated May 18, 1942, is worth quoting in full:

Dear Mr. President:

Last night I listened to the "I Am an American" broadcast, sitting in a primitive barrack in an internment camp, and I could not help feeling sadly disillusioned.

I had come to America as a poor young boy, thirteen years old, and have lived in this country ever since. In 1918 I became an American citizen and served with the A.E.F. [American Expeditionary Force] in France. I received an honorable discharge. I then married and now have a son, 17, and a daughter, 21, both born Americans. My son will join the armed forces soon and my daughter is to be married this summer to a man wearing the U.S. Army uniform.

I have always lived an honorable family life and am a businessman, head of the contracting establishment which I have created, of excellent standing.

Still, here I am in a prisoner's camp, forced to live in close contact with people whose countries are at war with mine. I have received the worst shock in my life when, on December 8, 1941, I was arrested in my home in Honolulu, torn away from my family, brought to the mainland under incredible conditions, and finally interned here, five thousand miles away from my home!

In Honolulu, I was given a so-called hearing which lasted five minutes. No formal accusation against which I could have defended myself was ever brought against me, nor were the reasons for my arrest ever disclosed to me.

There were twelve other naturalized American citizens in my company and subjected to the same odyssey, but ten of them have now been brought back from here to Hawaii, and only myself and two others have—I don't know why—been left behind.

Quite apart from the serious material damage which I have suffered through such cruel and arbitrary proceedings, the dishonor which has fallen upon my dear ones is terribly unjust and painful to bear, for them as for me.

I always thought of myself as an excellent American citizen. I am ready, at any time, to do my duty in this war towards my country as I have done it in the last war. I would consider it an honor and a privilege to serve in the most exposed and dangerous spot, on an oil tanker, anywhere. I would gladly sacrifice my life for my country.

But I find it profoundly shocking to be treated in my own country like an enemy alien and to have been subjected to proceedings unworthy of the American administration.

Hoping that you will believe in my sincerity and that you will give orders so that the wrong done to my family and myself will be straightened out,

I remain, Mr. President,
very respectfully yours,
Mario Valdastri[10]

It is not clear whether the letter to President Roosevelt had any effect. It bears a cryptic note in the bottom left-hand corner, "no further action necessary," and an indecipherable signature.

Valdastri did not end his writing campaign with the president. On June 1 the indefatigable internee wrote to Provost Marshal General Allen Gullion—the man in charge of all domestic military affairs. Judging from the opening paragraph, it appears that Valdastri was acquainted with Gullion, perhaps due to their both having served in World War I, and thought a letter to him would be effective. Valdastri reviews his service to America in World War I, tells about his internment and his innocence, and concludes hopefully:

> I know your high sense of justice. You will, I am sure, see to it that the obvious error committed in my case shall be promptly straightened out, that I shall be released from detention and allowed to join my wife and children, who are morally and materially suffering—unjustly—as much as I am.[11]

For good measure, he included a copy of his earlier letter to the ACLU. Of course, Gullion had already received a copy of that letter as well as Valdastri's letter to the president. Those, together with the new letter, may have been what helped to get Valdastri sent back to Hawaii, but apparently it wasn't enough to have him released, nor to merit a reply from the general. We know this because a month and a half later, on July 18, the provost marshal general was to receive another letter, handwritten on Valdastri company stationery, from the internee's daughter Frances. In it she writes:

> Dad has begged me to write to you for help. He has been returned here, to the detention camp at Sand Island. He mentioned writing to you, but has, as yet, received no reply. Is there something—anything, that can be done for him? He suffers so! He feels so intensely that he should be free to fight for his country. I should like very much to receive even a short note from you.[12]

The stiff-necked General Gullion—he it was who had urged upon Lieutenant General John DeWitt of the Western Defense Command many of the harshest measures against Japanese Americans; he it was, too, who had suggested to Edward Ennis, head of Enemy Alien Control in the Justice Department, early in December 1941 that not just enemy aliens but *every single person in the United States* should be forced to register for a new census (one had been taken less than two years ago in 1940) so that the army could compile fresh data on every living resident—finally responded to this letter. But it was not the response Frances Valdastri had hoped to get. On July 28, General Gullion sent a reply that completely ignored the specifics of Mario Valdastri's case, especially his citizenship, and treated him by the book—as if he were, indeed, an enemy alien:

> I am sorry to tell you that the release of your father, about which you wrote me on July 18, 1942, is wholly within the jurisdiction of the Commanding General, Hawaiian Department, Fort Shafter, T.H. It was by his order that your father was interned, after a hearing before a board comprising three civilians.
>
> The hearing thus accorded was not held as a matter of right but was allowed in order to avoid injustice. Considerations of national security, dependent upon the military factors involved, governed the decision of the general who interned your father.
>
> In order to have him released, it will be necessary to prove to the satisfaction of the Hawaiian Department that such release would in no way endanger the public safety of the United States or be detrimental to the war effort.[13]

In other words, Sorry, my dear, but your father is out of luck. He's been caught in the enemy-alien net and the fact that he is not an enemy alien profits him nothing. Nor does the fact that he has served his country before and would serve it again, nor the fact that he has done nothing wrong. What matters are rules, orders, military jurisdiction, considerations of national security, mysterious "military factors," and that terrible mandate given to each and every enemy alien taken into custody: *You must prove your innocence.* You must prove that your release will not "endanger the public safety of the United States or be detrimental to the war effort." Never mind that you must prove this in the absence of any charges, of any hint of what the authorities might have in mind about your past actions or sentiments or inclinations or associations or words that may be weighing against you. Never mind that you are not permitted any legal counsel. Never mind that your rights as a citizen have been abrogated. Never mind that the Constitution has been turned upside down and your guilt is here assumed until you can demonstrate otherwise. *You must prove your innocence.* And bear in mind, your opportunity to do this is itself a gift from the United States government, in that the hearing you have already been given and the new one you may yet be granted are not a matter of any right you may think you are owed, but are dispensed by those in charge of your fate out of their deep commitment to *avoiding injustice.*

What makes this all the more poignant is the fact that another letter in his file indicates a largeness of spirit in Mario Valdastri that might have counted in his favor but probably counted against him. This is a letter to the *Honolulu Star-Bulletin* in which Valdastri describes conditions at Camp McCoy, Wisconsin, particularly the humanity and cooperative spirit of the Japanese Hawaiian citizens with whom he is billeted. He describes the diligence with which they set up kitchen facilities and scientifically gauged the dietary needs of men in prison. He marvels at the speed with which they established medical care and cultural and educational activities. He waxes almost poetic about the unique activities and skills of the men:

> A curious sight was the picture of dignified men, their backs bent and their eyes glued to the road, collecting colored pebbles. An occasional stroll through their barracks revealed the purpose of this enterprise: they played "go." Also "mah-jongg" and Japanese chess were frequent pastimes...Amazing was the dexterity which some fellows showed in their hobbies. Some made sandals, some built nests for the birds who gradually returned from their winter quarters down south. All over you could find little flower beds in empty cans salvaged for this purpose. One fellow made rope out of grass and knotted a little mat, a craft that had come to him from his ancestors. Even a turtle was trained as a pet, whereas some rabbits refused to be tamed.[14]

He even admits that while in such company his health has "improved to the point where I feel moderately well again." But though a copy of this letter was made and inserted into his official War Department file, it availed him nothing. He remained interned at Camp McCoy even after all but two of the internee companions he wrote about were returned to Hawaii.

What makes the Valdastri story more disturbing still are several factors not contained in his file but supplied by his son, who still lives in Hawaii.[15] When asked what might have landed his father in detention, Mario Valdastri Jr. mentioned two possibilities.[16] First, the land upon which the Valdastri house was built bordered the Waimanalo Sugar Plantation. A nearby swamp supplied irrigation water for the plantation, to facilitate which, concrete berms had been built near the Kailua bridge. The berms, in turn, contained slots with removable planks designed to let excess water flow out from Kawainui swamp when necessary. When the planks were in place damming the water, however, the swamp level rose and flooded the Valdastri property, and even the Valdastri home. Mario Valdastri asked several times that the plantation alter its procedure. Then he simply told them flat out, "Don't do it any more." When none of this had the slightest effect, says his son, "He took me with him one day and we removed the planks from the berms to let the water run off." The plantation workers put them back, of course, and with the next flooding Mario Valdastri became even more heated. "If we're flooded again," he said, "I'm going to blow up the berm." The owner of the plantation, says Mario Valdastri Jr., "was one of the most powerful men in Hawaii, and my father always thought he reported that statement to the authorities." To those authorities, at that time, the mere mention of blowing up anything, even years before the war, may have been sufficient to land the man who mentioned it behind barbed wire.

The second factor seems even more tenuous, though it, in fact, is supported by corollary events. When Mario Valdastri first came to Hawaii to work on the Bank of Hawaii, he went to collect his first check for his efforts from the president of the subcontracting company for whom he worked, J. G., who said, "I have a check for M. V. Morris." Though the initials matched, the name itself was wrong and Valdastri replied, "No, that's not my name, I'm Mario Valdastri." The contractor had little patience with this kind of impudence from an immigrant and reportedly said, "Do you want the f—— check or don't you?" Seeing that it was futile to argue with such a man, Valdastri took the check. That might have been the end of it, but J. G. seemed to regard this as an amusing joke, and continued thereafter to call Valdastri by the mistaken name, Morris. Years later the joke came home to roost. One of the questions Mario Valdastri was asked at his hearing was "Why did you come to Hawaii under a false name?"[17]

Tenuous and circumstantial as all the evidence against him may have been, it took the authorities another seven months after his return to Hawaii to decide to give Mario Valdastri a second hearing. Those seven months turned out to be critical: first, his daughter got married, but Valdastri was not allowed to attend the wedding. Not long after, Frances Valdastri was involved in an automobile accident that ended her life. Though this time the authorities did allow Valdastri to view his daughter's body in the funeral home, it was but once, after he agreed to be accompanied by two armed guards.

At last, in late February 1943, a second hearing board concluded that Mario Valdastri was not, in fact, a danger to his country, and he was released. Thus had a remark made in the heat of the moment and a supposed alias pinned on him by a bigoted banker, and perhaps other as yet unknown factors, cost him more than a year of his life.

When the army did release him, it was partly under pressure from his army lawyer, who had vowed that if Valdastri's release were not granted, he would quit his work with army intelligence; and partly because the military needed Valdastri's skills in construction, and in fact gave the formerly "dangerous" internee a special pass a few days after his release to enter any military base or construction area in Hawaii.

Like most other internees, and despite the obvious violations of his rights, Mario Valdastri said very little about his ordeal once it was over. His constant comment, both ironic and philosophical, linked his honorable World War I army service with his World War II internment by means of a wry double entendre: "I served my country in both wars."[18]

Valdastri's wife, Josephine, was not so sanguine. According to Mario Jr., she "never forgave them for what they did to us." The result was that eventually, in 1967, she persuaded her husband to return to Italy and retire on her family's property near Lago Maggiore in the Piedmont region of northern Italy. There, notwithstanding how ill he had been in 1939 and the ordeal of internment, Mario Valdastri seemed to thrive; he lived to be eighty-two years old.

The United States government has neither accounted for nor apologized for its actions in his case.

Endnotes:
1. It is not clear whether to include Domenico Trombetta in this category. A naturalized U.S. citizen, the editor of the profascist *Il Grido delle Stirpe* was denaturalized on September 28, 1942, and taken into custody on the same day. According to his file, he was not paroled until May 1945. Trombetta file, RG 389, Records Relating to Italian Civilian Internees During WWII, 1941-46, Boxes 2-20, Provost Marshal General's Office, National Archives and Records Administration, College Park, Md. (hereafter RG 389 NARA II).

2. Pasquale DeCicco initially applied to the district court in Connecticut, asking for release on bail pending habeas corpus. On June 15, 1942, his motion was denied on the grounds that the court had no jurisdiction with respect to enemy aliens. See *United States ex. rel. Pasquale DeCicco vs. Longo*, Civil No. 768, United States District Court, June 15, 1942.

3. Pasquale DeCicco, Letter to Attorney General, Jan. 16, 1943, RG 389 NARA II.

4. Ibid., p. 5.

5. Ibid., p. 6.

6. Memo, "Points concerning my case before the U.S. Federal Court," RG 389 NARA II.

7. Mario Valdastri, Letter to American Civil Liberties Union, May 10, 1942, Mario Valdastri file, RG 389 NARA II.

8. Mario Valdastri Jr., personal interview.

9. It is interesting to note that very little information exists on the interment facilities at Camp McCoy. Indeed, in *Reflections of Internment: The Art of Hawaii's Hiroshi Honda* (Honolulu Academy of Arts, 1994), doubt is expressed that it was used for internment at all: "There is no documentation of an internment camp location in Wisconsin, although there was a Camp McCoy in which the 100th Battalion (composed of nisei volunteers) trained. A notation in one of Honda's sketchbooks, translated from the Japanese, makes reference to a 'Camp Ma-koe,' suggesting that the facility could have been used for different purposes during the course of the war." Given the testimony and records of Valdastri, there can be no doubt that Camp McCoy did indeed accommodate internees, including Japanese Americans from Hawaii, and that Honda's "Ma-koe" was probably Camp McCoy.

10. Mario Valdastri, Letter to the President of the United States, May 28, 1942, RG 389 NARA II.

11. Mario Valdastri, Letter to Allen W. Gullion, June 1, 1942, RG 389 NARA II.

12. Frances Valdastri, Letter to General Gullion, July 18, 1942, RG 389 NARA II.

13. Allen W. Gullion, Letter to Frances Valdastri, July 28, 1942, RG 389 NARA II.

14. Mario Valdastri, Letter to Riley H. Allen, *Honolulu Star Bulletin*, undated, RG 389 NARA II. According to Mario Valdastri Jr., the letter was never published, probably because Hawaii was under martial law and news was heavily restricted.

15. Mario Valdastri Jr., personal interview

16. A third is mentioned in a letter from Mario Valdastri Jr.: "Dad was a member of an Italian American club in Honolulu in 1938. He was elected president and felt pretty good about it, as did the whole family. Then he stopped going to meetings, and when I asked him why, he said that they talked too much about Fascism. That was his only answer and he never went to a meeting again." Based on what is known about other internees, that brief membership probably added to the suspicion of authorities.

17. Ibid.

18. Ibid.

Two Men in Suits

by Mario Valdastri Jr.

Mario Valdastri's internment* violated not one but several areas of rights: where most internees were noncitizens, Valdastri not only was naturalized but had earned his American citizenship by serving with the United States armed forces during World War I. Nonetheless, he was arrested at his home in Hawaii and sent to the mainland to be interned.

Mario Valdastri Jr. remembers all this vividly. He recalls the day of his father's arrest, the bitter frustration of a family rebuffed in their attempts to get the authorities to reconsider, and the apparently petty reasons for the government's suspicions. He also makes plain that the losses suffered during those years touched not only the person interned, while he was interned, but every member of the internee's family for years to come.

Dad and I were working on the exterior balcony to his bedroom the afternoon of December 8, 1942. This was the same place we were when we saw the Japanese planes attack Kaneohe Naval Air Station the morning before. "The Star-Spangled Banner" came on over the radio, and Dad had us both stand at attention and sing.

A while later, a car came down our entry road and into the parking yard. Two men in suits and ties (rare on Monday in the country) got out and asked Dad if he was Mario Valdastri. When Dad said yes, the men said, "Will you please come with us?" My father asked if he could change, but the men told him to come as he was dressed. Dad, however, took off his sweaty t-shirt and put on a sweatshirt. He said to my mother that they probably needed him as an interpreter, and they left in the FBI agents' car.

Later my dad informed me that many Italians, Germans, and other Caucasian men and women, not Japanese, were taken to a large barred room upstairs in the immigration building. They were there for many hours, with no

---

*For a full account of Mario Valdastri's internment at Camp McCoy, see "A Tale of Two Citizens," page 137.

chairs, furniture, or toilet facilities. After some time, the people behind the bars began to protest loudly, and a soldier with a rifle guarding them said, "Shut up, you goddamn spies!"

Sometime in February 1942, he was shipped to the mainland United States with only the Hawaiian clothes he had. He tried to keep warm by putting newspapers under his clothing. Eventually he arrived at Camp McCoy, Wisconsin, where he was reasonably well treated. At Camp McCoy, he appealed to the camp commander that, as an American citizen, he had the right of habeas corpus and he wanted to see a lawyer. I think the camp commander bluffed as long as he could, because Dad waited several months. Finally, an appointment with a lawyer was scheduled, but before it happened, he was shipped back to Hawaii, which was still under martial law, where his incarceration continued.

In late 1942, we could visit him in the concentration camp's enclosure. We went across Honolulu harbor by boat to Sand Island, walked about a half mile to the gates at the double, twelve-foot-high barbed-wire fences, and met in a tent inside the enclosure that held about six picnic tables. The tent we met my father in housed specifically Italians, while other tents housed Germans and other ethnicities. There were no Japanese evident.

On December 6, 1942, my older sister, Frances, was killed in an accident....Dad was allowed to view her once in the funeral home for about an hour, although two guards escorted him.

Sometime in February 1943, Dad was finally given a new hearing. His attorney was very eloquent, explaining that "Morris" [the name to which his paychecks had been written by a subcontractor he had worked for] did not mean he came to Hawaii under an assumed name, that he had never threatened to blow up Kailua bridge, and evidently clearing up all the other accusations. His attorney then (Dad told us this later) showed his credentials as an intelligence officer or FBI agent and threatened to resign if Dad were not released immediately.

Dad was told to go back to camp and get his things and go home. He walked out of the immigration building and onto Ala Moana Boulevard, stunned at the suddenness of his release. On the street in front of the immigration building was a public phone where he called home. After receiving the call, I jumped in my Model A (it was the only car that had any gas in it, because of rationing) and drove up the Pali road (the mountain pass between Kailua and Honolulu) and down the Honolulu side. I ran out of gas after coasting as far as I could and walked to where Dad had been, but he wasn't there. I had no money, so I walked to his shop and called home. He was home! An architect friend was driving by on Ala Moana, saw him, and took him home. I stayed at a friend's house that night so Mom and Dad were home alone.

He had been in business from the 1920s until his incarceration, at which time his shop shut down. When he was released in February 1942, he was only home a few days when the United States Engineering Department (USED) hired him and gave him a badge and pass for all military bases and construction areas throughout Hawaii. He soon became the foremost concrete, acoustics, and plastering expert in Hawaii.

I was away at school in New Mexico in 1945, and it came as a surprise to me when he sold his business and property in Honolulu, his home and nine acres of land in Kailua (a booming bedroom community eleven miles from Honolulu), and moved to California. Within two years he returned to Hawaii and started his business again, from scratch. I joined him in 1954. In 1968 he retired and returned to Italy with my mother for their remaining years, coming back to Hawaii occasionally and once specifically in 1975 to 1976, at the age of 78, to personally do the decorative plaster repair work on Iolani Palace. He died in Italy at age 82.

I am very interested in finding the report on Dad's hearing in February 1942, and the intitial interview with the army and three civilians. I remember that when we lived in Los Altos, California, between 1945 and 1947, two army officers and a uniformed female stenographer came to our house and interviewed Dad for a long afternoon. I didn't pay much attention then, but he later told me he thought they were trying to make sure he did not sue the government.

Exclusion Is a Four-Letter Word

by Colonel Angelo de Guttadauro

Like Remo Bosia, Nino Guttadauro fell victim to the frustration of Lieutenant General John DeWitt. Unable to rid his Western Defense Command of all "enemy aliens," DeWitt had to settle for exclusion orders aimed at naturalized citizens of Italian descent who had been declared suspect. In October 1942, therefore, Nino Guttadauro was ordered to vacate not just Military District One (the western states), but coastal states in all other military districts as well. The once prosperous accountant ended up combing the nation in search of any work he could get to support his family, which eventually joined him in Reno.

Angelo Guttadauro was six at that time. Subsequently, he served in the United States armed forces for more than thirty years and was the only Italian American to testify at the Civil Rights Commission Hearings in 1982. Here he remembers his father's ordeal, its effects on him and his family, and the little-known fact that FBI investigations and interrogations of the individuals it suspected of disloyalty began well before the United States had entered the war—in Nino Guttadauro's case, in the spring of 1941.

The gratuitous and malicious exercise of exclusion by private and public bodies transforms exclusion into a four-letter word because of its devastating effect on the individuals and groups affected. One need only consider the far-reaching consequences of excluding African Americans from certain sectors of public schooling to understand how exclusionary practices can be permanently damaging.

One of the most gratuitous exercises of exclusion by a sovereign state was America's exclusion and subsequent expulsion of United States citizens of Italian descent from twenty-nine states during World War II. Not only was this done in the absence of even the most basic constitutional rights of those excluded, but it has remained an almost unknown secret story to the general American public for almost sixty years.

It is time that this veil of secrecy is lifted and that the United States government acknowledge that fundamental injustices were practiced against its loyal citizens of Italian descent.[1]

Last winter, my son Andrew, a graduate of the United States Military Academy at West Point, sent me a copy of Tom Brokaw's 1998 best-seller, *The Greatest Generation*, as a Christmas present. It is a riveting account of personal integrity and courage as documented by the lives of Americans who were destined to confront World War II. But I was totally dismayed and offended that Brokaw continues to assert the widely held canard that Italian Americans were not persecuted during that period. The following passage makes this fictitious position quite clear:

> Italian and German aliens living in California coastal areas were ordered to move in early 1942 but by June of that year the order had been rescinded, and there was no major relocation for those groups. Italian and German immigrants were picked up and questioned closely; they may have had some uncomfortable moments during the war, but they retained all their rights.

Some moments, some rights.

My father, Nino Guttadauro, was born in Italy in 1899 and as a teenager was commissioned an infantry second lieutenant in the Italian armed forces. He served for over a year in combat against the Austrian army in World War I, until he was seriously wounded on the front lines. At that time, Italy was allied with America, England, and France to defeat the invading German and Austrian forces in Europe. For his gallantry in action, he was awarded Italy's War Cross for Military Valor, the equivalent of America's Silver Star.

Following the war, my father emigrated to the United States, married my mother (a native-born American citizen), continued his profession as an accountant, and became a naturalized American citizen residing in San Francisco, California. Because of his status as a veteran of World War I, he joined the Federation of Italian World War I Veterans in the U.S.A., Inc., an organization very similar to America's VFW. His later position as president of the federation's San Francisco branch, however, would have very damaging consequences for him and his entire family.

Under the provisions of the Freedom of Information and Protection of Privacy Act (FOIPA), I have received dozens of documents from the FBI covering the period from 19 March 1941 to 13 July 1944. A number of these documents were signed by John Edgar Hoover, director of the FBI, and by Wendell Berge, assistant attorney general of the United States. A brief summary of these documents will illustrate the unconscionable manner in which

Josephine and Angelo de Guttadauro with their father in Reno in 1943, where the family moved to comply with Nino de Guttadauro's exclusion order. Courtesy of Josephine Guttadauro

my father's most basic civil liberties were abused and the core principles of the Constitution abrogated. Even today, almost sixty years after the fact, the names of my father's accusers to the FBI and, indeed, their very allegations, have been blacked out, or sanitized, in these documents.

My father's interrogations by the FBI began in March 1941—well before the nation was at war—and continued until September 1942. At no time was he allowed to know the names of his accusers or the nature of their accusations. During his 29 March 1941 interrogation, the FBI agent recorded that the "Subject denied there was any Fascist activity in the Italian Colony in San Francisco" and further noted my father's statement that "Communism was an international ideology and Russia sought and would, if the chance came, inflict its system on the whole world." History has proven my father correct on both counts.

Notwithstanding my father's consistent denials over a period of one and a half years of any inappropriate or illegal activities, a board of officers was convened by the commanding general, Western Defense Command and Fourth Army, to determine if he should be issued an exclusion order prohibiting him from living in over half of the United States. The hearing was held in Room 483 of San Francisco's Whitcomb Hotel at 9:30 A.M. on Tuesday, 8 September 1942. As Lieutenant Colonel Frank E. Meek, the board president, informed my father in writing, "Materials in the hands of the Board will not be made available for your inspection," and you will not "be permitted to examine witnesses." These are exactly the arbitrary procedures exercised by the infamous "Star Chamber" courts of the Middle Ages, and these same processes were utilized during the FBI interrogations.

The board's decision, for which there was no appeal, resulted in my father's being served Exclusion Order F-1 at 10:18 A.M. on 29 September 1942. He was ordered to report two days later at 10:00 A.M. to a Major Ray Ashworth for "processing." This processing included having a photograph and fingerprints taken and a specimen signature supplied. Documentaries of military tribunals treating civilian citizens in such an arbitrary manner can be seen almost weekly on the History Channel, but most such examples were filmed over half a century ago in Nazi Germany or Communist Russia.

The immediate results of Exclusion Order F-1 were my father's automatic explusion from California, the loss of his professional position, and, most importantly, his forced separation from his wife, his seven-year-old daughter, and his five-year-old son. In fact, he was not only expelled from California, but he was also prohibited from living in or traveling to the following states:

Totally Prohibited:

Arizona	Massachusetts	Rhode Island
California	New Hampshire	South Carolina
Connecticut	New Jersey	Vermont
Delaware	New York	Virginia
Florida	North Carolina	Washington
Georgia	Oregon	The District of
Maine	Pennsylvania	Columbia
Maryland		

Partially Prohibited:

Alabama	Mississippi	New Mexico
Idaho	Montana	Texas
Louisiana	Nevada	Utah

Prior to departing California, my father was ordered by Lieutenant General John L. DeWitt, commanding general of the Western Defense Command and Fourth Army, "to communicate in writing the time of your departure, initial and ultimate destinations, route to be followed, and means of travel; upon arrival at ultimate destination, you will report in person the fact of your arrival and your address at such destination to the Special Agent in Charge of the nearest office of the Federal Bureau of Investigation, Department of Justice." This military notification and personal reporting mandate remained in force any time my father traveled more than five miles or changed his residence, even in the same city. Although an American citizen, my father was, in effect, a prisoner in his own country.

It was impossible for my father to find qualified accounting positions, because he would have to inform prospective employers that he was excluded on security grounds from half of the United States. It is understandable that employers would not trust such an individual with financial ledgers and cash payments. After an extensive search, the first job he was able to find following the exclusion was as a grocery clerk in Salt Lake City, Utah. This economic disruption and hardship, as well as the psychological scars, remained with my father for the rest of his life.

But the entire family also suffered. Due to the swiftness of the expulsion order, household goods were either stored or simply abandoned. We were forced to rent, in numerous cities, furnished apartments or homes at high costs due to our transient status. We had become, by military fiat, a family of involuntary gypsies. It fell upon my mother to create an artificial home atmosphere as best she could while my father roamed the Rocky Mountain states (in the non-prohibited areas), searching for a living. Because of this arbitrary and coercive action, a man's value to himself, to his family, and to his community and society was dramatically and permanently diminished.

Despite the hardships and injustices inflicted on a loyal citizen by his government, my father was always proud of my decision to enter the United States Army, from which I was honorably retired as a colonel after almost thirty-two years of commissioned service.

Had he lived, my father would have been one hundred and one this year. By exposing the indignities he was forced to endure, we can relay to his spirit, and to all citizens, that our country is truly based on liberty and justice for all. Not only is this the right thing to do; it is the American thing to do.

Endnote:
1. Since the time when Colonel de Guttadauro gave essentially this testimony about his father's ordeal before the House Judiciary Committee on October 24, 1999, the Wartime Violation of Italian American Civil Liberties Act was passed by Congress and signed into law. The law formally acknowledges that civil liberties violations against Italian Americans took place during World War II.

Unwelcome in Freedom's Land
The Impact of World War II on Italian Aliens in Southern California

by Gloria Ricci Lothrop

Gloria Ricci Lothrop is the W.P. Whitsett Professor of California
History at California State University, Northridge. Professor Lothrop
received her doctorate in the history of California and the American
West from the University of Southern California in 1970. Lothrop's
publications include *Recollections of the Flathead Mission: Le Memorie
di Gregorio Mengarini, S.J.* (Glendale, Calif.: A. H. Clark Co., 1977),
Pomona: A Centennial History (Northridge, Calif.: Windsor
Publications, 1988), and *Chi Siamo: The Italians of Los Angeles*
(Pasedena, Calif.: Tabula Rasa Press, 1982). She has co-edited *A
Guide to the History of California* (New York: Greenwood Press, 1989)
and is co-author of *California Women: A History* (Sparks, Nev.:
Materials for Today's Learning, 1987). A fellow of the California
Historical Society and the Southern California Historical Society, she
has received a Fulbright fellowship, the Haynes and Oakley fellowships, and two Haynes/Huntington Research fellowships. Among her
civic activities, she has served as president of the Historic Italian
Hall Foundation of Los Angeles and received the Targhe d'Oro award
conferred by the government of Puglia, Italy, and the Columbian
award presented by the Federated Italo Americans of Los Angeles.

Introduction

The World War II experiences of non-naturalized United States residents born
in Axis countries have been consigned to memory and assigned a marginal
place in the historical record. Nevertheless, the wartime policies of restriction,
internment, and exclusion enforced upon enemy aliens, particularly along the
Pacific slope in a region designated as Military District One of the Western
Defense Command, radically altered the leadership structures within many

"Unwelcome in Freedom's Land," first published in *Southern California Quarterly*, vol. 81 (Winter
1999), pp. 507–544, is reprinted here courtesy of the author and the Historical Society of
Southern California.

Italian American communities, resulted in a deliberate alienation from the parent culture and affected profoundly the individuals involved....

The presence of large numbers of noncitizen residents in the United States who had emigrated from belligerent nations posed a unique challenge. Federal policy, which evolved during the first months of the war, developed three components: (1) the immediate detention of enemy aliens who were deemed potentially subversive; (2) the imposition of restrictions upon resident enemy aliens, which included limitations on travel, registration, the surrender of enumerated articles, and the imposition of a curfew; and (3) the exclusion of enemy aliens from designated zones and their relocation in less strategic areas.

These policies were not consistently enforced. For example, Italian noncitizens were exempted from enemy-alien status on October 12, 1942, while the majority of Japanese aliens and citizens remained interned for the duration of the war. It should be noted, however, that sixty-four percent, or 10,775, of those detained by the Federal Bureau of Investigation between December 7, 1941, and June 30, 1945, were Europeans or European Americans. Enforcement of enemy-alien regulations varied according to expediency and practicality. For example, ninety percent of the enemy aliens were concentrated in eleven states, with fifty-one percent of the enemy aliens (approximately 1.5 million) living in the vicinity of New York, New Jersey, and Connecticut. The size of such a population made it too unwieldy to relocate or incarcerate.[1] In addition to their sheer numbers, the political influence of Italians, particularly in eastern seaboard states, defied any efforts at regulation beyond the registration mandated in February 1942.[2]

In contrast, along the Pacific slope, a declared military zone, enemy-alien groups were subjected to the full range of alien regulation, including detention, restriction, and relocation from specific areas, for limited periods of time. In the early months of the war these policies affected the lives of three alien groups: 38,171 Japanese, 19,417 German, and 52,008 Italian residing in California.[3] This study will examine the experiences of Italian enemy aliens living in the Los Angeles area in the early months of World War II.

Historical Background

The wartime policies and subsequent events are best understood within the context of the preceding three decades. Following the successful march on Rome in 1922 by Benito Mussolini and his black-shirted followers, Italy's new leader curried the support of the international community, particularly the United States. His efforts reaped benefits. As early as 1926, Congress approved a comparatively lenient settlement of Italy's World War I debt. In addition, between 1925 and 1930, Italy's new Fascist government was extended loans of more than $300 million, provided by the New York financial organization Morgan, Blair and Company.[4] Italian relations were further reinforced by a meeting in 1931 between Italian foreign minister Dino Grandi and President Herbert Hoover. The amity continued into the New Deal. In correspondence with Franklin D. Roosevelt, his ambassador to Italy, Breckenridge Long, praised Mussolini's dignity and energy.[5] In personal letters, FDR observed that he was deeply impressed by what Mussolini was accomplishing, adding that he kept in close touch with that "admirable gentleman."[6] In a letter to *Fortune* magazine written in the early months of his administration, FDR went so far as to describe Mussolini and Stalin as his "blood brothers."[7]

The signing of the 1929 Lateran Accords, bringing to a welcome end the strained relations with the Vatican and Italy, garnered support for Mussolini from the U.S. Catholic hierarchy. In Los Angeles, Archbishop John J. Cantwell joined the editor of *L'Osservatore Romano* to address one hundred thousand members of the Italian Catholic Federation at an outdoor Mass at the Coliseum.[8]

Through the mid-1930s, Mussolini's Fascist credo not only assumed legitimacy within the Catholic Church, among conservative financiers and leading academics, but also among fringe groups like the Silver Shirts and the Knights of the White Camellia. From his small studio in Des Moines, Iowa, the singularly popular Father Charles Coughlin, the radio priest, broadcast to more than fifteen million listeners a variation of the Fascist agenda adapted to American culture."[9]

Praise of the "new Italy," echoed throughout the international press, was a source of pride for Italian Americans, who were being urged by the Fascist government to celebrate their *Italianità*.[10] As a result, they became members of the Italian Touring Club and joined the growing number of language classes subsidized by the Italian government. In nostalgic celebration of their roots they became members of the Sons of Italy and the Italian war veterans' association, *Associazone Ex Combattenti e Reduci,* and enrolled their offspring in the youth club, *Gruppo Giovanile*.

Recognizing that emigrés represented potential troops, revenues, and public relations, especially in the United States, where in the 1930s they represented the largest group of foreign-born, Mussolini's government took every opportunity to remind Italian Americans that they remained Italian to the seventh generation. To reinforce this bond, subsidies were made available to the Italian language press, and local consulates were increased to seventy, including one in Los Angeles. In an effort to strengthen local loyalties, the Italian government dispatched dignitaries, including flying ace General Francesco Di Penedo and arctic explorer Umberto Nobile, to Los Angeles. Both were feted at the Italian Hall at Main and Macy Streets. Mussolini's son Vittorio was among the dignitaries. In addition to attending a reception at the Guasti mansion in Rancho Cucamonga, young Mussolini toured Hollywood, where he represented his father in negotiations for the establishment of the RAM production company with Hal Roach Studios.[11]

Despite increasing criticism of the growing Fascist activity in the United States, in 1934 the Congressional McCormack-Dickstein Committee, investigating un-American activities, concluded that there was little reason to investigate Italian American organizations. The next year, however, relations between the two countries became strained as Mussolini launched his invasion of Ethiopia. The United States ordered embargoes on oil and raw materials. But the promise of a new empire ruled from Rome led Italian wives in the United States to donate their wedding rings for the war effort and young men to pay the Fascist bachelor's tax. A U.S. embargo on copper shipments led to the mailing of eight hundred tons of copper postcards to Italy.[12]

Mussolini's entry into the Axis alliance with Adolph Hitler in 1936 stimulated additional criticism. Aware of this, the Fascists attempted to keep the international goodwill garnered through their propaganda campaigns by avoiding any outreach efforts with their new military ally. The German American Bund was notorious for its overt tactics and aggressive propaganda. But in Los Angeles the shared political aims of the new allies brought some Italians together with the German American Bund at Deutsches Haus, located in the 600 block of West 15th Street. This was the meeting place of one of the most active Bund chapters in the United States, having the responsibility for distributing propaganda, much of it printed in Mexico City, throughout the United States and Canada. There on June 12, 1937, a new group was formed. The National Protective Order of Gentiles was organized to include Germans, White Russians, Latin Americans, and Italians. News photos also reveal members of Italian organizations in attendance at other festivities sponsored by the German American Bund. They were also among the crowds participating in Bund activities at Hindenburg Park (now part of Crescenta Valley Park).[13]

By the late 1930s, local criticism of the Axis allies increased. In 1938 the *Los Angeles Daily News* published a letter in which the writer's argument acknowledged the dichotomy posed by the two major political philosophies which would plague the world for decades to come. He asserted:

> The safety of our country is being undermined not by Communism
> but by Hitler's and Mussolini's underground propaganda. Our
> democratic institutions are denounced and ridiculed by Italian
> and German officials, professors in our colleges, teachers in our

public and parochial schools, and those who refuse to join Nazi and Fascist organizations are called Communist.[14]

La Parola, the antifascist paper published in New York City, proposed a unique strategy. On its front page it listed all the U.S. recipients of decorations conferred by the Italian government, inviting the recipients to renounce the recognitions granted by Italy's Fascist regime. Among those listed were Romolo Cacciarella, manager of the Italian Cruise Lines with offices in Los Angeles, retired Los Angeles banker Armando Pedrini, and Gaetano Merola, impresario of the San Francisco Opera.[15]

Despite rising criticism of Mussolini's propaganda policies, *La Direzione Generale degli Italiani all'estero,* the ministry for Italians abroad, administered by Mussolini's son-in-law Count Galeazzo Ciano, accelerated its outreach programs to the emigrés and their children, particularly through the after-school language programs. In addition to offering prizes, including trips to Italy, the Italian government provided stipends to the host schools, paid teachers' salaries, and supplied curriculum materials. Orders were also issued that classes were to commence with the singing of the Italian national anthem. Curriculum became increasingly assertive in proclaiming the Fascist message, leading the Los Angeles Unified School District to withdraw two books, *Andiamo in Italia* (We're Going to Italy), which contained a lengthy discussion of the advantages of Fascism, and *L'Italia Nel Passato e Nel Presente* (Italy in the Past and in the Present), which contained pages of quotations from Mussolini.[16]

According to Maria Ricci, assistant director of *Le Scuole Giovanni Pascoli,* the Italian language program in Los Angeles, language teachers who objected to the increasingly partisan slant of the curriculum were summarily dismissed and barred from their facilities. Confronted with such policies, Los Angeles Italian school director Dr. Angela Spadea wired Count Ciano, offering her opinion in but one word: "Scoundrel!"[17]

The United States reacted to the escalating propaganda and threat of war with increased vigilance. In June 1940, President Roosevelt signed into law the Alien Registration Act, which required the fingerprinting and registration of 4,921,452 alien U.S. residents over the age of fourteen. In May 1941, Italian personnel at the World's Fair at Flushing, New York, including several renowned musical performers, were taken into custody, 125 in all. In June 1941, the Axis allies were ordered to close all consulates in the United States. As a result, on July 15, 1941, six-foot, six-inch tall Los Angeles Consul-General Dr. Dino Simplicini, accompanied by his wife and staff, joined other consular officials bound for Lisbon aboard the SS *West Point.* That same month, Italian public information libraries ceased operation in the United States.

Since 1939, when war broke out in Europe, ships belonging to the Axis powers had languished in twenty-one United States ports. The British government adamantly refused to assure safe transatlantic passage to ships carrying able-bodied men from countries with whom the British were at war. In March 1941, President Roosevelt ordered the seizure of sixty-nine Italian, German, and Danish ships. The Danish sailors were allowed to remain aboard their ships, but the 775 Italian and 69 German seamen were served warrants for having overstayed the sixty-day limit allowed to alien seamen in any United States territory. All the captured seamen, along with the orchestra and entertainers, multilingual athletes, medical staff, and a Catholic priest who were aboard the Italian luxury liner *Il Conte Biancamano*, which had been stranded in the Panama Canal Zone, were sent to join the World's Fair personnel at Fort Missoula, Montana, which would soon become the wartime home of a number of Los Angeles residents.[18]

Fort Missoula, located near the confluence of the Blackfoot, Bitteroot, and Clark Fork Rivers, was established in 1877. During World War I it became a training camp for mechanics, and in the 1930s it served as headquarters for the Civilian Conservation Corps. During World War II the camp, isolated by mountain ranges, was used as an internment center.

Even as the nation was assuming a wartime posture, the Italian media carried an appeal issued by Spartaco Bonomi, vice president of the Italian Catholic Federation in Los Angeles, requesting funds for food and medicine to be used by Italians displaced by the ongoing European military conflict. In May 1941, the local press reported that nearly $11,000 had been raised. That campaign did not go unnoticed by government officials.[19] Cautioning against such activity at ceremonies marking "I Am an American Day," a representative of the U.S. attorney general warned that it was the duty of noncitizens "to remain loyal to the United States, their host," adding, "We have a right to expect loyalty that leads to no division."[20]

As World War II hovered on the horizon and Americans were called upon to pledge allegiance to the national cause, Italian Americans quickly solved a seeming paradox. While they had earnestly reaffirmed their cultural roots, they had long before committed themselves and their futures to their newly adopted country. Thus, they dedicated themselves wholeheartedly to the war effort; Italian Americans represented the largest percentage of enlisted personnel at the onset of World War II. Nevertheless, for some the earlier political dalliances with Il Duce would exact a price. For those, particularly in Military District One, who had not completed the U.S. naturalization process, the months ahead would be filled with apprehension, confusion and fear.

The First Component of Alien Regulation: Detention

While the world and the nation had for some time anticipated the escalation of the war in Europe, events on December 7, 1941, stunned Americans. The ensuing state of war called for the rapid implementation of federal policies regulating resident aliens who were citizens of belligerent countries.

Federal plans for enemy alien detention had been drafted many months before the start of war. By the late 1930s, four cabinet offices were actively engaged in intelligence gathering, and after June 26, 1939, the FBI joined the efforts of the Office of Naval Intelligence and the G-2 Branch of the army in compiling lists of resident aliens considered dangerous. These names were subsequently collated by the Special Defense Unit (SDU) in the Justice Department into A, B, and C lists of those to be arrested immediately in the event of war and those to be placed under surveillance.

Individuals whose names were on the A list were considered dangerous because they were influential in their communities or their work could facilitate espionage activity. The second group was viewed as potentially dangerous, and the final, or C, group merited vigilant observation. The names on the lists, which included teachers, travel agents, and a variety of *prominenti* (community leaders) within the Italian community, had been gleaned in part from the columns of the ethnic community press, provided by informants, or drawn from membership lists of selected organizations. Particular attention was given to the members of the Italian media who were believed in some cases to have informal connections with the Italian Ministry of Popular Culture and to the staffs of the Italian-language schools which were directly administered by the Ministry of Education.[21] Unfortunately, by their own admission, agents were impeded in their compilations by their unfamiliarity with the language, culture, and organizational structure of the alien communities they were investigating.

On the afternoon of December 7, 1941, Edward Ennis, director of the Enemy Alien Control Unit of the Justice Department, undertook the first phase of the government's program to regulate enemy aliens, issuing the orders for summary apprehension of German, Italian, and Japanese aliens determined by the attorney general or the secretary of war to be dangerous to the public peace and safety of the United States. The legal justification for the action was cited as Section 21, Title 50 of the U.S. Code, as well as the Alien Enemies Act of 1798, as amended in 1918, which allowed the government to hold alien enemies and seize enemy property. Arrests began even before President Roosevelt had signed Proclamation 2525.[22]

On December 8, the day following the initial apprehension of enemy aliens, the *Los Angeles Times* reported that "a great manhunt" was underway in Southern California.[23] In theory, every enemy alien in the United States was subject to internment for the duration of the war, with no provision for legal appeal. Instead, only about 1,000 aliens were apprehended in the first twenty-four hours after the attack on Pearl Harbor, and 2,000 more by February 1942.[24] In that same twenty-four hours, 77 Italians were taken into custody.[25] On December 10, FBI Director J. Edgar Hoover reported that 147 Italians were among the 2,295 arrested nationwide.[26] However, these figures are not consistent with those issued on December 15, 1941, by William F. Kelly, Chief Supervisor of the Border Patrol, who reported 41 Italians arrested with warrant and an additional 85 arrested without warrant, totaling 126. A total of 48 aliens from the A and B lists were arrested in Los Angeles in the initial sweep, as the government implemented the first phase of its alien regulation program.[27]

Among the Southern Californians taken into custodial detention were radio broadcasters Filippo Fordelone and Giovanni Cardellini, and Secretary of the *Ex Combattenti* Spartaco Bonomi, who at one time had also served as president of the Italian Catholic Federation. Also arrested were the editor and assistant editor of *La Parola,* Dr. Giovanni Falasca and Capitano Zaccaria Lubrano. At least three of the detainees had no immediate families in the United States. Hence their apprehension went undetected and their disappearance remained unexplained as they failed to answer phone calls or appear at scheduled meetings. Friends reported that with the passage of time, the tires on their cars, left at curbside, gradually flattened from loss of air.

Families who had witnessed the arrests were confounded by the unfolding events as to the fate of their spouses, and particularly their own financial solvency, since detainees' assets had been frozen. Mrs. Fordelone, faced with caring for three young daughters without funds, repeated over and over again in her native dialect, as she methodically prepared tomato conserve, "*Mi mari, mi mari, dov e' mi mari.*" ("My husband, my husband, where is my husband?")[28] San Francisco attorney John Molinari described the parallel course of events in San Francisco as wives and mothers sought his assistance in securing the release of their loved ones....

The Los Angeles detainees were first taken to federal facilities on Terminal Island. While there, they were not formally charged; the only explanation given for their seizure was a prepared statement authorizing the apprehension of potentially dangerous alien enemies. Ultimately, each appeared before a three-person hearing board, without being advised of charges and without benefit of counsel.

While the government's position was legal, the accusations which caused individuals to be included on the "ABC lists" often consisted of no more than gossip or innuendo, allegations based on hearsay, and not uncommonly, vengeful accusations. In the estimation of most Italian Americans, those apprehended had not been disloyal to the United States. They viewed their relationship to the United States as a marriage of choice. This, however, did not in their minds negate their loyalty to Italy, their mother country, regardless of its current leadership. As a result, they expressed their pride in Italian accomplishments at public meetings and in print, while at the same time pledging their fealty to the United States. By January 30, 1942, 135 Italian aliens were held in Southern California camps, including one in Tujunga, as well as in the Santa Ana Jail and Camarillo State Hospital. Ultimately, female detainees were housed separately, some of them in six centers spread across the nation operated by the Sisters of the Good Shepherd.[29]

While the detainees were at Terminal Island, valuables, money, and identification were taken from them and they were officially registered. The accused were then assigned to barrack-like facilities under military guard. A few were released after preliminary hearings. On December 16, the fourteen remaining detainees from Los Angeles were transported to railway cars. The trip to their final destination, Fort Missoula, Montana, was spent in day cars with barred and darkened windows, under the watchful gaze of armed military personnel. On December 19, at 3:00 P.M., FBI agent Ed Kline reported by phone to William F. Kelly in Washington that he had arrived at Missoula at 2:45 P.M., where he delivered 364 Japanese and 25 Italians, and was continuing on to Fort Lincoln with 110 Germans. He added that the rail trip transporting the class A and B detainees had been uneventful. Although Fort Missoula was the initial destination, some of the internees, including 79 Italians from Peru, were rotated from one camp to another. As a result, Falasca and Lubrano of *La Parola* were first dispatched to Fort Lincoln, North Dakota, but were returned to Missoula on May 22, 1943.[30]

According to Lemuel Schofield, administrative assistant to U.S. Attorney General Francis Biddle, Fort Missoula had been in readiness to receive internees since April 1941. Kitchen appliances and bedding, including 3,800 sheets, had been requisitioned from other military bases. Medical supplies, some requisitioned from the Civilian Conservation Corps, included 250 sets of dentures, but initially, no X-ray equipment. An operating budget of $750,000 had been allocated, which, based upon the demographics of the anticipated detainees, included funds for burial expenses.[31]

The facility had been surrounded by twenty-four hundred feet of chain-link fence topped by barbed wire, anchored by guard towers, which were manned around the clock. Dominating the scene was a fifty-foot iron search-light tower. The fifty-five buildings within the enclosure included former CCC barracks, each accommodating forty men, which had been shipped from as far away as Alabama and the Pacific coast. In accordance with the guidelines established under the Geneva Convention governing the treatment of political internees during time of war, the government had provided a hospital, a school, a library, a theater, and a two-winged mess hall designed to provide meals for both the resident Japanese and Italians. Particularly impressive was the recreation hall built of lodgepole pine by the CCC, which seated over 800.[32]

The first residents at the commodious facility were the 125 Italians associated with the World's Fair, detained in May 1941, along with the seamen from the twenty-eight impounded ships and the entertainers from the Italian cruise ship *Il Conte Biancamano*. By the time Agent Ed Kline's charges arrived from Los Angeles, there were nearly 1,000 inmates at the camp.

Careful to observe the protocols of the Geneva Convention and inspections by the International Red Cross, and eager to assure reciprocal treatment for captured American nationals, officials had been attentive to making the camp comfortable and well supplied with library books and athletic equipment. There was even space for individual flower gardens, which the Southern California prisoners avidly cultivated. The food at Bella Vista, as the Italians named the facility, was more-than-adequate army issue, enhanced by familiar Italian breads. For their duty assignments the Italians had been given the bakery, while the Japanese had been dispatched to the laundry. On occasion, Fordelone, who had been assigned to kitchen duty, enhanced the daily diet with extra steaks he brought to the barracks to share with Falasca and Lubrano.[33]

There was a clearly established camp routine. Following a 6:00 A.M. reveille and roll call, detainees were assigned to camp maintenance projects. If the men provided any specialized services as carpenters or mechanics, they were paid eighty cents an hour.

According to Alfredo Cipoleto, the camp program also offered opportunities for musical entertainment, enhanced by the orchestra and entertainers from the impounded cruise ship. Missoula residents were permitted to attend for a small admission fee. The high quality of the performances, however, elicited protests from local musicians of Missoula who claimed the Italian prisoners represented unfair competition.[34] In due course the Italians also had cause to protest. On July 5, 1943, the musicians filed a formal complaint because they felt they had been misled into entertaining at an American patriotic holiday the day before.

Despite Geneva Convention stipulations which precluded labor by prisoners of war, accommodations were made to allow those detainees who wished to work for the Western Montana Beet Growers Association, which had requested approximately 1,850 workers to do so. At first, heavy security surrounded the transport of workers to the beet fields. But the degree of vigilance was gradually reduced, and policies were sufficiently relaxed to allow internees to serve on Forest Service crews, on the staff of St. Patrick's Hospital in Missoula, and even work on the Great Western Railroad and at the Garden City Floral Company in downtown Missoula.[35] By July 1, 1943, 800 of the 1,300 detainees, having received clearance from the FBI, were granted work paroles. Supervision was relaxed to the extent that Italian detainees were permitted to address service clubs in Coeur d'Alene, Sandpoint, Newport, and Priest River.

The diaries kept by Italian detainee spokesman First Captain Allesandro De Luca and his successor, Captain Paolo Stephano Saglietto, reveal that the routine included occasional highlights. The dreary routine at Fort Missoula was relieved by holiday celebrations, beginning with the first Christmas in camp in 1941, when a lottery was conducted in order to distribute one thousand gifts presented by the YMCA. Easter of 1943 was marked by religious observance and the pouring of glasses of wine from a supply sent the previous Christmas by the Italian Cruise Lines.[36]

Such festivities occurred against a background of stern surveillance as thirty-nine patrol inspectors observed from the towers, and officers within the camp censored mail, monitored for possible escapes, and maintained discipline, alert to such infractions as fermenting small amounts of raisins purloined from the larder to make wine. Given the surrounding wilderness and the snow-covered mountain ranges, the ratio of 53 enforcement officers to a maximum capacity 1,650 detainees was considered adequate. Sometimes, however, disputes called for armed response. On one occasion the melee between camp factions resulted in the hospitalization of five.[37]

Care in the camp hospital was one of the issues of contention, which resulted in appeals to the Spanish and Swiss embassies, who were responsible for enforcing the protocols of the Geneva Convention. Walter de Boury, first consul of the Swiss legation in Washington, D.C., representing the International Red Cross and the Geneva Convention, arrived at the camp on August 4, 1943. In the ensuing interviews some Italian seamen employed outside the camp expressed displeasure at paying a worker's tax, which, in their estimation, aided their nation's wartime adversary.[38]

The degree of conflict, frustration, and despair among the men was most apparent in the medical records, which reveal commitment to the state mental hospital of three inmates suffering deep depression. The records also revealed that cases of neurosis and neurogenic illnesses were increasing alarmingly. Such a condition plagued Aurelio Mariani, one of several suicides, who before plunging from the third story of the hospital wrote, "I kill myself because I am tired, tired of being closed in a cage..."[39]

In the meantime, the Italian community in Los Angeles observed in stunned silence. Not until January 23, 1942, after more than a month, did the Italian American press report the detention of Italian prisoners. The shocking news was announced in conjunction with the publication of a speech made by Attorney General Francis Biddle, who reported that three thousand arrests had occurred to date, and added that information about the detainees could be obtained at the nearest offices of the FBI or the Immigration and Naturalization Service. He explained that those arrested could send and receive letters, as well as visits from their families and from friends directly involved in their business affairs. In addition, detainees could also avail themselves of phone service. Biddle attempted to clarify the government's position by observing, "The enemy aliens will be held if and when their segregation is deemed necessary for the peace and security of the nation. Only when there is great reason to fear for the internal security of the nation, the enemy alien will remain interned for the duration of the war."[40]

To implement this policy, the attorney general announced the formation of Alien Enemy Hearing Boards, to be established in each federal judicial district, composed of three civilians in that locality. For those who had been detained, the boards could recommend unconditional release, release with parole, or detention for the duration of the war. Biddle outlined the following procedures:

> Each enemy alien may be accompanied to the hearing with a family member or a friend, but not an attorney, because hearing boards are not courts of justice and the United States has no constitutional obligation to provide recourse to the law in the cases of arrest of enemy aliens in time of war, and the procedures of boards are merely extensions of democratic principles....People brought before the board will be permitted the opportunity to present reasons for their release, including affidavits and testimonials....[41]

In Missoula, hearing boards consisted of local townsfolk, characterized by some of the detainees as inexperienced and prejudiced. Nevertheless, the prisoners appeared for interviews armed with affidavits and testimonials. In August 1942, Attorney General Biddle also allowed rehearings, by Special Hearing Boards, of those alien enemies whose cases deserved review, or about whom additional information was available.[42]

As a result of the work of the hearing boards, a number of enemy aliens were released. On June 5, 1942, the Los Angeles paper *L'Italo Americano* reported that of the 8,500 enemy aliens arrested, 2,548 cases had been heard to date. Among the Italians, 73 had been freed, while 91 were on parole and 113 remained detained, for they had "failed to prove beyond any doubt their loyalty to the United States."[43] By October 12, 1942, when Italian aliens were withdrawn from the enemies list, 228 remained in camps.[44]

By July 16, 1943, the procedures used to identify the detainees and those to be excluded from militarily sensitive areas were terminated. In a stinging letter to J. Edgar Hoover and the Special Defense Unit at the Justice Department, Attorney General Biddle directed that the keeping of detention lists on aliens was no longer necessary. He observed:

It is now clear to me the evidence used for the purpose of making these classifications was inadequate; the standards applied to the evidence for the purpose of making the classification were defective; and finally, the notion that it is possible to make a valid determination of how dangerous a person is…without reference to time, environment, and other relevant circumstances is impractical, unwise, and dangerous."[45]

Restricted Movement, Identification Certificates, Household Searches, and Curfews

While some enemy aliens were forced to endure custodial detention, those who remained at home were also affected by the national emergency as a result of the second and third components of the government's program to regulate resident enemy aliens. Italian noncitizens who remained in Southern California were subjected to restrictions on their movement, additional certification procedures, household searches for illegal contraband, and curfew restrictions.

The regulations were outlined by the U.S. attorney general in early January 1942. Enemy aliens were not to travel outside their immediate communities without first securing official permission. Additional authorization was required if such travel was to be undertaken by aircraft. Aliens were forbidden to enter strategic areas, including power stations, airports, docks, or elevated areas where they might send or receive signals. Furthermore, aliens were not to have in their possession, or on premises they owned or occupied, any weapons, explosives, photographic equipment, binoculars, or shortwave communication or signaling apparatus, including flashlights. Enemy aliens were not to possess any rendering or reproduction of military installations, or any written matter containing writing in invisible ink.[46]

The new rules created immediate confusion in Southern California. It was observed that residents of Los Angeles were allowed a wider range of movement than their friends and relatives in smaller towns like San Gabriel or Santa Monica. At the same time, enemy-alien residents of San Francisco were allowed to travel within a fifty-mile radius. It was also observed that the office of the U.S. attorney, which granted travel permits, was located in the federal building on Spring Street in Los Angeles, which was beyond the area in which suburbanites were permitted to travel.[47]

On January 14, 1942, Biddle introduced another element into the program of enemy-alien regulation. He announced a presidential order calling for the issuance of identification certificates bearing a likeness, fingerprint, and signature, which would be required of all enemy aliens fourteen years of age or older who had not received their final papers. Biddle explained that the requirement reinforced national security and protected loyal foreigners.

The registration issue was also addressed by Lieutenant General John L. DeWitt, commander of the Western Defense Command for the Fourth Army:

> I want to clarify that in no sense should the issuance of
> identification cards be construed as a second registration of the
> foreign-born population. We are fully satisfied with the results of
> the national registration of 1940. We consider this essential for
> the protection of enemy aliens and to obtain supplementary infor-
> mation from them and to provide them with identification cards.[48]

The January 23, 1942, issue of the local Italian newspaper, carrying news of the issuance of the certificates, also conveyed the intensifying war atmosphere. In addition to the headline bannering the alien registration to be held from February 2 to 7, there was another ominous one announcing "300,000 Japanese Against the Limited Forces of General MacArthur," portending the fall of Corregidor, an event which would heighten further the fears of a Japanese attack on the Pacific coast. Indeed, the wartime mood permeated the paper.[49] The writer of the column *"La Cronica di San Pedro"* likened the war to the Battle of Lepanto and urged prayer, while William G. Bonelli, member of the State Equalization Board, reported that at a meeting on January 20 the board had refused license applications of five Japanese and one Italian, suggesting that enemy aliens should not attempt to apply for liquor licenses in California for the duration of the war.

The following week another local Italian newspaper carried detailed instructions for registration, in the form of a series of questions and answers prepared by immigration attorney F. M. Andreani. In addition to routine information, he pointed out that applicants would be required to answer fourteen questions soliciting such information as the names and addresses of all relatives residing outside the United States, as well as all organizational affiliations during the past five years. If respondents had been residents of this country for less than five years, they would be required to list former places of residence, and all former political party affiliations. They were also required to present receipts as evidence of their August 1940 alien registration.

Despite wartime difficulties, including the effects of enemy-alien regulation, routine events continued to absorb the attention of the local Italian community. Accompanying reports of the expected arrival of the San Carlo Opera Company, there were relieved assurances that the Garibaldina Society, having acquired blackout curtains, would proceed with plans for its annual Valentine's Day dance. Advertisements for citizenship schools increased to three, and one entrepreneur, demonstrating that it is an ill wind indeed that doesn't blow some good, offered three passport photos, suitable for the soon-to-be-required registration cards, for seventy-five cents.[50]

In the first two days of filing, 6,800 grim-faced enemy aliens stood three and four across in a block-long line which circled the county offices at East 22nd and South San Pedro Streets, the registration site for all Los Angeles County residents with the exception of those living at great distances. Because of the numbers and the burden on the 160 clerks, the filing period for photo identity cards was extended two days, through Monday, February 9.[51]

At the same time it was dispensing information about the required registration, the Justice Department continued to urge enemy aliens to turn in all contraband items. Although the January 30 deadline had passed, they were still being directed to turn in those items listed in section 5 of the presidential proclamation of December 7, 1941. As encouragements, the aliens were assured that U.S. marshals would provide an inventory of all that had been consigned to them and would keep the enumerated articles on deposit for the duration. In the interim, it was promised that radios would be returned once their shortwave capabilities had been removed. Furthermore, it was announced that application could be made to the attorney general for the return of such items as antique muskets and ceremonial swords. Finally, photographers and other professionals needing their equipment for business purposes could contact the FBI, which would conduct an examination of each applicant's professional records to determine if equipment could be released.[52]

Strongly suspecting the presence of potential saboteurs among the enemy aliens, the unrelenting Lieutenant General DeWitt prevailed upon the Justice Department to issue special search warrants allowing access to residences and other premises owned and/or occupied by enemy aliens. In response, on January 1, 1942, the FBI telegraphed four forms to be used as executive search warrants. DeWitt's staff was also directed to examine bank records for evidence of any suspicious financial contributions.

The implementation of the special warrant program, soon authorized in most of the states and territories, was outlined in the FBI's Bureau Bulletin No. 2, First Series, 1942. In a supplementary memo issued on February 25, J. Edgar Hoover advised divisions that they were being held responsible for local infractions of section 5 of the presidential proclamation forbidding enemy-alien possession of contraband items. He urged them to use all resources, including game commissions and related agencies, in gathering data. He also urged multiple spot searches on succeeding days, particularly in the vicinity of military and naval installations and war industries, as well as other areas where recently collected registration data revealed a concentration of enemy aliens. Hoover added that simultaneous spot searches were to be developed with the cooperation of appropriate U.S. attorneys and were to be followed with reports to the FBI offices in Washington of the numbers of enemy aliens apprehended and the enumerated articles, including binoculars and flashlights, which had been confiscated.[53]

In the wake of the investigations, *L'Italo Americano* reported: "In recent days numerous homes of enemy aliens in the harbor area have been searched by FBI agents and it was announced that a considerable amount of contraband material was found." While expressing the hope that no Italians were guilty, the editors noted that they had repeatedly advised Italians about the dangers of keeping contraband items, explaining that, "It doesn't matter if this enemy alien is the mother or father of one of the citizens in the family. In that home, as long as an enemy alien resides there, no one can possess enumerated articles."[54]

The bureau chief of the FBI office in Los Angeles advised, after the San Pedro raid, that while no one was arrested, "such action will be taken against those who will be found in possession of interdicted items." He added, "We will consider it our duty to sequester and punish the transgressors."[55] Indeed, Giuseppe Guarini of San Francisco was arrested on April 9, 1942, when it was discovered that he possessed a rifle.

In a memo from Edward Ennis to Lemuel Schofield dated May 27, 1942, Ennis warned: "… all persons, aliens or citizens, believed to be dangerous by the War Department are to be detained on whatever grounds possible. Possibly hundreds of persons will be apprehended for violations of regulations beginning tonight, and not immediately released."[56] However, two female curfew violators apprehended in Los Angeles on June 4, 1942, were ordered released the next day. Between June 4 and 10, eight more were arrested. According to DeWitt, those arrested for curfew or contraband violations should not be released until consultation with appropriate military authorities. They could, however, be retained in their localities and need not be sent to camps at Missoula, Bismarck, or Santa Fe.[57]

In another series of sweeps which included the home of Luigi Franceschini, former president of the disbanded *Ex Combattenti*, agents searched from attic to basement several times. The investigation yielded only a table-model radio having a shortwave band, which belonged to his teenage daughter, Velma. The cause of the search was not Franceschini; he and his wife were citizens, but his aged noncitizen in-laws lived with them. Later, when the family recalled a carton of long-forgotten *Dopo Scuola* textbooks in the basement, they immediately consigned them to a backyard bonfire.[58]

In one of the FBI's frequent visits to the home of Italian alien writer and community activist Maria Ricci, a shortwave capacity of which no one in the family had been aware was detected in the deluxe floor-model Philco radio. Even greater concerns were raised by the revolvers in the possession of Mrs. Ricci's husband, Leo, a deputy sheriff and U.S. citizen for over twenty-five years. Ricci, a World War I veteran and founding member of the Dante Post of the American Legion, had concluded that his personal record exempted him from the enemy-alien household status. Some time would pass, however, before his revolvers were returned. In the meantime, Maria Ricci, a prolific writer of political satire as well as poetry, was directed to compile all her work for official translation by someone to be selected by the FBI. In addition, for the next ten months she and her family were visited at least once a month by FBI agents. To everyone's relief, no subversive activity was ever detected.[59]

The actions of the FBI were driven largely by Lieutenant General DeWitt's single-minded concern about enemy aliens as potential saboteurs and by a ground swell of public reaction against enemy aliens along the West Coast.

United States defeats in the Pacific in the early months of the war raised the issue of vulnerability along the coast. Indeed, on December 20, 1941, near Crescent City, the tanker SS *Emedio* became the first United States vessel sunk within coastal waters in World War II. On December 23 a Japanese submarine torpedoed the Union Oil Company tanker *Montebello* near Estero Bay. The next day the U.S. lumber carrier SS *Absaroka* was torpedoed off the coast near Los Angeles, resulting in the death of one crewman.[60] The shelling of the wharf at Goleta by an enemy sea-borne craft on February 23, 1942, while President

Roosevelt was delivering a fireside chat on nationwide radio, and the Los Angeles blackout and artillery response, possibly activated by unidentified planes in the early hours of February 25, heightened these concerns.[61]

Columnist Walter Lippmann was among those who warned of an imminent attack aided and abetted by a fifth column, adding, "The enemy-alien problem on the Pacific coast, or more accurately the fifth-column problem, is very serious and it is very special....The Pacific coast is in imminent danger of a combined attack from within and from without." To reduce this danger Lippmann urged that the nation forget about "...enemy aliens, dual citizenship, naturalized citizens, native citizens of alien parentage...and consider instead [the threat to] an airplane plant in Los Angeles." He concluded with a recommendation that the federal government should undertake a mass evacuation and internment "of all those who are technically enemy aliens."[62]

Lippmann's was but one voice in a rising chorus. On February 11, 1942, the Los Angeles County Defense Council approved a resolution calling for the evacuation to working internment areas of all able-bodied enemy-alien males.[63] On February 11, the Los Angeles County Board of Supervisors led the way in approving a resolution, the draft of which had been circulated at a statewide meeting of county supervisors, that urged the evacuation of all enemy aliens. More than a week earlier, while urging the passage of the resolution, Supervisor William A. Smith observed that this was the only nation where enemy aliens enjoyed such freedom, a condition which should be remedied by internment. Also on February 11, the Colton Chamber of Commerce called for the evacuation of enemy aliens and all others sympathetic to the enemy nations. Draconian as it may now seem, the resolution was less sweeping than that adopted by the Orange County grand jury on February 2, which called for the removal from the county of Orange of all enemy aliens, their children, and all those of enemy alien extraction. The following day the Orange County board of supervisors reiterated the request.

California Attorney General Earl Warren, at a conference of sheriffs and district attorneys, warned that the nation was at war with Axis powers whose activities included organized infiltration and sabotage. He followed with a letter on February 18 polling the law enforcement officials with regard to the enemy-alien situation. Twenty-eight of the 118 responding felt that all enemy aliens should be treated the same. However, J. C. Gregory, chief of police in Fullerton, felt that not only had the Japanese been more cooperative than either the Germans or Italians, but also that they were more readily identified, and therefore, their internment was not as urgent. On the other hand, the Huntington Park chief of police urged that all enemy aliens be moved inland and added that descendents of enemy aliens should be regularly investigated.[64]

Organizations also took positions on the issue of alien internment. On January 29 the 22nd district of the Native Sons of the Golden West asked for the summary arrest and internment of all aliens on the Pacific coast. On February 19 the American Legion adopted a statewide resolution stating that Axis agents and aliens, along with sympathizers, should be removed from California. As federal officials became increasingly apprehensive about possible violent confrontations between factions in Southern California, assertions escalated. Los Angeles was described as a center of enemy-alien activity and the second most dangerous area in the state.

Los Angeles Mayor Fletcher Bowron, in a February 5 radio broadcast on KECA, alleged that there were among the local enemy-alien population some who were bent on treason. He added that Los Angeles had become "the hotbed, the nerve center of the spy system, of planning for sabotage."[65] Some days later he added that it was the offspring of the German and Italian enemy aliens who posed the greater threat to the security of the nation in time of war. On December 8, 1941, while assuring Angelenos that no enemy bombing was expected, Bowron advised that if it occurred, citizens should not be on the streets or in their automobiles.[66]

Adding to this climate of heightening ethnic tension, the Los Angeles Council of California Women's Clubs recommended that all enemy aliens be immediately placed in concentration camps. These sentiments were echoed by the Young Democratic Club of Los Angeles, which approved a resolution also calling for the West Coast evacuation of Germans, Japanese, and Italians born in the United States.[67]

A memo from a committee of California church leaders headed by Galen M. Fisher, president of the board of trustees of the Pacific School of Religion, cautioned Colonel W. L. Magill, provost marshal and director of evacuation:

> We believe that a mass evacuation of women, children, and aged
> is not necessary except in Class A military zones. It is of course
> possible for the army to place the 115,000 Italian, 72,000
> German, and 33,000 Japanese aliens in California on trains and
> transport them to a distant place, but the care of the many elderly
> people would be very difficult, if they were uprooted.[68]

There were a few who expressed opposition to the potential suspension of civil rights. Among them was Ruth Benedict, chair of the legislative committee of the Los Angeles branch of the Women's International League for Peace and Freedom, who wrote to President Roosevelt commending Congressman John H. Tolan of Oakland, who headed the House Select Committee Investigating

National Defense. She warned, however, that private economic interests as well as growing hysteria could result in alien policies which could create economic problems, as well as long-term resentment.[69]

Despite this warning and the detainment of the potential subversives on the A, B, and C lists, the heated public debate hastened the government's formulation of the third component of its enemy-alien program, a plan of evacuation, relocation, and internment. Its implementation would reveal differences between Lieutenant General DeWitt and the Department of Justice. These disagreements would result in an uneven and sporadic enforcement of the plan. It would fall heavily on West Coast Japanese aliens and affect Italians and Germans to a much lesser degree.

Before turning to an examination of the halting implementation of the third component of alien regulation, it is important to take note of the economic effects on alien lives that can be traced to war fever in general but are often directly attributable to the regulations already discussed. Despite the fact that the War Department and the Navy Department had approved ninety-nine percent of the aliens' requests to work on government contracts, and despite Attorney General Biddle's warning that job discrimination would deprive the United States of a valuable labor resource, enemy aliens were reporting a high incidence of job discrimination. On January 9 Biddle again declared that the exclusion of aliens from private employment is "a most effective method to create disunion and to break faith with a people who came seeking liberty and equity." Citing numerous cases where workers had been dismissed simply because of their foreign names, he observed that such policies were shortsighted, wasteful, and unmindful of the fact that sons of these dismissed workers were serving in the cause of national defense. He characterized such action as "a complete rejection of our American institutions and principles upon which our democracy is founded." He also publicly challenged the board of trustees' decision to bar enemy aliens from the University of Missouri as being inconsistent with federal policy.[70]

In an open letter to Alien Control Coordinator Tom Clark published by the local press, attorney and community leader F. M. Andreani provided specific examples of employment discrimination. "They are not only being discharged wholesale as wage earners, but their relatives, native-born young men, armed with birth certificates, cannot approach an employment office window...for consideration because such applications bear Italian names."[71]

Andreani's complaints were directed to both the private and public sectors. Despite the admonitions from Attorney General Biddle, and overriding the official dissent of California Attorney General Warren, even the California State Personnel Board, on February 1, 1942, issued a directive barring descendants of enemy aliens from civil service positions. To assure this exclusion, state employment applications issued pursuant to a state senate concurrent resolution reflected an added degree of vigilance, requesting a vast amount of information including the names of physicians or midwives in attendance at birth. If applicants were foreign-born, they were asked to supply information about the reasons, condition, and mode of their entry into the United States.[72] Even Italians who were naturalized citizens employed by such public agencies as the United States Post Office were personally questioned by their superiors about their entry and citizenship status.[73]

Despite calls for moderation issued by the president and by the Justice Department, members of the California congressional delegation lobbied for the removal of all aliens from the coastal zone. With the added support of representatives from the other Pacific states, they called upon the president to order a mass evacuation of all enemy aliens.[74]

The Joint Fact-Finding Committee on Un-American Activities in California, which held sixteen of its thirty days of hearings in Los Angeles, also ignored the admonitions for moderation. In its final recommendations, presaging a disdain for civil rights which would be a hallmark of the McCarthy era, it urged that members of un-American and subversive groups should have professional licenses revoked and be ousted from civil service positions. Furthermore, if they were aliens, it was recommended that the suspected subversives should be prohibited from holding any official positions in labor unions and, if they were naturalized, their citizenship should be revoked. In addition, the committee recommended that there be close supervision and censorship of the foreign press.[75]

In San Francisco hearings, there were also attacks against enemy aliens from the Italian community, generated by such antifascists as A. M. Cogliandro, the mysterious Mr. X-2, who in one executive session categorically condemned the *Dopo Scuola* program. Another witness was Carmelo Zito, editor of *Il Corriere del Popolo*, who in testimony before the Joint Fact-Finding Committee lashed out at longtime adversaries. Under oath, Zito attacked as Fascist sympathizers San Francisco Mayor Angelo Rossi, the Italian Chamber of Commerce, and the Bank of America. In testimony he accused Los Angeles residents Giovanni Cardellini and Luigi Colombo of Fascist affiliations, despite the fact that FBI files listed Giovanni Valperga as the only member of the Fascist Party in Los Angeles. He also claimed Falasca's Los Angeles paper, *La Parola*, was definitely profascist, although, in point of fact, Falasca had fled Italy in protest against Mussolini.[76] As a result of this testimony, exclusion orders were issued to twenty men and women, all naturalized American citizens, requiring them to leave Military District One within ten days.[77]

Barracks at Fort Missoula, Montana, during World War II. Courtesy of National Japanese American Historical Society

Members of the antifascist Mazzini Society also became involved in the debate. Amerigo Bozzani, a successful Los Angeles businessman and a leader in Southern California Democratic politics, tried to persuade Maria Ricci to participate in international broadcasts urging the Italian people to support the resistance movement. The young writer, who in the late 1930s had been approached for support by Fascist operatives in the offices of Vice Consul Ernesto Arrighi, noted the irony of these two conflicting appeals. Since she was currently under regular surveillance by the FBI, she chose to decline the invitation and continue to maintain a low profile.[78]

In the midst of these heated debates, the Italian American population faced a series of vexing problems. Mail service to loved ones in Italy had been interrupted by the war. On January 16, federal censor Byron Price prohibited any postal communication, with the exception of that transmitted by the Red Cross, with residents of any areas occupied by the enemy. The Red Cross had been authorized to make available RC forms, on which correspondents could write no more than twenty-five words in English, with no mention of defense employment, with no codes or abbreviations used. Nothing was to be conveyed regarding politics, weather conditions, ship departures, military matters, or geographic descriptions. Despite the philanthropic assistance of the Red Cross, Italian nationals still had to contend with the impossible difficulties in transmitting funds to families in Italy for whom they were often the sole source of support.[79]

An outgrowth of these legal complications confronting enemy aliens was a victory in court by California Attorney General Earl Warren regarding aliens whose estates had been bequeathed to persons in Italy. Warren argued, successfully, that since no reciprocal agreements existed with that nation after July 1, 1941, when there were no heirs within the United States, estates should pass to the particular state within the U.S. where the deceased had resided.[80]

Evacuation and Internment

While seemingly arcane legal issues were being decided by the courts, enemy aliens were informed of the third component of the government's enemy-alien regulation policy: their restriction from designated geographic zones and their relocation and possible internment. On the evening of January 29, Attorney General Biddle ordered all German, Italian, and Japanese enemy aliens to vacate, by February 24, certain areas in California, specifically in the Bay Area and Los Angeles, promising that additional restricted areas would soon be announced....In Los Angeles, the initial restricted zone was the coastal area extending from the intersection of Sepulveda Boulevard and Rosecrans Avenue to Western Avenue and north to Manchester Avenue.[81]

Reminding its readers that California was not only a war zone, but also an essential war industry area, on February 6 L'Italo Americano explained that newly restricted areas too numerous to list had been designated. Enemy aliens were requested to vacate by February 15 all areas around oil fields, aircraft plants, munitions factories, hydroelectric installations, and other areas where there would be posters listing evacuation procedures. It was added that additional restricted areas would be announced on February 24.[82]

On Sunday, February 1, the Los Angeles Times reported that Germans, Italians, and Japanese would be barred from sixty-nine war zones in the state, but noted that to date there had been few indications of alien departures from the coastal area. The article concluded with assurances from Tom Clark, the newly appointed alien control coordinator, who warned that aliens who had not voluntarily left by the deadline would be ejected under whatever procedure was necessary. Three days later, in an article describing farm colonies to be set up for the enemy nationals who were being evicted, the *Times* reminded read-ers that, in the process of enemy-alien evacuation, "the aged and infirm will not be permitted to remain with naturalized sons and daughters in such areas."[83]

By February 13, posters listing evacuation instructions, printed in English, German, Italian, and Japanese, appeared in seventeen localities around Los Angeles County. Enemy aliens were informed that within two days, on February 15, they were to vacate such areas as West Hollywood, sections of Santa Monica, Huntington Park, Burbank, Inglewood, Long Beach, Downey, Vernon, central Los Angeles, and south central Los Angeles, among others. The prohibited list also included the various pumping stations operated by the Metropolitan Water District. Aliens were informed that service committees had been established by the Social Security Administration offices at 623 East 8th Street and 435 South Boyle Avenue for those seeking assistance and clarification. In the face of these new proposed evacuations *L'Italo Americano* continued to advise patience, explaining that since Los Angeles was an impor-tant military and industrial area, the government was forced "to adopt policies more stringent than those adopted in other states of the Union."[84]

The enforcement of the evacuation order was sporadic. It was compre-hensive at Terminal Island and in Northern California coastal communities. In other areas regulations were not invoked, creating both confusion and relief among the alien residents, who now focused on a new concern.

Beginning in January, rumors had circulated concerning the extension of the curfew that had been imposed in Northern California. The curfew soon reached as far south as Santa Maria, and on March 24, 1942, it was applied to enemy aliens remaining in Southern California. Regulations stipulated that enemy aliens could travel any required distance back and forth to work but were required to be in their homes from 8 P.M. to 6 A.M. No exceptions would be permitted to those with nighttime employment. Finally, when not working, enemy aliens could not travel more than five miles from their homes.[85]

Perhaps because the government's orders for evacuation and relocation had thus far been generally unenforced in Southern California, many southland enemy aliens at first honored the curfew in the breach. The casual observance of the curfew invited a brisk warning from Attorney General Biddle, contained in a telegram directed to U.S. Attorney William Fleet Palmer in Los Angeles. Biddle's message was to the point: "All enemy aliens arrested for violating regu-lations issued by the president regarding contraband material or military regula-tions regarding the curfew will be placed in confinement and not released."[86]

The press continued to carry warnings about the importance of observ-ing the curfew. On June 5, *L'Italo Americano* added, along with the warning that those arrested would not be released, the news that the newly appointed government hearing officer was a member of the Italian American community, Assistant U.S. Attorney Attillio Di Girolamo. The appointment was auspicious in light of the sweeps by the FBI and local police and sheriffs which occurred in the middle of June. They resulted in the apprehension of 45 and the eventual arrest of 25.

Newspaper editor Cleto Baroni took the opportunity to remind readers that, although by June 6 only the Japanese had been evacuated and interned, in his opinion Executive Order 9066 was not specific to the Japanese, adding: "Keep always in mind that the order to evacuate enemy aliens from California was not abrogated after the evacuation of the Japanese...if the authorities see Italians and Germans do not observe the law, they could order their exodus as well."[87]

The raids, which continued through June and often included several consecutive visits to the same home, were usually conducted in the dead of night. The practice elicited the only expression of impatience found in the pages of *L'Italo Americano* during these difficult times. The practice of nocturnal visits provoked the editor to observe, "It does not seem logical or humane that for a simple verification it is necessary to waken and frighten people in the middle of the night."[88]

Although enemy-alien Italians had been subjected to many restrictions and limitations, most of them in Southern California escaped the evacuation and internment that had been imposed on their confreres in Northern California and on the Japanese. The vacillation regarding orders for evacuation from restricted districts was the result of conflicting opinions regarding strategy. During the first two months of war, the Western Defense Command had determined that it was essential to remove all enemy aliens from sensitive areas along the Pacific coast. When Executive Order 9066 was drafted in early February it was still understood that all enemy aliens would be evacuated.

As noted earlier, the calls for removal were echoed in numerous resolutions approved by local governmental agencies and organizations. Alien exclusion was also supported by the Congressional Committee on Handling Enemy Aliens on the West Coast, which at the behest of the California delegation urged the War Department to assume responsibility "to effectuate the evacuation, resettlement, or internment of enemy aliens and of United States citizens holding dual citizenship with enemy nations."[89]

Although encouraged by widespread calls for wholesale internment, Lieutenant General DeWitt was also receiving an increasing number of indications of insufficient personnel and organization to move the 85,000 German and Italian aliens. He was also confronted with the continuing resistance of the Justice Department and the president to full-scale evacuation. As a result of these factors, by March 24 DeWitt was finally persuaded that the strategy of full-scale evacuation, relocation, and internment was not feasible in Military District One. By April he conceded to the Department of Justice that there would be no mass evacuation of Germans and Italians. He agreed that severe restrictions on travel and a curfew had already imposed sufficient regulation. Furthermore, there was a growing acceptance of the fact that there was slight prospect of an Italian or German attack along the Pacific coast.[90]

By August, DeWitt was under the impression that the Department of Justice had agreed to an alternative procedure in which the majority of aliens would be saved from exclusion through broad categorical exemptions. The possible security risks, amounting to 25,000 names compiled by security agencies, would be reviewed by hearing boards, who, after reviewing files and interrogating subpoenaed suspects, would submit recommendations regarding possible exclusion from Military District One to officials of the Western Defense Command.[91] The procedure was soon repudiated by Attorney General Biddle in a memo issued in September 1943....

The utilization of hearing boards had been proposed in the first report of the House Committee Investigating National Defense Migration. As early as February 28, in a telegram to Attorney General Biddle, Congressman John H. Tolan of California, chairman of the committee, had advised the formation of hearing boards to examine the loyalty of German and Italian aliens. In its fourth report, the committee also raised questions about the logistical burden of a massive internment process which had already removed an entire Japanese community from the population:

> This is in the nature of an exodus of a people. The numbers
> involved are large, but they are by no means as large, for the
> whole country, as those who will be involved if we generalize the
> current treatment of the Japanese to apply to all Axis aliens and
> their immediate families. Indeed this committee is prepared to say
> that any such proposal is out of the question if we intend to win
> the war.[92]

In a press conference held in early June, Tolan had received sufficient assurances from the government to declare confidently that the War Department did not contemplate any additional mass evacuation of aliens from the Pacific coast.[93] The committee had helped convince the government that to move the 85,000 German and Italian aliens in the three coastal states, who had an average age of sixty and an average length of residence of twenty-four years, was impractical. Furthermore, it was pointed out that such a move would also dislocate members of their families, requiring, as a result, the actual movement of 145,000 people.[94]

Federal policy was also being shaped by political realities, not the least of which was the fact that Roosevelt's earlier election victories had been strongly supported in eastern urban states where Italian Americans were most heavily concentrated.[95] It was a fact which the Italian political community and labor unions did not allow to be overlooked. The administration was also concerned about the morale implications of Italian alien internment upon relatives in military service, since a large percentage of the military were Italians or had one or more parents who were Italian.[96]

The composition of the enemy-alien community was also a factor. Nationwide, the average age of Italians was forty-four; ten percent were over sixty-four years of age. Furthermore, it was generally accepted that their failure to file for U.S. citizenship grew not from disloyalty, but from educational impediments and long traditions of regional rather than national allegiance. The alien German community presented its own complexities. The West Coast population, which had burgeoned to over 60,000 during World War II, included approximately 20,000 refugees from Nazi Germany. Clearly, the enemy-alien classification did not apply to these new American residents.[97]

The exemption of most Italians and Germans from the third phase of the government's enemy-alien regulation program, consisting of evacuation, relocation, and internment, was in part also the result of racial bias. This became clear in policy statements made by the attorney general and the president. In a memo dated April 17, 1943, for the president in which Biddle strongly opposed Lieutenant General DeWitt's efforts to initiate exclusionary proceedings against Sylvester Andriano of San Francisco, the attorney general reminded the president, "You signed the original executive order permitting the exclusion so the army could handle the Japs. It was never intended to apply to Italians and Germans."[98] The position was reiterated by Roosevelt in a letter to Governor Herbert H. Lehman of New York on June 3, 1943, in which the president assured him that "no collective evacuation of German and Italian aliens is contemplated at this time."[99]

Increasing support for designating Italians as non-dangerous aliens met with some opposition in the War Department, where it was argued that such a designation would embolden Italian operatives working under German direction, and also "create bitter resentment within the antifascist Communist Party, as well as the Soviet government."[100]

Nevertheless, policies were relaxed. In May the Italian press heralded the Second War Powers Act, in which the administration simplified citizenship procedures for foreign-born soldiers in the United States military, waiving the residence, language, and literacy requirements. Later that same month it was announced that male enemy aliens, with or without first papers, were being reclassified from IV-C to a military service classification.[101] In July, another presidential order, urged by the Sons of Italy, embraced all enemy aliens who had served in the armed forces, all those with continued residence in the United States since 1916, all those married to U.S. citizens who had not returned to their homelands since 1924, and all those who had applied for their first papers before December 7, 1941.[102]

Within months the policy of exclusion was terminated and the release of interned Italian aliens soon followed, hastened by Italy's realignment as an ally of the United States. In an effort to make amends for the disruptions which had occurred, the U.S. government offered to subsidize the detainees' return to private life. Falasca, released November 16, 1943, had lost his newspaper. He was now offered a a government subsidy to launch a literary magazine, an invitation the disenchanted newsman declined.[103]

In June 1942, Biddle proposed to the president an idea originally advanced by Edward Ennis, head of the Enemy Alien Control Unit, to completely remove Italians from the enemy-alien category. Roosevelt welcomed it as good statesmanship and politics and regretted that he had not come up with the idea himself.[104]

On October 12, Columbus Day, Attorney General Biddle was introduced to a Carnegie Hall audience by Mayor Fiorello La Guardia to make his announcement, which was broadcast throughout the United States, Latin America, and Europe. Biddle began by praising those of the "free Italy of the people," the land from which came "Dante, who ripped through the fog of antiquity, Galileo, navigator among the stars...Leonardo da Vinci, Michelangelo, Tasso, and Ariosto." He continued, "When America was forging independence, Italian patriots were also calling for it, and Leopardi was praising it in poetry."

Following his fulsome praise of the Italian cultural heritage, the attorney general addressed the current state of affairs. He announced that after ten months of surveillance, "We found that 600,000 enemy aliens were in fact not enemies." As a result, he offered as the highlight of his message the announcement that from October 19, Italians would no longer be classified as enemy aliens in the United States. The news was carried in a banner headline in *L'Italo Americano*, "*Non Piu'—Nemici—!*" (No Longer Enemies!).[105] Italians were no longer unwelcome citizens in freedom's land!

Endnotes:
1. "Ninety Percent of Enemy Aliens Live in Eleven States," *L'Italo Americano*, March 2, 1942, p. 2.
2. For a fuller discussion of the role of Italian Americans in U.S. politics, see Philip V. Cannistraro, "Generoso Pope and the Rise of Italian American Politics, 1925–1936," in *Italian Americans: New Perspectives in Italian Immigration and Ethnicity*, edited by Lydio Tomasi (New York: Center for Migration Studies of New York, Inc., 1983), pp. 264–285.
3. *L'Italo Americano*, March 2, 1942, p. 2.
4. "Italy's War of Nerves in America," *Fortune*, 22 (November 1940): 85–86.
5. John Patrick Diggins, *Mussolini and Fascism: The View From America* (Princeton, N.J.: Princeton University Press, 1972), p. 72. See also Gloria Ricci Lothrop, "Shadow on the Land: Italians in Southern California in the 1930s," *California History*, 75 (Winter 1996–97): 338–353, 385–387
6. Ibid., p. 279.
7. Arthur Schlessinger, *The Politics of Upheaval* (Boston: Houghton Mifflin, 1960), p. 648.
8. Interview with Peter Bonino, Glendale, California, July 14, 1991; *Los Angeles Times*, September 14, 1937, p. 8.
9. Dale Kramer, "The American Fascists," *Harper's*, 170 (September 1940): 380–393. See also Morris Schoenbach, *Native American Fascism During the 1930s and 1940s: A Study of Its Roots and Its Decline* (Hamden, Conn.: Garland Press, 1990).
10. Constantine Panunzio, "Italian Americans, Fascism and the War," *Yale Review*, 31 (June 1942): 771–782; Givacchino Panettoni, "Professionisti Italiani e Funzionari Publici Italo Americani in California" [Italian American Professionals and Public Officials in California] (Sacramento: n.p., 1935); Alan Cassels, "Fascism for Export: Italy and the United States in the 1920s," *American Historical Review*, 69 (April 1964): 702–712. Important insights into the effects of Fascism upon Italian Americans is provided in Philip V. Cannistraro, *Blackshirts in Little Italy: Italian Americans and Fascism 1921–1929* (Lafayette, In.: Bordigliera, Inc., 1999).
11. Interview with Charles Highham, Los Angeles, California, June 27, 1991. Criticism of Vittorio Mussolini appearing in the Hollywood trade papers evoked a spirited response in letters of support published in *La Parola* of Los Angeles, October 20, 1937, p. 2. See also Marcus Duffield, "Mussolini's American Empire: The Fascist Invasion of the United States," *Harper's*, 159 (November 1929): 24–33.
12. Brice Harris, *The United States and the Italo-Ethiopian Crisis* (Stanford, Calif.: Stanford University Press, 1964), p. 139.
13. Record Group BB IIC, File 1434, Community Relations Committee Papers, Los Angeles Jewish Federation collection, Los Angeles Urban Archives, California State University, Northridge. (Hereafter cited as CRC.)
14. *Los Angeles Daily News*, October 28, 1938.
15. *La Parola di New York*, November 29, 1941, pp. 1–3. For a discussion of the Fascist and antifascist debate in the Italian press, see Andrew Canepa, "Profile of Italian-language Freemasons in California (1871–1966)," *Studi Emigrazione* XXVII (March 1990): 87–107; James Bruce, "California Gets Tough: Mood of the State as War Draws Closer," *New York Times*, March 6, 1942, M3–4.
16. Record Group 2B IIC, #7641, CRC.
17. Interview with Maria Ricci, La Verne, California, July 7, 1991.
18. Record Group 85, Entry 282, Box 1, File 4250, National Archives, Washington D.C. See also Carol Van Valkenburg, *An Alien Place: The Fort Missoula Detention Camp 1941–1944* (Missoula, Mont.: Pictorial Histories Publishing Co., Inc. 1995). Though the overall interpretation is deeply flawed, the account provides useful details about the camp.
19. Letter from Spartaco Bonomi, secretary of the Italian Catholic Federation, Los Angeles, to Maria Ricci, February 7, 1941. In the author's possession.
20. "Attorney General Affirms that the Recent Arrests of Aliens Should Not Cause Anxiety Among Foreigners," *L'Italo Americano* June 6, 1942, p. 1. See also "Alien Mop Up: Drive on Spy Subjects Pushed: Expelled Subjects to Sail Soon," *Newsweek* (July 14, 1941): 16; John Norman, "Repudiation of Fascism by the Italian Press," *Journalism Quarterly*, 20 (March

1944): 2; "Italo-Americans and World War II," *Sociology and Social Research*, 29 (July–August 1945): 470–471.

21. Dale Kramer, "The American Fascists," *Harper's*, 170 (September 1940): 380–393; Ralph T. Tucker, "Tools of Mussolini in America," *New Republic*, 52 (September 14, 1927): 89–91; Raymond Moley and Charles Jedel, "About the Aliens in Our Midst," *American Mercury*, 53 (October 6, 1941): 481–486; Among the organizations under scrutiny were the Sons of Italy, American Italian Sports League of the U.S., Council of Marconi, Dante Alighieri Society, Federation of Italian War Veterans, and the National United Italian Association. "Schematic Chart of Italian and Italian American Organizations. Supplemental Report, Western Defense Command and Fourth Army Western Civil Control," (Declassified), n.d., Italian American Collection, the Immigrant Research Center, University of Minnesota, St. Paul.

22. Randolph Boehm, ed., *Papers of the U.S. Commission on Wartime Relocation and Internment of Civilians* (Fredericksburg, Md.: Government Printing Office, 1984), 9:10378 (hereafter cited as CWRIC). "Rules for Apprehension for Those on 'A' List," Record Group 85, Access 85–58A734, Box 1765, File 560351, National Archives, Washington, D.C. Between December 7, 1941, and June 30, 1945, 6 Italians had been apprehended in San Diego, 458 in San Francisco, and 142 in Los Angeles. Similar sweeps occurred simultaneously in Latin America and Canada. Early in 1942, 2,364 aliens from Axis countries residing in Latin America were interned in INS centers, including Crystal City, Texas, and Ellis Island. CWRIC, p. 308. Ten Italians in this group remained in custody as late as June 30, 1945. Grace Shimizu, "Report of the Japanese Peruvian Oral History Project," Japanese American Historical Society, San Francisco, 1995. On June 10, 1940, between 600 and 700 Italian aliens, including four women, residing in Canada were arrested and interned as being threats to Canadian security. Luigi Pautasso, "La Donna Durante Il Periodo Fascista in Toronto, 1930–1940," in *The Italian Immigrant Woman in North America*, edited by Betty B. Caroli, Robert F. Herney, and Lydio F. Tomasi (Toronto: The Multicultural Society of Ontario, 1978), p. 185.

23. *Los Angeles Times*, December 8, 1941, quoted in Peter Irons, *Justice at War* (Berkeley and Los Angeles: University of California Press, 1983), pp. 19–23; Rose Scherini, "Executive Order 9066 and Italian Americans: the San Francisco Story," *California History*, LXXI (Winter 1991/92): 367–377, 422–424. See also Gloria Ricci Lothrop, "The Untold Story: The Effects of the Second World War on California Italians," *Journal of the West*, 35 (January 1996): 7–14.

24. James Rose Jr., "Keeping Our Heads on the Enemy Alien Problem," *The American City*, 57 (February 1942): 56–57. See also Peter Sheridan, "Internment of German and Italian Aliens as Compared with the Internment of Japanese Aliens in the United States during World War II: A Brief History and Analysis," Library of Congress, Congressional Research Service, November 24, 1980, and Rose Scherini, Lawrence DiStasi and Adele Negro, *Una Storia Segreta: When Italian Americans Were "Enemy Aliens"* (Oakland, Calif.: Western Chapter of the American Italian Historical Association, 1995).

25. Memorandum for Lemuel B. Schofield, Immigration and Naturalization Service," December 8, 1941, CWRIC 9:10371.

26. "Memo to Mr. Ennis," December 10, 1941, CWRIC 9:10373.

27. William F. Kelly, "Memo for the File," December 15, 1941, CWRIC 9:10375–10376. By February 18, 1942, it is estimated that 267 Italian aliens had been apprehended in the U.S.

28. Personal experience of the author, Los Angeles, California, December 1941. Government assistance was available to the families of detainees through a grant jointly administered by the Social Security Administration and the California Department of Public Welfare, and later by a separate board called Services and Assistance to Enemy Aliens and Other in Need Because of Restrictive Action of the Federal Government. It was reported to the Tolan Committee that by February 21, 1942, while 5,500 individuals had visited Social Security offices in Southern California to make inquiries, only 150 dependents of detainees had sought assistance. U.S. Congress, Report of the Select Committee Investigating National Defense Migration. 77th Congress, 2nd Session, CWRIC 10:11420; Stephen Fox, *Unknown Internment: An Oral History of the Relocation of Italian Americans during World War II* (Boston: Twayne Publishers, 1990), p. 154.

29. Interview with Maria Ricci; Scherini, "Executive Order 9066," p. 366. Despite efforts to observe the provisions of the Geneva Convention, Secretary of War Henry L. Stimson complained in a January 12, 1942, letter to Attorney General Biddle that 106 enemy aliens, including 5 Italians, were confined to city and county jails. CWRIC 1: 56–57. See also "The Wartime Reminiscences of Umberto Benedetti on the Life of Italian Internees at Fort Missoula, Montana, 1941–43," American Italian Historical Association Depository, San Francisco Public Library, and Umberto Benedetti, *Italian Boys at Fort Missoula, Montana 1941–1943* (Missoula, Mont.: Pictorial Histories Publishing Co., Inc. 1991).

30. James Brooke, "After Silence, Italians Recall Internment," *New York Times*, August 11, 1997, A8.

31. Fort Missoula Internment Camp Record, Record Group 85, Box 1, Number 425–282–299 National Archives, Washington, D.C.; Van Valkenburg, *An Alien Place*, pp.16–17.

32. Ibid.; Benedetti, *Italian Boys*, p. 12.

33. Interview with Giovanni Falasca, Los Angeles, February 19, 1975; CWRIC 2: 1286–88; Fox, *Unknown Internment*, pp. 164–165; John Christgau, *"Enemies": World War II Alien Internment* (Ames: Iowa State University Press, 1985), p. 36; Benedetti, "Wartime Reminiscences."

34. Fox, *Unknown Internment*, p. 165.

35. Captain Paolo S. Saglietto, "Diary," Book 3 (Translation 3348), Record Group 85, Number 58–A–734, File 56/25/162. National Archives, Washington, D.C.; Van Valkenburg, *An Alien Place*, p. 81.

36. Ibid.

37. Fort Missoula Internment Camp Record, Box 1.

38. Saglietto Diary, Book Two.

39. Saglietto Diary, Book Three; Van Valkenburg, *An Alien Place*, p. 32. In the 1980s the graves of three Italian detainees who died at Fort Missoula were marked by a stone memorial erected by several of the detained seaman who had settled in the United States. The deceased were Giuseppe Marrazzo, age 47, Giuseppe Marchese, age 24, and Aurelio Mariani, age 32. Benedetti, *Italian Boys*, pp. 80–83.

40. "Announcements from Francis Biddle," *L'Italo Americano*, January 23, 1942, p. 2. See also Francis Biddle, "Axis Aliens in America: Statement of Policy Issued December 19, 1941," *Survey Graphic*, 31 (October 1942): 13–14. Though figures vary, it was estimated that 260 Italians were included among the 3,000 aliens interned nationwide. Scherini, "Executive Order," p. 368.

41. Ibid.

42. Christgau, Enemies, p. 117; Scherini, "Executive Order 9066," p. 369. For additional discussion of the nation's internment policy see Richard Drinnon, *Keeper of the Concentration Camps: Dillon S. Myer and American Racism* (Berkeley and Los Angeles: University of California Press, 1986).

43. "Enemy Aliens Are Loyal to the United States," *L'Italo Americano*, June 5, 1942, p. 2.

44. *San Francisco Chronicle*, October 13, 1942.

45. Christgau, Enemies, pp. 82–83.

46. "New Rules for Enemy Aliens," *L'Italo Americano*, January 2, 1942, p. 1. See also "Aliens in Prohibited Areas," WPA Writers Project, Group 306, Boxes 5 and 6, Department of Special Collections, Young Research Library, University of California, Los Angeles.

47. Ibid.

48. "From February 2 through 7 Italian, German, Japanese Non-citizens Will Have to Secure Identification Documents," *L'Italo Americano*, January 23, 1942, p. 1. Plans for the registration of aliens had been drawn up by the FBI in December 1940. Conference in Lt. Gen. DeWitt's office, January 4, 1942, CWRIC 2:1251. See also Michael Van De Water, "U.S.A. Being Fingerprinted: Identification, Registration Required of All Aliens," "Science Newsletter," 38 (August 10, 1940): 86–87.

49. Ibid., p. 4.

50. *L'Italo Americano*, January 30, 1942, p. 2.

51. "Aliens Flock to Register Unit," *Los Angeles Times*, February 4, 1942, p. 6.

52. "Restitution of Various Objects Consigned to the Police by Enemy Aliens," *L'Italo Americano*, February 27, 1942, p. 2.
53. J. Edgar Hoover, "Multiple Spot Searches of Premises Inhabited or Controlled by Alien Enemies—Internal Security Alien Control," Washington, D.C., February 25, 1942. CWRIC; J. Edgar Hoover, "Alien Enemy Control," *Iowa Law Review*, 29 (1944): 398–399.
54. "Homes of Enemy Aliens Searched by FBI," *L'Italo Americano*, May 1, 1942, p. 4.
55. Ibid. See also Jerome S. Bruner and Jeanette Sayre, "Shortwave Listening in an Italian Community," *Public Opinion Quarterly*, 5 (Winter 1941): 640–656.
56. Memo to Lemuel Schofield from Edward Ennis, May 27, 1942. Record Group 85, Number 58-A-734, File 56 1251B, National Archives, Washington D.C.
57. Memo to Lemuel Schofield from Edward Ennis, June 16, 1942. Record Group 85, Number 58-A-734, File 561 25173, National Archives, Washington D.C.
58. Interview with Velma (Franceschini) Pagliossotti, West Covina, California, July 5, 1991; see also George E. Pozzetta, "My Children Are My Jewels: Italian American Generations during World War II," *Home-Front War: World War II and American Society*, edited by Kenneth P. O'Brien and Lynn Parsons (Westport, Conn.: Greenwood Press, 1995), pp. 84–103.
59. Interview with Maria Ricci, July 7, 1991.
60. Suzanne Dewberry, "Perils at Sea: the Sinking of the SS *Montebello*," *Prologue: Quarterly of the National Archives*, 23 (Fall 1991): 260–265. See also *Union Oil Company v. War Damage Corporation*, Civil Case 24101, U.S. District Court for the Northern District of California, Southern Division, RG 21, National Archives, Pacific Sierra Region, Laguna Nigel; Arthur C. Verge, "The Impact of the Second World War on Los Angeles," *Pacific Historical Review*, LXIII (August 1994): 295.
61. Dillon S. Myer, *Uprooted Americans* (Tucson: University of Arizona Press, 1971), p. 24.
62. Walter Lippmann, "The Fifth Column on the Coast," *Washington Post*, February 12, 1942. CWRIC, RG 107, Box 6, ASW 014,311.
63. CWRIC 1: 108.
64. Fox, *Unknown Internment*, pp. 43–53; Jacobus ten Broeck, Edward Barnhart and Floyd Matson, *Prejudice, War and the Constitution* (Berkeley and Los Angeles: University of California Press, 1954), pp. 38–81, n. 98, n. 102, and n. 103; CWRIC 9:10475, 9:10649–50; *Los Angeles Times*, February 2, 1942, p. 3.
65. Verge, "Impact of World War II on Los Angeles," p. 295.
66. "Speeches and Press Statements, 1938–41," Fletcher Bowron Papers, Box 33, Huntington Library, San Marino, California.
67. CWRIC 2: 412–14; Fox, *Unknown Internment*, pp. 48–50.
68. CWRIC 10: 11478.
69. CWRIC 9: 10674.
70. "Important Declaration by Attorney General Biddle," *L'Italo Americano*, January 9, 1942, p. 1.
71. F. M. Andreani, "The Italian Enemy Alien Situation," ibid., March 27, 1942, p. 1.
72. State Personnel Board Application Form, CWRIC 9: 10707. "Aliens Have a Right to Work," *Christian Century*, 58 (July 9, 1941): 876.
73. Interview with Peter Bonino.
74. CWRIC 5: 6212–6216; "Enemy Within," *Time* (July 13, 1942): 13; "Moving Aliens," *Business Week* (March 7, 1942): 26; "Safety First: Ban Aliens from West Coast Defense Areas," *Newsweek*, 19 (February 9, 1942): 27. See also Stephen Fox, "General John DeWitt and Proposed Internment of German and Italian Aliens During World War II," *Pacific Historical Review*, 57 (November 1988): 407–438.
75. State of California, Summary Report of Joint Fact-Finding Committee on Un-American Activities in California (Sacramento, California: State Legislature, 55th Session, 1943), pp. 383–385. See also "What to Do with Foreign Press Puzzles Officials," *Advertising Age*, 22 (April 20, 1942): 25.
76. Summary Report of Joint Fact-Finding Committee, pp. 286, p. 299; CWRIC 24: 25998.
77. Scherini, "Other Internment," p. 12.

78. Interview with Maria Ricci, July 7, 1991. See also Diggins, "Italo-American Anti-Fascist Opposition," pp. 579–598.

79. Interview with Fernando Castagnola, Alhambra, California, July 2, 1991; personal papers in the author's possession; "To Send Letters to Your Dear Ones in Italy," *L'Italo Americano*, February 27, 1942, p. 4.

80. "New Rules Regarding Successions of Deceased Aliens," July 24, 1942, p. 4 and "All Aliens Will Be Reclassified for Military Service," *L'Italo Americano*, May 29, 1942, p. 1. See also "More Assets Iced: Treasury's Control over Enemy Alien Funds $8,000,000,000," *Business Week* (February 27, 1943): 95–96; "2000 Alien Patents Seized by United States Aviation," *Aviation*, 41 (July 1942): 184.

81. "Enemy Aliens Will Have to Evacuate the Entire Coastal Area of Los Angeles By February 24," *L'Italo Americano*, January 30, 1942, p. 1.

82. "Placards Posted," *Los Angeles Times*, February 7, 1942, p. 1; "New Restrictions for Enemy Aliens," *L'Italo Americano*, February 6, 1942, p. 1. It is interesting to note that in the same issue an advertisement for Jesse Piri's market included the notice: "We deliver in the country and nearby towns." There was an added explanation: "Given certain restrictions existing at the moment, many non-naturalized fellow Italians living in the country and nearby towns may come to Los Angeles only with the permission of the authorities, we have decided to make available the acquisition of imported foods, wines and olive oil." Obviously, the restrictions outlined in the December presidential proclamation had their desired effect. Ibid., p. 4.

83. "More Listed in County and 69 in State," *Los Angeles Times*, February 1, 1942, p. 3; "Farm Colonies to Be Set Up for Evicted Enemy Nationals," ibid., February 4, 1942, p. 6.

84. "Prohibited Zones for Enemy Aliens," pp. 1 and 5; "To Assist Enemy Aliens Who Will Have to Abandon Various Zones," pp. 1 and 2; "While We Are Studying the Problems of the Enemy Aliens," *L'Italo Americano*, February 13, 1942, pp. 1–2. For a comprehensive discussion of the political infighting which surrounded the imposition of evacuation regulations, and particularly their effects upon the coastal communities of Northern California, see Fox, *Unknown Internment*, pp. 173–177. In early 1942 civilian leaders were well aware of Lt. Gen. DeWitt's plan to move all enemy aliens out of California. See Roger Daniels, *Concentration Camps USA: Japanese Americans and World War II* (New York: Holt, Rinehart and Winston, 1972), p. 75.

85. "No Changes in the Curfew Orders," p. 4 and "Rules and Regulations for Enemy Aliens," p. 2, *L'Italo Americano*, April 17, 1942.

86. "Prison for Those Who Break Curfew Laws," ibid., May 29, 1942, p. 4.

87. "Curfew Violators Arrested," ibid., June 19, 1942, p. 4.

88. "Of Interest to Enemy Aliens," ibid., June 26, 1942, p. 4.

89. "The Internment of German and Italian Aliens," CWRIC 24:25888; "CRS-9," CWRIC 1: 1–9.

90. CWRIC 24: 25886–25888.

91. Ibid.

92. House Committee Investigating National Defense Migration, Findings and Recommendations, Fourth Report, p. 31.

93. "Italians and Germans Will Not Be Evacuated," *L'Italo Americano*, June 5, 1942, p 1. See also Carlo Sforza and Gaetano Salvemini, "Biddle's Order: Two Views on the Removal of the Enemy Alien Stigma for Italians," *Nation*, 155 (November 7, 1942): 476–478.

94. "For an Equitable Treatment of the Enemy Aliens," *L'Italo Americano*, May 8, 1942, p. 2.

95. Franklin D. Roosevelt's 1936 victories by margins of three to one in the densely populated Italian American New York community of Queens, two to one in Staten Island and Richmond, and four to one in the Bronx had been followed in 1940 with a marked voter shift toward the GOP. In the Bronx the Republican presidential vote more than doubled from 93,000 in 1936 to 198,293 in 1940. For a fuller discussion of Italian American voting patterns see Michael Barone, "Italian American Politics," *Italian Americans: New Perspectives in Italian Immigration and Ethnicity*, edited by Lydio F. Tomasi (New York: Center for Migration Studies, 1985), pp. 378–384. See also "Intelligence: Oval Room" Folder, Box 107, Ernest Cuneo Papers, Franklin D. Roosevelt Library, Hyde Park, N.Y.

96. Italian aliens had 60,000 of their husbands and/or sons in the U.S. military, and 500,000 Italian Americans would serve in the U.S. military before World War II was concluded. Lawrence DiStasi, "Schizoid America," unpublished manuscript in possession of the author.

97. Memo from Mr. Jaretzki, War Department to Colonel Tate, June 4, 1942, CWRIC 6:6697–6699.

98. Michi Weglyn, *Years of Infamy: The Untold Story of America's Concentration Camps* (New York: William Morrow, 1976), p. 200 and *Personal Justice Denied*, p. 78, n. 149.

99. Ibid., p. 134.

100. "Memorandum for the Hon. J. J. McCloy: Suggested Preferential Treatment of Italian Citizens in the United States," June 8, 1942, CWRIC 1:148–49.

101. "Naturalization Process Simplified to Accommodate Alien Soldiers," *L'Italo Americano*, May 1, 1942, p. 2.

102. "All Aliens Will Be Reclassified for Military Service," May 29, 1942, p. 1 and "Orders to Aliens Reflect Good Sense by the Executive Leadership," *L'Italo Americano*, July 24, 1942, p. 2.

103. Interview with Maria Ricci, July 7, 1991. Among the detainees only Spartaco Bonomi returned to his previous employment as a travel agent. Upon his release Zaccaria Lubrano relocated to Paso Robles. Filippo Fordelone established the successful Angelus Concrete Block Company. Instead of launching a literary review, which the U.S. government had offered to subsidize as restitution for the demise of his newspaper, *La Parola,* Dr. Giovanni Falasca opened a restaurant in a section of Los Angeles where residential patterns gradually shifted. In August 1975, he was beaten to death by young gang members who had broken into his establishment.

104. Francis B. Biddle, "Americans of Italian Origin: An Address by the Honorable Francis Biddle Delivered at the Columbus Day Celebration, Carnegie Hall, New York…October 12, 1942," United States Congressional Record, 76th Congress, p. 11134 ff. See also Francis B. Biddle, *In Brief Authority* (Hartford, Conn.: Greenwood Press. 1976), p. 229. See a contrasting view in "Concerning the Exemption of Italian Aliens from Alien Enemy Classification," *Interpreter Releases*, 19 (October 20, 1942): 353–362.

105. *L'Italo Americano*, October 17, 1942, p. 1. See also Joseph S. Roucek, "Italo-Americans and World War II," *Sociology and Social Research*, 29 (July/August 1956): 465–471; Gary R. Mormino and George E. Pozzetta, "Ethnics at War: Italian Americans in California during World II," in *The Way We Really Were: The Golden State in the Second Great War*, ed. by Roger W. Lotohin (Urbana: University of Illinois Press, 2000), pp. 143–163.

Rejected First-Generation Enemy Alien

by Carolina Constantina Bracco

> Carolina Bracco grew up in California's Central Valley, in the town
> of Modesto. Here she makes it plain that during wartime, no one
> with an Italian name was ever fully safe from suspicion. Bracco notes
> that neither her birth in the United States nor attending the
> University of California failed to protect her from employment dis-
> crimination.

My mother and father were from the towns of Torino and Brozzolo in Italy. I
was born in Ripon, California. Italian was my first language. I learned English
very rapidly when my mother sent me to an all English-speaking school in
first grade.

I went to UCLA in 1942. At UCLA I needed to work to support myself
and so applied for a job with Douglas Aircraft Company in Santa Monica. One
week later, the application was shown to me: *"Rejected First-Generation Enemy
Alien"!* I was born in and had lived in the Modesto area *all* my life! What a shock.

My two older brothers and two older sisters always thought I was nuts
when I told them Mama and I might be incarcerated. They were all older than
me—the youngest of the four—nine years older. Too bad I can't show them this
book. One brother has died; one sister is in a cult; one sister has full-time care
due to Alzheimer's. And so it goes. That's life.

Alien in Texas

by Gloria Micheletti Sylvernale

> Gloria Micheletti Sylvernale was thirteen when the wartime events
> occurred. She here recounts the unsettling story of her father's arrest
> and detention for six months in Galveston, Texas. Absent any formal
> charges, Sylvernale, like countless others, can only speculate about
> what her father's offense may have been.

Kelly Air Force Base during the early 1940s was used as a camp to intern many
(I'm not sure of the numbers) Japanese, German, and Italian immigrants from
Galveston and Friendswood County, Texas. Friendswood County had a large
concentration of Japanese who were cotton farmers. Also, among many other
missions, Kelly was an advanced flight-cadet training base.

I was thirteen years old when my father was taken away from our home.
My father had failed to become naturalized, even though he had been in this
country for many years—he was too busy feeding a large family and trying to
make a success of his grocery store.

Soon after the start of World War II, my father, having already given up
the grocery business, went to work at Todd Dry Docks in Galveston. He went
to work very early each morning to get as much overtime as he could. Early one
morning after arriving on the job at Todd's, he was met by an FBI agent, an
Immigration and Naturalization agent, and a police sergeant, who handcuffed
my father and drove him to our home with a search warrant. It was 5 or 6 A.M.
when they arrived at our home, woke us up, completely searched the house,
tore it apart as they did, and left it that way. The search resulted in their finding
and confiscating a household radio, a flashlight, a sunlamp that my mother used
on her sore shoulder (with the comment that it could be used to signal enemy
aircraft!) and a small Brownie box camera that was given to my seventeen-year-
old brother by my father. My father had received it as a prize when in the grocery business.

They then took my father into custody, even though there was no reason
to suspect he was a threat to the United States, but just because he was an

enemy alien. Of course, my mother was devastated. She was left with ten children, the oldest seventeen years old, and no income!

My father was taken to a guarded facility at Fort Sam Houston in San Antonio, Texas, for a while and then to Kelly Air Force Base, also in San Antonio. I visited my father with several members of my family at Fort Sam Houston and remember that the internees were housed in tents, in a double-fenced enclosure made of heavy cyclone fencing with barbed wire across the top. Also, two armed guards were sitting in towers at each corner of the enclosure.

After my father was investigated for six months, he was released from detention along with a few other people being held, but with restrictions imposed on him, i.e. no travel without permission, could not move from his residence, and had to report to the immigration department every week. His only "crime" was his Italian ancestry.

My father had been drafted into the Italian army during World War I at a young age and served from 1918 to 1921 as a telegraph operator. He arrived in Galveston, Texas, from Santa Maria del Giudice, Lucca, Italy, in April 1921. In Galveston he was a member of the Knights of Columbus, the Sons of Italy (he served as their secretary and considered it a social organization), and the Galveston Retail Merchants Association.

My oldest brother reminded me that he was going to be drafted into the service at this time and found it hard to reconcile the fact that our father was in an enemy-alien camp and he was about to put on a uniform for the country that had our father in detention. My father was released several months before my brother left for military service.

As we were growing up, we were taught to be proud to be Americans and we all were! My husband was a B-24 pilot in the U.S. Air Force during World War II and became a career officer in the Air Force for twenty-two and a half years.

This is an experience my family and I will never forget.

Let's Keep Smiling
Conditions of Internment

by Lawrence DiStasi

Much of what we have been able to learn about the conditions for the resident aliens who were interned during World War II has come from sources other than the internees themselves—in particular from the diaries and books of Italian merchant seamen who were interned at the camp run by the Immigration and Naturalization Service (INS) at Fort Missoula, Montana. These were mostly younger, unmarried Italian nationals who were interned when their ships were caught in American ports in 1940, and their impressions of their internment at Missoula typically convey a kind of bon-vivant quality, perhaps due to the fact that many were relieved to have avoided the grim wartime conditions prevalent in their own country.[1]

Testimony from the permanent resident aliens interned has always contrasted sharply with that of the seamen, for many of the former resented what they considered an unjust incarceration by the country in which they had chosen to live. This is particularly true of those held in camps other than Missoula, i.e. camps run by the War Department. Until recently, little was known about these camps, but newly discovered files from the Provost Marshal General's Office have now provided documents which testify to the feelings of these men, as well as to the conditions in the army-run camps where the majority of them were interned. They tell a story quite different from what we have come to expect.

Mario Ricciardelli, a china and glassware repairman, was picked up on December 9, 1941, by the FBI, held at the INS detention station at Fort Howard, Maryland, and subsequently interned as a dangerous enemy alien.[2] Like most other Italian-born internees, he was moved from camp to camp, spending time at Fort George Meade in Maryland, the McAlester Internment Camp in Oklahoma, and finally at Fort Missoula in Montana. His War Department file contains two letters that convey some sense of what it was like to be a civilian internee during World War II, particularly at the internment facilities run by the War Department. The first expresses his appreciation to Colonel Hutchins, commander of the Internee Section of Fort George Meade, Maryland, for the colonel's humane treatment of his prisoners. This puts into context the second letter, written just before his rehearing, which Ricciardelli addressed to H.E.N.D. Borgue, the Swiss minister in Washington, D.C. The letter was translated from its original Italian, and though the typed copy has no inside address, it appears to have been written from a government station near Ricciardelli's hometown of Washington, probably the INS station at Fort Howard near Baltimore, from where his second letter derives. Here is what it says:

Excellency:

On leaving Camp McAlester, the colonel commandant in chief, the major, and all the officers there had encouraged me, thanking me for my cooperation and conduct during the period of internment.

At this scene of courtesy and of grand emotions there were present two U.S. marshals, sent from Washington to escort me to this center. At the railroad station in McAlester, to my surprise, a pair of handcuffs were placed on me hand to hand with one of the marshals and my objections availed me nothing.

During the two nights passed in the Pullman, after having consigned pants and shoes to my custodians, another pair of manacles, more firm, secured me by one ankle to the middle of the berth above. Always manacled, I have traversed and paused along the stations where it was necessary to change trains and in the restaurants to be the object of the gaze of citizens and passengers.

I call to your Excellency's attention, incidentally, that I have never before been place in handcuffs when transferred to the various camps, and therefore I find it rather stupid and vile when I was returning toward my home and perhaps toward liberty.

But apart from this consideration of inadequate personnel I beg your Excellency to let me know if the use of handcuffs conforms with the Geneva Convention and if such is the treatment of civilian internees.

In case [your answer to this is] affirmative, I have nothing but to maintain philosophically the humiliation suffered and much other suffering by circumstances of the actual situation, but in case [your information to me] is to the contrary, I beg your Excellency's interest in interpreting and more so to vigorously protest the abuse and the humiliation inflicted upon me and thus to avoid in the future that other fine Italian citizens in that concentration camp, model fathers, honest and decorous professional men, and all in expectation of rehearings of their cases, must in turn undergo the same outrage of which I have been an object.

Infinite thanks, Excellency, and I will be very grateful if you would courteously reply to my letter.[3]

We do not know if Ricciardelli received a reply from the Swiss minister. What is obvious is that his letter was forwarded to (if not outright intercepted by) the U.S. government, made its way into his War Department file, and indeed, may have negatively influenced the hearing he mentions: Ricciardelli's file records him as being sent to Fort Missoula in May 1943, so his hearing apparently failed to secure his release.

This, in itself, is one of the conditions of internment that bears discussion—to wit, that whatever an internee wrote, and in many cases what he said, was routinely observed, recorded, inspected, and placed in his file. In Ricciardelli's case, this is fortunate, because his first letter indicates the surprising fact that being interned, at least for Ricciardelli, proved more humane than being transported for possible release. Written to Colonel Hutchins after Ricciardelli had been transferred from Fort George Meade to McAlester, and then to Fort Howard, the letter begins with a request for his pay, eighty cents per day, earned while working for ten days in the kitchen at Meade, and apologizes for even asking for such a paltry sum: "I would have never requested such little sum of money but I am practically penniless." Then it goes on to thank the colonel for his "courtesies":

> I also wish to thank you very, very much for the courtesies you have use it to the Italian group during the period we were there, and I will never forget you kindly farewell you give us when we left the camp the night of September 17th. I am here pending a decision to go free after a rehearing and I hope very much to go back to my house and work in Washington.
>
> I also left at the camp a one-foot-square black and nickel-plated electric stove which will be very useful to me if I can have it back.
>
> I hope all the flowerbeds we build there someone take care of it. I miss them very much and I hope the soldiers there will enjoy them.
>
> In Washington I have a laboratory for the repairing of china, glass and antiques in generally (2333-18th St. N.W.), and if you have anything to repair on that line I will be happy to do something for you to show my appreciation to your courtesies.
>
> I thank you very much again and I remain, Yours respectfully[4]

Several points are worth noting. First, the internees were paid for certain work, such as kitchen service, and some seemed to depend on the paltry income it provided.[5] Second, Ricciardelli and the other internees occupied themselves by gardening, among other things, and felt some pride in the work they had done. Finally, some internees, at least, developed a certain amount of attachment not only to their fellow internees, but also to their jailers. Ricciardelli's offer to do some repairs for the colonel as a way of repaying his kindnesses seems quite genuine, especially remembering his reference to the "grand emotions" present when he left Camp McAlester. This makes all the more jarring the treatment he received from the U.S. marshals, who insisted on escorting him to Washington as if he were an escaped convict rather than a civilian internee possibly about to be paroled. Thus, from Ricciardelli we get one crucial aspect of the internee portrait: notwithstanding the fact that they had never been tried or convicted or even accused of any crime, the internees were never allowed to forget, even when out of the camps, that they were prisoners.

A more extreme example of such severity can be found in the file of Modesto Sabini. Sabini, a janitor, had been picked up in San Francisco on February 22, 1942. After a rehearing of his case, he was ordered paroled by the attorney general on November 6, 1942, and deemed eligible to return to his home in San Francisco. His homecoming was short-circuited, however, for in a letter to Colonel B. M. Bryan, chief of the Aliens Division in the Provost Marshal General's Office (PMGO), sent by Earl Harrison, commissioner of the INS, on November 24, the commissioner asks for a clarification of Western Defense Command (WDC) policy ruling that, parole or no, Sabini could not return to California at all:

> In view of the denial of permission for subject to enter the military area on the West Coast and in order to effectuate the attorney general's order of parole, it is now requested that you issue the necessary authority to the internment camp commander at McAlester, Oklahoma, for the alien's release for travel without guard to whatever place outside the military area the district director at Kansas City, Missouri may designate after appropriate investigation has been conducted by this service.[6]

In other words, if Sabini could not go home to San Francisco, where could he go? Colonel Bryan then wrote to General DeWitt of the Western Defense Command, asking about travel to his area. Two other internees of Italian descent from that command besides Modesto Sabini had been released and were also awaiting permission to travel there without guard. Since Sabini's request had been disapproved, Colonel Bryan wanted to know what the policy was, and cited a WDC communication dated November 30 concerning parole:

> The policy of this Headquarters requires that a guard accompany all such aliens entering or traveling within the states of Washington, Oregon, California, and Arizona. Aliens paroled or released to the other four states (Idaho, Montana, Utah, and Nevada), are not required to have a travel permit or to be accompanied by a guard.

Then Colonel Bryan cited another directive given to INS director Harrison by the Western Defense Command, i.e. "that General DeWitt by proclamation exempted Italian nationals including parolees and internees who have been unconditionally released from custody from requiring travel permits to enter military areas in the Western Defense Command." Since Sabini, an Italian, had been denied permission, the two WDC policies seemed to be totally contradictory, and Bryan wanted to know (a) if the policy had been changed, and (b) "if changed as to whether such change may be regarded as a general expression of policy or whether each individual case must be submitted to the Western Defense Command as in the past and its particular disposition determined upon its own merits."

Sabini's file does not contain the response from the Western Defense Command. But it does contain a new parole order, dated January 12, 1943, though whether he had to go under guard is not clear. In any case, the major point at issue remains the conditions that prevailed for internees, even upon their release. Mario Ricciardelli was not only accompanied by a guard to his home area, but was placed in handcuffs, a practice that general policy seems to have opposed. And Modesto Sabini was denied entry to California, for reasons that were not clear even to Colonel Bryan of PMGO. After all, he states, Italian nationals had been exempted from the requirement to carry travel permits, probably as a result of the lifting of the enemy-alien classification from all Italian resident aliens on October 12, 1942. Why would Sabini be held up? The answer must lie either in the fact that policy in the WDC, and indeed everywhere else, was thoroughly inconsistent (which it was, especially when moving from one jurisdiction to another, as internees did), or that a clerical error in Sabini's case caused his trouble. That is, on the original letter from Earl Harrison to Colonel Bryan, the designation for Sabini identifies him, in spite of his serial number's "I" for Italian, as Japanese; the heading says, "In re: Modesto Sabini, Japanese internee, ISN-19-4-I-23-CI." If this error were repeated elsewhere, especially in the offices of General John DeWitt, it may have set off alarm bells which caused Modesto Sabini's otherwise normal return to his home in San Francisco to be rejected. Even when returning to "normal" life, that is, the enemy alien who had been interned could not expect "normalcy" to prevail.

As to life within the camps, it surely varied with the camp, with the commander of the camp, and with the agency that had jurisdiction over the camp: some camps fell under the jurisdiction of the army (Provost Marshal General's Office, War Department), while others were run by the Immigration and Naturalization Service, Department of Justice.[7] War Department rules, in general, seem to have been more severe.

For one example, photos and other testimony indicate that the INS-run camp at Missoula, Montana, allowed internees to work outside the camp with local growers, organize orchestras, soccer matches, and other cultural activities, and remain in civilian clothes. But testimony from Albert Berizzi, who visited his father, Louis, at Fort Meade (War Department), indicates that the internees there wore shirts with "POW" printed on the back.[8] Evidence from internee files confirms this observation: in the file of Ubaldo Guidi-Buttrini is a record of a visit made to him by his son, Private Mal Guidi. One paragraph in the recorded conversation refers to "uniforms" as follows:

> Pvt. Guidi asked about the uniforms. Internee Guidi-Buttrini stated that the Italians probably would not have had to wear the uniforms if they had not been in the same area with the Germans. The Japanese were in an area to themselves and they were permitted to wear civilian clothes.[9]

The same memo also indicates that the living quarters at Meade, internee Ricciardelli's compliments notwithstanding, consisted of tents. Indeed, the army may have been somewhat embarrassed about this, because when internee Guidi-Buttrini asked if he could show his living space to his son, the response was negative:

> As the time was now twelve o'clock the conversation was brought to an end. Internee Guidi-Buttrini requested permission to show his son inside his "hut." This privilege was denied him.[10]

Another private reference confirms that internees in other army-run camps were housed in tents. Prospero Cecconi* kept a notebook of his internment experience, which he called "Via Crucis," and which notes with the utmost

---

*This is the same Prospero Cecconi who appears in "Morto il Camerata," p. 1.

brevity Cecconi's travels from camp to camp. On May 23, 1942, Cecconi writes that, having left Fort McDowell in San Francisco, he and his fellow internees traveled for three days and arrived at Fort Sam Houston, in Texas. The brief entry for May 23 says simply: "We found there fine tend [tents] and plenty innabitant."[11] It would seem that the U.S. Army, though it had insisted that it should be given custody of the civilian internees, was not really prepared to house them.[12] Accordingly, internees in at least three camps—Camp Upton, Fort George Meade, and Fort Sam Houston—lived in what could only have been temporary quarters.

Several other references in the record of Mal Guidi's visit testify to the conditions under which such visits, limited to two per month, were conducted, and of the camps in general.[13] At one point during the visit, other internees entered the "recreation hall," where visitors met with internees, and shook hands with Private Guidi, promising the internee's son they would take good care of his father. Apparently, their emotions got the better of them: "When one attempted to embrace Pvt. Guidi they were all ordered to leave." One wonders why. Was even the touch of an internee considered somehow toxic? Dangerous to security? Apparently it was, as was waving to other internees; when, upon leaving, Private Guidi tried to wave to the internees he had recently met, "this was stopped."

We also learn from this exchange that the food was quite good, especially breakfast. On the other hand, like so many internees, Guidi-Buttrini complained of stomach trouble.[14]

> ...there were some foods he could not eat. Consequently he had
> to keep a supply of spaghetti on hand, which he cooked on a little
> stove in his tent.[15] Upon being asked by his son if he could get his
> black coffee, he answered, "Plenty of it."

This accords with Ricciardelli's request for his electric stove, with which he was also allowed to cook.

On the other hand, though internees were allowed a great deal of latitude with foods and food preparation, they were not given a free hand altogether. In one rather amusing exchange of letters, Remo Fioroni, a language teacher who functioned as internee spokesman, attempts to disburse among himself and some thirty-four other internees recently moved to McAlester the proceeds from a "special concession granted for the sale of soft drinks in the compound in order to create a fund for the Italians." Having originated at their previous place of internment, Fort Meade, the concession would have to be disbanded and its profits disbursed. Fioroni wrote a letter requesting this disbursement:

two internees were to get ten dollars each to cover the cost of a gift, and the remaining sum, $54.24, was to be divided among the rest, amounting to $1.64 each. Word of such a concession took the army by surprise, setting off a flurry of memos between the Provost Marshal General's Office in Washington, the commander at Fort Meade, and the commander at McAlester, wondering how to handle this request. The officers at McAlester, clearly baffled, wrote, "No mention of this fund was made by officers transferring the Internees from Camp Meade. Request information as to disposition."[16] General Bryan at the Provost Marshal General's Office was clearly miffed at such laxity, and wrote dismissively, "This office knows of no provision whereby individual internees may benefit from profits realized through the operation of a camp canteen."[17] Yet the funds were there, creating a financial tangle whose resolution does not appear in Fioroni's file. What does appear is evidence that the Italian internees had created a rather messy and all-too-visible breach of regulations.

More important breaches involved the regulations governing the types of conversation allowable to internees and their visitors. Any mention of other internees, or other camps, or an impending move to those camps was forbidden:

> Pvt. Guidi asked his father if he had received the chair. Internee Guidi-Buttrini said that he had not, but that it might be in today. If not, the authorities would ship—(a warning was given by the undersigned so the statement was not finished).

Equally severe was the restriction on speaking Italian. On August 30, 1942, for example, internee Guidi-Buttrini was visited by his daughter, Temi Guidi, a conversation observed and recorded by Sergeant Caton J. Marconi:

> The undersigned was unable to prevent Miss Guidi from saying "how are you" to her father in Italian. Miss Guidi said that she was sorry, said that it would not happen again. The undersigned felt justified in allowing her to proceed, in view of the fact that she had only uttered two words, which he understood, being conversant in that language (*Come stai*), and felt that the rebuke that she had received was severe enough so that it would never happen again.[18]

On the basis of this incident, it seems fair to conclude that speaking the "enemy's language"[19] was strictly prohibited during these visits.[20] It also seems that if Temi Guidi had spoken longer and uttered a more significant sentence in Italian, her visit with her father would have been summarily terminated. As it was, her departure upset Sergeant Marconi considerably, because she flouted other rules and procedures:

> The departure of Buttrini and Miss Guidi was in violation of regulations. Buttrini attempted to introduce Miss Guidi to another internee, but was informed that this was prohibited. At the final parting Buttrini again attempted to say something to his daughter in Italian, but was prevented from doing so.
>
> Miss Guidi also waved at another internee on the way out, in defiance of regulations. On the way out, beyond area "C," Miss Guidi attempted to wave at her father again. When the undersigned told her that this was in defiance of regulations she made no answer to this statement.
>
> The undersigned feels that, even though Miss Guidi seemed well mannered, that she exhibited no sense of tact, and no desire to cooperate with the rules and regulations established by this Headquarters. This was done, not by opposing them, rather, by simply ignoring them.

The violations in question seemed to involve contact, even at a distance, with any other internee. Was this out of fear that people in the Italian American community might thereby learn more about who had been interned? We do not know, though we do know from Jerre Mangione's account of his experiences in Alien Control that the Justice Department had a general policy of keeping information about civilian internments as far out of the public eye as possible.[21] In any case, about three weeks later, Private Mal Guidi *was* allowed to meet, if not embrace, other internees, but again, not to wave to them!

The army apparently saw an even more serious threat in one or more remarks made by Bianca Berizzi to her husband, Louis, on a visit to the internee at Fort Meade on February 7, 1943. The visit apparently did not elicit censure at the time, but a February 12 letter from the headquarters of the 1343rd Service Command Unit in charge of internees to the director, Military Intelligence Division, Third Service Command, printed the following excerpts from the recorded version of the visit for the intelligence division to consider:

> "Mrs. Berizzi mentioned her daughter's being in love. If said daughter got married, Mrs. Berizzi pointed out, she, Mrs. Berizzi, would have to stay here rather than return to Italy. The daughter, Mrs. Berizzi intimated, would soon tell her father all about it.

"Regarding Internment, Mrs. Berizzi, surveying the Internment Camp, remarked, "They don't do things like this in Italy.""

"Mrs. Berizzi stated that her son, Albert, would be inducted into the army on the 16th of this month, and would be stationed at Fort Meade. It was her impression that the son would arrange to pay daily visits to his father at the Internment Camp. Mrs. Berizzi said that Albert was trying to get into the Intelligence Service. Internee Berizzi expressed doubt as to the possibility of this, despite the fact that the dean of Albert's school would recommend him.

"Mrs. Berizzi said that she was again going to talk to Major Cavanough of the Army and Navy Club in Washington, among other things, about her insurance problem."

This information is forwarded your office for whatever action might be deemed advisable.[22]

The writer does not state which of these bits of information might require action: was it the implied criticism in "They don't do things like this in Italy"? Or the suggestion that their daughter's marriage might interfere with plans to repatriate? Or, more likely, the fact that the son of an internee might be admitted to army intelligence? The truth is, Albert Berizzi *was* accepted into military intelligence. Indeed, the contradiction of his being assigned to intelligence, awaiting orders to proceed to battle in Europe at the very time his father was interned as a dangerous alien, ultimately led to a new hearing for Louis Berizzi, and his parole.[23] At the time, however, those in charge of internees clearly drew the opposite conclusion—that the local director of military intelligence ought to know about this and might want to intervene to prevent it.*

When it came to material in letters, the military was equally sensitive.[24] One letter in the Guidi-Buttrini file complains about the time allowed for visits. It seems that visitors were given no more than twenty-five minutes to spend with internees. Velleda Guidi tried to explain to Colonel Hutchins why this was insufficient:

> I take this opportunity to make a request. You probably are aware
> of the fact that to visit Camp George Meade, from Boston, Mass.,
> it takes quite a number of hours, and is very expensive. Also, on
> arrival there, we, his children, are so tired, that before we even get
> our breaths, the 25 minutes allotted us are up, and we have had

---

*See "Orders to Take Him Away," p. 217, for more on the Berizzi family.

very little, if any, of that satisfaction of being with our father. We
know well that according to regulations, each internee is allowed
two visits a month, of a 25-minute duration. We are wondering if,
in our case, we couldn't be allowed but one visit a month, and
allowed to be with him a little longer. You may well imagine the
satisfaction this would be granting his seven children...[25]

Colonel Hutchins's response is handwritten at the top of this letter. It says,
"write sending regulations and advise that internees may have two visitors per
month. Regulations the same for each internee, 25 min." A formal response,
written August 6, 1942, is also included in the Buttrini file and conveys the
same message: "an extension of time cannot be granted."

An earlier reference to the same issue seems to have alarmed the army
censors even more. In Guidi-Buttrini's file is a fragment of a May 7 letter from
the same daughter with the note, "the following passage deleted":

It seems to me that it was very mean that we were allowed only
25 minutes with you. I thought sure, where we were two people,
we would be allowed 25 minutes apiece. It doesn't seem fair to
me. Imagine, we traveled 30 hours straight to be allowed only 25
minutes with you. Well, I suppose that's the way it is and that's all
there is to it.[26]

Why the mention of this in a letter to an internee should be considered threatening, or even dangerous to security, especially when a subsequent request to
the commander concerning the same issue was considered legitimate, is hard to
fathom, but apparently such complaints in letters to or from internees were so
categorized and routinely censored.

Other deletions from correspondence, found in numerous internee files,
confirm that the army was hypersensitive to anything that might be either
detrimental to morale, or to its role as the imprisoning agency, or to security.
Most striking are the routine deletions of *x*'s, normally used as a sign of affection between loved ones. On May 22, 1942, for example, Mrs. Anna Andresino
wrote to internee Michelangelo Scicchitani. Scicchitani's file contains the
handwritten note, "The following kisses extracted"; the offensive "K is," and
"xxxxxxxxx," having been cut from the letter, are attached.[27] In the same vein,
curse words were apparently forbidden and routinely excised. Thus, in a letter
from Maria Favoino to her husband, Giovanni Favoino, the Italian word
maledetto is deleted, along with its translation, "damn."[28]

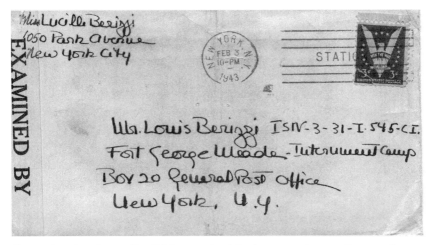

The envelope from Lucetta (Lucille) Berizzi to her father has a censor's stamp. Courtesy of Lucetta Berizzi Drypolcher

In the file of Alfredo Tribuani is a more puzzling deletion. In a letter written to Tribuani by Ralph Ottaviano on or about August 10, 1942, there was included a verse, "Let's Keep Smiling," illuminated with flowers and fancy script in the manner common to greeting cards

LET'S KEEP SMILING

Just a friendly little word
May make some heart grow lighter
Just a little smile may help
To make someone's day brighter
So let us keep our courage high
And give that smile today
For we owe it to our fellow man
To help him on his way.

This was deleted with the following explanation: "deleted because of possible hidden meaning."[29] The irony is all too apparent: in the cases cited above, the authorities worried about sentiments in letters—kisses or curses or complaints—that might negatively affect the morale of internees; here a bit of doggerel intended to *raise* Tribuani's morale is found equally suspect.

"Let's Keep Smiling," the verse sent from Ralph Ottaviano to Alfredo Tribuani, was deleted by army censors because of possible hidden meanings. Courtesy of National Archives and Records Administration, College Park, Md.

In perhaps the most stunning example of all, we find these lines written to internee Tullio Verrando on July 12, 1942, from a Sister Vincent of St. Lucy's Convent in New Jersey:

> Try to unite your sufferings with those of Jesus Christ. Remember, he suffered unjustly just to save your soul and mine and all other children. Therefore, give Him your Heart.[30]

The censor deleted the passage because, he noted, "it is a false analogy." The censor apparently felt that encouraging an internee to compare his suffering to that of Jesus Christ might lead to what? Mistaken pride? The false notion that he was interned unjustly? Whatever it was, in retrospect, the action borders on cruelty—depriving the internee of what may well have comforted him. Oddly, Verrando's mail seems to have been more prone to such deletions than most. In a June letter to his wife, the following line was deleted: "because I can't see me any more in this place which I don't belong." An earlier letter in June, also to his wife, lost yet another line to the censor's scissors. Verrando had written "because I see that there is no justice," prompting a deletion and the explanation, "the following passage was deleted as criticism."[31]

So there it is. Possible hidden meanings, forbidden. Cursing, forbidden. False analogies, forbidden. Despair, forbidden. Criticism, either direct or implied, doubly forbidden. On the other hand, internees were urged to maintain contact with loved ones. In Verrando's file just a week later is a poignant letter from one of his daughters addressed to Colonel Hutchins:

Dear Colonel Hutchins,

It is one week that we didn't receive news from my Daddy, we have been worrying very much. Please let me know if my Daddy (Tullio Verrando, Internee) is allright. I would appreciate it very much and I thank you immensely.

Truly yours,
Elaine Verrando[32]

At the top of the letter is a handwritten comment by Colonel Hutchins to Captain Relles: "Advise Internee Verrando to write a letter to his family." Perhaps the colonel should have added, "and make sure he sounds cheerful."

Of course, being cheerful didn't always suffice either. In the file of Alfio Carta is a letter written to him at Fort Meade by another internee, A. Kappus, with whom he had been detained at Fort Howard. Carta never saw the letter himself, because it was censored and returned to Kappus with the following explanation from the commanding officer at Fort Meade:

According to present regulations correspondence between internees is prohibited except in cases of close family relationships. Your letter to Internee Alfio Carta is therefore returned to you herewith.

The offending letter, kept from its intended recipient, goes as follows:

Dear Carta:

Some time ago I was informed that it might be possible to write to you directly at Camp Meade. Please excuse me for not having written immediately; some confusing happenings made it impossible.

First of all I should like to thank you very sincerely for the letter and the $1.00 which your brother sent me; and, thanks too for the regards which he forwarded to me. I am very glad, indeed, that you do not regret having been transferred to Camp Meade.

Here, everything has changed considerably. However, it is not advisable to report about that; necessary information could have been found in the *Baltimore Sun*.

The garden is in a satisfactory condition, although I have not had enough time to fight the beetles. Some plants die suddenly; apparently a disease of the roots kills them, or some parasites eat the roots. We already picked about half a dozen very beautiful tomatoes and expect a rich harvest. All the zinnias have been blooming; most of them are white. Mr. Carney told me that all the zinnias he received were white ones and he is disappointed about this monotony....The radishes will be harvested in a few days; because of the ants or other parasites they are not good. On July 29 we admired the first moonflower which was a perfect beauty.

Your shorts are of great help to me; they are light and very cool. Unfortunately, we have myriads of biting flies; and on certain days

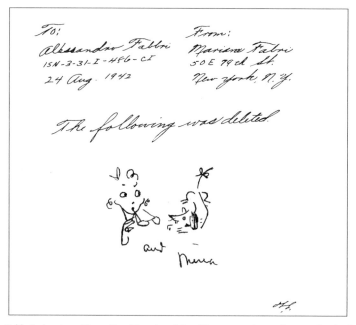

Mariam Fabbri's drawing of herself and her dog, deleted by censors from a letter to her husband. Courtesy of National Archives and Records Administration, College Park, Md.

and hours it is almost impossible to stay outside the screened rooms...

I should like to take this opportunity to thank you again for all your kindness and for your help and assistance. Be assured that I and all of us still miss you and very often think of you. I hope and wish sincerely that we do meet again after these hard times are over and that, then, I can prove to you the deep devotion I have for you and the confidence I shall always have in you.

> My best wishes and kindest regards,
> A. Kappus[33]

It is hard to see what harm might have resulted from such a letter, or how letters between internees at different camps could be considered more dangerous (collusion in escape attempts? gathering information about more than one camp?) than conversations among internees at the same camp, especially with the censors combing through every line of mail, but that was the rule.

Finally, it appears that drawings—not just maps, or drawings of important facilities, but drawings of any kind, were prohibited. In the file of Alessandro Fabbri, in addition to letters expressing his mystification over why he should have been interned, several parts of letters written to him from his wife Mariam are deleted. An August 1942 letter from her contains the following deletion:

> She was telling me about the food situation there [handwritten: *Italy – censor*]. It's really bad, Sandro. No potatoes, very little bread, no spaghetti, no butter, coffee, tea, sugar, cheese—wine is becoming scarce, half a kilo of rice per month, no lard, very little meat—in fact practically nothing but turnips, zucchini, and one other vegetable—I forget what. Coffee in the black market is one hundred lira a pound—tea, two hundred. It was terrible to hear her—and the stories about Greece that her friend was telling would make you weep. There is just nothing there to eat at all. It sounds very much as if unless this damn war doesn't end soon, the world will have returned to...

These deletions evidently were due to the references to Italy, a nation with whom the United States was at war. But what in these references could be considered damaging to security? In fact, quite the contrary, the references would seem more likely to discourage anyone contemplating a return to Italy, or a continuation of the fight. No matter. The mere mention of "there" was enough.

More astonishing still are the cartoon deletions. It appears that Mariam Fabbri was something of a cartoonist, having developed funny, self-deprecating cartoon renderings of herself and her dog, Mina. One depicts her washing her hair and putting on clothes, with the caption: "The next hour of my life will be consumed thusly." Others show her trying to think of something to write, and there are several of her dog.

All have been deleted. It appears that the prohibition on drawings brooked no exceptions; to the censor, drawings were drawings, and all were equally suspect.

In some ways, the same was true of the entire program of internment. If one fit a certain category—Italian war veteran, journalist, community leader—one did not have to do anything to be arrested; one's beliefs, real or inferred, were enough. As Jerre Mangione admitted when he toured the internment camps: "The war had thrust us into the shameful position of locking up people for their beliefs."[34]

The censored material accords with that principle exactly—if in doubt, cut it out—except that for many internees, it must have seemed that what was being scissored from their lives was their very selves.

Endnotes:

1. See Umberto Benedetti, *Italian Boys at Fort Missoula, Montana 1941–1943*, (Missoula, Mont.: Pictorial Histories Publishing Co., 1991). Though Benedetti has continued to testify to the "pleasant" conditions at the camp they christened "Bella Vista," or "beautiful view," other documents indicate that even among the merchant seamen, what Jerre Mangione termed "barbed-wire sickness" led in some cases to suicides, at least four of which were recorded at Missoula.

2. Most Italian resident aliens were initially picked up and processed by the INS under Justice Department jurisdiction. When a hearing recommended internment, the internee would be turned over to the PMGO under War Department jurisdiction to be formally interned, usually at an army base, at which point the PMGO Form No. 2 would be initiated. The first internees turned over to army custody for internment were sent to Camp Upton, New York in February 1942.

3. Mario Ricciardelli, Letter to Swiss Minister, Ricciardelli file, Dec. 9, 1942, RG 389, Records Relating to Italian Civilian Internees During WWII, 1941-46, Boxes 2-20, Provost Marshal General's Office, National Archives and Records Administration, College Park, Md. (hereafter RG 389 NARA II)

4. Mario Ricciardelli, Letter to Col. Hutchins, Dec. 4, 1942, RG 389 NARA II.

5. In the recorded conversation between internee Guidi-Buttrini and his son, Guidi-Buttrini refers to the fact that internees were paid ten cents for each day of internment, "his share coming to better than $14." Guidi-Buttrini file, RG 389 NARA II.

6. Thomas McDermott, acting supervisor for Earl Harrison, INS, to Col. Bryan, PMGO, Nov. 24, 1942, in Modesto Sabini file, RG 389 NARA II.

7. Roland Becsey, Letter to PMGO, Jan. 12, 1943, in Sabini file, RG 389 NARA II.

8. The INS camps run by the border patrol were at Missoula, Montana; Bismarck, North Dakota; Fort Stanton, New Mexico; Santa Fe, New Mexico; Crystal City, Texas; Kenedy, Texas; and Seagoville, Texas. The PMGO had camps at several army bases, including Fort George Meade, Maryland; Fort McAlester, Oklahoma; Fort Sam Houston, Texas; Camp Forrest, Tennessee; Camp McCoy, Wisconsin; and Fort McDowell on Angel Island in San

Francisco Bay. The INS also had detention stations at Ellis Island, New York; East Boston, Massachusetts; Gloucester City, New Jersey; Detroit, Michigan; Seattle, Washington; San Francisco, California; and San Pedro, California. As the war progressed, the INS opened temporary detention facilities at Portland, Oregon; Salt Lake City, Utah; St. Louis, Missouri; St. Paul, Minnesota; Kansas City, Missouri; Cleveland, Ohio; Houston, Texas; Hartford, Connecticut; Niagara Falls, New York; Chicago, Illinois; Miami, Florida; Pittsburgh, Pennsylvania; Nanticoke, Pennsylvania; Ft. Howard, Maryland; and more permanent facilities at Sharp Park, California, and Tuna Canyon, California. Finally, War Department facilities for civilian internees were run by the army, with military discipline. INS facilities were run by the border patrol, with a far different attitude.

9. Albert Berizzi, personal interview.

10. Harry Lucas, Memo of Monitored Conversation between Internee Ubaldo Guidi-Buttrini and his son, Sept. 17, 1942, in Guidi-Buttrini file, RG 389 NARA II. It should be noted, however, that Guidi-Buttrini's inference may not have held elsewhere, for in his notebook, Prospero Cecconi also makes note of uniforms at Fort Sam Houston: "May 28, 1942, I received prisoner clothing." As to the uniforms for Japanese internees, Kiku Funabiki actually has in her possession her father's internee uniform, with "PW" printed on it. This suggests that internees at camps run by the War Department were considered prisoners of war and were treated as such.

11. Ibid.

12. Prospero Cecconi, "Via Crucis," unpaginated.

13. In its *Administrative History of the Immigration and Naturalization Service during World War II*, dated Aug. 19, 1946, the INS confirms this: "the first internees...were accepted at a temporary camp the Army had established at Camp Upton, New York. The housing facilities provided were 16' x16' pyramidal tents with wooden floors and boarded sides." Eventually, however, the War Department's need to accommodate hundreds of thousands of prisoners of war led it to wash its hands of civilian internees altogether. In May 1943, it turned over all the Italian resident aliens in its custody to the Immigration and Naturalization Service, ending three years of bickering over the proper policy to be applied. The Italian aliens were then sent to Fort Missoula and remained there until their release or transfer, in March 1944, to Ellis Island, from where many were repatriated.

14. Rules and regulations governing mail, telegrams, and visits were sent to the families of internees upon the arrival of each internee. Among the rules about visits were these: "Each internee is allowed to submit the names of five (5) persons whom he desires to visit him. Passes are issued only upon direct written request to this Headquarters for Sundays only during the hours of 1:00 P.M. to 4:00 P.M. Internees are limited to two visitors per month not on consecutive Sundays...*Foreign Language Monitors*—All conversations must be in English...All visitors will call at Headquarters, 1343rd Service Unit, before presenting passes at gate for entry into Internment Camp." from "Revised Regulations Governing Mail, Telegrams and Visitors to the Fort George G. Meade Internment Camp, Fort George G. Meade, Maryland," by permission of Lucetta Berizzi Drypolcher.

15. Stomach trouble was clearly, for Italian internees, the most common ailment. One internee, Giobatta Gasparini, even died of it: Gasparini's death, on January 17, 1943, was attributed to gastric hemorrhage, ulcer of the stomach, and cancer of the stomach. Death certificate, Gasparini file, RG 389 NARA II.

16. This in spite of the fact that in a previous visit by his daughter Temi Guidi, the internee noted that "now that the Italians had a separate kitchen with an Italian cook who cooked Italian dishes for them, they had good food, and that it was not necessary for them to send in food." Marconi memo cited in note 19, Guidi-Buttrini file, RG 389 NARA II.

17. Memo, HQ McAlester Internment Camp to PMGO, Dec. 7, 1942, Fioroni file, RG 389 NARA II.

18. PMGO to Commanding General, 3rd Service Command, Baltimore, Md., Dec. 14, 1942, Fioroni file, RG 389 NARA II.

19. Caton J. Marconi, Memo, August 30, 1942, Guidi-Buttrini file, RG 389 NARA II.

20. On the other hand, another recorded conversation at this same camp between Margherita Ricciardelli (wife of Mario referenced above) and another internee, Enrico Torino, apparently was allowed to take place in Italian; the monitor, Private Jos. Gravino, noted at its inception: "Conversation was conducted in Italian." The contradiction can be attributed either to the general inconsistency in rules and their application, or to the fact, as evidenced in the file of Angelo DiCarlo, that internees could conduct visits in Italian if they applied for permission ahead of time. See Memo in Torino file, and letter in DiCarlo file: "As I do not speak English, I respectfully request the authorization to talk in Italian before an interpreter." RG 389 NARA II.

21. See Jerre Mangione, *An Ethnic at Large: A Memoir of America in the Thirties and Forties* (New York: Putnam, 1978), p. 322: "At the outset of the war, in the interests of national security, the media had cheerfully acceded to the Department of Justice's request that as little as possible be said about the arrest and detention of alien enemies since any publicity given to the subject might seriously interfere with the government's observance of the Geneva Convention of 1929. Based on the concept of reciprocity, the pact provided the government with its only means of assuring the safety and humane treatment of Americans who became prisoners in enemy countries. It protected all interned men and women from acts of violence as well as from insults and public curiosity…"

22. Capt. David A. Wiley, Letter to Military Intelligence, Feb. 12, 1943, Berizzi file, RG 389 NARA II.

23. Albert Berizzi, personal interview.

24. Rules and regulations about mail were extensive. "Each internee is allowed to name five (5) persons with whom he desires to correspond. Two letters, not to exceed 24 lines each, and one post card weekly may be written by internees, on approved stationery…*Rules Governing Correspondence:* 1. Not to be of inordinate length. 2. Be written on one side of paper only. 3. Be legibly written. 4. Be clear in meaning. 5. Have no writing on margin. 6. Show the full name and address of the sender. 7. Show return address on envelope. 8. Show internee's name, serial number, company or group identification, name of Internment Camp. 9. Contain no deletions, erasures, strikeovers…*Telephone Calls:* Internees will not be permitted to make or receive any telephone calls." "Revised Regulations Governing Mail,…"

25. Velleda Guidi, Letter to C.O. 1343rd Service Unit, Fort George G. Meade, Guidi-Buttrini file, RG 389 NARA II.

26. Velleda Guidi, Letter to her father, May 7, 1942, Guidi-Buttrini file, RG 389 NARA II.

27. Deletions, Michelangelo Scicchitani file, RG 389 NARA II.

28. Deletion, Giovanni Favoino file, RG 389 NARA II

29. Deletion, Alfredo Tribuani file, RG 389 NARA II.

30. Deletion, Tullio Verrando file, RG 389 NARA II.

31. Ibid.

32. Ibid.

33. A. Kappus, Letter to Alfio Carta, Aug. 8, 1942, in Carta file, RG 389 NARA II.

34. Mangione, *An Ethnic at Large*, p. 352.

Orders to Take Him Away

by Lucetta Berizzi Drypolcher

The first roundup of Italian Americans took place almost immediately after Pearl Harbor. Louis Berizzi, a raw-silk importer, was included in that early roundup, but strangely, he was detained on Ellis Island for nearly a year after his arrest before the authorities decided to formally intern him. The authorities offered no explanation to Berizzi or his family for this or for any other circumstance of his arrest.

Recently, with the help of letters and documents she saved, Berizzi's daughter Lucetta has been able to remember those days with some precision, including what it felt like to visit her father at both Ellis Island and the internment camp at Fort Meade, Maryland. She also testifies to the collateral effects of being related to an internee in those days, socially, financially, and in her employment.

In the very early hours of December 8, 1941, FBI agents came to our apartment at 78th Street and Park Avenue in New York City. We were all sound asleep. My father was in his pajamas; they told him to get dressed, as they had orders to take him away. No explanation was given. They would not divulge where they were taking him. They stayed in his bedroom while he dressed, so we had no time to speak to him privately. They did not even give him time to gather personal effects or toiletries. I believe it took several days [for us] to find out that he had been taken to Ellis Island. We were pretty shaken.

On December 11th, a telegram came from him requesting personal items to be taken to the Barge Office for Ellis Island. The telegram also requested news about us. On December 14th another telegram arrived advising that we would get information regarding visitation. I cannot remember now the exact date those visits started.

Several days after his arrest, we learned that my father's office at Rockefeller Plaza had been locked and sealed by the Enemy Alien Custodian, and all my father's assets were blocked. In time we learned that when my brother's tuition was due at Lehigh College, we had to petition the Enemy Alien Custodian for the money to pay it. For other money, my stepmother had to make a special trip to Ellis Island to obtain my father's co-signature on three postdated checks for $500 for our expenses. It was our money, but we had to justify our need for it and get approval from the Enemy Alien Custodian.

The next big event for us was a notice that a hearing would take place on January 12, 1942....[1] The hearing was to be held before the Alien Enemy Hearing Board at the courthouse at Foley Square, New York City. The hearing was for my father and his business associate, Prince Boncompagni-Ludovisi. Only family and friends could speak for the defendants. No legal representation was allowed....

I was twenty-two at the time and was asked many questions about our trips to Italy. These trips were our summer vacations. We would first go to Rome to visit our mother's relatives. Then our father would join us to go to my grandmother's house in the mountains near Bergamo. Aunts and uncles and a cousin would be there too. The hearing board also wanted to know what other places we visited that might be important. I mentioned that once we had visited a silk-spinning mill to see how the cocoons were harvested and the silk extracted and put on spools.[2] The question I found rather amusing was about languages. How come I spoke French and Italian, they wanted to know. I told them that when my mother died (I was eleven years old), we had a French governess, so we spoke French, which my father also spoke. With our parents we spoke Italian. I had also had classes in German at Lenox School and had graduated from the Spence School in 1938. There I was enrolled in French and Italian classes, which were part of the curriculum.

I'm not sure if they questioned my stepmother; she was pretty hysterical. We had other people who vouched for him, to see if we could obtain his release. We didn't, and he remained at Ellis Island.

At the time of my father's internment I had a job at Saks Fifth Avenue. I was a salesperson and worked in different departments at first. I would also be called upon to escort customers who did not speak English, so my

Albert, Louis, and Lucetta Berizzi on a trip to Italy before the war (ca. 1934), near Bergamo. Courtesy of Lucetta Berizzi Drypolcher

languages were useful in helping people to shop; "subversive" I don't think they were. Nonetheless, the FBI showed up at Saks one day and I was called up to the personnel office. The meeting did not take very long, but I was subsequently fired. I guess they found what I was doing suspicious.

The irony is, sometime after that I got a much better job at the United States Cane Sugar Refiners Association. My immediate boss was Ellsworth Bunker, who was head of the association and in charge of all sugar allocations, which could have been very sensitive. The FBI didn't seem to mind that. After six months as

Louis Berizzi in Central Park, a few years after his release from internment. Courtesy of Lucetta Berizzi Drypolcher

a receptionist, I became office manager. Bunker later became ambassador to India, and I resigned in April of 1946 to get married and move to New Mexico.

While my father was at Ellis Island we could visit every week. We were allowed to bring him changes of clothes and food. In one telegram, "Bonny" (Boncompagni) asked my stepmother to buy him, at Macy's, "three pairs of white cotton banjo seater pants with lastex belt, size 36." Visitation was in a very large room with tables and benches—no privacy whatsoever.

Some of the Italian enemy aliens were given the choice of returning to Italy with their families. An Italian actor named Tullio Carminati, I remember, was going to go to Rome, and we were able to ask him to inform our relatives of our situation. I don't remember when my father's associate, Boncompagni, left Ellis Island. I know he eventually went to Switzerland. We were also offered the possibility of leaving the United States. This was just not an option for us. My brother was in college here and would shortly be called to serve in the United States Army. None of us had any desire to make such a change in our lives.[3]

Towards the end of 1942 it became apparent that many interned Italian resident aliens would be transferred to concentration camps. It was then that we learned that my father would be sent to Fort George Meade in Maryland. Still no reason why! On December 4, 1942, we were advised of his arrival there and given his new mailing address.[4] We were also sent a copy of regulations and restrictions governing mail and visitation.

In January, my brother's request to visit our father on January 24, 1943, was denied. Our stepmother had visited on January 10th and had just been issued a pass to visit on January 24th. These two visits were all that were allowed that month. For this reason, and the fact that my stepmother needed to see him to discuss many family matters, I only went with her to visit once. My brother also saw him only once.[5]

Shortly after my father's transfer to Camp Meade we moved to a smaller apartment. Our finances were being stretched to the limit and we had no assurance that this would end any time soon. During that time, my father's letters to us were always heartbreaking. He tried to be reassuring. He wished us to know that he had always wanted the best for us. He was so sorry that these hard times were upon us. He apologized and promised to make it up to us.

As I mentioned before, conditions at the camp were so alien to what my father was accustomed to. Visitation was infrequent and under strict surveillance. We could only speak English. The meeting room was cold and crowded, and he didn't look well. He was underweight—just not the same, in a fatigue uniform with "PW" on the back. There was sort of a general room where we met with him. The internees would come from their quarters. They were behind barbed wire, we could see that as we entered. We were very close, so it

Albert Berizzi (far left) and friends in the U.S. Army at a Milan airport during World War II. Courtesy of Lucetta Berizzi Drypolcher

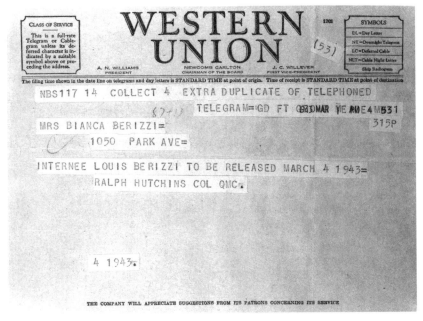

Telegram informing Bianca Berizzi that her husband would soon be released from Fort Meade, Maryland. Courtesy of Lucetta Berizzi Drypolcher

was very difficult being there. Albert said he was crushed, and he was. But I never saw him be angry about it, just sort of incredulous about it. In his letters he would say always, "Don't worry; this will end."

While my father was still interned, my brother was inducted into the army and reported for duty at Camp Wheeler in Georgia. From there he was transferred to Camp Ritchie in Maryland, where he trained for military intelligence. His division was to have landed in Sicily, but due to some delay they were ordered to land at Salerno....As the war in Italy progressed, he was transferred to the Office of Strategic Services, again because of his knowledge of Italian.

It was when we learned that he was being trained for military intelligence that we decided I would go to Washington, D.C., with a lawyer, I think to the Justice Department, to plead for my father's release. Aside from the fact that conditions at Camp Meade in winter were causing my father to have some health problems, and that the food was certainly not what he was accustomed to, it just seemed so unjust to have a father interned as an Italian enemy alien in a POW concentration camp, and a son about to go overseas to fight for his country. That was my case: my brother is going to land in Italy to fight for America, and my father is interned here. How can you hold my father when my brother is going to fight in Italy?

Finally, on March 1, 1942, we received a collect Western Union message from the Commander at Fort Meade confirming that our father would be released on March 4....My stepmother sent a telegram to my father the same day asking for his train arrival so we could meet him at the station. We were all overjoyed.

———

Senator Robert Torricelli of New Jersey says about the legislation he introduced into the Senate[6] to acknowledge that Italian Americans suffered these events, "I don't think there's a lingering anger about it."

In me it is not anger, but in recalling what that time was like I find that much pain is still there. Now I am sort of having to deal with it again.

I hope that the recognition and apology we are seeking will help us to finally put the matter to rest.

My heart goes out to all who I am sure went through similar anguish and perhaps had greater losses. They must all be acknowledged, even if the past cannot be changed.

Endnotes:
1. Standard procedure called for three hearing board members, all from the detainee's community.
2. Louis Berizzi "was in the raw silk importing business, and the company was an Italian company in Bergamo. So his brother became an American citizen to do business here, and my father kept his Italian citizenship so he could go back and forth." Albert Berizzi, personal interview.
3. Documents in internee files indicate that the offer to repatriate was made to internees at least twice: once when they were under INS jurisdiction, and again when they were formally interned and consigned to the Provost Marshal General's jurisdiction. Each internee had to fill out a Repatriation Form stating whether or not he would agree to repatriate "in the event of internment" or "whether or not I am interned." A number of Italian-born internees were repatriated in mid-1942; whether they, or others, were used in civilian prisoner exchanges (as Japanese Peruvians brought to the United States most definitely were) has not yet been determined.
4. The first letter from Camp Meade stipulates that mail should be addressed to: Internee Louis Berizzi, ISN-3-31-I-545-CI, Area "C", Alien Internment Camp, Fort George G. Meade, Md. A second letter, a month later on January 18, 1943, changes the address to name, serial number, name of internment camp, Box 20, General Post Office, New York, New York. This was said to expedite "censorship." No postage was required if in the place for postage was written "Prisoner of War Mail—Free."
5. "They were wearing fatigue uniforms with a big "PW" on the back. He was a pretty crushed guy." Albert Berizzi, personal interview.
6. S. 1909 was the companion bill to the Wartime Violation of Italian American Civil Liberties Act, H.R. 2442, signed into law November 7, 2000.

Letters to 3024 Pierce

by Rose D. Scherini

Carmelo Ilacqua was living an ordinary immigrant's life in San Francisco when World War II changed his family's life. He was one of many immigrants residing in a city where foreign-born Italians made up nine percent of the city's residents. Prior to the war, San Francisco had the largest number of Italians in the West.

Ever since September 1939—when the war began in Europe—the immigrants from potential enemy countries had held an uncertain status. Those who had not obtained United States citizenship feared they would be perceived as enemies of their adopted country, even though their native-born children and often their spouses were U.S. citizens. At the same time, the Italian Americans were gravely concerned about their relatives in Italy.

Carmelo, a U.S. resident since 1924, was married to Bruna Giusti, a naturalized immigrant. Ilacqua had not become a U.S. citizen because the conditions of his employment at the Italian consulate required him to maintain his Italian citizenship.[1] Carmelo and Bruna had one child, Costanza Gioia, then six years old. The family lived on Russian Hill in a flat they were buying.

On December 19, 1941—less than two weeks after the attack on Pearl Harbor—Ilacqua was arrested and then interned as a "dangerous" enemy alien. It was to be a major disruption in his life and those of his wife and small daughter.[2] His early years had not been free of disruptions: in the Messina earthquake of 1906, when he was eleven, he was buried in debris for three days until rescued. During the First World War, he served in the Italian navy. Then in 1924, as a merchant seaman, he jumped ship in Seattle, Washington, and was on his own in this new land until he got established. In 1928 he moved to San Francisco, where he found employment at the Italian consulate. He married Bruna Giusti in 1932, and three years later they had a daughter.

On the evening of December 19, 1941, an FBI agent and two San Francisco policemen came to 3024 Pierce and arrested Carmelo "by order of President Roosevelt" on the authority of a warrant signed by the U.S. Attorney General. They searched his desk for "incriminating papers"—and found none. Costanza, his six-year-old, asked the agents if they wanted to search her little desk. Then the agents took Ilacqua away, without advising his wife what was to happen.

Several days later, Carmelo phoned home to say he was being held at 201 Silver Avenue, an Immigration and Naturalization Service facility, but was expecting to leave soon by train for another facility. He mentioned several other local Italians in the same situation. He asked Bruna to bring him some clothing, and she and Costanza were allowed to see Carmelo briefly.

The next news was a telegram, dated December 29, 1941, from Fort Missoula, Montana. For almost two years he was moved from camp to camp in places like Tennessee, Texas, and Oklahoma before being released in late 1943 when Italy became a U.S. ally.

Internees were allowed to mail two letters and one postcard per week. Bruna saved this correspondence in a brown valise, and in 1990 Costanza Ilacqua Foran let me read the material saved by her mother. More recently, Costanza found a small number of letters written by her mother, Bruna ("Buba"), to Carmelo during his time at Missoula and Camp Forrest, Tennessee.

Why was this man interned? In fall 1939, when Britain declared war on Germany, President Franklin Roosevelt directed FBI head J. Edgar Hoover to compile a list of individuals who should be detained in case the U.S. entered the conflict. At first, lists were compiled of German Americans, then—as the war came closer—Italians, Japanese, and some others were added to the lists. In addition to the FBI, the Office of Naval Intelligence and the Army's G-2 Branch also added names of "potentially dangerous" naturalized citizens to these lists.

According to my research, Italians from San Francisco who were on these lists fell into one or more of the following categories:

1. Members of the Federation of Italian War Veterans (primarily veterans of the First World War)
2. Employees of Italian-language newspapers
3. Teachers in Italian foreign-language schools, i.e., the *Dopo Scuola* financed by the Italian government.

Carmelo Ilacqua had served in the Italian navy, was a member of the Federation of Italian War Veterans, and was the consulate liaison with the San Francisco chapter. His FBI report describes him as chancellor (their translation of *cancelliere*, which also means "registrar") of the consulate, whereas he was only a local employee assigned to administrative and clerical work relating to immigrants. Furthermore, the FBI reported "subject was observed to leave the *Tatu Maru* by special agents" without noting that during the early days of the

European war, all diplomatic pouches traveled across the Pacific, as the submarine war in the Atlantic made that crossing too dangerous. Ilacqua was merely picking up the mail for the consulate. The FBI report also notes Ilacqua's membership in the Fascist Party without explaining that it was another condition of his employment.

The report says, "subject not apprehended previously because a former consular employee." And, in fact, Ilacqua was asked by the consulate if he wished to return to Italy along with the other staff when the U.S. ordered the closure of Italian and German consulates in June 1941, but he refused to do so, as he wanted to remain here. The returning consular staff were treated quite differently by this government, being housed in elegant East Coast resorts like Greenbrier and Saratoga Springs until neutral registry ships such as the *Gripsholm* could return them to their own countries.

Bruna and Carmelo Ilacqua with daughter Costanza at their home at 3024 Pierce in San Francisco, ca. 1945. Courtesy of Costanza Ilacqua Foran

After the aliens were interned, their cases were reviewed by Alien Enemy Hearing Boards, with the only facts presented being those in the FBI reports; no legal counsel was provided or even allowed. Ilacqua's hearing was held on February 10, 1942, and his internment was confirmed. When families learned later that they could request rehearing and present letters of character recommendation, they did so, although it took many months for the rehearings to be scheduled. Thus, in August 1943, at Ilacqua's second hearing, the board—composed of army officers, civilians, and FBI agents—recommended his release, but final approval by the attorney general was withheld for almost two months because of FBI objections. Did the FBI actually believe its own reports, while the hearing board believed Ilacqua and his references that he was loyal and truthful? Ilacqua finally returned home in October 1943, almost two years after his arrest.

Internee families were given no financial assistance by the U.S. government, although there were reports that the American Red Cross and the Federal War Relief Agency would help the families. However, when Bruna Ilacqua went to these agencies, she was turned away. Since the family was without a breadwinner after Carmelo's arrest, Bruna's sister and brother-in-law moved into the flat and helped with the household expenses. The Bank of America—which held the mortgage on their flat—allowed the family to pay interest only and skip payment on the principal while Carmelo was interned, thereby placing the Ilacquas in a position similar to servicemen for whom the bank had created this provision.

The correspondence among the family members over the two years of Ilacqua's internment reveals some of the stresses and strains of their situation. What follows are excerpts from letters between Carmelo and Bruna and occasional postccards and greeting cards from Costanza. The collection of letters from Carmelo cover the period from December 1941 through September 1943. Bruna's letters cover a short period, mostly in 1942.

December 29, 1941. Western Union Missoula Mont. Arrived In good health after a nice trip. Am comfortable and warm. Dante and others here well. Kisses to you Costanza Beppina Bastiano. Follows letter, Carmelo Ilacqua.

December 30, 1941. Buba dearest: 2nd day at Missoula. I'm in a view barracks with the other Italians from San Francisco. I placed my bed near Dante Francesconi and Dr. Santini.

January 10, 1942. I'm beginning to be a little restless as no mail from you yet. Also, Immigration in S.F. hasn't sent my belongings yet. Don't worry and get sick because Costanza needs you more than ever....I can only write 2 times a week and not more than 29 lines. Lovingly, Carmelo.

January 10, 1942. It's below freezing here (28°). Hope to have my hearing soon. Confident they will be fair. Think of you two constantly. Bertoletti and others felt humiliated. Ask Mrs. Walsh, Mr. Donahue, and Mr. Couch to write the authorities on my behalf. But don't spend any money as that little you have left must be used for Costanza and you. The morning we left—I knew you were there, and they allowed me to kiss you goodbye....The ravioli you left for me I shared with della Maggiora, who is still at Silver Ave. There were guards and some Japanese Americans on train to Missoula; the guards were kind.

January 15, 1942. [telegram] Written already several letters. Don't worry. Received only your letters 12/27 and 1/7. Kisses, Carmelo.

January 17, 1942. While I write there is music coming out from the radio Ghirardi received. I would write long letters but the rules does not permit.

January 26, 1942. Last night we had the first show in the auditorium—a musical program and sketches by Ghirardi. Francesconi was *maestro di ceremonie*. Trento was supposed to present a few numbers but on account of a cold could not take part....I received letter from Patrizi. He sent Trento some books and cigarets for us.[3]

January 30, 1942. As far as my hearing is concerned, I think it takes time both for the hearing and for the decision from Washington. It might take months. Anyway, keep your chin up.

February 6, 1942. One has the impression to be in a military camp. Reveille at 6:30 A.M., silence 10:30 P.M., and so, at 47, I experience again "military life"— this time in an internment camp.

February 10, 1942. I was called for the hearing. The board was nice and there was one of the board that...allowed me to talk with you and Gioia at Silver Ave. I don't know the result but my impression is that I will be a resident of Ft. Missoula for a considerable time. Anyway, let's hope for the best. Kisses to you and Gioia.

February 13, 1942. So I had my hearing and all those of San Francisco had theirs. I hope they will free us as we are innocent of anything against this country.

February 23, 1942. From the papers I see that more arrests are being made and it makes me doubt an early release, so the best thing is to place ourselves in the hands of God and pray that his will be done.

February 26, 1942. We must be patient and meet adversities with courage and strength because justice will be done eventually to those who are innocent because God is infinitely good.

February 27, 1942. [postcard] Thank you, Gioia, for the Valentine and liquorice [sic] you sent me. A Big Kiss from Daddy.

March 6, 1942. The sailors are beginning to get busy outside.[4] Near my barrack a *gioco di bocce* [ball court] is being built. Some are planting sweet peas and other flowers; others are preparing the ground to plant vegetables....Yesterday we had a snowstorm with a high wind. Now we're in another storm, but meeting this storm with courage and fortitude, we will be able to withstand it and we, too, will see the sunshine again.

March 20, 1942. I had a dream in which I was home again. I'm giving English lessons to two of the Italian merchant marine officers.

April 9, 1942. I'm sending a ship model to Bobby [nephew], one for you, and another one for the house. Please send $12.50 to Egidio Dordoni, the merchant marine who made the boats.

April 10, 1942. Today at noon we leave Ft. Missoula for the South. We made gnocchi for our table as a farewell special. It is a moving experience to leave the many friends among the Italian merchant seamen. [Bruna also received a letter at this time from another internee, Dr. Ruggero Santini, informing her that Carmelo was going to Ft. Sam Houston, Texas.]

April 17, 1942. [telegram] Just arrived. Everything ok. My address: Dodd Field Internment Camp, Ft. Sam Houston, Tex.

April 17, 1942. I live in a tent with 3 others: Dante Francesconi, Filippo Molinari, and Gianni Cardellini. There are 4 Japanese internees living in next tent.

April 29, 1942. The tents of us Italians are better kept and more attractive than the Germans and the Japanese. From Baccocina's friend I heard that you and the other ladies were together to see what could be done for us.

May 2, 1942. [to San Francisco florist Elia Durisotti] Please send flowers to Bruna for Mother's Day and I will pay you when I return home.

May 21, 1942. The German internees' homemade orchestra played and sang several popular German songs.

May 24, 1942. Wish I could telephone home but not allowed. Some of the other Italians are Eduardo Dinucci, Bossoni, Aliotti.

May 29, 1942. Dinucci is now in charge of kitchen and for 3 days we've been eating food cooked Italian stile [sic].[5] Molinari receives *L'Italia* so we keep posted on the life of dear San Francisco.[6]

June 2, 1942. We have been told that the families of those interned, if American citizens, should apply to the American Red Cross for help. Those who are still subjects of Italy should instead apply to the Swiss consulate.[7]

June 14, 1942. [from Bruna] Dear Babbo [Daddy]: I received your letter of 6/8 last Friday, you seemed to be kind of sad. But dear Daddy, you have to be patient and have faith that this cruel war will finish soon. I am sorry that from now on you will write only on special forms....Why don't you write as much as you want, keep the letters, and I shall read all when you come back? It will be something like a diary....I would like very much to visit you but don't like to take C. as I hear the voyage is kind of strenuous. What do you think, Babbo? Shall I come or wait for you to come back? Lovingly, Buba.

June 15, 1942. If you see Mrs. Dinucci pay her my compliments for the way her husband manages our kitchen. Thanks for the poem. I like it very much.

June 16, 1942. I'm moving again, to Camp Forrest, Tenn. Sorry to leave Ft. Sam Houston as treated very well, much better than at Missoula where authorities attitude was as though we had broken laws.

June 19, 1942. [from Camp Forrest, third camp in seven months] This is my first letter from Camp Forrest where I arrived 3 hours ago after a...trip of about 30 hours. On the train we ate in the diner and for the first time since...they took me away from home, I ate at a table set with tablecloth and napkins, and myself and the others felt again that we are human beings.

June 21, 1942. Now we start the Camp Forrest chapter of this tragic-comedy of my internment. During Mass could hear the melancholic chant of a Buddhist service in the Japanese quarters.

June 23, 1942. [from Bruna] Dearest Babbo, I received your 1st letter from Tenn....Tears came down and dampened my face when I was reading that for the first time you had tablecloth and napkins and you felt like a human being again. Poor Daddy! You have no idea how that made me feel.

Carmelo Ilacqua when he was in the Italian navy during World War I. Courtesy of Costanza Ilacqua Foran

June 26, 1942. You would like me to write a diary, at present I don't feel like doing it, maybe later. Forget visiting me here, it is too far, and to see me for about one hour and be separated again is too painful, and besides the expenses of the trip are too high. Life here [3 lines here were deleted by censor.]

June 28, 1942. This is not like Ft. Missoula, it is a new camp. I am glad that you and Gioia work some in my garden. Write me how the flowers came out this year, if the rhododendron is in bloom and if the crab apple made many flowers.

July 5, 1942. [from Bruna] Dear Carmelo, The Red Cross here does not know a thing about help-ing the families of the interned. Patience. Let's hope that you will be back soon, then you will work for us and we won't need nobody's help. Relatives and friends send you their regards, and from me and Gioia many, many kisses.

July 5, 1942. Yesterday we elected Dinucci as camp leader. The magazine pic-tures I used to send Gioia from Missoula are now being removed from my let-ters by the censor even though I asked the censor to let them pass.

July 10, 1942. Did you go to the Federal Emergency Board? I hope that the authorities who took me away from my family will at least give assistance to my family, American citizens, left without support by the internment of its bread-winner.

July 14, 1942. [from Costanza] Dear Daddy, How are you? I am fine. Thank you for the dollar that you send me. Come home soon. Love and kisses, Gioia.

July 15, 1942. [from Bruna] Dearest Carmelo, Beppina [sister] cannot go out after eight o'clock in the evening as she is not a citizen and this is the law now. I wish I could be home alone when I write you but I have to do the best I can. I am including 2 air mail stamps and the two 3-cent stamps. Many kisses, Bruna.

July 16, 1942. We received a food package from Italian Welfare Agency. Dinucci received herbs and garlic and so yesterday we tasted the best spaghetti sauce since we left S.F. Did you go to the Federal Emergency Board?

July 19, 1942. Please send me some books, one on real estate law and an Italian-English dictionary.

July 20, 1942. [from Bruna] Dear Carmelo: And finally we received the pictures for C's scrapbook. She was very happy about it. Now that she is home for vacation, she is waiting near the window or outside for the mailman. She still thinks that you are working for the government as a farmer and she is surprised that, with so many aliens, they just took you and not everybody. But I explained that you are very capable and this is the reason they had you.

I have been to the Fed. Emergency Board but they won't give me a thing. They suggest that I could work. I told them C. is too small to be left here and there and since my brother and sister are living with us, they want their money's worth. Love and kisses, Buba

August 2, 1942. Enclosed are photos of an amateur program with both German and Italian performers. [A note from censor who had removed the photos: "No pictures allowed."]

August 5, 1942. I'm in good health, we're all treated equal, do our share of upkeep, but not hard work....You should go out more because you need relaxation. We still don't know about a new hearing....I found a nest of baby thrushes.

August 12, 1942. [from Bruna] Dear Carmelo: Your book *The Business Encyclopedia* has arrived so I shall mail it to you tomorrow. Last Sun. my brother took us in Marin County. C. talked about the picnic we had last year with you. But everything is sad and even beautiful Marin has changed its appearance....I am so sorry that it is almost 8 months that you are missing your little girl. All her little and cute ways, the way she is progressing, rather intelligent and pretty. She is not the baby that was hiding under your coat that evening you left the house, when the authorities took you away from us. She is a big girl now and she is very tall for her age. Love always, Buba.

August 15, 1942. Saw a travelogue through Europe and Asia. Wish they had more movies especially of this type.

August 22, 1942. I'm giving lessons in English and citizenship. I'm reading about U.S. history in the camp library.

August 23, 1942. The authorities are treating us better now that they know us. I don't consider myself an enemy alien.

August 26, 1942. [from Costanza] Dear Daddy, I went over Egisto's place last Sat. and Sun. I wish you were with me. Love, Costanza.

September 3, 1942. I'm being called for naturalization....We're being moved again.

September 9, 1942. [from Bruna] Dearest Babbo: The letter I had last week, it is just marvelous. Every word shows your feeling, your refined and honest sentiment and also your resentment to be over there in a [censored] far away from us just because the world is in a mess. I enjoyed the letter in which you described your cabin. But, Daddy, I didn't know you had no sheets. You had them in Montana....Don't you think I better send you some? And how about blankets? Let me know and I shall send what you need. C. has decided that when you will be back we shall move in the country. She is so cute and is making herself friends. I am so glad that some of the internees are send back to their homes and families. I hope your day won't be very far. We will be so happy again. Love and many kisses, Buba.

September 14, 1942. [from Bruna] Dear Carmelo: What an anniversary, eh, Daddy? So far away from each other. But my soul is with you and on that day my thoughts will be all yours more than usual. Let's hope that next year we will have a regular anniversary and a happy one too, with the world at peace. Love and kisses. Yours always, Bruna.

September 21, 1942. [from Bruna] Dearest Carmelo, I had your letter today....I really was worrying, not knowing where you had been sent. I looked at the map right away to see just exactly where Oklahoma is situated....The roses and gardenia you sent me on our 10th anniversary were just too beautiful for words. I still have them in vases. I want to keep them long as possible. Best regards to Bertoletti and Cesana and all the others. Love and kisses, Buba.

September 24, 1942. [Ft. MacAlester, Okla.] There are 24 of us in the barrack including Dinucci, Bossoni.

September 25, 1942. [from Bruna] Dearest Carmelo, At times, if all this won't be so cruel and tragic, I would like to think that you are kept over there, so far away from us, because the authorities think that you are an enemy of this country. Then I say to myself: in war and in love everything is permissible. And so, reconcile with the fact that you are over there…We miss you very, very much—in many ways and in every way. Love and kisses, Buba.

September 26, 1942. [birthday card from Bruna: "With love to my husband on your birthday and always"] Dear Carmelo, Holy days, anniversary, and birthday are passing by—and you are still away. I wish you Daddy, with all my heart, that the authorities will send you home as soon as possible. I shall pray on your birthday that God will give you health, strength, and patience. And I shall also pray that you will write us soon. With love and kisses, Buba.

Internees at Fort Missoula, Montana. Courtesy of Costanza Ilacqua Foran

October 6, 1942. Italian Welfare sent us a box of fresh fruit and vegetables....Guido Trento performed last night....I resumed my study of Spanish, English, and real estate. There are no movies, no church services. Not allowed to receive the Spanish paper *L'Opinion* although received at Camp Forrest.

December 8, 1942. Mrs. Francesconi visited Nereo. I'm thinking about our Christmases together.

December 17, 1942. It's one year since my arrest.

January 18, 1943. There's a long delay between your letters as they now go through the censor in New York. I received a letter from the federal attorney in S.F.

January 26, 1943. I just now received my Xmas cards and mail from 12/14 to 12/28.

January 28, 1943. [written in Italian; trans. by author] I am happy because one of my mates dreamed that I, Carmelo, was going home.

February 8, 1943. Received package with dates and almonds, chocolate, your cake, and Valentine. For lunch we had veal cutlets, baked potatoes, and green beans. At night, risotto alla Milanese, Swiss cheese, fruit salad. It's different from my five years in the First War.

March 4, 1943. I'm sending you $11 to buy Easter gifts.

March 11, 1943. It's Ash Wednesday. I hope for peace, that our great country will succeed soon in bringing peace and liberty to all those subject to injustice.

———

The last letter to Carmelo in these collected letters was sent to Ft. Missoula the last day of August 1943. He had returned to Missoula to await his rehearing there. According to Immigration and Naturalization Service records, on June 30, 1943, the hearing board had unanimously recommended his release, noting, "the board is thoroughly impressed with the alien's loyalty to the US...that he had always been opposed to the Axis...that he fought the Germans once and would fight them again...this man impressed the board with his truthfulness." Despite FBI objection to Ilacqua's release, the attorney general gave final approval for parole on September 4, 1943. Carmelo finally returned to his family at 3024 Pierce.

Shortly after his return, the U.S. Army hired Ilacqua to teach Italian to officers in training at Stanford University for assignment to the occupation of Italy.[8] One day a "dangerous" alien—the next day training army officers!

Endnotes:

1. Current regulations now allow naturalized citizens to maintain dual citizenship.
2. This narrative is based on correspondence and interviews with Costanza Ilacqua Foran, Sacramento, Calif., 1989–1993 and records in the National Archives and the FBI.
3. Patrizi was the editor/publisher of *L'Italia;* he received an exclusion order in September 1942 as a naturalized citizen on the "dangerous" list.
4. The sailors were Italian national merchant seamen interned at Missoula in May 1941. Their ships had been stranded in Atlantic ports after the war began in Europe; the crew had been taken into custody when it was reported that they were sabotaging their ships so the ships could not be used against Italy.
5. Missoula archives report a "food riot" in 1942 by the Italian merchant seamen who complained about the cooking, especially the use of suet. They were allowed to do their own shopping and cooking after that.
6. *L'Italia* was the San Francisco-based foreign language newspaper that before the war had extolled Italy's Fascist government.
7. However, neither agency could help the internee families.
8. At least one other internee from San Francisco, Angelo Baccocina, was similarly employed by the army after his release.

New Discoveries, Old Prejudices
The Internment of Italian Americans during World War II

by Guido Tintori

Guido Tintori is a doctoral candidate and teaching assistant in the department of history at the University of Milan. His undergraduate thesis, "Italian Americans: Alien Enemies or Opera Singers? A History of the Italian Community in the United States from 1920 to 1942," was based on a two-month research trip to the National Archives in Washington, D.C. He presented a shortened version of this thesis dealing with the internment of Italian Americans during World War II at the American Italian Association's national conference in 1999. He is the recipient of numerous research scholarships, most recently to study the Italian American wartime story at the Franklin Delano Roosevelt Library in Hyde Park, New York.

When President Roosevelt, neglecting the fact that the United States was not yet formally at war with Mussolini, signed Public Proclamation 2527 on December 8, 1941, declaring all the Italian resident aliens in the country "alien enemies,"[1] an agreement between the War Department and the Department of Justice had already occurred on the matter some months before.[2] Attorney General Francis Biddle was to monitor every issue concerning the enemy aliens, and his personal approval would be required in order to proceed with the internment of any alien. The FBI, under the Department of Justice, was supposed to arrest those who, on the basis of the previous two years of investigations, had been listed as "dangerous to the public peace and safety of the United States." In fact, on September 6, 1939, President Roosevelt had officially instructed the FBI to investigate acts of sabotage and espionage by foreign agents on American soil. This had led to nothing but lists of Axis nationals, and to a control on German American, Italian American, and Japanese American associations.[3] Furthermore, after the Voorhis Act against subversive activities in the United States was ratified in 1940, the Department of Justice had intensified its investigations and made a list of roughly 3,700 suspected associations, of which 350 were said to have "pro-Axis tendencies."[4]

The Aliens Division of the Provost Marshal General's Office (PMGO),[5] within the War Department, and the Immigration and Naturalization Service (INS), within the Department of Justice, were to provide locations and staff for internment camps. Finally, a joint committee, with two members from each department, was to coordinate all operations.

At this stage, the enemy-alien *affaire* seemed mostly to be a job for civil courts and the interdepartmental machinery created to rule it, and it looked perfect on paper. But things were far from being that simple. During what came to be called the "phony war," a real contest of wills had developed between the two departments concerning the method by which the Roosevelt administration should face the problem of the Axis aliens on American soil. The War Department did not trust the Department of Justice to handle the issue, and deemed not very practical its policy of considering each case on an individual basis, especially in an emergency.[6] The creation of a new agency, the Provost Marshal General's Office, on July 3, 1941, totally dedicated to operations relating to prisoners of war and alien enemies, testified to this distrust. The army wanted to act as it saw fit, and within the Justice Department, only the head of the FBI, John Edgar Hoover, proved to be at ease with it.

In fact, the army's distrust and intentions were evident as far back as August 21, 1940, when Major General Allen W. Gullion, who was to be appointed chief of the PMGO one year later, drew up a memorandum for the assistant chief of staff, Liaison Branch. Gullion was asked to provide answers on a strictly legalistic basis to two questions of vital importance for the War Department:

> a. In the zone of the interior, as differentiated from the theatre of
>   operations under military control, to what extent can the
>   Military legally, actually control through Provost Marshal
>   Generals, local forces, police or constabulary, any operations
>   against "Fifth Columnists"?
> b. Can the Military in the zone of the interior participate in the
>   arrest and temporary holding of civilians who are not alien ene-
>   mies but citizens of the United States?

It is not only the War Department's intention of taking control of the situation that is clear here; so is the policy adopted by Lieutenant General John L. DeWitt against American citizens of Japanese descent in the Western Defense

Command, a policy which can no longer be considered an hysterical reaction to the bombing of Pearl Harbor.

On October 14, 1941, another memorandum, by Joseph C. Green, Special War Problems Division of the State Department, responded to the inquiry made by Gullion about the policies to be adopted in the first two years of war toward civilian internees. Green informed Gullion that there were no international law conventions on the subject. Yet Harvey H. Bundy, special assistant to the secretary of war, had forwarded the inquiry in a strictly informal but confidential way, adding that actually, the real aim of the military was to test whether the State Department would give support to the question concerning the enemy aliens. In fact, the secretary of war would not even discuss the matter with Attorney General Francis Biddle without knowing the State Department position. Green stated that his department was not interested in taking sides with any of the two contenders, but in finding instead a "solution of the question at issue which will be least likely to cause difficulty for this Government in the conduct of its foreign relations."[7] The State Department was to act as a go-between.

A few days later, acting Secretary of State Sumner Welles informed Secretary of War Henry L. Stimson that the nations in conflict had reached a semi-official agreement, extending to civilian internees the terms stated in the Geneva Convention (1929) for prisoners of war. He added that it would be the best solution if the joint management of the issue between the War Department and the Department of Justice were put into practice. The War Department had more proper locations in which to detain the internees than the incarceration quarters usually used for federal prisoners, and as they were civilians, it was better if civil forces handled their cases.[8] The news turned out to be intolerable to Major Bresee, PMGO, who on December 3 phoned Mr. Clattenburg, Special Division. He complained that it was an injustice that the prisoners of war were not to be treated better than civilians.[9]

But the men around the attorney general had learned an important lesson from what had happened in the United Kingdom in the first year of the war. The astonishing advance of the *Wehrmacht* on the Continent and the raids of the *Luftwaffe* had thrown Great Britain into a state of hysterical xenophobia. In response, the British government, in the spring of 1940, launched a policy of indiscriminate mass internment of all enemy aliens. This policy was to prove a complete failure, especially when it was realized what a great waste it was of human resources needed for the common war effort. Roughly 50,000 of the more than 62,000 Germans interned in the United Kingdom had been welcomed as political refugees from Nazi Germany, and eighty-five percent of the Axis nationals turned out to have been usefully employed in British industries before their internment. The House of Commons had to set up a helter-skelter system of hearing boards in order to be able to identify the "loyal aliens" for release. By November 1941, only 1,903 out of 19,217 Italians and 1,156 Austrians and Germans were still detained.[10]

Francis Biddle was determined to avoid such a mass internment of enemy aliens. Just a few days after Pearl Harbor, he appointed civilian boards in each judicial district, called Alien Enemy Hearing Boards, to proceed with the hearings of those arrested by the FBI.[11] This was done despite the fact that, under the Trading With the Enemy Act, an enemy was prohibited from prosecuting suits in any court of the country prior to the end of the war. As Biddle put it, "all alien enemies are subject to detention and internment for the duration of the war without hearing, which hearing has however been provided, not as a matter of right, but in order to permit them to present facts in their behalf."[12] Moreover, on December 22, 1941, a new agency in the Department of Justice, the Enemy Alien Control Unit, headed by Edward J. Ennis, started the "identification program," a wartime measure with the noble aim of certifying the allegiance of enemy aliens on an individual basis. Then, beginning February 5, 1942, a free booklet with all the regulations concerning enemy aliens was made available in every post office and U.S. Attorney's office throughout the country. Ominously for all the Axis nationals, however, this identification program turned into more bureaucratic obligations: all enemy aliens had to provide a photograph and fingerprints, which would appear in the pink booklet they had to carry at all times or risk being interned for the duration of the war.

Meanwhile, the internment of the targeted enemy aliens had begun on the night of December 7, 1941. Those who failed to obey the registration laws—either the 1940 registration under the Smith Act or the later one that went into effect in February 1942—or who were considered dangerous on the basis of FBI investigations, or who were accused by a private citizen, were apprehended by the FBI and conducted to so-called INS "receiving points." From there, they were transferred to "temporary internment camps," some under INS jurisdiction and some under the PMGO, to await their hearings. The Alien Enemy Hearing Boards were made up of three citizens (of whom at least one had to be an attorney) living in the same area as the accused person and called to judge the case under the supervision of the U.S. attorney of the district. After hearing the evidence, the board would recommend the disposition of the case to the attorney general, who could declare the detainees dangerous aliens and intern them in "permanent internment camps" wholly under PMGO control.[13]

Most of the detained enemy aliens of Italian descent came from the eastern states: New York, New Jersey, Pennsylvania, Massachusetts, Ohio. They were first kept in custody in INS detention centers like Ellis Island or Camp Upton, New York. Then, after a hearing determined that they were to be interned, they were transferred by the army from camp to camp, usually to the interior, clearly to remove them from the coast and from their acquaintances. There were numerous camps in which Italian enemy aliens were interned: Fort Meade, Maryland; Stringtown, Oklahoma; Camp McCoy, Wisconsin; Camp Forrest, Tennessee; and Fort Sam Houston, Texas (all subject to War Department control). The War Department intended that the permanent internment camps for Italian internees were to be the McAlester Internment Camp at McAlester, Oklahoma, and the Fort Missoula Camp at Fort Missoula, Montana, a former INS camp.

For those who came from the West Coast, mainly from California, the route to their final destination proved more varied. The first internees were sent to the Missoula camp soon after being apprehended; most were thereafter transferred to other camps, including McAlester. Later internees from California followed the East Coast pattern of being shifted from the coast to the interior: usually, they were sent first to Sharp Park (INS) or Angel Island (WD), near San Francisco, and then were moved to Fort Sam Houston and Fort Bliss (WD), or Seagoville and Kenedy (INS) in Texas.[14]

The two departments' dual jurisdiction generated such confusion that, in the end, the total lack of collaboration between their agencies damaged the enemy aliens. There were two sets of regulations concerning the internees' camp life: "Instructions Concerning the Treatment of Alien Enemies," issued by the Department of Justice,[15] and "Tentative Internee Regulations Governing Civilian Enemy Aliens and Prisoners of War," issued by the War Department.[16] The latter was a little more strict, mostly with regard to visits and mail for the internees. For the same reason—dual jurisdiction—the internees were registered twice: first by the Department of Justice, which had initially taken them into custody, and then by the PMGO, which received them for internment. In fact, the regulations stated, "The initiation of permanent Army custody will commence as of the date when the responsible officer in custodial charge receives a copy of the internment order of such alien from the Department of Justice."[17] Upon receipt of this order, the Aliens Division of PMGO would record the internee's data on the War Department PMGO Form 2.

Despite Department of Justice goodwill, even the Alien Enemy Hearing Boards did not seem to work well. Significantly, Francis Biddle was forced to ask the civilian boards, on more than one occasion, to provide him with more of the data on which their opinions were based.[18] On August 21, 1942, Biddle issued a circular to assure a rehearing to those interned, as abuses and misconduct had been perpetrated by the boards.[19] This was based on a 1941 joint agreement of the Justice and War Departments regarding enemy aliens that read, in part:

> The combined effort of both [departments] will be directed
> toward the avoidance of difficulties arising from:
>   a. Over-internment
>   b. The unnecessary creating of situations in which dependency
>   of family, infirm persons, or minors presents a problem
>   c. Interference with labor through reckless internment
>   d. The internment of persons solely for careless statements
>   made prior to the outbreak of war."[20]

Unfortunately, these provisions were not complied with and not enforced. John Galeotti, a 54-year-old fisherman from Anchorage, Alaska, in bad health, was denounced by his former landlord, Mr. Hagen, because when he got drunk he "continually boasted about Mussolini and Hitler and what they would do to England and the United States." He was interned at Fort Lewis, Washington, until he was paroled on March 23, 1943, and forbidden to go back to Alaska until the end of the war. All this occurred even though, at his hearing on February 5, 1942, a clerk of the U.S. Commissioner's Office, Miss Rose Walsh, and a sergeant of the United States Army, Benjamin G. Helmlinger, bore witness to Galeotti's loyalty to the United States. The board's recommendation was very confused: it suggested placing Mr. Galeotti under the surveillance of the military police while further investigations were made. It also recommended internment for the duration of the war "if it is the policy of the United States Government that all enemy aliens be interned"; at the same time, it recommended releasing Galeotti from internment because "there is considerable suspicion that John Galeotti was turned in to the Army authorities as an enemy alien to satisfy a personal grudge rather than because of any subversive activities," and "there has been produced absolutely no evidence of subversive activities or tendencies" on his part. Galeotti's wife, Lorna, who was a U.S. citizen and pregnant at the time, did not have any support except the money that her husband could earn. (As if things weren't bad enough, she explained in a letter to a PMGO officer on November 12, 1942, that when her husband was out fishing in Bristol Bay, some neighbors had approached her and tried to force her to prostitute herself. When John Galeotti came back and learned about this, he threatened them.)[21]

John Picco, fifty years old and also from Alaska, was interned on June 19, 1942. At his hearing there was absolutely no evidence of his involvement in any political activity. He was arrested because he was unemployed, after being blackballed by his former manager in a mine, and interned simply because of his nationality. During a visit to Fort Missoula in October 1943, Edward J. Ennis took up the case, noticing that Picco could not speak Italian anymore and kept on complaining about the Italians' way of cooking, calling them "dagos" and "wops." Picco was released in January 1944, after a year and a half of internment.[22]

Sabri Appoloni,[23] twenty-nine years old, a young employee of an American company in San Francisco, had worked for Banca Nazionale del Lavoro in Italy. In 1940 he managed to obtain a permit of expatriation from the Italian government and married an American girl. All this was enough to brand him a dangerous alien. He was interned on April 14, 1942, although Gilson G. Blake, an officer of the State Department, had declared that he had known Appoloni since 1937 as "a thoroughly sincere and honest young man, very much opposed to the present regime in Italy…and one who can be trusted to do his best in any work which may be assigned to him in the present emergency. I am most certainly of the opinion that to keep him in an internment camp is a waste of good material."[24] Appoloni eventually collaborated with the Office of Strategic Services, but he was not to be released before September 3, 1943, after which he became an American citizen.

Many more Italian resident aliens were interned under PMGO control, awaiting their hearings or rehearings for months. Even though some of them, like Giovanni Favoino di Giura,[25] Frank Macaluso,[26] the radio star Ubaldo Guidi-Buttrini,[27] or the irrepressible Baron Cocco Osvaldo,[28] had played a role in the diffusion of Fascist propaganda before the war, as regards the vast majority, the impression remains that the inefficiency of the people called upon to judge their cases, rather than their own activities or beliefs, was at the root of their internment; the military's and the FBI's irrational phobia against fifth columnists and aliens and the old prejudices against "dagos" and "wops" all played an important part in shaping the fate of Italian resident aliens in the United States.

With regard to such prejudices, the following conversation between President Roosevelt and Francis Biddle appears in Biddle's memoir, *In Brief Authority*:

> "And you're going to intern all of them," said the president in a tone that suggested he approved of the idea.
>
> "Well, not quite," replied Biddle.
>
> "I don't care about the Italians," continued Roosevelt. "They are a lot of opera singers, but the Germans are different; they may be dangerous…."[29]

On the other hand, it may well have been this American bias of considering Italians to be a people who love *"la dolce vita"* that helped in the removal of the enemy-alien stigma from the Italian American community on October 12, 1942 (in contrast to German Americans, who were considered to be hard workers and feared as hard fighters, and so remained enemy aliens until the end of the war). In addition to bias, however, three specific factors led to the early lifting of restrictions on Italian Americans.

First, there were about six million Italian American voters, most of them tired of being treated like second-class citizens. The rising star of Luigi Antonini[30] had replaced President Roosevelt's old friend Generoso Pope[31] as the spokesman of this Italian American electoral machine because, by wartime, Pope was too compromised by his profascist statements prior to Pearl Harbor to remain in favor. Following a gentlemen's agreement, Antonini was to overlook Pope's pre–Pearl Harbor Fascism in exchange for the leadership of the Italian American community and be a liaison to the Roosevelt administration. Gaetano Salvemini, a leading member of the Italian *fuorusciti* (exiles) and the antifascist Mazzini Society,[32] tried to block Antonini, denouncing him as if he had come to terms with the devil (i.e. Pope), and remaining ever afterwards persuaded that Pope was behind every initiative brought on by Antonini:

> I am deeply disturbed by your attitude towards such Italo-
> Americans as Pope and Corsi, who have contributed to poisoning
> the Italo-Americans with Fascist misinformation. I do not think
> we have to fight them now that they have changed with the wind.
> But we have to maintain that people who have been helping
> Mussolini for the last twenty years should not claim leading posi-
> tions in the present political set-up. I know that the administra-
> tion wants us to put ourselves at the service of Pope and Corsi. But
> I am not an agent of the administration, and the Mazzini Society
> ought not to act as a transmission belt of the administration.[33]

Despite such opposition, it soon became evident to the members of the Mazzini Society that Italian Americans like Antonini were essential to get funds, political connections, and above all, an actual mass of militants.

To make a long story short, Antonini worked on his own, and Americans of Italian descent were again able to rely on a respectable, prominent leader to exert pressure on the Roosevelt administration in their behalf. By November 1943, Vanni Montana, a man Antonini could completely trust, had joined the Mazzini Society and gotten control over it. With Italy by that time having joined the Allies, Antonini could thenceforth act totally free from the moral attacks of the Italian exiles regarding his political conduct. He even joined an association, the American Committee for Italian Democracy (ACID) of which Generoso Pope was the treasurer, and which included many *prominenti* of New York City who had boasted of Fascist Italy's prestige in the thirties, as members of the board.[34]

Second, the outstanding contribution of the Italian community in the military and on the home front gave moral force to lifting the restrictions. In each division of the army there were at least 500 soldiers of Italian descent, for a total of roughly 750,000 regulars. The very first casualty suffered by the United States was an Italian American, Rudolph Lupino.[35] It seemed as if a real contest had started among the families of the Little Italies throughout the country to provide the army with as many troops as possible. Antonio De Palma,[36] of Hudson City, New Jersey, had all six of his sons enlisted, as did Frank and Maria Armogida, from the youngest (Dante, age 20) to the oldest (James, age 32).[37] Peter Anthony Perri, fourteen years old, "added four years to his age and fooled the recruiting officer of Philadelphia"[38] in order to join the army. He spent a whole week at Fort Meade as a member of an infantry training battalion before his age was discovered. On the other hand, "Big Ralph" Mastalio,[39] fifty-two years old, succeeded in eluding the age limit (thirty-nine) to join the army by simply dying his hair. He was wounded in action and won a medal for valor. Many other Italian Americans distinguished themselves in the war: Joseph Tasca was cited for "sticking to his anti-aircraft post during the bombing of Hawaii and for shooting down several Japanese planes." First Lieutenant Willibald Bianchi was "wounded three times, was cited for heroism and awarded the medal of honor by President Roosevelt for his bravery in the Philippines."[40]

The commitment on the home front was even more remarkable: 800,000 war workers out of a total of 17 million, i.e. nearly five percent, were of Italian descent. In addition, Italian Americans proved to be very generous by giving blood, working as volunteers in the hospitals, and buying war bonds. The campaigns to sell war bonds promoted by the Sons of Italy and the Italian newspaper *Il Progresso Italo-Americano* totaled, respectively, $10 million and $6 million. International Ladies Garment Workers Union members would invest ten percent of their wages in war bonds, while in 1942 the Italian Americans of New York State alone bought war bonds that totaled $220 million.[41]

Last, but by no means least, was the enlightened campaign waged successfully by the Office of War Information (OWI) toward Italian American communities in the United States "to organize their full participation in the huge ideological struggle of the century."[42] It is worth analyzing this campaign in detail. OWI was a federal agency established by President Roosevelt on June

13, 1942, by means of Executive Order No. 9182, to monitor U.S. newspapers and magazines published in languages other than English.[43] As far as Italian Americans were concerned, one of OWI's tasks was also to prepare a weekly bulletin in Italian, called "Notiziario Italo-Americano," which was to work as the official "press service" for Italian newspapers throughout the country.

After Attorney General Biddle's October 12, 1942, speech at Carnegie Hall, many activists, from the Mazzini Society's leaders to Luigi Antonini's Italian American Labor Council (IALC), claimed that they had originated the idea of lifting the enemy-alien stigma from the Italian American community. Jerre Mangione would ascribe it to Edward J. Ennis, head of the Enemy Alien Control Unit.[44] But it was Joseph Facci who originally proposed the idea to his OWI chief, Alan Cranston.

Facci was an American citizen of Italian descent who had worked at the chamber of commerce in Milan in the twenties. At the beginning of the thirties, he immigrated to San Francisco, where he was employed in the California chamber of commerce. From 1940 to 1941 he took a job with the Special Defense Unit, Department of Justice, and from 1941 to 1942 with the Federal Communications Commission, where his task was to analyze Italian language newspapers and radio broadcasts in order to point out those that spread Fascist propaganda.[45] He was then appointed by Alan Cranston as Italian adviser to the Office of Facts and Figures (OFF), within OWI, "to win maximum support of Italian Americans for the war effort, to increase their willingness to participate in fighting, production, civilian defense and all other war activities."[46] Eventually, when an informal interdepartmental task force was set up in order to find a better solution than internment for the enemy aliens, Joseph Facci would emerge as one of the leading advocates not only for the Italian American communities, but also for the Italians in Italy. On the task force, there were representatives of the aliens division of the Departments of Justice, War, and State; Elmer Davis, the OWI director; Alan Cranston, head of OFF; and DeWitt Poole, coordinator of information for both OWI agencies.

By this time, even the War Department representatives had come to the conclusion that a new policy toward enemy aliens was needed. They lamented the lack of personnel for a job that was becoming more and more onerous, especially following Lieutenant General DeWitt's orders of mass evacuation from the restricted areas.[47] As early as January 26, 1942, Facci had drawn up a memorandum for his boss, entitled "Italian Americans and 'Morale,'" in which he maintained that "It is unfortunate that a super-legalistic approach of the problem and circumstances have made it expedient to leave, for the time being, undisturbed and protected behind the second papers, and behind political influence, some of the people most responsible for the Fascist propaganda of the last seventeen years," (the names of Generoso Pope, Domenico Trombetta,[48] and Luigi Criscuolo[49] come to mind) "while at the same time burdening with largely unnecessary regulations, which hurt economically and morally, thousands of innocent and loyal aliens. This error will certainly be corrected soon, I hope." Facci also added that the main mistake in the policy pursued up to that moment was that Italian Americans "are suspected as a group, that they do not belong." According to Facci, the government was missing its greatest opportunity to achieve the full Americanization of the rank and file in Italian communities once and for all, because it was "absent, or at least, not ready right now to strengthen through education, information, and service, the upsurge of loyalty and patriotism of these people and to organize their full participation in the huge ideological struggle of the century."[50]

Renzo Sereno, group analyst for the Office of Facts and Figures, wrote another report at the request of Facci, corroborating his theory:

> The Italians suffer from mass guilt. The anxiety aroused by this guilt is cultivated by their leaders and increased by the impact of discrimination. The enemy registration card is per se a stigma; it means that the bearers, through events beyond their control, lost their civil rights and that they are now on probation. It means a revival of all the feelings connected with the most humiliating phase of immigration, the passport phase. Restrictive measures tend to precipitate these feelings into a subjective crisis. These people are forced to identify themselves with the clichés with which they are associated. A prolongation of the discriminatory system may well transform these people from potential fifth columnists, potential saboteurs, into actual fifth columnists, actual saboteurs. A revocation of their alien enemy status would produce such release of tension as to simplify enormously the security problem presented by these people."[51]

The main obstacle to overcome, in order to carry out such a far-sighted policy, was the stubborn xenophobia of J. Edgar Hoover and of some men around Henry L. Stimson in the War Department. But Facci was to find two valiant allies in Eleanor Roosevelt and in Max Ascoli, the former chairman of the Mazzini Society, who, in the meanwhile, had started working for the Coordinator of Inter-American Affairs (CIAA). On February 4, 1942, under a suggestion made by the first lady, Max Ascoli wrote a short booklet, entitled "On the Italian Americans," whose contents were very similar to those stated by Facci just a week before. Better than Facci, though, Ascoli expressed in ten typewritten pages a complete synthesis of the Italian Americans' assimilation process into the American community, their relationship to Fascist propaganda and Mussolini's myth, and their present state of confusion between the two allegiances. Like Facci, Ascoli thought the Italian American communities were at a historical crossroads, and that it was the right moment for the Roosevelt administration to exert pressure on them to make the right choice. What follows are some excerpts from Ascoli's booklet:

> The problem of the Italian Americans is one of complete assimilation in the American community of a very large stock of recent immigrants. In the abnormal conditions created by the war, this process of assimilation may be arrested and the bulk of the Italian Americans, which means five to seven million people, transformed into an alien body or into a national minority. If we realize the gravity of the problem and deal with it realistically, we can render a great service to the United States and to Italy…It can be said that they became Americans before ever having been Italians…They were unified into a racial bloc by other Americans with whom they came to live and who called all of them Italians—or rather, "wops."…There is no reason to be surprised if large sections of Italian Americans felt the spell of Mussolini's myth…Those of them who could read were proud in seeing how the most prominent Americans, bankers, university presidents, writers, were paying tribute to Mussolini and extolling Fascist Italy as an example to the world. Yet, it would be a gross exaggeration to say that the large majority of the Italian Americans were for Mussolini. Their problem was, and still is, that of winning social and economic equality in the American community…And, of course, Fascist propaganda played abundantly on their hunger for recognition…The American politicians were never too fastidious, particularly in our great metropolitan centers, about getting the support of Fascist consulates. Even today in New York City the man who comes nearest the dignity of being the boss of the Italian Americans is a man who was until a few months ago a Fascist propagandist and who is still a power in Tammany Hall….In the meanwhile the rumors are spreading among the masses of Italian Americans of discrimination against Italian laborers in the defense program, of widespread suspicion, of a tendency to consider the Italians, no matter whether American citizens or not, on the same level as the Germans or the Japanese.

Instinctively, the Italians over here feel that it is unfair to treat them like Germans. Instinctively they started doubting about Mussolini when Mussolini went to war on the side of Germany. But the American authorities call "alien enemies" those of them who are not yet American citizens."[52]

On February 9, 1942, Eleanor Roosevelt forwarded these pages to Earl G. Harrison, special assistant to the attorney general, with a message from Ascoli in which he expressed a desire for the creation of an advisory board on Italian American affairs "to explain America and the advantages of American life to the American people of Italian descent." Three days later, in his answer to Mrs. Roosevelt, Harrison was glad to inform her that "much of this...is now being planned. It will be carried out under the leadership of Archibald MacLeish in OFF. He has associated with him my good friend Alan Cranston."[53]

As a matter of fact, after it reached Cranston and DeWitt Poole's offices early in March, Ascoli's booklet was to work as a fundamental source for most of the OFF's reports on Italian Americans.[54] And Facci proved to be the most attentive and sensitive reader. In fact, he embraced Ascoli's idea at once. Ascoli did not want to limit the administration's action only to Italian Americans; he also aimed at taking advantage of the still-strong bonds between them and the Italians of Italy in order to have a decisive influence on the Italian peninsula's revolt against Fascism. Ascoli wrote:

Gradually the Italian Americans can be led to realize that America's victory in the war will mean the liberation of Italy. They can be educated to consider themselves as the trustees of a better Italy. By being shown what harm Fascism has done to the country of their origin they can be made into convinced opponents of any Fascist tendency over here. There can be no problem of divided allegiance when the goal is absolutely identical...Our aim should be not to force the Italian Americans to compulsory sudden Americanization, but rather to have them develop an American interpretation of their Italian heritage...It would be incorrect to say that Italian Americans are not good Americans or good democrats. The truth is that they are in danger, and because of this danger, adequate steps should be taken...The lesson of these last twenty years is that the events in Italy, the rise of the Fascist state, the conquest of Ethiopia and of Greece, [and] the defeat of the Fascist armies have deeply affected the morale of the Italian Americans, and their status in the American community.

The success or the plight of men of Italian descent in America has always had far-reaching influence on the Italians in Italy…Now the war situation, the fact that the obstacle on the way to peace is only one, Fascism, has made infinitely closer the inter-relation between Italian Americans and Italians in Italy. The participation of the Italian Americans in the war effort will and must have a decisive influence on the Italian revolt against Fascism.

In these words, Facci found the inspiration for his strategy, or as he used to call it, the "powerful psychological offensive":

It is my plan to mobilize the Italian Americans in a direct, daily, devastating appeal to their home folks. It would cost nothing to the government; it would be paid by the Italian Americans; above all, it would come from their heart and would go to the heart of their brothers—something new and explosive in the ideological warfare field. I am so sure of the astounding results of such a plan that I would stake everything I have in the success of such a drive.[55]

Facci showed himself to be sensitive to Antonini's "qualities" as well. Thus, OFF and OWI started a close collaboration with the ILGWU leader, promoting rallies together in the Italian communities and adopting Antonini's slogan, "America's victory is Italy's Freedom," in "Il Notiziario Italo-Americano"[56]

Nevertheless, the Department of Justice, and especially the War Department, seemed to be more oriented towards putting into effect a policy of small steps toward enemy aliens. Meanwhile, time was running out fast. On May 12, 1942, an eager Facci wrote to Alan Cranston that "the legalistic approach of piecemeal amendments to the 'enemy aliens' status, at least as far as the Italians are concerned, is typical 'too little and too late.' Time marches on. We might be compelled to do later as an act of weakness what we have the opportunity to do right now as an act of strength, intelligent defense, and true broad-minded democracy, [and] also as an act of political justice."[57] On the other hand, the Department of Justice was also concerned that Facci's proposal could turn out to be a slap in the face for German Americans.[58] But Facci's obstinacy got the better of every difficulty.

A public-opinion poll conducted by the Bureau of Intelligence of the OFF to analyze which of the enemy-alien groups was considered most dangerous had stressed that forty-six percent of United States citizens were concerned about Germans, another thirty-five percent about Japanese, and only two percent about Italians. The survey explained:

Although this comparative ranking cannot be regarded as an indication that the American public is unconcerned about Italians, it does show plainly that it distinguishes them sharply from the Germans and Japanese. A similar distinction may be valid in governmental handling of the three alien groups...Selective and special treatment could be accorded to the Italians apparently without arousing American fears in a high degree. Separation of them from the other enemy alien groups in this country may prove a useful first step in separating Italy itself from the other members of the Axis.[59]

This gave enough confidence to Edward J. Ennis to find a way to overcome J. Edgar Hoover's resistance, which was simply to present him with a fait accompli.[60] Reading the speech that Francis Biddle delivered on October 12, 1942, releasing Italian resident aliens from all restrictions, it is easy to pick out all the references to Ascoli's and Facci's papers.

Looking back on it, the whole policy adopted toward German, Italian, and Japanese aliens by the Roosevelt administration has to be regarded as one of the lowest points for democracy in United States history. The power conflict between the Department of Justice and the War Department, the FBI's attitude, and the faulty functioning of the system appointed to govern the whole question of the enemy aliens created favorable conditions for abuses to be perpetrated against thousands of loyal aliens, and thousands of citizens as well.

Fortunately, OWI's efforts to remove the humiliating stigma of enemy-alien status from Italian Americans prevented the continuation of such a policy toward them. As Alan Cranston stated at the end of their successful, democratic campaign: "Hats off to Signor Facci!"[61]

Endnotes:
1. Under sections 21–24 of the U.S. Code, title 50.
2. Joint Agreement of the Secretary of War and the Attorney General with respect to Internment of Alien Enemies, July 18, 1941. RG 389, Subject correspondence 1942–1945, Executive Division, Legal Office, Office of the Provost Marshal General, National Archives and Records Administration, College Park, Md., hereafter PMGO NARA II.
3. In order to make out the list of the "potentially dangerous" civilians in the Italian communities, FBI officers read all the back numbers of the main Italian American newspapers and magazines and asked Gaetano Salvemini to be an adviser on the matter. In 1940, Salvemini issued his pamphlet "Italian Fascist Activities in the U.S." (C. Killinger, "Gaetano Salvemini e le Autorità Americane." Documenti inediti dal FBI, Storia Contemporanea, *Il Mulino*, XII, 3, June 1981, pp. 403–442).
4. A detailed list of all the Italian American associations investigated for possible subversive activities is to be found in RG 60, Records of the War Division, General Index 1928–1951, Records of the Department of Justice, NARA II.

5. Major Karl R. Bendetsen was appointed chief of the division. On February 10, 1942, Colonel B. M. Bryan Jr. took his place. Subject correspondence 1942–1945, Executive Division, Legal Office, PMGO NARA II.

6. The study conducted by Stephen Fox on the relocation of the Italian Americans of the West Coast comes to this same conclusion. Stephen Fox, *The Unknown Internment: An Oral History of the Relocation of Italian Americans during World War II* (Boston: Twayne Publishers, 1990) and "General John DeWitt and the Proposed Internment of German and Italian Aliens during World War II," *Pacific Historical Review*, LVII (4), 1988, pp. 407–438.

7. Mr. Green, Special Division, to Mr. Long, Alien Legislation, Department of State (SD): Copy of memorandum from Mr. Green, Special Division, SD, to Provost Marshal General Gullion, War Department (WD), Civilian Internees, RG 59, Subject files 1939–1954, Records of the Special War Problems Division, SD, NARA II (hereafter RG 59 SD NARA II).

8. Memorandum of conversation, Custody of Enemy Aliens in the United States, October 31, 1941. RG 59 SD NARA II.

9. Major Bresee, PMGO, WD, to Mr. Clattenburg, Special Division, SD, Memorandum of Conversation Telephone, December 3, 1941. RG 59 SD NARA II.

10. Survey edited by The British Library of Information, reported in U.S. Congress, House of Representatives, 76th Congress, 3rd sess. Special Committee on Un-American Activities, Report No. 1476, "Investigations of Un-American Propaganda Activities in the United States" (Washington D.C.: Government Printing Office, 1940).

11. Most of the enemy aliens were apprehended by the FBI in the days between December 8 and December 12. It is difficult to provide the exact number of enemy aliens taken into custody by the FBI. J. Edgar Hoover, at the end of 1944, talked of a total of 14,807 enemy aliens seized by the FBI. Earl G. Harrison, INS, claimed some 15,000 detainees (quoted by R. Daniels in "l'Internamento di 'Alien Enemies' negli Stati Uniti durante la Seconda Guerra Mondiale," *Àcoma, Rivista Internazionale di Studi Nordamericani* 11, Estate-Autunno 1997, Giunti, pp. 42–44). Moreover, Daniels states that other agencies such as the Office of Naval Intelligence and the army intelligence branch (G-2), together with the FBI, contributed to making up the so-called "ABC Lists" of potentially subversive individuals.

12. Instructions to Alien Enemy Hearing Board. Supplement #1. January 7, 1942. RG 85, General files 1942–1945, Ft. Missoula, Mont., World War II Internment files, Immigration and Naturalization Service (INS), National Archives and Records Administration, Washington D.C. (NARA I).

13. There were fourteen camps (and another twenty-two would be finished by 1943). The thirty-six camps were intended by the War Department to have a total capacity of 91,300 internees. RG 389, Subject correspondence, Executive Division, Legal Office, PMGO NARA II.

14. RG 389, Records relating to alien civilian internees during World War II, 1941–1964. Records of the Information Bureau, PMGO NARA II.

15. RG 59 SD NARA II.

16. Published in April 1942, it was replaced by "Regulations Concerning Prisoners of War" on September 24, 1943. RG 389, Historical File 1941–1958, PMGO NARA II.

17. RG 389, Supplementing Circular No. 32, War Department. Processing of Alien Enemies, February 12, 1942. Records relating to alien civilian internees during World War II, 1941–1964, Records of the Information Bureau, PMGO NARA II.

18. Instructions to Alien Enemy Hearing Board. Supplement #2, January 9, 1942. RG 85, General files 1942–1945, Ft. Missoula, Mont., World War II Internment files, INS, NARA I.

19. RG 85, Rehearing of Alien Enemy Cases, Department of Justice Circular No. 3589, Supplement No. 12, August 21, 1942, General Files 1942–1945, Ft. Missoula, Mont., World War II Internment files, INS, NARA I.

20. Joint Agreement of the Secretary of War and the Attorney General with Respect to Internment of Alien Enemies, July 18, 1941, reported in Don Heinrich Tolzmann, ed., German-Americans in the World Wars (München: Saur Vol. IV, *The World War Two Experience: The Internment of German-Americans*; documents edited by Arthur D. Jacobs and

Joseph E. Fallon. Section 1 (1995): "From Suspicion to Internment: U.S. Government Policy Toward German-Americans, 1939–1948," pp.1539–1547.

21. RG 389, Civilian Internee Cases Files 1941–1945 (decimal file #291.2), American Prisoner of War Information Bureau, Alien Enemy Branch, PMGO NARA II.

22. Ibid.

23. RG 389, Records Relating to Italian Civilian Internees During WW II, 1941–1946, Boxes 2-20. Alien Enemy Information Bureau, PMGO NARA II.

24. RG 226, Records of the New York Secret Intelligence Branch. Records of the Office of the Strategic Service, NARA II.

25. Giovanni Favonio di Giura, coordinator of the Fasci abroad for the state of New York (1928–1930) and one of the editors of *Il Progresso Italo-Americano*, was arrested on December 9, 1941, and interned after Biddle's sentence on January 26, 1942. RG 389, Records Relating to Italian Civilian Internees During WW II, 1941–1946, Boxes 2-20. Alien Enemy Information Bureau, PMGO NARA II.

26. Arrested on December 9, 1941, Macaluso was sentenced "to be interned for the duration of the war" on February 4, 1942, and released on May 30, 1944, after being detained in Camp Upton, N.Y.; Fort Meade, Md.; McAlester, Okla.; and Ft. Missoula, Mont. Macaluso was editor of the Italian newspaper *Giovinezza* and spread Fascist propaganda through Italian communities of the East Coast in the twenties and thirties. He was married to an American citizen and his three sons were all American citizens, one of them a private in the U.S. Army. In his internment correspondence to his wife, Macaluso sounds depressed and tired, always complaining about the work he was forced to do together with the other internees. RG 389, Records Relating to Italian Civilian Internees During WW II, 1941–1946, Boxes 2-20. Alien Enemy Information Bureau, PMGO NARA II.

27. Arrested on December 9, 1941, Guidi-Buttrini was detained in Ellis Island, N.Y.; Fort Meade, Md.; McAlester, Okla.; Fort Missoula, Mont.; and from April 4, 1945 on at Fort Stanton, N.M. RG 389, Records Relating to Italian Civilian Internees During WW II, 1941–1946, Boxes 2-20. Alien Enemy Information Bureau, PMGO NARA II. On his activity and on his profascist statements as radio announcer and accountant for the station WHOM of Boston, see S. J. LaGumina, *Wop! A Documentary History of Anti-Italian Discrimination in the United States* (San Francisco: Straight Arrow Books, 1973).

28. Art collector and dealer, arrested on October 1, 1942, in Englewood, N.J., he was sent to Ellis Island, N.Y.; then to Fort Meade, Md.; McAlester, Okla.; and Fort Missoula, Mont., where he refused to collaborate with camp authorities and went on writing profascist letters to his relatives in Italy. Cocco di Tione was repatriated to Italy on October 23, 1945. RG 389, Records Relating to Italian Civilian Internees During WW II, 1941–1946, Boxes 2-20. Alien Enemy Information Bureau, PMGO NARA II.

29. Francis B. Biddle, *In Brief Authority* (Hartford, Conn.: Greenwood Press, 1976).

30. President of Local 89 of the International Ladies Garment Workers Union (ILGWU), with 33,500 members in New York City, he was known as an "antifascist of the very first hour" in the Italian community, together with Girolamo Valenti, Giuseppe Lupis, Vanni Montana, Frank and Augusto Bellanca, and Carlo Tresca. He was, though, on friendly terms with members of the Roosevelt administration and of the American Federation of Labor. ILGWU, as a matter of fact, was closely linked to the Democratic Party and a strong supporter of the New Deal. See P. V. Cannistraro, "Luigi Antonini and the Italian Anti-Fascist Movement in the United States, 1940–1943." *Journal of American Ethnic History*, V (1), Fall 1985.

31. Generoso Pope, in the twenties and thirties, got control of the Italian American electoral machine of New York City. He was a businessman, chief of the Democratic Council of Americans of Italian Origin at Tammany Hall, editor of the largest Italian newspaper in the United States, *Il Progresso Italo-Americano*, and had connections with Italian authorities of the Fascist regime, spreading Fascist propaganda amongst Italian Americans in collaboration with the Ministero della Cultura Popolare (MINCULPOP). Only in September 1941 did Pope disavow his strongly profascist past, candidly declaring, "my attitude has changed."

32. Maddelena Tirabassi, "Enemy Aliens or Loyal Americans? The Mazzini Society and the Italian American Communities," in *Rivista di Studi Angloamericani* (Abano Terme: Piovan Editore, 1985).

33. Salvemini to Antonini, June 29, 1942, ILGWU Archives, quoted in P. V. Cannistraro, "Antonini and the Italian Anti-Fascist Movement in the United States, 1940–1943," *Journal of American Ethnic History*, V (1), Fall 1985.

34. Judge Ferdinand Pecora was chairman of the committee, while Antonini was vice chairman. In any case, Pope's prestige and credit were by then irreparably on the way out. A report of the Office of Strategic Service about ACID read: "It's Mr. Gualtieri's opinion, and that of other Italian labor leaders that the Committee is a dead issue, because of Pope's presence. He is the stumbling block. No central, Italian organization can be organized nationally as long as Pope is a part of it. Antonini will fight for him and Pope will fight for himself. That makes his presence doubly certain of being there. That means failure for a national organization of Italians which takes in all people." RG 59, "Latest Status of Activities of Italian American Committee for Democracy," 20 December 1943, OSS Foreign Nationalities Branch Files 1942–1945, Microfiches INT-17IT-927, State Department, NARA II.

35. "Italian Americans Help Win the War," RG 208, Subject File of the Chief, Feb 1942–Jan 1944, Office of War Information (OWI), NARA II (hereafter Subj. File/Chief, NARA II).

36. Ibid.

37. "The Armogida Family," Foreign Language Information Service (FLIS) Press Releases, January–April 1942, Records of the American Council for Nationalities Service, 1921–1971, IHRC, general editor Rudolph J. Vecoli (hereafter FLIS).

38. "14-Year-Old Italian American Boy Joins Army," March 20, 1942, FLIS.

39. S. J. LaGumina, *From Steerage to Suburb: Long Island Italians* (New York: Center for Migration Studies, 1988) pp.156–157.

40. "Italian Americans Win Medals for Valor," April 6, 1942, FLIS.

41. "Italian Americans Help Win the War," RG 208, Subj. File/Chief, NARA II.

42. "Italian Americans and 'Morale,'" January 26, 1942, Ibid.

43. Ibid.

44. Jerre Mangione, *An Ethnic at Large: a Memoir of America in the Thirties and Forties* (New York: Putnam, 1978) p.287.

45. "Draft Deferments for Foreign Language Division Staff," October 1, 1942, RG 208, General Correspondence of the Chief, Dec 1941–Jan 1944, OWI, NARA II (hereafter Gen. Corr. NARA II)

46. Ibid.

47. RG 389, Decimal Subject File 1941–1945, #320.2, Administrative Division, PMGO NARA II.

48. "Dominick" Domenico Trombetta, editor of the openly Fascist magazine *Il Grido della Stirpe*, American citizen since 1924, lost his citizenship on September 28, 1942, because of his political conduct as an agent of a foreign government. Trombetta was the first Italian to be sentenced for violating the Foreign Agents Registration Act. *New York Times*, "Citizenship Lost by Fascist Editor," September 29, 1942. RG 208, DOJ release on Trombetta, May 24, 1943, Subj. File/Chief, NARA II.

49. Luigi Criscuolo, American citizen, was an ambiguous person, editor of the fortnightly magazine, *The Rubicon*, that Cranston's staff defined simply as "Fascist." Under the Rubicon's headline there was a note reading: "Published for Private Circulation by Luigi Criscuolo. An American publication, established in 1941 to: re-affirm the principles in the Declaration of Independence, the Constitution and the Bill of Rights; fight for all good causes as Citizens of the United States; instill loyalty to the Flag and the Nation especially in time of War and industrial stress." He always claimed that the only "ism" he could have been charged with was that of Americanism. His personal enemies were the OWI staff and its chief, Elmer Davis, the congressman Vito Marcantonio, because he "certainly did not support the president in everything until after the Russians got into the war against Hitler, with whom they had been previously allied," and firstly Luigi Antonini, or as he used to call him, the *"Duce delle sartine."* In 1942 he founded the Council of Americans of Italian Origin, "organized under the auspices of the

New York State Department of Education and State War Council to further Americanizations of Italians and to enlist their loyal co-operation in the present war program." *The Rubicon*, August 15, 1942, volume 2, number 1. RG 208, L. Criscuolo to A. Cranston, August 26, 1942, Gen. Corr. NARA II.

50. "Italian-Americans and 'Morale'," January 26, 1942, RG 208, Subj. File/Chief, NARA II.

51. Facci entered in the margin of the page: "I think it is very good. J.F." RG 208, Renzo Sereno, "Enemy Aliens," written at request of J. Facci, Gen. Corr. NARA II.

52. Max Ascoli, "On the Italian Americans," February 4, 1942, RG 208, Gen. Corr. NARA II.

53. Earl G. Harrison to Mrs. Roosevelt, February 12, 1942, RG 208, Gen. Corr. NARA II.

54. Alan Cranston to Mrs. Roosevelt, March 3, 1942; DeWitt C. Poole to Cranston, March 3, 1942, RG 208, Gen. Corr. NARA II.

55. Joseph Facci to Alan Cranston, June 18, 1942, RG 208, Subj. File/Chief, NARA II.

56. On June 2, 1942, OWI and IALC commemorated the anniversary of Garibaldi's death together with a rally in Washington, D.C., in which Cranston, Antonini, Sforza, Dean Acheson (assistant secretary of state), Max Ascoli, Hon. D'Alessandro and Hon. Voorhis took part. RG 208, J. Facci to A. Cranston, "Italian American Rally for the Commemoration of Garibaldi," May 12, 1942. A. Cranston to H. Harris, "Departmental Auditorium Needed for Italian American Rally, May 25, 1942. "Notiziario Italo-Americano," *Edizione Speciale* (Special Release), *"Vittoria per l'America-Libertà per l'Italia,"* *Garibaldi Commemorato dagli Italo-americani a Washington,* June 3, 1942, Subject File of the Chief, Feb 1942–Jan 1944, OWI, NARA II.

57. Joseph Facci to Alan Cranston, "Dear Alan," May 12, 1942, RG 208, Gen. Corr. NARA II.

58. M. E. Gilfond, Director of Public Relations, DOJ, Memorandum for the Attorney General, June 6, 1942. Copy in attachment from Alan Cranston to Archibald MacLeish, "Italian Aliens," June 12, 1942, RG 208, Gen. Corr. NARA II.

59. OFF Bureau of Intelligence, Intelligence Report # 19, "Distinction Among Alien Groups," April 21, 1942, RG 208, Subj. File/Chief, NARA II.

60. J. Facci, "In order to overcome...," June 18, 1942, RG 208, Subj. File/Chief, NARA II.

61. Alan Cranston to Foreign Language Division Staff, "Italian Aliens," October 15, 1942, RG 208, Subj. File/Chief, NARA II.

Pippo l'Americano

by Joseph DeLuca

Joseph DeLuca and his family suffered a double violation during
World War II. The firstborn of his family, Joe was unable to emigrate
with his parents to America because, as the son of a father who had
fled from Fascism, he was essentially held hostage in Sicily during the
war, where he was under suspicion by Mussolini's government for
being an American, subject to curfew and travel restrictions, and nar-
rowly escaping internment. At the same time, his father, Pietro
DeLuca, became likewise the object of suspicion in America, the difference being that he did not escape arrest as a dangerous enemy
alien and was detained for several months on Ellis Island. What follows is the late Joe DeLuca's account, as he told it in October 1993,
of how all this came to pass.

I came from Italy in 1947—February 20, 1947—and landed in New York at age
sixteen. That was the first time I met my parents, because they left Italy when
I was a baby—my father when I was three months old, my mother when I was
nine months old.

My father did not go straight to New York when he left Italy in 1931,
because the first place he could find a job was in British Honduras. And his life
there was rather difficult, because they were also trying to expatriate him back
to Italy because of his opposition to Fascism.

Actually, initially he was supportive of the Fascists. There was constant
turmoil in Italy after World War I, not just in the north but also in the south.
My father was a student, trying to study to be an engineer, and like many Italian
students now, they like to participate in *sciopero* [strikes]. So my father became
an active supporter, because he felt it was a way for Italy to redeem its national
and international stature as well as provide a uniform government to address
the needs of that time.

He became a supporter, and at the same time he slowly became disenchanted with the Fascists. As time progressed, the economic and social conditions, particularly in Sicily, were very difficult, and so a lot of the supporters
became disenchanted with the way the government was going about land

reforms or other economic benefits they had promised. My father was also one of six children, and the family was split among the different parties. My grandfather, whose name I bear, was an old monarchist. On the other hand, my father's older brother, Nino, was a strong socialist. His middle brother, Gaetano, was a republican, a Mazzini republican.

My father became particularly upset when *his* father—you know, the Fascists had a way of going about getting obedience, and one of the ways was to beat you up and force you to take in a substantial dose of castor oil. Well, my grandfather was objecting to Mussolini, and so he got this treatment. My father did not like that, particularly since he was a supporting member in the region, only to find out what they did to his father. So antagonism began to arise and my father fell out of favor. At the same time, it was very difficult economically and socially to stay there, and he sought to get a visa to go abroad to America. Well, he was not given a visa, because the Italians were no longer a favored immigrant group in the early 1930s. He then learned that if he did not escape soon, he was going to get it—one of our relatives who was a *maresciallo di questura* learned that there was an arrest order for him and said, "Nicola, *scappa:* Get out or they're going to give it to you."

So my father escaped and landed in Honduras. He sought asylum there but it was not given. By that time, I was already born and was about three months old. My father wrote to say he needed to escape Honduras, and the family realized that the only way he could come to this country was by way of my mother, who had been born in Philadelphia. Her parents were part of that immigrant group that in the late 1890s came to the United States, lived for a number of years, accumulated some fortune, and then returned to Italy to form a new life. She was five or six years old when she returned, but she always retained her American citizenship, and as such, she was able to get a visa to come back to the United States.

The only problem was me. I was a babe in arms, and she sought to give me an American passport, but it was denied because I'd been born in Italy. And so now it's split—they gave me an Italian passport. However, even though I was able to get a passport, the Italian government refused me the visa, the idea being that by denying my mother a visa for me, they could hold her and me as hostages to get my father. Those were the machinations.

So the first time my mother was scheduled to leave, I was six months old. We got to Palermo and the consulate denied the visa. And now she has to return to Nizza, and the question is what to do. I don't think it was that simple. My mother was barely twenty-two at that time, a very young woman with a child of six months, but eventually my grandparents on both sides were able to persuade

Giuseppe and Giuseppina Di Bella (brother and sister) with their nephew Joe (Pippo) DeLuca in Italy ca. 1934. Courtesy of Barbara DeLuca

my mother to leave me with them. She could then be free to leave Italy, come to the United States, and, as a spouse, bring her husband into the country.

After much consideration and much pain, my mother left Palermo when I was nine months old. It was October 1931....By that time, her older brother Sebastian, my uncle Buster, had been able to come to this country and was living in Boston. Therefore my mother at least had a place where she could live. So she lived with her brother for a period of months and during that period was able to activate the necessary documents so that my father was able to come to this country by early 1932. They lived in Boston for a few months and ultimately got to New York.

My father was able to get a job, whatever he could....He started to get handyman's work and [since he had been trained]...in Italy in industrial technology, was able to get better ones. At one time I remember hearing he had a job with the Sealy Mattress Company, where he was hooking springs together, and rose to various other jobs.

During this period they were trying to get me over, but I was too young to be able to travel by myself, and my father didn't dare to come to Italy, and my mother could not leave, because she was taking care of my father, and she soon became pregnant with my brother John. By 1933 he was born, and then in 1936 my sister Terry was born, and the hope was that by then they would have accumulated sufficient money for my mother to make a run and come over, pick me up, and come back. But things didn't work out that way.

By 1940, they were able to get me a visa to leave Italy and a tutor. [He was] a friend of my father's who was from Naples [and] had come to Naples to visit his family; and the understanding was that he would gain legal custody of me and therefore become my guardian, with whom I would be able to travel. Because I was a minor, eight years old, they wouldn't let me travel by myself. Again, I don't know whether it was a legal technicality they were using....But then finally, this friend of my father's was able to get me a visa, and we were scheduled to leave Italy in May—May 10, 1940—aboard the *Rex*, from Naples. Those were the plans.

June 1940, Italy declares war on France. So we couldn't leave, because in May, the Italian government, knowing something was going to happen, would not let the *Rex* leave Italy. So now the *Rex* is still tied up in Naples. Had it left Italy in May, I [would have been], when war was declared, subject to being captured—twist of fate.

So every day we are scheduled to leave, but the go-ahead is never given. I learned later why, but not then—I would not have known too much. But you are aware that there is something, particularly [because]—and I am not saying this to brag about it—I was somewhat precocious. Because here I am, as a child, living part of the time with one set of relatives and part of the time with another, both because of financial necessity and because of custodial responsibility. And after 1936 my grandmother died, and by 1938 my grandfather—these were my paternal grandparents—became blind, so their ability to take care of me was diminished. So I started to spend more time with my maternal relatives. My mother's father had died before she got married, so the only ones on her side of the family who could care for me were her mother and her older brother and younger sister....By way of history, my maternal grandparents had founded a factory in Messina after they returned from the United States for the production of citrus products, spirits from lemon and things like that, and they had a very flourishing business. But when the depression started, a lot of the bills were not paid, and it got to the point where my grandfather became very sick and had a heart attack and died. And during that period, my maternal grandmother had to declare bankruptcy and turn the company over to the protection of the court, the understanding being that if by a given date they could not come out of it, the court would dissolve the company. Well, the company was dissolved, so we moved from Nizza—this was 1936—to the village of Santissima Nunziata in Messina....

So I spent most of the winter months in Messina, where I was enrolled in school, and the summer months in Nizza with my paternal relatives. So, when you are that young and you move around, you get conscious of the things that go on. By 1940, when I was scheduled to leave on the *Rex*, I knew that things were not working out.

So now, with the war, I was suspect in Italy—suspect in the same sense my parents were suspect in America. By the time America came into the war, I was literally an enemy of the state, even though I was born and raised in Italy, because my parents were American—all of which I was aware of, though not as to its full meaning....People used to refer to me as *Pippo l'Americano*. Pippo—my nickname, from Giuseppe, my full name....When the war started and I stayed in Italy, some of my friends were not quite as friendly as otherwise, because America was the enemy and I was Pippo l'Americano....

Meantime, my father was working various jobs, and by 1940 he was working more in war-supportive industries. During that period my father had...his personality was socially oriented, so he had formed an Italian club called Tito Minitti. Minitti was evidently a person who had risen within the Fascist ranks in Italy [and] who had become somewhat like a role model to some people, I think. And I recall my brother saying they used to go there to the club, with the Italian flag on one side and the American flag on the other, and my father was the president and the main force in what was basically a social club...They would have fund-raisers for school, various social events, dances, which was one way of keeping the Italian community together in New York. Politically, he was proud of being Italian, as Mussolini had finally, through the Fascist regime, been able to achieve that Italy now was a country of presence. The nationialism that had arisen in Italy as a *paese riconosciuto* [recognized country, or country to be reckoned with] was also translated and transferred to the involvement [in Italian American communities] in the United States. So where there was no Fascist activity, there was more of a social support and association, taking pride in the fact that Italy was now a power. These were not just immigrants, second-class citizens, as many Italians were being considered then—and partly in the United States still are. The pride that associated with it [Fascism] may have made them *simpatici*, if not supportive....They recognized Italian holidays, they would recognize events abroad—for instance when Italo Balbo had made a solo flight. These were events where they would rally, *viva Italia* and *viva America*.

But [my father] also had a certain amount of antagonism, not only because he had to leave Italy, but also because he was deprived of his son—me. So in that sense, it's one of those conflicts between ideology and reality. He was not necessarily averse to the principles of Italian Fascism, but he was averse to the way they were implementing it.

All this continued through the 1930s and early 1940s, and I know they would hold many social events, because when I came in the 1940s they still had a lot of the memorabilia—the records (musical records), operas. So it was social, political, but more cultural. They would have plays among themselves, they would show movies—Beniamino Gigli, Tito Gobbi, DeLuca the famous baritone—and they would participate in picnics, dances, parades, and things like that. And my father continued as president of the club.

Then, lo and behold, the war takes place. Meanwhile, communications between us were more difficult, because of the situation where I became suspect in Italy, and I became like a parolee. I had to check in periodically to let them know where I was going and so forth, to the point that the communication with my parents was via the Red Cross. And it got to a point where we lost communication altogether when they tried to put me in a concentration camp in Italy. I was trying to go to school, but war was marching on, and [while] this was not like it was in Germany, where they would put you in a real concentration camp, it was sort of a loose parole situation, where you had to stay within an area. If I wanted to go from Messina to Nizza to visit my paternal side, I had to have permission.

And my father, in this country, was subject to the same thing.

So then, by the time the war broke out and the United States entered the war, my father was arrested by the FBI. The war was declared December 7, 1941, and that very night, in the middle of the night—my mother says, "*Era mezzanotte, e son venuti e battuti la porta, e chi è, siamo l'FBI, vogliamo parlare a Signor DeLuca."* [It was midnight, and they came and knocked on the door, and who is it, it's the FBI, we want to speak to Mr. DeLuca.] So they opened the door and, *"Sei Pietro DeLuca? Si, cos è? Sei arrestato come nemico di paese."* [Are you Pietro DeLuca? Yes, what is it? You are under arrest as an enemy of the state.] So they arrested him because he was an Italian. They arrested him and put him in the concentration camp on Ellis Island, took him directly to Ellis Island. And there were others. In fact, I know of two others—they were friends of my father's—because I met them when I came to this country, who were also members of the same club, you might say officers or directors of the club. I remember meeting one, a fine gentleman from Napoli, another from Genoa. [They] were picked up that same night, only they were released later.

So my father was on Ellis Island, and here is my mother, alone with two children, and not informed where they were taking him. Finally, there was communication. What length of time transpired between the arrest and the notification as to [my father's] location, I'm not aware. But they learned where he was, and my mother was able to visit my father on Ellis Island and commenced a program for the discharge of my father. And I think that there was Fiorello La Guardia, being the mayor of New York, and there was Mr. Impelliteri, he was the lieutenant governor of the state. So then my mother [wrote] letters to the mayor and Impelliteri and to the bankers, [and] then was told to appeal directly to Mrs. Roosevelt. I know—I've seen letters addressed to Mrs. Roosevelt as well as a letter in response to my mother's appeal to her, under her signature—that she had received my mother's appeal and was looking into the matter and would see what she could do.

Whether it was through that intervention or through others, my father was released about eight or nine months later, but on parole, meaning under surveillance, having to check in with the authorities. When I'm saying "parole," I'm using the word to mean there is a controlled element. And I learned about this through the American Red Cross in Italy. And my parents, my father specifically, learned about my escape from the condition that I was in through the Red Cross as well.

They were going to put me in a concentration camp; but I escaped and joined the guerillas in the mountains in Sicily, *i partigiani*. That was 1942, I was eleven years old—young, yes, but you had to be somewhere, you had to do something, and in Sicily the *partigiani* was more in name than in activity....People knew us—the neighbors and friends, the police knew who we were—but we were sort of a group of outsiders who lived in the mountains and lived from foraging and whatever other resources were available to us—not really attacking anyone. I mean, we made a couple of raids—I recall a raid particularly on the Germans in Fiume di Nizza...primarily to gain food and clothes, and ammunition and whatever else we could gain. More like, you might say more like a robbery than an attack.

Meantime, in New York, sometime in 1942, my father was released. How the final release came about I don't know—whether it was through political influence, or an evaluation of the fact that here's my mother with two little children, and my father was not an enemy of the state, he was an Italian, proud of his heritage but also proud to be an American. My father had not yet obtained his American citizenship; he was still operating on what was referred to as *la mezza carta*, half papers, and the reason I know that is that when he finally became an American citizen, which was I think sometime in '44 or '45, he had me included in his papers as a minor child living abroad, which then facilitated my finally getting my visa from Italy to come over.

After his release, he went to work. And I know that for a while...[my] father would go to the club with his friends, the *circolo*. So I know that it remained in composition. I don't know if they kept the name. I know that it retained a social activity more than before, because I recall meeting people that my mother and father would introduce to me as *l'amici* [friends] *di circolo.*

As to how he was after the war, I know my father as being a deep thinker. He was socially sensitive and very philosophical. And I never heard him complain. He was not one that would say, "Had it not been for this, this is what I would have been."...But within his own makeup, there were scars. And I think there was suspicion or resentment, a type of reaction that was antagonistic, because there were people in the Italian community, [with] their sons or husbands in the service, and [they] therefore felt, "You are not fighting me, but you must be a spy. Otherwise, if you weren't, they would not have arrested you. They would not have kept you for so long." So that suspicion was damaging.

...I recall the way...the Sunday afternoon dinner became really a classroom for us, because we would talk about events of the day, relatives, activities of the past, take positions on events—that's why the part that I enjoyed best were our Sunday dinners, because of family participation. I remember Zio Natale would come and have dinner with us, and sometimes other friends. And my brother would come in with three or four friends from school and it was dinnertime—okay guys, sit down and eat. That's why I called it a classroom—well...it was more like a forum. And I recall Zio Natale, Zio Gaetano—not so much Zio Nino, who was the old socialist, there was some antipathy...that lasted even to the days I remember. I mean, they were brothers, they loved each other, but there was not the kinship, for instance, that there was between Gaetano and my father. I don't know if it was because of their political philosophy, or because my Uncle Nino used to say, "Look, you continue in this manner and you end up being in a concentration camp. I did not participate and they left me alone."...So in that sense there was a bitterness. And my father was more the center than his older brother. His older brother, he left Italy, [he might say], "I am of Italian descent," but he left it. That's it.

My father left, but emotionally he did not leave. Whether that...[was] because of me, I don't know—because his son was there. And if there was any bitterness, it would have been that because of his political involvement, I was left in Italy and therefore subject to the suffering of the war and all that. Because I remember he always used to say, *"Se non fosse stato per me, tu avresti stato con me."* [If it had not been for me, you would have *been* with me.] And this I recall not so much as an antagonistic feeling between my mother and father, but *quasi*....I'm not casting any ill feelings on either [one], but I recall sometimes getting into an argument with my mother and my father and saying, *"Basta. Sono qua ora."* [Enough, I'm here now.] I mean, *è passate* [it's over]....To this day, my mother sees me as a nine-month-old baby that she left on the dock at Palermo. Like,..."I had to come and rescue you and I had to leave my child for you, and therefore a part of me was left behind."...Sometimes it would cast me against my mother in saying, "But mother, I'm here now. It's all forgiven." But my mother is eighty-six, and she has been sick most of her life, and...I visit her on Sundays—the two of us have lunch—to give her something to do, to look forward to. She's alone, she wants to live alone, and...she gets into these emotional memories.

...My mother would say, *"Tuo padre, a canciata,"* using Sicilian. "Your father has changed." My father became moodier....The whole thing, you might say it became a demarcation point. *Tuo padre a canciata.* And when I'm trying to ask my mother more, well, *come si fa*, you know, more by mannerism, by expression, but no direct reference to any one particular. So you might say, well, the passage of time. Age. Conditions. War. Suffering. Jobs. Could be any one of those. But there is a point from which you could see a change, during the war, from that point on. And I know this also, that it became a focal point, because my brother...sometimes used to tease me. [He would] say, *"Se non fosse stato per te, non avrei mangiare spinacc'."* [If it hadn't been for you, I wouldn't have had to eat spinach.]...Here I am in a country that is the subject of bombardment, invasion, deprivation of foods and conditions, and whenever my mother cooked and my brother would say, "I don't like it, I don't want to eat it," they would say, *"Mangitulo, il fratre non a li."* [Eat it, your brother isn't here.] And so my brother would eat [spinach] or any other food, because my mother and father would say, "Look how lucky you are, you have food on the table and your brother doesn't have any, he has to go foraging," and so forth.

So all throughout, I was this presence. And this presence is more revealed through the memories and the activities and the references of my brother and sister, because they knew they had a brother whom they did not know.

So when my father would say to my brother, *"Mangia"* [Eat], you could see a resentment. These are the things that temper moods and people....

———

I finally came here on February 20, 1947. It was my third attempt. The first had been 1940. The second attempt was in 1946. The war was already over, I had finally gotten my visa and a tutor, again, because I was still a minor (under sixteen), and the tutor was again a friend of my father who had come over, and I could come over under his tutelage....[Booking] passage was very difficult. First passage rights were given to Americans, and I was not an American, therefore I had to take my turn....Finally, I had obtained a visa to leave aboard the *Prince Albert,* debarking from Bari. And it would have landed in New Orleans, which to me—I didn't know what that meant. And I remember leaving—this was in the winter, about November of '46—leaving Messina with my cousin Luciano, and we got on the train to Bari. Never made it. Because by the time we got to Paola—it was not a regular passenger train, it was a...freight car—the train could not go any further, because there had been a storm, and the bridge had been washed [out], and we got stuck. We could not go forward, we could not go back, we are in *carro di merce* [freight car], no food, no heat, nothing. And I became very *affezionato di grappa* [fond of grappa] because of that....Signor Piccioni, who had been engaged by my father...to become my guardian and facilitate the papers for me to get my visa and embarkation, and who had worked for La Grande Adriatica, which was a shipping line, and therefore knew the ins and outs...[had] booked this trip for me and was accompanying me to Bari, where he would turn me over to this friend of my father. And when we got stuck, [after] a couple or three days, he went into the area, found a farm, and the only thing that he could buy was a bottle of grappa; and that bottle of grappa kept us alive and warm for three days....So there was no point even continuing to Bari, because we'd already missed it. And I'll never forget the return back to Messina, to my grandmother and my aunts. Came back, knocked on the door, alone. *"Che fai?"* [What are you doing?] And [we] had to communicate to my parents that the trip had been aborted—which in a way was a partial blessing, because the *Prince Albert* was some sort of a merchant ship, stopping to pick up passengers at various ports, and would have taken something like forty days.

Ultimately, I got a visa to leave and left out of Palermo, in 1947, aboard the *Marine Shark,* which had been a converted troop ship. It took us twelve days to cross the Atlantic, which was a long time by comparison—the *Rex* used to do it in five days—because in the Atlantic we struck a mine, and we lost the bow, and we had deaths, and a fire on board. So my parents always said how ironic, how tragic was my coming. And I recall when we first came into New York harbor and I saw the Statue of Liberty for the first time in my life, and it was the most beautiful thing that I could have seen.

Then I recall coming to the wharf in New York City, and my father was the first one, he recognized me and I recognized him, and I remember he broke through the line, jumped aboard, and met me on the stairwell going down. And it had been so cold—you know New York in February—and I remember all I had on me was a suit, a light serge, navy blue suit which had been sent to me through a CARE package; it had been the suit of my Uncle Guy, who was smaller, and therefore didn't necessarily fit me that well. And I was so cold that I felt my nose and my ears had been cut off. And I recall, my sister and my mother and my uncle Buster and my two cousins had come for the event—I mean, this was an event. And my mother was crying so much, from joy and all, that as she was waving the handkerchief at me, the handkerchief *froze*. And Uncle Buster had a car—it was a Hudson—and on the way from the port to the house, he stopped. And I couldn't figure out why he had stopped in the middle of the street, so I asked him. And his answer was *"Il semaforo,"* the traffic light. I'll never forget that.

...Then I got to meet a lot of my father's friends. He used to take me around—you know, the prize. I was literally like I'd gotten my prize, I'd won the lottery. I'll never forget the joy and the pride in my father taking me around, introducing me....[We went to] the marketplace, Grand Central Market, and I'd never seen a market like that. Everyone had his own little *banco* [stall]. And my Uncle Natale and three other friends—their name was DeMarco—were selling vegetables and fruits and dried goods. And I remember when my father brought me there, and this Patsy said to my father, *"Ma questa una fortuna e brave, prendi whiskey."* [This is a great event—break out the whiskey.] And my father said, *"Si, per mio figlio, uscire il cappellacio,"* which is to say, "Yes, for my son, break out the good stuff"—which I learned only later referred to Lord Calvert, who had a big hat, *il cappellacio*—a prize whiskey.

And so, my coming into America was the goal, my aspiration. If anybody would say to me, *"Che cosa vuoi fare quando tu fai grande?"* [What do you want to do when you grow up?], my answer was *"essere l'Americano"* [to be American]. Because from the moment that I first learned what my life was about, which was at age five, when my aunt and my uncle told me that they were not my parents, the only thing that kept me going was *essere un Americano*. To be an American.

That's why they used to call me Pippo l'Americano.

Impersonizing Columbus

by Joseph L. Cervetto

> Joe Cervetto came to San Francisco in 1933 aboard an Italian mer-
> chant marine ship and, at the urging of family members, jumped ship
> and stayed to build a window-washing business into a highly
> profitable office-cleaning venture. But he found his real metier play-
> ing the role of Christopher Columbus each year in the annual
> Columbus Day pageant, playing the part with such fidelity and com-
> mitment for thirty-three years that for most people, including him-
> self, Cervetto was Colombo, and vice versa. Before his Columbus
> days, however, Cervetto was arrested by the FBI following Pearl
> Harbor and detained for several weeks, narrowly escaping intern-
> ment. What follows is his version of that wartime episode, as he told
> it in a 1992 interview.

LAWRENCE DISTASI: Where did your family originate?

JOE CERVETTO: Varrazze. My parents came from Genoa. My father was a contractor and moved to find work, and Savona was a city building up—it was a
port, that's where Colombo's (Columbus's) family moved too. And they used to
make mattresses. And my mother used to make mattresses too. And my father
made buildings, he used to make buildings that—in Savona there are still buildings he made. Then, my father married my mother, and they stopped there in
Varrazze. But it's really a little fraction called Pero.

LDS: And from there…

CERVETTO: First, in 1892, my brother Tony came over. Tony invite Charlie, the
other brother. And then a cousin Charlie. And then they invite, in 1914, my
sister Rina, and brother Jack. In Oregon.

LDS: And you came later, in 1933. And there's a story that in World War II
you were actually interned.

CERVETTO: Yeah, they put me on Angel Island. Then from Angel Island[1] to Sharp Park....Before they sent you to Missoula, they questioned you for a month or so, to find if you were a Fascist. When I came here, in 1933, I was not a Fascist. But [before coming], I did make application to be a Fascist, because everybody did. I had a good job....

The police, one night they come in, took me from the house, two FBI, one policeman, I didn't even finish my dinner, I remember it was risotto...and I was eating...

LDS: Funny, how you remember what you were eating.

CERVETTO: And I was having dinner, and...I was listening to the radio. Francesconi,[2] you remember him? And he was joking about smoking the Toscanelli's—cigars you know—and he said, "Now we're going to sing a beautiful song from Italy." And all of a sudden, nothing happened, and I said, "What the hell happened to the radio?" So my wife, she said, "I don't know." Then an American voice come on and said, "Francesconi is temporarily disconnected." Hah-ha, and then, "Sorry, we'll sing some martial songs." And they took over the station. And then ring the bell, and police said, "Joe Cervetto there?" "Yes," my wife said, "he's having dinner."...

I went over, saw them, say to myself, "Oh boy." They said, "Come with us." "Can I get my coat?" "No coat. Come the way you are." I said, "How about my pocketbook?" "You don't need no pocketbook. Come like you are."

They took me to the Salvation Army. I slept there in a bunk, one blanket. Then, in the morning, got that little bus, and I remember was with me an officer of the *Graf Spee*,—you remember? In Montevideo [the German ship was] sunk by the queen's destroyer from England. Uruguay was neutral, so they couldn't stay, Valparaiso didn't want them, so...they sent them to San Francisco. And he was in the same boat with me to Angel Island.

LDS: Did they tell you what you were being arrested for?

CERVETTO: Nothing. So they put me there in one of the cabins. They told us if we wanted to make our own dinner...they gave us tomato sauce, and a pot, and dishes....They had a big kitchen, you ever been to Angel Island? And we was on top of the hill, and they treat us good.

LDS: Why didn't they send you to Missoula, or Colorado?

CERVETTO: Because I was able to answer the questions. They want to find out about the Fascists, why I came here—to bomb the bridges? "Why did you come here, you had a good job," and, "Did you join the Fascist Party?" I said I was in the merchant marine, and didn't need to join. Then they say, "But after, were you instructed [in how] to take care of explosives?" I said, "I made application, but one year before I left for the U.S." Again, "How come?" I said, "My other ship went out, so I went ashore and made application with another company." So he said, "But didn't you do anything, become a Fascist?" "No, the 24th of April, the day they wrote me to buy a black shirt, that was the day I left for the U.S." And it was true. So, by golly, they left me there. And then they repeat the same questions. "What about the explosives?" No explosives. "What about the bridges?" What bridges? "You came to the U.S. to bomb bridges, didn't you?" "No," I say. "I came to wash windows!"

LDS: How long did they hold you altogether?

CERVETTO: Four weeks. Because one day, this captain, the interrogator says, "How come you tell me the same bullshit all the time, you talk, talk, talk, and you tell the same thing?" I said, "My mother told me, when you say the truth, you should not be scared to make a mistake, because it's got to be the same." He said, "Your mother told you that?" I said, "Yes, my mother's still alive. In North Beach." And they laugh like hell.

LDS: Okay. But this happened when you were in the Italian community organizations. How did you first get involved?

CERVETTO: I guess that was the time around 1935, I joined the Sons of Italy, then became president, Piemonte Social Club. All of a sudden I got involved. I talked good Italian and that was my downfall, because one day I saw Judge Molinari, [he] was an attorney then…I saw him over the Buon Gusto Market, and he said, "You, Joe Cervetto—listen, you showed some pictures of Mussolini and Hitler at a meeting, four in the afternoon." I said, "Mr. Molinari, those pictures, I don't have no camera. I bought those films, they are Castle Films, on Market Street, made in this country. I didn't put Mussolini there."

LDS: And that's what got you in trouble?

CERVETTO: Yeah. They put me in the concentration for showing propaganda.

LDS: But that didn't stop your activity in the community after that?

CERVETTO: That didn't. You're Italian—I was in the navy—I mean, you couldn't forget your country. I was Italian, admired Mussolini. But I was not Fascist; I never was a Fascist. So I got involved here. Then, one of the guys, an Italian prisoner that worked for me, fell in love with my wife. Before you knew, they was—uh, my wife went there...

Still, I'm Italian, but never against America. I was in Italy, they ask me, "How come you talk good Italian?"...This lady says, "You talk good Italian, in America fifty years, and uh, how you like the country? I mean, you have an English [speaking] woman." I said, "Well, I had an Italian woman, she run away with a goddamn prisoner." Of course, she came back and she was sorry. But this lady, she said, "What do you like better, Italy or the U.S.? You must have some kind of attachment to either country."

And I said, 'To tell you the truth, you cannot...You have a mother, and you have a wife. You love both of them, different love. You cannot go in bed with your mother, but you love your mother, and you love your wife. You can't say I want one to love or the other. It's the same thing like your country. I said I would never go against the United States. Because the U.S. is my country."

LDS: And is the United States your wife or your mother?

CERVETTO: Doesn't make any difference. My mother country is Italy. That's where I was born. In the U.S., England is the mother country. In the south, Spanish is the mother country. And I call Italy my mother country.

LDS: And where does Columbus fit in? Is Columbus—in your thinking about him, being him—I mean, you've visited every place, you've walked the beach in San Salvador where he landed...

CERVETTO: I even have some rocks from that beach. I gave some to Judge Molinari...

LDS: You saw the bed in the house where he died, the house in Savona where he was born, the cathedral in Santo Domingo where he's buried—is Columbus your mother or your wife?

CERVETTO: Well, love of Colombo is a different thing. The love of Colombo is the same thing like a son. You know you have the same love you have for a son.

LDS: You mean that Columbus is like your son, something you created all those years in the pageant?

CERVETTO: No. See, I have a daughter, she's fifty years old now. She does some things, you know, but she's my daughter. You have a son, it's the same, he can do some things wrong, but you don't just get rid of him. It's flesh and blood. No matter what, he's your son. You still love him.

Endnotes:
1. Fort McDowell, an Army camp for internees, was located on Angel Island in San Francisco Bay. Sharp Park was a temporary Immigration and Naturalization Service detention center located in the town of Sharp Park (now part of Pacifica), just south of San Francisco. Missoula, referred to in the next sentence, was the INS internment camp in Montana.
2. Nereo Francesconi was a San Francisco radio announcer who was picked up in the first wave of arrests made by the FBI. He was sent to the internment camp at Missoula, Montana, in December 1941 and spent two years in various internment camps.

War within War
Italian Americans and the Military in World War II

by Lawrence DiStasi

When the United States entered World War II in 1941, Italian immigrants comprised the largest foreign-born group in the United States. Congruently, their children comprised the largest ethnic contingent in the United States armed forces, with estimates of their numbers ranging from 400,000 to one million.

Of those hundreds of thousands, many served with distinction, but none more so than Sergeant John Basilone of Raritan, New Jersey. The son of Italian immigrants, Basilone holds the distinction of being one of the very first enlisted men in World War II to receive the Congressional Medal of Honor as well as the only soldier in U.S. history to earn both this medal and the Navy Cross, the two highest American awards for heroism. He was granted both honors because he seemed incapable of sitting out a battle.

Basilone first joined the army in 1933 and served four years in the prewar period, receiving an honorable discharge in 1937. But as he saw war drawing nearer in 1940, he not only reenlisted, but this time joined the marines. Within two years he had his first medal, earned while serving as a sergeant on Guadalcanal. On October 24 and 25, 1942, Basilone and his vastly outnumbered unit were defending a pass leading to Henderson airfield. At one point, Basilone was reduced to only a revolver with which to hold off the Japanese attack, but he and his men prevailed. He returned to the United States a hero, not only receiving the Congressional Medal, but also agreeing to travel the country to drum up support for the U.S. war effort by raising over $1.3 million in war bonds. This would have sufficed for most people, but once again, Basilone was not content to rest on his considerable laurels. Refusing a safe domestic assignment, he volunteered to rejoin the combat raging in the Pacific in late 1944 and wound up in the bloody battle for Iwo Jima on February 19, 1945. He was single-handedly destroying a Japanese blockhouse while under a withering artillery bombardment when an enemy shell caught up with him, and he died as he had lived, fighting against enormous odds. His posthumous honors, besides the Navy Cross, include the naming of both a bridge, the Basilone

Memorial Bridge on the New Jersey Turnpike, and a destroyer, the USS *Basilone*, in his memory.[1]

John Basilone was not the only member of his large Italian family to serve. Three brothers followed him into the service, two in the marines and one in the army. This same pattern was repeated countless times among the children of Italian immigrants in World War II, and it is one that only heightens the irony of the other, more suppressed story of the wartime period—that while many of these Italian American sons and daughters were fighting and dying in the U.S. armed forces, 600,000 of their parents were stigmatized on the home front as enemy aliens and forced to endure various levels of suspicion, restriction, and incarceration.

Catherine Buccellato of the little Delta town of Pittsburg, northeast of San Francisco, felt this irony firsthand. Because she had never become a citizen, Buccellato, like nearly 2,000 other Italian-born resident aliens of Pittsburg, had been forced to evacuate her home in February 1942, when the whole town had been declared a prohibited zone. Like much of the California coast, it was thus off limits to enemy aliens. Along with her minor children and several relatives, Buccellato moved into cramped housing normally occupied by migrant farmworkers in the nearby town of Oakley. All the while, two of her sons were serving in the U.S. Navy, and it wasn't long before her son Nick came home on leave to find his home empty. It took him a while to learn from local authorities that, as an enemy alien, his mother could no longer live in the home that proudly displayed two stars in the window—for two sons in the service.[2] This same rude awakening would befall countless others. Steve (Ghighi) Ghio of Santa Cruz, for example, arrived home on leave from the navy to find his house boarded up and his parents, fisherman Steve Ghio and his wife, gone he knew not where. He had to ask the local police to find them, at a time when not just he but two of his brothers were all in the service.[3]

For Rosina Trovato of Monterey, a similarly painful contradiction applied, only in reverse. On one day in early 1942, she received the terrible news from the War Department that in the battle of Pearl Harbor both her son and her nephew had been killed in the attack on their ship, the *Arizona*. Notwithstanding her ultimate sacrifice, Mrs. Trovato was then informed that, as a resident alien of Italian birth, she would have to leave her home in Monterey because the area in which it was located had been declared a prohibited zone.[4] Leo Giorgetti, whose parents had a farm west of Highway 1 near Half Moon Bay, had a similar experience, only he tried to do something about it. Having enlisted in the U.S. Navy four days after Pearl Harbor, he came home on leave to find his mother forced to evacuate across the highway, a half mile from the home in which her husband, Federico, who was a citizen, could remain. From her place of exile, Maria Giorgetti could see the family's home, Leo Georgetti said, "and my father and their animals. It just killed her. Deep in my heart, I thought it was unfair. I knew it hurt my mother, but I couldn't do anything about it. Everyone was bewildered."[5]

Leo Giorgetti refused to accept his mother's exile and traveled to San Francisco to plead his case with Lieutenant General John DeWitt, head of the Western Defense Command. Though he could not see the general, he got to see a colonel in DeWitt's office:

> I made a deal. I said, "You've got me in the service. The day my mother betrays this country, you take me out and shoot me. I'm here to beg. I want my mother home, and she belongs there."

In Giorgetti's case, the deal worked; three weeks later, his mother was back on the family farm. But for the vast majority of those evacuated, there was no deal; they were treated by the book.

Nor should it be thought that only evacuees in California endured these bitter contradictions. Josie Patania of Boston remembers that "during the war, they took my father off the fishing boat" because he and Josie's mother were both enemy aliens. At the same time, "my brothers Carmelo, Angelo, and Vincent were all in the service. Carmelo and Vincent weren't even citizens. They swore them in before they went, Vincent to Normandy and Carmelo to the Philippines."[6]

Perhaps more striking, and certainly more ironic, was the situation of the internees. In the early days and months of the war, hundreds of resident aliens of Italian descent who had earlier been designated dangerous were picked up by the FBI, taken to detention centers maintained by the Immigration and Naturalization Service (INS), and questioned as to their past activities. Most were given hearings to determine if their continued freedom was inimical to the public safety of the United States. Some 260 of them were eventually judged too dangerous to remain at large and were sent to internment camps in various parts of the United States. The fact that many of these internees had sons either already in the service or about to join seemed to make no difference to the authorities deciding their fate.

Louis Berizzi, for example, was picked up on December 9, 1941, two days after Pearl Harbor, and two days before the United States and Italy were formally at war.[7] He was held at the INS detention center on Ellis Island for almost a year and formally interned at Fort Meade in Maryland in December of 1942. Early in 1943, his son Albert, an ROTC student at Lehigh University, joined the army as an officer. The army did not seem to notice that Albert Berizzi, having been accepted into the intelligence service, was awaiting transport to Europe to join the Allied invasion of Italy—at the very same time that his father was interned as an enemy alien. It took a vigorous legal campaign by Berizzi's daughter Lucetta to force the authorities to take note of this, reconsider Louis Berizzi's case, and eventually parole him.*

Ubaldo Guidi-Buttrini endured a similar irony. The radio broadcaster from Winthrop, Massachusetts, was picked up on December 9, 1941, and soon interned. Records show that on September 17, 1942, he was visited by his son, Private Mal Guidi, of Company H, 11th Armored Regiment, 10th Armored Division, Ft. Benning, Georgia.[8] Overcome with emotion when he first greeted his son, he was stopped by the corporal monitoring their conversation until the internee could control his voice so as to be understood and monitored. There ensued a long conversation, all of it recorded, about Private Guidi's enthusiasm for the army, his furlough in Boston, and other matters. At one point,

> Internee Guidi-Buttrini turned to the undersigned and stated that he had four children, born in this country, that were ready for military service. Private Guidi remarked, "We were educated in America and we are all good Americans."

Whether or not this impressed the monitor is not recorded. It did not seem to impress the authorities, for Guidi-Buttrini is recorded as having been transferred to the internment camp at Missoula, Montana, on May 18, 1943, and his incarceration continued.†

More extreme still was the situation of Alfredo Tribuani, a newspaper reporter for the Italian newspaper in Wilmington, Delaware, as well as a member of the Advisory Board for Adult Education and Americanization there. According to a memo in his War Department file dated June 20, 1942,[9] at the time of his internment, Tribuani had contributed no less than four sons to the United States armed forces: Ralph, a member of the Delaware National Guard since 1928, with one year's regular army service; Armand, a corporal in the Delaware National Guard, also with one year's regular army service; Dino, a private in the same unit of the National Guard; and Lambert, a private in the 198th Coast Artillery. Since January 1942, moreover, his sons in uniform numbered only three, for on January 5, Lambert Tribuani died while serving in his regiment at Denver, Colorado. The memo relates that "following the death of his son, a soldier in the U.S. Army, he [Tribuani] was temporarily released."

---

*For more on the Berizzi family's wartime experiences, see "Orders to Take Him Away, p. 217.
†Guidi-Buttrini's case is also discussed in "Let's Keep Smiling," p. 198.

But not for long. Tribuani "was again arrested in April 1942 and reinterned on May 15, 1942."

We do not know precisely how the War Department responded to the information in this memo, but the fact that it was developed at the request of the intelligence section at Fort Meade did not bode well for the internee. On June 22, 1942, a copy of the memo was sent to the assistant chief of staff at G-2 headquarters in Baltimore, Maryland, by way of the post intelligence officer at Fort Meade with the information on Tribuani's sons in service repeated. At the end is this comment: "This information is forwarded to your office for whatever action may be deemed appropriate."[10] One would like to think that "appropriate action," given the three sons he had still serving in the military, might refer to some sort of mitigation of Tribuani's sentence as an internee. But since the information was sent to G-2, and had been developed for the intelligence section in the first place, "appropriate action" may well have been intended to alert G-2 to the fact that, given the father's questionable status, *the sons themselves might need to be investigated.* We do know that sons or no, on September 17,

Albert Berizzi (right) with an army buddy in Lucca during the war. Courtesy of Lucetta Berizzi Drypolcher

1942, Alfredo Tribuani was transferred to another internment camp at Fort McAlester, Oklahoma, and he remained interned until June 1943.

At this point it might be relevant to quote a relative of the writer Jerre Mangione about the effect of long residence in the United States and having American-born children: "Don't those imbeciles in Washington understand," he said, "that to have American-born children is to become an American for the rest of your life?"[11]

Apparently the United States government during World War II knew nothing of the kind. Its primary concern in those dark early days of the war seemed to be not the positive influence American-born children might have on an immigrant parent's future, but on the degree to which actions or sentiments favorable to Italy in the past might possibly contaminate the present. Among the most significant of those past actions was service in the Italian military during World War I—with its likely corollary, membership in a veterans' organization known as the Federation of Italian War Veterans, or, in Italian, the *Ex Combattenti*. This was an organization about which the FBI had grave concerns, categorizing it as a highly dangerous group which took its orders directly from Rome. Notwithstanding the fact that the organization had been granted a permit by the U.S. government to carry on its activities, most notably the collection of gold rings and other donations to help the Italian war effort, including war widows and orphans; nor the fact that its permit had been rescinded in May of 1941 and it had completely disbanded on December 13 of that year; nor the fact that the Justice Department found in August 1942 that there was no evidence whatsoever of subversive activities on its part; nor the fact that the veterans comprising it had fought, like Italy, on the Allied side in World War I against Germany—all these facts notwithstanding, the FBI targeted virtually every member of the organization and interned those who were not citizens. In the fall of 1942 it also went after those who were naturalized citizens, successfully obtaining exclusion orders for a dozen or more with past ties to the group.[12]

Unfair and contradictory as this might seem today, government suspicion of Italian ex-combatants from World War I might be granted a shred of reasonableness—they had, after all, been trained as soldiers and might therefore have tendencies that could prove dangerous during a war. More difficult to understand are the government's actions against someone like Fred Stella. Stella, it is true, had also served in the First World War. But the resident of Indiana had served not in the Italian army, but *in the army of the United States of America*. This is testified to by several letters written by Stella, and also by a letter from the national director of the American Legion, T. O. Kraabel.[13] What we learn in Kraabel's letter is that either the government mistakenly thought Stella was a WWI veteran of the Italian army or it arrested him for failing to register under the Alien Registration Act of 1940. But the letter makes clear that at the time he was supposed to register, Stella was in a Veterans Administration hospital run by the United States Government. Fred Stella himself wrote a letter to the provost marshal general, Allen Gullion, on September 25, 1942, in which he made this clear:

Dear Sir,

My name and address are the above ones. I am a veteran of the last war, when I enlisted voluntarily to fight on the Allied side in the American army.

At present I am, as you can judge by the address, an alien enemy in a camp for internees. The reason for this has not been made clear to me, and in consideration of my past record of loyalty to this country, I consider the treatment given to me hardly fair.

For about five years and a half I was laid up in a hospital of Denville, Illinois. When, in 1940, all aliens were supposed to register, according to a new law, I was not only unaware of this fact, but would also have been unable to comply with the regulation, had I known about it, for the very reason of my illness. I think, therefore, that in all justice, I cannot be held responsible for my failing to comply, in view of the reasons just told.

Could you be so good as to send me a copy of my record, as held in your care, to the above address. I shall be looking forward to your reply and remain in the meantime,

Yours very truly,
Fred Stella

[P.S.] I should also like to add that I am still ill, having only recently come out of hospital, and that moreover I am without resources, since I am not able after my long illness to do any physical work. However, I have not drawn on my bonus since 1936, which my brother, who was appointed as my guardian during the time of my illness, is holding for me. I wonder whether you could assist me in returning home so that I might get this money which is due to me and live on its proceeds.

My brother's address is 845 Matthew Street in Clinton, Indiana. He is a widower of six years standing and over seventy years of age. My presence would be a great comfort and almost indispensable help to him.

I shall be much obliged for your giving this letter your prompt attention and answering at your earliest convenience.[14]

Colonel Bryan, chief of the Aliens Division of the Provost Marshal General's Office, replied to Stella on October 5, informing him that since he had been interned at the direction of the attorney general, any change in status fell under the jurisdiction of the Justice Department. Thus, "In the event you care to do so, you may direct any request you wish to make regarding such matters to the Director, Alien Enemy Control Unit, Department of Justice, Washington, DC."[15] Stella, still ill, may have found all this bureaucratic delay and buck passing too much to bear. On April 6, 1943, he was remanded, along with eight other Italian internees, to Borden General Hospital, Chickasha, Oklahoma. It was a hospital for the insane.

It is too bad that Fred Stella never had the opportunity to learn that he was not alone, nor even the Italian internee whose rights had been most egregiously violated. It might have comforted him to meet another internee who had fought for the United States in World War I and shared a similar fate. But this second internee never got to McAlester nor to Borden Hospital, where he might have met Stella, for virtually alone among Italian American internees, he ended up at Camp McCoy in Wisconsin. His name was Mario Valdastri, and he had lived in Hawaii for many years, building up a successful contracting business there.* On December 8, 1941, he was picked up by the FBI and taken to the detention center at Sand Island in Honolulu. Failing to convince the hearing board that he was not a threat to public safety, in January he was transported to the mainland for internment in Wisconsin, five thousand miles from his home in Hawaii. Like Stella, he could not understand why. Having come to the United States as a thirteen-year-old from his native Italy, Mario Valdastri had lived in the United States (or its Hawaiian territory) ever since, going to school, building businesses, becoming fairly prominent, and along the way, enlisting in the United States Army, serving in France *as an American soldier* during World War I and receiving an honorable discharge in 1919 as an American citizen.

And yet, on December 8, 1941, Mario Valdastri was interned as an alien enemy of his adopted country. The question he kept asking was, why? On what possible grounds could an American citizen who has served his country in one war be interned as a dangerous alien in another?

---

*For more about Mario Valdastri, see "A Tale of Two Citizens," p. 137, and "Two Men in Suits," p. 153.

Valdastri never got an answer. Neither has his family or anyone else. All that can be gathered from his War Department file is that in those days, with the United States at war with Italy, anyone, indeed everyone, with an Italian name and any connection to the military whatsoever was suspect. Consider those who innocently and patriotically answered the call printed on posters everywhere, "Uncle Sam Needs You," which seemed to be reinforced by the enthusiastic reception they got when they joined up and reported for duty. How dismaying, then, to find out, which several did, that the United States military was not exactly wholehearted in its welcome; that, in fact, it harbored serious reservations about the loyalties of those with Italian names and was taking covert steps to investigate them.

This was what Harold Ferrari of Lafayette, California, found. Once he had completed basic training, Ferrari noticed that he was being held back as the rest of his outfit moved on. He then discovered why. Not only was he interrogated carefully about his willingness to fight in Italy and specifically to "kill Italians," but when he was finally allowed to proceed to his unit, he was given a lower priority—he was a machinist in the navy—that kept him apart from the "sensitive" materials accessible to his peers.[16] Sergio Ottino, who had attended the same after-school Italian language program as Ferrari, had a similar experience, only his was compounded by a further and more specific insult.* The native of Berkeley was likewise asked questions about his loyalty, held apart from his navy comrades in San Diego, and given no access to certain high-priority areas. Even prior to this, however, Ottino felt a more dispiriting backlash from the fact that his mother, as an enemy alien, had been forced to move from her home in Berkeley. While in training at Farragut, Idaho, Ottino had taken a standard aptitude test for placement. When the results came in, Ottino was told that he and another candidate had achieved the highest scores ever recorded there and would be receiving orders for pre-flight school as officer candidates. Within weeks, the other man did receive his orders, but Ottino did not. After an additional wait, Ottino inquired about the delay and was made to understand that his mother's status as an alien had compromised her son's candidacy.[17]

Still, to openly question Italian American recruits about their willingness to fight in their ancestral homeland would be one thing. To spy on them would be quite another. But the United States military apparently saw fit to indulge in that activity as well. This astonishing fact is confirmed not by any of those spied upon (for how could they know?), but by one of the GIs who did the spying. His name is Dan Dougherty, and without knowing anything about the restrictions on Italian Americans during the war, he wrote an account of his brief career as

---

*See "A Tragic Episode," p. 59, for Sergio Ottino's recollections.

a spy in a July 1998 newsletter prepared for comrades who had served with him in C Company, 157th Infantry Regiment, 45th Division, Seventh Army during World War II. Here is the item he headlines "Clarence Toon":

> My army basic training in 1943 was at Ft. McClelland near Anniston, Alabama, which operated as a huge infantry replacement training center. Shortly after our arrival I was called to company headquarters where I was shown into the office of the executive officer. He greeted me with "Private Dougherty, from this day forward you will be a member of army intelligence!"
>
> You could figure that being one month out of high school I wouldn't be assigned to breaking the Japanese code and you'd be right. Turns out the GI who had the bed next to mine was an Italian American from New York City whose family still owned property in Italy. The army had no reason to suspect his loyalty, but to make sure, I was to ask him leading questions and report what I learned in a weekly letter to be mailed each Friday to a post-office box in Anniston. No one was to know about this and my letters were to be signed Clarence Toon. Nor was I to use my franking privilege. A three-cent stamp would be provided each week at company headquarters!
>
> I monitored this fellow for several weeks. I never had anything to report because my inquiries served only to confirm his interests in girls and sports. Eventually he had an emergency appendectomy and I visited him one time in the hospital. He never returned to the unit, so my career as a crack army intelligence operative (blarney) was cut short.
>
> I was really impressed with the importance and secrecy of it all, until one day when I went to the orderly room to get my three-cent stamp, the first sergeant bellowed, "Here comes Detective Dougherty!" A few years ago I met a fellow who had a similar assignment in World War II and he, too, signed his letters Clarence Toon. I tell my wife we Clarence Toons may be unsung heroes of World War II. When our covert actions are eventually declassified (big blarney), look for a book with glossy pages and lots of photos entitled *Top Secret: Clarence Toon*, probably written by Stephen Ambrose![18]

When Dougherty read a Sacramento news story about the exhibit *Una Storia Segreta* detailing the Italian American experience during the war, he suddenly saw the larger significance of "Clarence Toon" and sent his newsletter to the exhibit sponsors.

Among the many questions Dougherty's revelation raises, one that deserves mention is this: How did the military come to know that the parents of the Italian American soldier from New York still had property in Italy? Perhaps the answer comes from an email recently received from Nicholas D'Antona, who writes that though his father never experienced any difficulties or restrictions during wartime, "after my father was drafted into the army in early 1942, he did recall a friend telling him that FBI agents did ask around the neighborhood [Scranton, Pennsylvania] about my father's character and loyalties."[19]

Thus has it become known that the largest ethnic group to serve the United States in World War II not only served under a general cloud of suspicion, which in some cases led to outright discrimination, but also, in an as-yet-undetermined number of cases, was secretly spied upon as well—all this as its members were preparing to give their lives to defend the rights and property and lives of those engaged in the spying.

———————

What the aforementioned cases reduce to is the following: the United States military during World War II decided, reasonably or not, that it had to separate from its ranks those who might fall prey to divided loyalties. That is, the military high command seemed to believe that were an Italian American in a combat situation faced with enemy troops which he had reason to believe might include his relatives, he might be inhibited from taking the appropriate action, thus risking lives and/or victory. Those in charge devised measures to search out and eliminate anyone whose commitment to battle might be less than zealous. They could do this by discharging those whose loyalties they found questionable; by sending them to a theater of operations, such as the Pacific, where those conflicted loyalties would not be tested; or by redirecting suspect individuals to noncombat units within the continental United States where, presumably, they could be rendered harmless.

We now know that each of these expedients was implemented, though the degree to which each was used remains unclear. Recent research, for example, has confirmed what Remo Bosia,* an excludee from San Francisco who joined the army to prove his loyalty, discovered in 1943 when he was sent to Camp Ripley in Minnesota: the War Department had set up bases deep in the interior

———————

*See "The General and I," p. 290 for more on Remo Bosia.

of the continent manned by segregated units, often engineer units, of Italian American and German American soldiers whose loyalties it suspected.[20]

In writing about his discovery, Bosia says that the Italian Americans in his battalion at Camp Ripley were there "as the subject of suspicion or distrust of some sort."[21] Though none of them were sure about the cause of that distrust, Bosia's conversations with several soon revealed that for the Italian Americans, it had to do with their one reservation about the military: they did not want to be sent to fight against Italy. As one of them put it,

> After all, my father, mother, brothers, and sisters are still in
> Italy. How can you be expected to shoot at your flesh and blood?
> But America is at war with other countries. Why can't we be
> given proper, adequate training and be sent to fight the Germans
> or the Japs?[22]

The soldiers at Camp Ripley never got an answer to this question. All they knew was that the duties they were given "…left no doubt as to our status in the army."

> We shoveled snow, sawed wood, unloaded trucks, policed the bar-
> racks, kitchens, and latrines, and so on. Except for a drill now and
> then, there was no basic training. And if that camp had been
> attacked by some sort of Axis airborne invasion, it would have
> been a pushover. There wasn't a single pistol, rifle, or machine
> gun in sight.[23]

On the other hand, extensive anecdotal evidence (to wit, the battles where John Basilone earned his medals) indicates that Italian American troops in very large numbers were indeed sent to fight in the Pacific—where the problem of encountering Italian relatives in enemy ranks would be moot. Vincent and Carmelo Patania, the two brothers from Boston mentioned earlier, were given assignments in Germany and the Philippines because one of their brothers, left in Italy when their mother emigrated, was in the Italian army.[24] The famed 442nd Regimental Combat Team, made up of Japanese American troops recruited from the relocation camps, supports this same conclusion in reverse: its battles, invariably fought with distinction, took place in the European the-ater of operations, where their loyalties would not be tested. Thus, it seems evi-dent that this segregation-by-theater expedient was also used to minimize conflicts of loyalty.

What has never been considered, however, is that the most extreme form of the military's segregation policy would be implemented. That is, until recently no one imagined that the U.S. Army would go beyond simply finding and then diverting to one of its segregated units a soldier it found less than enthusiastic, to taking the next step—punishing him for it. But that is what happened to Private Illidio DiBugnara.

DiBugnara came to the United States in 1935, when he was about sixteen, to join his father and brother in Brooklyn. In February 1941, despite the fact that he was not yet a citizen, he was called up for duty with the United States Army. The military was in desperate need of troops in those days before war was formally declared and took even noncitizens gladly. Private DiBugnara spent most of 1941 stationed at Fort Gordon, Georgia, no doubt hoping that he would be able to serve out his year of active duty without incident.

Then the Japanese attacked Pearl Harbor, the United States entered the war against the Axis powers, and on December 11, 1941, formally declared war on Italy. This meant, first, that all U.S. troops, including Private DiBugnara, were notified that they would now be required to remain on active duty indefinitely. Some weeks after that, a second bombshell arrived: the army circulated a bulletin addressed to servicemen who, like DiBugnara, were natives of the now-enemy nations and presented them with a choice. They could either stay in a U.S. military now at war and automatically become citizens; or they could choose to be discharged. While the former choice carried with it the considerable benefit of citizenship (as well as the substantially increased risk of going into battle), the latter choice carried with it an equally strong negative: as a native of an enemy nation, the discharged soldier, his loyalty now suspect, would be subject to internment as an enemy alien.

While the choice might seem obvious to some, Private DiBugnara found himself on the horns of a cruel dilemma, for there was another component to the choice he was given. In order to stay in the service of his adopted country, he had to answer the "loyalty question." Would he, as a native of Italy, be willing to fight against Italy and Italians? Could he actually kill Italians?

As noted above, numerous other Italian American servicemen reported being asked these same questions. Most, apparently, were able to answer in the affirmative. Private DiBugnara could not answer so easily, however, for as he explained to his superiors, he knew for certain that two of his own brothers were then serving in the Italian army. In effect, he tried to point out, he was being asked if he would, as the price of becoming an American citizen, be willing not only to risk his own life but to kill his own brothers.

Difficult as it must have been, DiBugnara said no. He could not and would not risk it. Did that mean he was choosing internment rather than citizenship?

Catherine Buccellato with her son Nick shortly after he entered the navy. Courtesy of Leo Buccellato

If citizenship meant killing his own brothers, it did. As he later put it in a letter to the U.S. district attorney in Savannah, Georgia, from his internment quarters at McAlester, "I know that I was interned because I did not feel as I should have fought against my native country because I wasn't yet a citizen of America and I have two brothers in the army in Italy."[25] In short, DiBugnara didn't want to fight in Italy because he knew he could not, under any circumstances, kill his own brothers. Who could? Who, indeed, could even come up with the notion of forcing a man to make so deadly a Hobson's choice? The military did, and even though Private DiBugnara took great pains to explain that though "my conscience did not dictate me to go to the front against my own brothers and family, I would have been more than willing to be a good soldier in continental United States or against another enemy such as Japan or any other nation on earth," his refusal to fight Italians had raised fatal questions about his loyalty. So much so that rather than allowing Private DiBugnara to go to another theater of operations, or stay in the United States (both perfectly reasonable options in other cases, as noted above), the army for some reason interpreted his choice as a wholesale refusal to defend his country and discharged him from the service—knowing full well what would happen; indeed, intending for it to happen.

And happen it did. Immediately following his discharge in July 1942, Illidio DiBugnara was taken to the INS detention center at Fort Screven, Georgia, classified as an enemy alien, and given a hearing before a civilian hearing board in nearby Savannah. The operations of such hearing boards are well known. The suspect alien was not allowed to know the charges against him, nor to have legal representation. In the absence of specific charges, he had to prove his innocence to all three hearing board judges. If even one judge found his "proof" a failure, he was interned. The Savannah hearing board apparently found that former Private Illidio DiBugnara's refusal to kill Italians had cast sufficient doubt upon his innocence to warrant internment. He was sent to Camp Forrest, Tennessee, and then transferred to Fort McAlester in Oklahoma, where he joined more than a hundred other civilian internees of Italian descent behind barbed wire.

DiBugnara's presence at McAlester no doubt disturbed the few who thought to ask why he was there. For here was a very young man, one who had already served his adopted country for fifteen months; a man who, as he told the hearing board:

> in civilian life, [had] never been arrested or been in any trouble;
> [whose] conduct and respect for all that is American [had] always
> been beyond any doubt; [who had] worked and studied to become
> a better resident of this country; never been associated with any
> club or society with a subversive purpose or against the welfare of
> America.[26]

Here was a man who had not only served, but even agreed to continue his military service in any other theater of war. And yet, because he had expressed scruples against killing his own relatives, he had been given what must have seemed a harsh punishment indeed to those who shared it.

Now he was ill—so ill with a stomach ailment that twice he had found it necessary to recover in the station hospital, because, as he wrote, "it is evident that life in the camp causes an incurable state of my illness."[27] He was asking the Justice Department for a rehearing.

Eventually he got that rehearing, and this time reason prevailed. DiBugnara was released from internment in early 1943, returned to his former job in Brooklyn, reported to a parole officer every six months, and in 1950 became a United States citizen.[28]

But the questions remain: Why put a man in such a situation? Why persecute someone who has already served more than the time he was drafted to serve? Why impose internment on someone already serving, especially when you demand the opposite—service in the military—from someone who has been interned? For this is what the military did in the case of Lanfranco Dwight Rasponi Dalle Teste.

Papers in his file tell us very little about Dalle Teste. All we know is that he was detained at Ellis Island sometime early in 1942, and that he apparently failed to prove his innocence at his hearing, for on February 13, 1942, he was ordered interned. A copy of the internment order is found in his War Department file.[29] Also in that file is a July 20, 1943, letter from FBI director J. Edgar Hoover to the assistant chief of staff, G-2 [Intelligence], in Washington. In it, the director refers to his previous letter of August 1, 1942, "in which you were advised that on June 24, 1942, the attorney general ordered the parole of Lanfranco Dwight Rasponi Dalle Teste." Thus we learn, to begin with, that Dalle Teste was paroled about six months after he was interned.

The letter goes on to its real point: "For your information, I have received from the attorney general a copy of another order, dated June 25, 1943, directing that Dalle Teste be released inasmuch as he has been inducted into the armed forces of the United States."[30] After being paroled, an internee had to report to a parole officer weekly until he was formally released—a procedure which could take two years or more. In Dalle Teste's case, the release was apparently hastened by the fact that the formerly "dangerous" internee had been drafted and had agreed to serve.

But what of the loyalty question? If someone like DiBugnara is interned after having already served loyally, simply because he honestly admits he cannot kill his brothers (making him, perhaps, *not* dangerous enough for the army), how can someone who has been judged so dangerous to the public safety that he is incarcerated suddenly be judged loyal enough to be drafted?[31]

And if someone like Dalle Teste, first interned as a dangerous alien, is judged, a few months later, fit to serve in the armed forces of his adopted country, why would someone else, a native-born American citizen, *not* be allowed to serve, this time because of the lesser restriction represented by an exclusion order? For that is what happened to Remo Bosia—the same Remo Bosia mentioned above.

Born in Madera, California, Bosia had returned to Italy at age six when a nervous ailment led his mother to resettle there. He had stayed with her until the age of eighteen when, to get away from Fascist rule, he returned to San Francisco. Fluent in several languages, he eventually became a translator for the Italian-language newspaper in San Francisco, *L'Italia*, and in 1937 was offered the job of editor. He took the job gladly, but what had looked like an opportunity in 1937 turned, in 1941, into a grave problem—for with the war, *L'Italia* was, like most Italian American newspapers, accused of having been profascist. Bosia maintained that he had vehemently disagreed with the political stance of *L'Italia*'s publisher, Ettore Patrizi, but the head of the Western Defense Command, Lieutenant General John DeWitt, was unimpressed. In August 1942, DeWitt served Bosia with an exclusion order mandating his removal from most of the western states.

As he explains in his book *The General and I,* the exclusion order ignored Bosia's attempts to join the army air force, and indeed ended them. Yet so eager was he to prove his loyalty that Bosia, with the tacit approval of the head of the local exclusion authority, Major Ashworth, enlisted immediately in the army as a private and proceeded to the Monterey Receiving Center for processing. There, on the basis of tests demonstrating his language fluency, he was admitted to the intelligence corps and thought his problems were over. They were not. Once again, his orders were delayed until he was suddenly confronted by MPs, who placed him under arrest.

Thus began a series of arrests initiated by Lieutenant General DeWitt, and temporary releases initiated by the army, which continued almost interminably. Eventually, Private Bosia was sent to Fort Douglas, Utah, for a court-martial, where he finally learned the charges against him: attempting to enlist in the armed forces under false pretenses and remaining in a prohibited zone after the date, September 19, 1942, of his exclusion order. The fact that he was already an enlisted man by then, and that leaving his post would have constituted a military crime, did not deter the court-martial or the general.

Bosia's court-martial began in December 1942, and in the end he was acquitted of all charges and returned to duty. But just as he had completed plans for his wife to come live in nearby Salt Lake City, he learned that the zealous general had still not finished with him. The very day his wife arrived, Bosia received new orders transferring him to an even more remote post, this time the camp for those with suspect loyalties, Camp Ripley, in Minnesota. Duty in that frigid place aggravated his bronchitis and eventually led to a medical discharge from the army.

At last his ordeal seemed over, but before he could completely recover, Bosia was served yet another order from Lieutenant General DeWitt—this one informing him that the original exclusion order remained in effect, and that the now-civilian Remo Bosia had to leave Military Zone One by the next morning. Too exhausted to fight any longer, Bosia left for Reno, Nevada, where he remained in exile until Lieutenant General DeWitt's transfer to an obscure post at the War College and Italy's surrender in September 1943 finally left him a free man.

Surely it would be asking too much of a government and its military branch to be consistent during wartime. Perhaps it would be asking too much of the military to be consistent even in peacetime. But during wartime especially, decisions are made on the run. Innocuous events seem fraught with significance and danger. All this is little consolation to those caught in the clutches of such a government or such a military, however. For the central point in all the above cases is that it was not actions, nor even intentions, that were at issue, but national origin. The central flaw was having been born in Italy, or in Bosia's case, having been born in America to Italian parents. Such an origin in enemy nations was a red flag during World War II and it elicited a wide variety of responses by military authorities. In some cases there was simply a question, clearly asked and easily answered, about a soldier's willingness to fight in Italy. In others, it inspired cloak-and-dagger measures. In still others, it led to delays in training, or rejection of candidates for certain jobs or ranks. In a few, it led to actual punishment, ranging from exile to remote posts to incarceration for disloyalty. And in at least one case, Bosia's, it instigated a full-scale persecution that went on for years.

The problem was that in the face of such treatment—which was seldom overt and so could not always be flushed out, much less opposed or protested—one never knew what might help. Doctors who were interned, like Domenico Rosati of Pittsburgh, offered to make use of their skills to aid the American war effort. They were rejected. Private DiBugnara offered to serve in any theater other than Italy. He was rejected. Remo Bosia offered to use his flying skills in the air force, and when he could not, agreed to take the lowest rank available to demonstrate his loyalty. In return, he was court-martialed and hounded so continuously that he ended up unfit for duty—and then hounded some more. The world he and others describe has often been called Kafkaesque, and that may be the best way to describe it still. For in answer to the Kafkaesque question "What have I done?" there come only bureaucratic responses, or contradictory responses, or silence.

Thus, in the end, one can understand those who retreat into irony. For what else but an ironic stance remains when those who served, or whose children served, are left with the knowledge that they and theirs were risking their lives to defend the very government that was accusing and judging and punishing them?

Endnotes:
1. "World War II Hero John Basilone Remembered," *Italian Tribune News*, Feb. 23, 1995, pp. 1–4.
2. Personal interview, John Buccellato.
3. Geoffrey Dunn, "The Unknown Internment," *San Jose Metro*, July 7–13, 1994, p. 21.
4. Personal story given at Open Forum, *Una Storia Segreta*, Conference Center Monterey, California, July 1994.
5. Heather Knight, "War Story Untold," *San Francisco Chronicle*, Oct. 8, 1999, Peninsula section, p. 8.
6. Josie Patania, personal interview, July 25, 2000.

7. Louis Berizzi file, RG 389, Records Relating to Italian Civilian Internees During WWII, 1941–46, Boxes 2-20, Provost Marshal General's Office, National Archives and Records Administration, College Park, Md. (hereafter RG 389 NARA II); also personal interviews, Albert Berizzi and Lucetta Berizzi Drypolcher.

8. "Memorandum of monitored conversation between Internee Ubaldo Guidi-Buttrini and his son, Pvt. Mal Guidi, Sept. 17, 1942," Ubaldo Buttrini file, RG 389 NARA II.

9. Memo by Henry B. Mohler, June 20, 1942, Alfredo Tribuani file, RG 389 NARA II.

10. Memo to Asst. Chief of Staff, G-2, HQ, Third Corps Area, "Sons of Internee Alfredo Tribuani," RG 389 NARA II.

11. Jerre Mangione, *An Ethnic at Large: A Memoir of America in the Thirties and Forties* (New York: Putnam, 1978), p. 286.

12. See Rose D. Scherini, "When Italian Americans Were 'Enemy Aliens,'" this volume, p. 10.

13. Letter to Major General J. A. Ulio, Adjutant General, Aug. 18, 1943, in Fred Stella file, RG 389 NARA II.

14. Letter to Col. B. M. Bryan, Chief, Aliens Division, Sept. 25, 1942, RG 389 NARA II.

15. Letter, Col. B. M. Bryan to Fred Stella, RG 389 NARA II.

16. Harold Ferrari, personal interview.

17. Sergio Ottino, personal communication.

18. Dan Dougherty, "Company C Newsletter," July 1998, pp. 2–3.

19. Nicholas D'Antona, personal communication, June 6, 2000.

20. Mary Ellen Reese, personal communication, Jan. 2, 2000.

21. Remo Bosia, *The General and I*, (New York: Phaedra, 1971), p. 105.

22. Ibid., p. 106.

23. Ibid.

24. Patania interview

25. Letter to J. Sexton Daniel, U.S. District Attorney, Jan. 30 1943, DiBugnara file, RG 389 NARA II.

26. Ibid.

27. Letter to Edward J. Ennis, DOJ, Jan. 5, 1943, DiBugnara file, RG 389 NARA II.

28. Illidio DiBugnara, personal communication.

29. Lemuel B. Schofield, Internment Order, Feb. 13, 1942, Dalle Teste file, RG 389 NARA II.

30. Letter, J. Edgar Hoover to Asst. Chief of Staff, G-2, July 20, 1943, Dalle Teste file, RG 389 NARA II.

31. Not to mention this Kafkaesque paradox: when DiBugnara is discharged from service, he becomes vulnerable to internment; when Dalle Teste is freed from internment, he becomes vulnerable to induction.

32. Bosia, *The General and I*.

The General and I

by Remo Bosia

> Remo Bosia was born in Madera, California, and moved to Europe at age six with his parents. As a young man, he returned to the United States, where he worked as a stunt pilot and then as a writer and translator for San Francisco's Italian American newspaper, *L'Italia*. After his World War II travails, described in his book *The General and I*, Bosia opened a jewelry store, which he ran until his retirement, at which time he began operating a motel. The multi-talented Bosia also composed several songs and painted landscapes which were exhibited locally. He died in 1989.

The trial by general court-martial in the case of the *United States of America* versus *Private Remo Bosia*, Serial Number 19085016, began at ten o'clock on a bitter morning, December 22, 1942, at Fort Douglas, Utah.

I was the private.

Until a few days earlier I had not known what I was accused of specifically, only in a most general way, although I had been in and out of military custody for weeks. My arrest had occurred at Monterey, a West Coast reception center for the army in California.

When I had been hustled into the post prison and recovered enough from my GI trauma to think a little, another inmate asked me what I had done.

"I don't know," I mumbled. "I'm at my wit's end."

"Not your wit's end," said he, "DeWitt's end, and I guess you know what end that is."

He referred to [Lieutenant] General J. L. DeWitt, commander of the Fourth Army defenses of the Pacific coast against the Japanese. The general had declared a personal war on me shortly after Pearl Harbor. Our mutual hostilities lasted until Italy surrendered and joined the Allies against the Axis.

By then he had been transferred to some desk job in the War College. His last tour of duty must have been frustrating, what with no people of Italian, Russian, or Japanese ancestry to shove around.

This selection is excerpted from *The General and I* by Remo Bosia (New York: Phaedra, 1971).

As the name Remo Bosia suggests, I am of Italian parentage. That was the origin of my troubles with the general, although I am a native American, born in Madera, California....

In May of 1937, I got married to Marcella, the daughter of one P. Pallavicini, a man of noble birth, noble in character, and a writer of considerable renown among the people of his race. At the time he was editor-in-chief of *L'Italia*.

About a year later we had our only child, Sandra; she was born the same day Mr. Pallavicini passed away.

Mr. Pallavicini dropped dead from a heart attack while trying to stop a fight between his beautiful alaskan husky and another dog in front of his house; he died in full view of the family. His death occurred at almost the same hour as Sandra's birth; we had a new life for the one we had lost.

The husky refused to eat from that moment on. Two weeks later, after one last visit to the spot where his master had fallen, he returned to his pallet in the garage, gave a last mournful howl, lay down, and died.

At my father-in-law's death, Mr. Patrizi, the publisher of *L'Italia*, promoted me to succeed him as editor-in-chief. For the next three years, life was relatively happy and serene. The one fly in my journalistic ointment was Patrizi's mounting enthusiasm for Fascism and Mussolini. We had discussions, sometimes arguments. I could admit the benefits of certain aspects of Il Duce's regime, but we differed fundamentally on the philosophies involved in a dictatorship.

I went about the business of putting out the paper. Mr. Patrizi and another member of the staff wrote the editorials, but Patrizi, only, dictated the policy.

Sunday, December 7, 1941, I left our home in San Carlos, a peninsula community twenty-five miles south of San Francisco. There was much work to be handled for the Monday edition, so I wanted to get to work a little earlier than usual. It was a beautiful sunny morning; the city, as I drove through it, had an aura of festive well-being. The Christmas holidays were close at hand. It seemed that everyone I saw was smiling and in a jovial mood. Church bells tolled joyfully, calling people to worship.

I entered the building of *L'Italia* and, in walking towards my desk to labor at the typewriter, paused a few seconds for a quick glance at the teletype machines that brought us news of events from all over the world.

The teletype bells suddenly clanged out their tocsin—the bulletin signal that news of momentous events was coming over the wires.

As I watched, the keys hammered out:

Attention all editors. The White House announces...Pearl
Harbor was attacked this morning by hundreds of Japanese

aircrafts....Tremendous losses suffered in men and ships by our Pacific Fleet...

My reaction, of course, was one of shock. I had feared we would eventually be dragged into the war, but not this way, through such infamous treachery on the part of Japan, whose ambassador and special envoy were even then sitting in Washington pledging peace and understanding.

That was a frenetic day for all newspapermen. Once the work was done, I took stock of myself and came to a decision. The next morning, December 8, I went looking for a friend, Major William Fillmore of the U.S. Army Air Force, and finally located him at the San Francisco Presidio, Fourth Army headquarters. He told me he would see me the following day.

When we met, Fillmore appeared grave, as any officer would at the grim turn of events. Coming right to the point, I told him I wanted to join the air force and asked him how to go about it.

"You're a good flier and the air force certainly could use you, but didn't you once tell me you majored in Italian and French?" he asked.

I nodded.

"In that case," he went on, "my advice to you would be to join the air force intelligence. The corps needs pilots, but more than pilots it needs men familiar with foreign languages for the intelligence."

I hadn't given this a thought, but it seemed more than reasonable. I told him that I liked the idea and proceeded to fill out an application. Bill said I would be commissioned a first lieutenant within two or three weeks. He advised me to get my affairs in order and be prepared to leave. I returned to *L'Italia* and informed Mr. Patrizi of what I had done. He congratulated me and promised me that my job would be waiting at the end of the war. This began the first phase of what was to become the most abominable period of waiting in my life.

Three weeks, a month, two months went by with no word. I called Major Fillmore. He was as baffled as I. He thought the delay must be due to the apex of red-tape confusion going on in Washington.

Late in August of 1942, two men walked into my office at *L'Italia* and presented credentials identifying them as secret service agents attached to the staff of [Lieutenant] General J. L. DeWitt, commander in chief of the Fourth Army. They said they would like to talk to me.

I greeted them warmly. I thought, naively, they had brought good news of my commission from the War Department.

They informed me they had come to serve a citation ordering me to "appear before a military board and explain why I should not be excluded from the Pacific coast, a war zone, as a potential enemy."

"Are you kidding?" I asked when I had recovered enough to speak. One of them handed me the citation. I was to be at the board hearing in the Whitcomb Hotel the following morning.

The hours before the hearing were terrible, beset with anguished doubts, momentary hope, sickening fear, and disgust. I had no sleep and neither did my wife, who was in a state of near hysteria.

I arrived at the hearing finally with only the determination to speak my piece as best I might. I thought I did so with convincing sincerity. I told the board I had never been a member of any political organization, let alone one inimical to the United States. I reminded them I was a Californian and to the best of my knowledge had been a good citizen. I confessed to some affection in my heart for Italy as it was before Mussolini; I had nothing but scorn for him. I avowed my willingness to serve my country, and pleaded at the end only for the opportunity to prove with deeds the statements I had made.

All of the board members were smiling when I ended; I thought I had won the battle. Actually, I believe now that the hearing was no more than a hollow routine. I doubt if any excludee obtained a favorable ruling, once his citation had been issued. We were condemned before the official machinery began grinding out its edicts.

Within a day or two I was told that, on the orders of General DeWitt, I had to leave San Francisco, my home, family, and job, and establish myself at a distance of not less than one hundred fifty miles from the Pacific coast.

My departure, however, was delayed by a period of humiliation that included session after session of questioning, posing stiffly for rogues'-gallery-type photographs, fingerprinting, and all the sorry procedure that the suspected or known criminal is subjected to.

Nor were my family and friends exempt. They too were grilled, as was—of all people—my little daughter, Sandra, at the time not quite five years old. She was questioned not in our home, but in her kindergarten class. I couldn't help but wonder, in God's name, what revelations of treason or of a traitorous father they hoped to get from so young a child.

These men, I supposed, had a job to do, but they pressed their efforts to astonishing extremes and seemed to enjoy it. The whole intolerable mess eventually drove me to a decision.

I went to see Major Ray Ashworth, head of the local Exclusion Authority, at his office in the Whitcomb Hotel. His secretary, a Miss Cornelia Matteson, was present at the meeting. I told him that rather than suffer the shame and stigma of exclusion as an enemy of the country, I wanted to enlist in the army as a private. The major listened in silence until I had finished. Then, looking straight at me, he curtly said I could enlist if I wished.

I left him and went to the nearest recruiting office. In a matter of minutes I was in the army, under notice to be ready for induction the next morning. From there, I went to my office at *L'Italia*, where I asked Miss Henrietta Setaro, secretary to the publisher, to take a letter to Major Ashworth informing him of my enlistment. Miss Setaro typed the letter, which I signed; at my request, she delivered it in person to the major's office. After this I went to the upstairs office of a friend, Dr. Richard Sabatini, and told him of the step I had taken. Finally, I went home to another unnerving night.

Unable to understand what I had done, Marcella wept and asked, again and again, "Why enlist to fight a war for people who treat you this way, people who consider you an enemy?"

The next day I drove back to San Francisco, my wife and daughter with me. I left them at Second and Mission Streets after a heartbreaking farewell. They were both in tears. When the family car turned the corner and disappeared, all of my heart and most of my hope went with them. It took me minutes to muster enough strength to walk on to the recruiting station at 444 Market.

There I was informed that I need not report until 6:30 P.M., when my group would entrain for the Monterey Receiving Center to be processed before final assignment.

A long wait was before me, but I felt I couldn't return home; it would have been inhuman to subject Marcella and Sandra to another prolonged farewell. So I walked aimlessly until I reached Union Square, in the heart of the city's downtown area, where I found a spot on the thick lawn in a clump of massive shrubbery that screened me from the eyes of the passing crowd. There I lay all afternoon in an emotional void. I felt drained. The passing hours were a complete blank.

The hour of departure finally arrived and with it a dismally long trip. A hundred or so men made up my group. Monterey was wrapped in a cold thick fog when we arrived shortly after midnight. After a thorough physical examination, we were given a couple of anti-something shots, divided into smaller groups, and sent to the barracks.

Bone weary, I threw myself on the nearest empty cot, aching for sleep. But only two men in that outfit got any rest that night. They took cots on either side of mine. Formidable snorers, they shook the barracks all night long with strange horrible gurglings, stranglings, and explosions until we were routed in the morning, after which, taken to a large assembly hall, we were put in uniform and questioned as to our qualifications, if any, for some particular branch of the service.

My preference was intelligence, as I had a college background and could speak, read, and write several languages as well as a number of Italian dialects.

My request was tentatively approved. So for the next three days I took a series of examinations that lasted from morning until late afternoon. On the fifth day, a Captain Riley summoned me to the Classification Office and cordially shook hands.

"Congratulations, Bosia," he said. "You made intelligence. In a few days you will leave for training in Florida."

It seemed my trouble might actually be coming to an end, so I hurried to a telephone and called my wife to give her the news.

During the next several weeks, thousands of men arrived in Monterey and left; for me, nothing but delay. Finally I was told to pack my gear, orders having arrived for me to leave that same day for the East. My hopes soared again. Several hundred of us assembled on a field for instructions, ready to move at once. The roll call began. When it was over, everyone had been called but me.

As I started towards an officer to ask if there had been an an oversight, two MPs appeared from nowhere, asked my name, and put me under arrest.

Within minutes I was in the guardhouse. As the barred door of my naked cell clanged shut, it closed on all my illusions, dreams, and hopes of doing honor to the uniform I wore.

I dropped onto a cot, sick with disgust, incapable of coherent thought. It was about an hour later, I guess, when one of my fellow prisoners asked me what I had done and made the crack about "DeWitt's end."

The men in this military jail were a cheerful bunch and several of them went out of their way to try to make me feel better. They played poker, told stories, and waited philosophically for whatever the morrow might bring. They were in for definite violations and crimes. I still didn't know what I was supposed to have done.

Days went by in this excruciating state of uncertainty, although an accused soldier is supposed to be informed of his alleged crime at once, even as a defendant in the civil courts. My repeated requests to see the chaplain were also ignored.

Each morning, instead, I was put to work digging ditches, planting trees and shrubs, sweeping halls, mowing lawns, cleaning latrines, and policing grounds.

The worst moment of that period came one gloomy October morning. Up to my knees in mud, I was busy planting a hedge along the highway that leads from Monterey's Presidio to the city proper when a car came to a stop a few feet away.

Looking up, I saw my wife and daughter getting out and, instinctively, ran towards them. My guard, who kept watch over me, aimed his gun and screamed, "Halt or I'll shoot!"

Marcella and Sandra, paralyzed with terror, stood still. I stopped and tried to reassure them. We exchanged a few words from a distance; then I was ordered back to the guardhouse.

Two weeks after my arrest I appeared before an officer of high rank, a Colonel Grier. Affable and courteous, a novelty in my recent experiences, he asked if I would be willing to meet with Major Ashworth, in his presence, the following day....I readily agreed.

In this session Colonel Grier seemed to be interested chiefly in whether I had informed Major Ashworth of my intention to enlist. Both of us were questioned at length. Then, to my surprise, Miss Setaro was summoned. She was my publisher's secretary, who had typed and personally delivered to the major's office my letter, informing him I had enlisted.

Two days later the chaplain of the post paid me his first visit. He, too, was courteous and brought great news.

"Take your things," he said. "I think you have been in here long enough. You're now a free man."

That was great news indeed. I hurried with my gear to the barracks of my original outfit, Company C, then walked soberly to the chapel to give thanks. My faith, however, was soon shaken.

Within a week, DeWitt made his next move in his cat-and-mouse game with me. Arrested a second time, back to the guardhouse I went, too numb emotionally to care much about what was going on. Another week passed, then Colonel Grier informed me I was to be taken under guard to Fort Douglas, Utah, new headquarters of the Ninth Service Command.

I was still ignorant of my crimes....

———

The abominable weather and my deepening anxiety remained my worst foes until one miserable afternoon early in December. An icy rain had been falling. I was back in my cell, half frozen, when two officers arrived to see me. They were Captains Frederick Bold and Lionel Campbell.

After introductions, Captain Bold said, "Both of us were lawyers before entering the service. We have been assigned to your defense."

"Defense of what?" I asked.

"Your defense at your general court-martial."

"General court-martial!" I gasped. "Have I killed somebody?"

Until they explained the charges, I was probably more terribly frightened and dejected than ever in my life. Then I took heart. They told me I had a right to a third lawyer, a civilian, if I wanted one; but I waived that. Now that I finally knew what I was accused of, I was ready to fight.

"We won't need him," I said. "The three of us will win.

I had been charged with violating the 54th and 96th Articles of War, plus a specification. The first charge, alleging violation of the 54th Article of War, stated:

> In that Private Remo Bosia, Company C, Service Command
> Unit 1930, at San Francisco, Cal., on or about September 15,
> 1942, by willfully concealing the fact that on or about September
> 9, 1942, he had received from [Lieutenant] General J. L. DeWitt,
> commanding the Western Defense Command and Fourth Army,
> a lawful exclusion order...which, among other things, prohibited
> him, the said Private Remo Rosia, after September 19, 1942,
> from being in, remaining in or entering into Military Areas Nos.
> 1 and 2 established by Public Proclamations 1 and 2 of said com-
> mander, did procure himself, the said Remo Bosia, to be enlisted
> in the military service of the United States by the recruiting
> officer at San Francisco, Cal.; and did thereafter at or near the
> Presidio of Monterey, Cal. receive allowances under the enlist-
> ment so procured.

Concerning the 96th Article of War, the second charge alleged:

> In that Private Remo Bosia...having, on or about September 9,
> 1942, and prior to voluntarily enlisting in the United States
> Army, received from [Lieutenant] General J. L. DeWitt a lawful
> Exclusion Order which...among other things, prohibited him, the
> said Private Remo Bosia, after September 19, 1942, from being in,
> entering or remaining in Military Areas Nos. 1 and 2...did, at or
> near the Presidio of Monterey, Cal., wrongfully and contrary to
> Public Law 503, 77th Congress, violate said Exclusion Order by
> then being and remaining within the said Military Area No. 1.

The third count, the specification, declared:

> In that Private Remo Bosia...having, on or about September 9,
> 1942, received from [Lieutenant] General J. L. DeWitt a lawful
> Exclusion Order...did, at or near the Presidio of Monterey, Cal.,
> on and after September 20, 1942, wrongfully fail to disclose to

Captain Winsor D. Wilkinson, his commanding officer, that he
had been served with said Exclusion Order, well knowing that he
was within said Military Area No. 1.

Boiled down, it amounted to this: I was accused of fraudulent enlistment, which
had damaged the honor of the army; of endangering the security of the country by remaining in a military area from which I had been excluded; and of con-
cealing the exclusion order from my commander. Come to think of it, there was
another point in that first charge: bilking the army out of my room and board.

None of it made any sense, and after hearing my side of it in detail the two
captains agreed with me. I've often wondered what motivated DeWitt in my
case, and what the rather staggering cost to the government must have been.

The general court-martial was set for December 22, now not many days
away. With the interminable waiting about over, I was tremendously encouraged. This is America, I kept telling myself, and they won't convict me of
crimes I haven't committed. The general, I thought, might have influenced or
even overruled the exclusion board in San Francisco, but certainly he would
have no control over a court-martial.

Conviction on any one of those three counts would have carried a minimum sentence of ten years at hard labor.

Each day after our first meeting, Captains Bold and Campbell spent a couple of hours with me, going over the case and planning the defense strategy. But
when not in conference with my attorneys, the sergeant of the guard saw to it
that I was not idle. Heavy snow had been falling again. I felt worse and worse
each day, until I knew I had a far more dangerous attack of bronchitis than the
first one. Fear of further delay, however, took precedence over fear of illness, and
I kept going until one night two medics came and took me back to the hospital.

The other prisoners had informed the officer of the guard I was danger-
ously sick, also that my nocturnal choking noises were ruining their sleep.

A young doctor I hadn't met before examined me and found I had a serious case of bronchitis with a high fever. He ordered me put under an oxygen tent.

I had the same room as before, with an armed guard at the door, but guard
or no guard, the place was a pleasant contrast. Outside it was snowing heavily.
Here, all was peaceful. I felt comfortably warm for a change. My breathing was
easier, thanks to the oxygen. The thought of not being routed out at six in the
morning to shovel snow was a deep relief. After taking a couple of capsules, I
settled down for what I expected would be at least one night of genuine rest.

It was not to be. As I was dropping off all hell broke loose in the form of
a 220-pound Negro soldier who was dragged into a room just across the hall
from mine. The man had gone berserk. He screamed, roared, and occasionally

grunted like a dying hog. Before entering the service I had had occasions to visit two of California's mental institutions, at Patton and at Ukiah, and thought I knew how furiously demented people acted and sounded. The poor fellow across the hall was in a class by himself. Four guards worked all night holding him in bed, although he was strapped into a double straitjacket.

He quieted shortly before morning, and I got a brief nap. But when I awakened, it was to new consternation. My voice was gone—not a sound, not a whisper left. And this was a problem if ever I'd had one.

It was the morning of December 18. My court-martial was to begin in just four days, on the 22nd. The mere thought of a possible postponement and what it could entail gave me the chills. Heaven only knew when the trial would be rescheduled, what with all the confusion of those early war days. Assembling the trial board of a dozen to fifteen officers, most of high rank, was no easy task. I had to regain my voice and regain it quickly and, above all, prevent the military authorities from discovering my predicament.

I sent a request for Captain Bold to come to me. He did so, promptly. I used a pad and pencil to inform him of the situation. I wrote that the court-martial must, under no circumstances, be delayed.

"How in the devil do you expect to face trial in your present condition?" he asked.

I scribbled assurances that I would be there and added, "Just get the hospital commander down here."

What went on between the captain and the commanding officer of the hospital I never learned. But Captain Bold must have won his sympathy and understanding. A colonel, he proved to be a man with an unusually pleasant personality. He took a great kindly interest in my case, showing me every possible courtesy.

I wrote, "Colonel, I have been waiting for this trial several months. You know what will happen if they postpone it—months more of waiting, in jail. I beg of you, restore my voice. I shall do the rest."

He shook his head dubiously but said, "Okay, I'll do my best."

He left the room briefly, then returned with some capsules and pills. His instructions were to take a white one and two of the blue ones every three hours.

"If," he said, "you can keep them down, you'll be able to talk again by tomorrow night."

I was too anxious to care about the ominous "if" in his statement. I started taking the pills at once and probably shaved the three-hour interval in my eagerness to regain my voice. Sometime during the night I became terribly nauseated. The seizure, with incessant vomiting, lasted for two solid hours, until I thought I had turned my stomach upside down.

When the colonel came again the next morning, I had my voice back, and the fever was gone. My first words to him were the question of what fearsome drugs went into those pills and capsules. He gently declined to discuss it. He approved my departure on the evening of December 21. Physically weak, but mentally full of fight, I returned to the guardhouse where the other inmates gave me a cheerful welcome. They too had feared I might not make it by the trial date.

Next morning two MPs escorted me to the building a few blocks away where the court-martial would be held. Twice on the way, I fell flat in the snow. Still, I remarked to the guard that at least this was one day I wouldn't have to shovel the stuff. They didn't answer, thinking I was a doomed man and hating their part in the procedure.

Shortly before we arrived at the building I saw an officer approaching and recognized him as an old friend, Dr. Richard Sabatini, then a first lieutenant in the air force at Kern Air Base. We nearly collided, except that Sabatini stepped aside, an unusual courtesy for an officer to show an enlisted man who was in the custody of guards. He looked at me but said nothing. I remained silent, thinking any overture on my part might embarrass him. The seeming snub hurt, though. I knew my lawyers had arranged for his presence as a witness on my behalf. I quickly wondered why he had come all the way to Fort Douglas if he were ashamed even to speak to me.

Later I learned the truth. My appearance had changed so much since we had last seen each other in San Francisco that he simply failed to recognize me. He more than proved his friendship, that same afternoon, when he faced the crossfire of prosecution questions on the witness stand....

"Gentlemen, you have heard the complete story from the defense," said TJA Sutter, and from his tone I sensed that he was coming to the close of his argument. "Bosia had an opportunity to tell you everything in his favor. But you have to start with that exclusion order and from there decide: "Did the accused have in his heart a dishonest intent?"

Lieutenant Sutter took his seat. Brigadier General Graham, president of the court, asked if anyone had anything more to offer. The TJA did not. Neither did my counsel.

"If there is nothing else," said the general, "the court will be closed and cleared."

The court was closed and cleared, ending the strange military trial of a man who was court-martialed because he had tried to prove his patriotism by enlisting. (Parenthetically, I would like to say that what I have recounted of the proceedings was taken from the trial transcript....)

The trial board, my jury, remained in closed session for half an hour. It was like waiting for a group of doctors to diagnose whether a piece of tumor they had cut out of you was benign or malignant. Then all hands—I, my counsel, the TJA, and the court reporter—were summoned to return.

We filed in and took our places. The verdict was at hand.

General Graham stood up. He was an erect elderly man, a fine specimen of the career soldier, severe but with kindness and fairness in his eyes. When he spoke, there was evident satisfaction in his voice. He said, "The general court-martial in the case of the *United States of America* versus *Private Remo Bosia* was closed, and upon secret written ballot the court finds Private Remo Bosia not guilty on all charges and specifications."

Me, yours truly, Private Bosia—not guilty! After one moment of heaven-sent bliss, I quietly keeled over in a dead faint.

———————

> Having been acquitted, Bosia resumed regular army duties at Fort Douglas, but not for long. Lieutenant General DeWitt next had him assigned to the battalion at Camp Riley in remote Minnesota reserved for soldiers of Italian or German descent whom the military found suspect. The cold weather there aggravated his bronchitis and he was transferred to the hospital at Fort Snelling in Minneapolis, from whence his military career ended with a medical discharge. This did not end his saga with General DeWitt, however.

I was reasonably happy as I headed for the railroad station, intent for the moment only on catching the first train for the Pacific coast, my family, warmth and sunshine, and freedom and forgetfulness from the now-ended nightmare. But on the way, the thought of DeWitt impinged itself and a lot of the old misgivings came rushing back.

Prudence, I counseled myself, is the better part of haste.

Fort Snelling is at Minneapolis. I hailed a cab and asked to be taken to the local offices of the FBI. I was lucky enough to get the agent in charge. After hearing my story, he could think of nothing except to call the commanding general at Fort Snelling.

There followed a long conversation, which I didn't hear, and then the agent returned to me with this assurance: "The general tells me you can go home and no one, from now on, will bother you."

With those lovely words singing in my heart I caught a train and headed west.

San Francisco, clean and shining on its beautiful hills, seemed to welcome me with open arms when I arrived at the Ferry Building. All of my family literally did. It was a joyous welcome on a joyous day, Easter Sunday, 1943.

The embracing, the tears, and the laughter quieted, I announced my intention of telephoning at once to the local FBI to let them know of my return with the blessing of the commanding general of the Fourth War Zone, headquarters in Minneapolis.

I was a minority of one on that proposal, but I did it anyway.

Then we went home to San Carlos for a family celebration by a long parade of guests and well-wishers. Finally, when all had departed, Marcella and I remained up late, reveling in being together and intermittently talking about the future.

We argued about it in friendly fashion. She thought I should return to my job on *L'Italia*. I had been thinking about a business of my own, perhaps a liquor store. We slept, finally, after compromising: I would return to *L'Italia*, but meanwhile we would keep our eyes open for private business opportunities. But first, we agreed, I should have two weeks of badly needed rest.

At breakfast the next morning things seemed to have returned wonderfully to a normal life. Then the doorbell rang. I answered. Two men were there.

"Are you Mr. Bosia, Remo Bosia?" one of them asked.

I nodded.

"We have this paper for you. Will you please read it and sign it?"

Before I looked, I knew what it was. The tirelessly vindictive DeWitt had issued a second exclusion order against me. I'm afraid I commented profanely to the effect that the old so-and-so still had not had his fill. I had twenty-four hours to get out or face arrest.

My visitors were brusque. One of them said, "We're just obeying orders. At what time will you leave tomorrow and what will your destination be?"

"I'll be at the Ferry Building at 9:30 in the morning and I shall go to Reno," I replied.

"Very well, we'll be there to see you off."

They left. Marcella burst into tears, but there were no tears left in me. The general, I guess, had become old hat, although the old hat was more like a Chinese boot that I could never shake off.

Editor's note: Shortly after Italy surrendered to the Allies in September 1943, and with Lieutenant General John L. DeWitt relieved of his Western Defense Command, the War Department canceled the exclusion order against Remo Bosia, and he was allowed to return to his home in San Carlos for good.

How World War II Iced Italian American Culture

by Lawrence DiStasi

In 1940, fifty years after their mass migration to the New World, Americans of Italian descent numbered over five million people. This made them the largest foreign-born group in the United States, and a force to contend with nationwide: they had mayors in New York City (Fiorello La Guardia) and San Francisco (Angelo Rossi), a lieutenant governor in New York State, and congressmen and representatives in various legislatures, including the irrepressible Vito Marcantonio representing New York's Harlem district in Congress. Joe DiMaggio, with his record-breaking assault on the consecutive-game hitting record was already revered as a quintessential American hero. In the arts, Italian Americans from the time of Jefferson had been recognized as seminal forces in music, painting, and sculpture. Now they were beginning to establish a presence in literature as well. Pietro Di Donato was being lionized for his best-selling novel *Christ in Concrete*. John Fante received critical acclaim for his *Wait Until Spring, Bandini*, and *Dago Red*. Jerre Mangione would soon find his *Mount Allegro* on best-seller lists. Other writers focusing on the Italian experience in America were already published or waiting in the wings.

When all this is added to the facts that the immigrant generation was steadily improving its economic prospects and its sons were joining the United States armed forces in record numbers—with well over half a million in uniform, they would become the largest ethnic presence in the American military—it becomes reasonable to posit that the Italian moment in America was at hand. The population was large, growing, and concentrated in Little Italys in all the major cities. The culture had the kind of unity of experience and vision that occurs only when its best and brightest are alive, together, and in possession of a healthy sense of entitlement. With Benito Mussolini apparently proving that Italy was now a world power to be reckoned with, strength was added to the growing feeling among Italian Americans that their time as a potent presence in the American institutions heretofore closed to them was at hand.

All this collapsed with World War II. The man whom President Franklin Roosevelt had once characterized as "that admirable gentleman," Benito Mussolini, with his attack on France in June 1940 became a "back-stabber." After Pearl Harbor, the friendly ally from World War I to which FDR had sent his cabinet officials (Social Security, the WPA, and other New Deal innovations were inspired by Mussolini's programs) became an enemy of the United States, the target of its propaganda and its bombs. As a result, anyone associated with Italy became likewise targeted—particularly those in the United States who, for various reasons, had failed to complete the process of naturalization. Whether they were columnists for Italian-language newspapers, or Italian-language teachers who taught in after-school programs from books provided by the Fascist government, or refugees from Mussolini's repression, or aging mothers who, without English, wanted to avoid the humiliating citizenship process of the time, all were branded "enemy aliens."

With this designation came a series of blows in 1941 and early 1942 that frightened, fractured, dispersed, and silenced much of Italian America for a generation. For some, the silence still prevails—a silence that until the 1990s included the very story of the events that did the job.

Those events, briefly summarized, included the following. On the night of December 7, 1941, the FBI activated the Custodial Detention List it had been preparing since 1939 and took into custody, over the next few months, much of the Italian American leadership throughout the country. Hundreds who, like Pietro DeLuca, led small Italian American social clubs, or who were writing or editing Italian American newspapers or broadcasting on Italian American radio shows were picked up and held on Ellis Island or at various INS detention centers in Boston, Cleveland, and other cities nationwide. After brief hearings, many were sent to internment camps run by the War Department. On the West Coast, the same scenario was enacted, with most of the aliens adjudged "dangerous to the public safety of the United States" sent to the internment camp at Fort Missoula, Montana.

This roundup of so-called dangerous aliens continued well into 1942 and sometimes beyond. Though it spared most of the six hundred thousand Italian immigrants designated enemy aliens, it and the measures that followed nonetheless accomplished their aim: to keep Italian Americans in a state of apprehension that any or all of them could be rounded up next.

The events of January and February 1942 underlined the threat. Despite the fact that they had just registered in 1940, all 600,000 resident aliens nationwide had to re-register and thenceforth carry their ID booklets at all times. Along with registration came restrictions—no travel of more than five miles without a permit, no move without notifying authorities, and no possession of so-called contraband (shortwave radios, weapons of any kind, cameras, flashlights). Those suspected of retaining such materials (and all enemy aliens were suspect) were subject to search, seizure, and summary detention.

In California, the threat intensified. In February came a curfew: enemy aliens were confined to their homes between the hours of 8:00 P.M. and 6:00 A.M. This hit hardest at those who worked odd hours—garbage collectors, fishermen, restaurant and bakery workers, truck farmers. Within days it hardly mattered, for the next blow was evacuation: almost the entire coast, and selected areas around sensitive installations like dams or power plants, were declared prohibited zones. After February 24, no enemy alien could live, work, or even be within such areas, or generally within five miles of the coast. Though no exact figures were kept, it is estimated that upwards of 10,000 Italian Americans had to leave their homes. A few were so undone by the prospect of pulling up stakes that they committed suicide. Others simply bent their heads and left, to endure the next months as best they could. The lucky ones found refuge with relatives; others, tired of the humiliation of being turned down by landlords who refused to rent to "enemies" judged too dangerous to be in sensitive areas, crammed into migrant-worker bungalows; Bettina Troia of Pittsburg could only find shelter in a chicken coop. To add to the threat, newspapers carried stories that the full-scale relocation of Japanese Americans had only begun a process that would soon include Italian Americans as well.[1]

As it turned out, most of the restrictions against Italian resident aliens were lifted the following October, but ironically, this was the time when some of the most flagrant abuses occurred. As Italian neighborhoods rejoiced in the return of evacuees and the lifting of the enemy-alien status, the recommendations made by Assemblyman Jack Tenney's Joint Fact-Finding Committee on Un-American Activities were going into effect. At the committee hearings in San Francisco in May 1942, several dozen Italian Americans had been accused of being the leaders of the West Coast's Fascist movement. Notwithstanding the fact that they were all U.S. citizens, or that no illegal action had been alleged, much less proved, against them, they were ordered to leave the state (and stay out of dozens of other states as well) for the duration of the war.[2] They would be allowed to return, with many of the internees, only in late 1943, after Italy surrendered.

It doesn't take much familiarity with civil rights law to conclude that the civil liberties of thousands of Italian Americans were violated during World War II. What is under discussion here, however, is not so much specific instances of injustice as their long-range effects. It is these subtler, longer-lasting ripples—some of which still endure—that constitute the enduring legacy of World War II.

Consider what happened to the traditional leadership in Italian American communities. Almost overnight, hundreds of teachers, newspaper editors, writers, and club leaders disappeared. Even their wives were not told where they were going nor what their eventual fate would be. The Italian-language schools staffed by many of those arrested were closed. Many of the Italian-language newspapers stopped publication. Anyone associated with them was automatically under suspicion.[3] Those trying to correspond with relatives in Italy found that letters were opened by censors, which reinforced the message that anything to do with that country or that language had become suspect. Within the community, suspicion grew and magnified. No one knew who might be informing on whom, or how the residue from an old rivalry might now bring one down.

The worst of it was, most of those affected were isolated. Until very recently, even those who were arrested or evacuated had only vague ideas about why they were targeted or how many others were affected. The internees, for example, were never informed of the charges against them; at their hearings, they were simply assumed to be guilty and then required to prove their innocence. Mary Lou Harris of San Mateo, whose gardener uncle was picked up and detained at Tanforan racetrack for several months, operated in a similar void: she and her family finally concluded that her uncle must have been arrested because he was a single Italian male and thereby suspect.[4] Such a lack of information, and the isolation that accompanies it, can only magnify feelings of guilt and shame.

How much the government intended its actions to appear arbitrary, and thereby more intimidating, is not clear.[5] What is obvious is that it intended to frighten people as efficiently as it could. A government poster of the time conveys this quite well: over cartoon figures of Hitler, Tojo, and Mussolini speaking such lines as "It's necessary to destroy democracy," there runs the upper-case admonishment: DON'T SPEAK THE ENEMY'S LANGUAGE. The double entendre here is clear, but the effect on Italian Americans was singular: many Italian-born parents admonished their children to stop speaking that "enemy's language." Italian stores and clubs put up signs that declared "No Italian Spoken for the Duration."

The net effect is evident. People who do not know what is happening to them, or why it is happening, end up feeling guilty. The syllogism infiltrates the soul: Italians were arrested; in America no one gets arrested without just cause; the arrestees must have been guilty. We all must have been guilty. But of what? Nothing was done. It must be what we are. Therefore, to the extent that it is possible, stop being that. Stop being Italian, stop using Italian, and as for one's name—necessarily a word in that enemy language—stop that too. Drop it: from "Ardente," drop the *e* to make it "Ardent," American, and this is precisely what

William Ardente of Pittsburg, California, and many others did.[6]

Studs Terkel's book *The Good War* contains a variation on this theme. In the interview he gave Terkel, the Italian American architect Paul Pisicano, with no apparent knowledge of the wartime restrictions, describes the change in his Bronx neighborhood after the war:

A poster issued by the U.S. government that associated foreign languages with disloyalty. Courtesy of the Center of Military History

> Since the war, Italo-Americans have undergone this amazing transformation…We stopped being Italo and started becoming Americans.
>
> We had all lived in one big apartment house my father built. He built a wine cellar. The guys, after they'd worked hard all day—not in offices, in factories—they'd have their dinner, there was no TV, they'd go downstairs, during the grape season, and they would crush. *It was a communal effort.* Everybody in the apartment house worked on the harvest…My father would provide the machinery. Big vats of wine. Everybody would have his own grapes. The whole cellar was a vineyard.
>
> After the war, nobody used the wine cellars. The whole sense of community disappeared. You lost your Italianness…Suddenly we looked up, we owned property. Italians could buy. The GI Bill, the American dream. Guys my age had really become Americanized. They moved to the suburbs.
>
> Oh, God, I see the war as that transition piece that pulled us out of the wine cellar. It obliterated our culture and made us Americans. That's no fun.[7]

Pisicano's theme has been repeated in countless variations by many others. World War II marked a watershed for Italian American culture. In the postwar years, large numbers moved out of the old colonies and into neighborhoods that were newer, trimmer, American. How many did this consciously, in response to the wartime stigma, cannot be ascertained with certainty. What is certain is that after the war the United States government implemented just such a dispersal program for others, particularly Japanese Americans and Native Americans. It even had a name for this: "mainstreaming." If you can induce a population to scatter, its coherence and strength as a unified force responding to discrimination and exerting pressure for justice is vitiated. Though this movement for Italian Americans was not forced or complete, it happened consistently enough to make a difference.

The difference can be gauged by the nation's lack of awareness of the very wartime experiences under discussion; the story has been suppressed and repressed. Like victims of abuse, Italian Americans took the blame on themselves and treated it as they treated all else—with silence. Even now, many Italian Americans would prefer to keep the story buried. It seems that the United States government, and those who write the histories, agree. Routinely, it has been stated that for Italian Americans, such wartime restrictions *never happened.*[8]

―――――

> The spirit of a community or collective can be wiped out, tradition can be destroyed. We tend to think of genocide as the physical destruction of a race or group, but the term may be aptly expanded to include the obliteration of the genius of a group, the killing of its creative spirit through the destruction, debasement, or silencing of its art. Those parts of our being that extend beyond the individual ego (i.e. that pertain to community) cannot survive unless they can be constantly articulated.
>
> And there are individuals—all of us, I would say, but men and women of spiritual and artistic temperament in particular—who cannot survive, either, unless the symbols of zoe [transcendent] life circulate among us as a common wealth.[9]

The above quotation is taken from Lewis Hyde's remarkable book *The Gift*. It raises the issue I have been aiming at all along: the silencing of a community's spirit. Where the Italian American wartime experience is even mentioned, the discussion usually focuses on the loss of physical community, with an agreement that, to one degree or another, such communities in America lost coherence and power after the war. Italian immigrants and their children Americanized, and not the least of that Americanization involved their tendency to lose their sense of place, their sense of culture tied to that place, their sense of themselves tied to both.

These are serious losses, but in some ways they have been reversed—not physically so much as organizationally—through the revitalization of some of the old clubs and the blossoming of new organizations in the late sixties and thereafter. Though there was a hiatus of twenty-five years or so, Italian Americans in many areas have renewed their affiliations with the Italian language, and with their ancestral *Italianità* in general. Under the influence of Italian "chic," many of the old Little Italys now prosper, even if in a more gentrified and artificial way than before.

Here, however, I am concerned with what Hyde refers to: the loss of spiritual community. This is a more subtle, but to my mind, more serious and permanent loss. Earlier I referred to the Italian moment that appeared to be gathering force just prior to the war. Artists and writers were expressing themselves with a vitality that bespoke confidence and entitlement. Di Donato, Fante, and others knew that they had something to say, knew it was challenging, and sensed that American audiences were ready and eager to hear it.

The war brought "Don't." It brought silence, and not just to those in the immigrant generation who were targeted. It silenced their spokesmen, too—their children, their teachers, and those ultimate community spokesmen, their writers. It diverted them into other areas. Who knows how many potential novelists became lawyers or ad writers?[10] How many poets became teachers or social workers? We shall never know. All we can do is look at some we do know and gauge the overall result.

After the war, Pietro Di Donato wrote little. Using the same material he had mined in *Christ in Concrete*, he reprised it in 1960 in *Three Circles of Light*, a little-read novel. Then a book about *Mother Cabrini*. Then silence. John Fante followed a different but no less discouraging trajectory. He went to Hollywood and wrote screenplays. As with Faulkner, this was death to him, but unlike Faulkner he lacked the confidence (or was it the cultural sanction?) to go home again. To his credit, he continued to write novels in his spare time, but had it not been for an offhand comment about him by Charles Bukowski, he'd still be totally unknown, rather than almost unknown. Jerre Mangione, it is true, published *Mount Allegro* in 1943, but it was really a memoir, not a novel, and its determined optimism fed into the climate expected of Italian America after the war: though we're exotic, we're American, we're loyal, we're happy to be, and happy to be here.

Michael de Capite wrote two novels, *Maria* and *No Bright Banner*, in the 1940s, and Mari Tomasi wrote her best work, *Like Lesser Gods*, in 1949, yet the climate for their work and the work of the few others writing truly about Italian America can be gauged by counting the handful who even know it exists. The case of Salvatore Lombino suggests why. He is the most widely published Italian American writer we know; his first book was a runaway best-seller; besides movies, television scripts, and plays, his detective novels are considered classics of that genre. Never heard of him? Perhaps that is because he has never written under his Italian name, and only late in life did he write about his Italian roots. Instead, he concluded early on that the name "Evan Hunter" (*The Blackboard Jungle, The Birds*) or Ed McBain (the pseudonym the already pseudonymous Hunter uses for his 87th Precinct crime novels) would serve an American writer better. It's an old story among Italian Americans, allowing authors as disparate as Frances Winwar (Francesca Vinciguerra), Hamilton Basso, and Don DeLillo to "pass."[11]

Mario Puzo confirms the pattern. He wrote a fine novel, *The Fortunate Pilgrim,* in 1964, but he saw the writing on the wall, as it were: America was massively uninterested in novels about Italian America. Conversely, it was massively obsessed by Italian Americans in crime. So Puzo decided to Americanize. In his case, that meant "give 'em what they want." His *Godfather* became a best-seller, and the rest is history.

The irony at this point is heavy, even grim, for there is evidence to suggest that even this pandering to a fascination with criminality has roots in the war. That is, at the same time that Italian Americans were being restricted and their community leaders interned for their now-suspect beliefs, the U.S. Office of Naval Intelligence was embarking on one of the darkest ventures of the war. It was choosing to court the mafia—specifically the imprisoned Lucky Luciano—in a deal that would obtain underworld help to secure the East Coast waterfront in exchange for the gangster's freedom after the war. The deal was proposed through intermediaries—and concluded. The waterfront experienced no repeats of the *Normandie* fire, in which a luxury liner being converted for military use had burned and sunk, possibly through the efforts of German saboteurs. In 1946 Luciano was pardoned by Governor Dewey and deported to Italy.[12]

This was only part one, however. The second part of the deal concerned the invasion of Sicily. Mussolini had been the first (and the last) Italian head of state to succeed in controlling the mafia: he simply jailed all suspected mafia figures, many on remote islands. Their hatred for him knew no bounds, so they had no hesitation in agreeing to the Allied proposal, brokered by Luciano and American organized crime, that they give all possible aid to the upcoming Sicilian invasion in return for their freedom. Thus was forged a second devil's pact, but the real devil was in the details. Not only were Sicily's crime bosses released; not only were they made mayors of the towns they had formerly terrorized; they were also reportedly given carte blanche to carry on the heroin trade, which thenceforth expanded from Marseilles to the cities of southern Sicily. It was a trade that would supply their organizations with far more money than they had ever amassed before—enough money, indeed, to gain them unprecedented influence in the postwar Italian government, right up to the most recent scandals over such mafia-government collusion in 1992 Italy.

These machinations reverberated through Italian America from 1941 on. They signified that the United States government, through its willingness to deal with organized crime, was elevating those criminals to abnormal, even heroic status. In other words, the U.S. government during World War II didn't just neutralize and devalue the traditional leadership in the Italian American community. It also helped, by example, to promote the claim to leadership of the criminals it preferred to deal with.

No wonder Italian American writers have been rejected for treating what is close to their hearts; no wonder they have been induced to write about crime. The American mainstream, aided and abetted by the federal government and a steady stream of media reinforcement, has concluded that criminals do in fact constitute the community's backbone. And this has contributed to the spiritual genocide Hyde refers to—not so thoroughly as to destroy Italian American culture, but sufficient to debase, divert, and silence it for a generation and more.

In a recent article in the *New York Times Sunday Book Review*, Gay Talese posed the question: "Where are all the Italian-American novelists?"[13] Where indeed. Though many Italian American scholars and writers took him to task for his ignorance, the question hangs over the community still. Where have they been for so long?

The answer, in my opinion, is that they, along with their audience, were silenced during the war. Since then, their art and their spirit have been debased by the continuing, repetitive message: "Give us gangsters. Give us crime. Or give us 'most happy fellas.' That's what Italian America is about. That's what we—the publishers, the editors, the arbiters of American culture—will listen to."[14]

It has been a spiritually crippling message. In the last two decades, to be sure, Italian American novelists have emerged who are trying to counter all this; Italian American scholars have emerged alongside them to try to resuscitate a more authentic tradition. But it is by no means certain that their work will amount to much more than the faint glow from a fire whose flame has already gone out.

That is the real tragedy of the war for Italian Americans. A community's moment may come but once. Miss that moment, and its vital spirit may be gone forever.

Endnotes:
1. See, among others, "Aliens in California: U.S. to Move Thousands Inland to Undisclosed Farm Colonies," *San Francisco Chronicle*, Feb. 4, 1942, p. 1, and "Enemy Aliens: 200,000 Face Internment, Evacuation Shortly," *San Francisco Chronicle*, Feb. 28, 1942.

2. It is worth noting that even before the war's end, the U.S. government recognized that it had erred. In a May 1942 memo, the Justice Department admitted that "persons are at times interned where there is considerable doubt as to whether they are guilty of conduct endangering the nation." Another memo from the attorney general to the FBI in July 1943 goes even further. It admits that the government's method of classifying aliens as to dangerousness was neither authorized nor justified, and that even the notion that such a thing could be done in the abstract is itself dangerous. Memo, Attorney General Francis Biddle to Hugh B. Cox and J. Edgar Hoover, July 16, 1943, in FBI file of Nino Guttadauro.

3. *La Parola* of Los Angeles and *Il Capitale* of Sacramento were two newpapers that closed down. Appearing too often in newspapers was itself suspect, as FBI officials combed community newspapers to find those who might be considered dangerous by virtue of their prominence.

4. Mary Lou Harris, personal interview, May 1994.

5. Jerre Mangione, who worked for the Immigration and Naturalization Service during the war, reports that the Justice Department did ask news organizations to limit their coverage of arrests and internments (Jerre Mangione, *An Ethnic at Large: A Memoir of America in the Thirties and Forties;* New York: Putnam, 1978). The ostensible reason was to reduce the risk of vigilante groups attacking those interned—but the corollary effect of heading off embarrassing questions by Americans about the arbitrary arrests in its midst appears obvious.

6. Angela Ardent, in a personal interview, June 1994, pointed out that it was her father-in-law's boss who suggested the name change in order to divert suspicion from Ardente and preserve his job. It didn't work—he was fired anyway.

7. Studs Terkel, *The Good War* (New York: Random House, 1985).

8. The examples of this are too numerous to mention. Tom Brokaw's *The Greatest Generation* is only the most recent, reducing the ordeal of Italians to "some uncomfortable moments." The federal government seems to agree. In a letter to Richard Armento of the Sons of Italy in California, Assistant Attorney General John R. Dunne, either ignorant or in denial, wrote on June 25, 1992: "a relatively small number of ethnic Germans and Italians received individual exclusion orders in contrast to the mass detention of Japanese Americans." The effects are numerous as well: Mary Lou Harris reported in 1994 that when she referred to her uncle's ordeal, her high-school-age son would vehemently insist that since no account of such restrictions on Italian Americans appeared in his history text, "It didn't happen, so stop saying that!"

9. Lewis Hyde, *The Gift* (New York: Vintage Books, 1979), p. 154.

10. The case of Giovanni Falasca, the interned editor of the Italian-language newspaper published in Los Angeles, *La Parola,* is one case we do know about (see p. 194, n103, in this volume).

11. "Passing" here means more than just changing one's name to sound American. It also means studiously avoiding anything that might get one tagged as an "ethnic" writer; or, as Lombino has his alter ego say in *Streets of Gold,* his one ethnic book, "I changed my name because I no longer wished to belong to that great brotherhood of *compaesani* whose sole occupation seemed to be searching out names ending in vowels." DeLillo came out (partly) in his most recent novel, *The Underworld,* after his reputation was firmly established.

12. Thus Luciano and many of the "dangerous" aliens were deported at about the same time—though in the case of internees, the government called this "repatriation." The difference, apparently ignored by authorities, was that Luciano had been convicted of numerous crimes; the internees, as Jerre Mangione put it, had been locked up "for their beliefs."

13. Gay Talese, "Where Are All the Italian-American Novelists," *New York Times Sunday Book Review,* March 14, 1993, p. 1

14. To read about this repressive literary climate in detail, see Helen Barolini's introduction to her anthology of writings by Italian American women, *The Dream Book* (New York: Shocken Books, 1985). There she points out the almost total absence of Italian American writers and their works from the accepted literary canon.

Appendix A
Timeline of Events

1939
November 9. FBI director J. Edgar Hoover orders the compilation of a Custodial Detention List of persons of Italian, German, and Japanese ancestry to be rounded up and imprisoned in concentration camps in the event of a national emergency.

1940
June 10. President Roosevelt, in response to the Italian invasion of France, accuses Italy of having "struck a dagger into the back of its neighbor," a statement that outrages many Italian Americans.

1941
March 31. FDR orders the seizure of Italian ships caught in American ports since Italy entered the war. This will be followed, in May, by the internment of some 1,000 Italian seamen aboard the ships, together with about one hundred Italian nationals from the World's Fair, at Fort Missoula, Montana.

June 28. Italian consulates in the United States are closed, and most consular personnel repatriated to Italy.

December 7. Immediately after the attack on Pearl Harbor, government agents begin to arrest the noncitizens on the Custodial Detention List. The following day the president signs Proclamation 2527, declaring that "an invasion or predatory incursion is threatened upon the territory of the United States by Italy." This turns 600,000 Italian immigrants without citizenship into "enemy aliens" and authorizes the apprehension of those deemed "dangerous to the public health and safety of the United States" and the confiscation of their property.

December 11. The United States declares war on Italy, and most Italian-language schools in California are closed and the teachers detained or interned. Most Italian internees from California are processed at Immigration and Naturalization Service (INS) facilities and sent directly to Fort Missoula, Montana.

Those on the East Coast are detained at INS facilities like Ellis Island to await a hearing; if ordered interned, they are transferred to War Department custody and sent to internment facilities such as those at Fort Meade, Maryland.

December 12. The FBI warns against the possession of cameras or weapons by suspected enemy aliens.

December 16. Dozens of fishing boats belonging to Italian Americans on the West Coast, most of them purse seiners, are requisitioned by the U.S. Navy and delivered to the 12th Naval District in San Francisco. Commercial traffic in and out of San Francisco has been suspended since December 8, when a huge submarine net was placed across the inner entrance of the Golden Gate.

December 19. Lieutenant General John DeWitt, commander of the Western Defense Command, sends a memo to the War Department demanding action to "collect all alien subjects fourteen years of age and over, of enemy nations, and remove them to the Zone of the Interior."

December 27. Attorney General Francis Biddle orders all suspected "enemy aliens" to surrender shortwave radios and cameras to local authorities; subsequent orders will extend the order to other so-called contraband, including flashlights, binoculars, and written matter in invisible ink. Failure to comply can result in internment.

1942

January 1. The attorney general issues new rules for enemy aliens, prohibiting travel without a permit beyond the city limits where an alien resides and ordering them to surrender all weapons.

January 4. Assistant Attorney General James Rowe meets with Lieutenant General John DeWitt at the Presidio in San Francisco to iron out serious differences between the War and Justice Departments over enemy-alien policy. The meeting results in the capitulation of Attorney General Biddle to DeWitt's demands for prohibited zones cleared of all enemy aliens, and for increased raids on homes to search for contraband; probable cause for a search warrant is reduced to the fact that an "enemy alien" resides in given premises.

January 14. General Biddle announces Presidential Order 2537, stipulating that enemy aliens will have to apply for and acquire Certificates of Identification bearing a photo, fingerprint, and signature. The new registration will be held from February 2 to February 7 in the Western Defense Command, and from February 9 to February 28 in the rest of the nation.

January 25. The Roberts Commission releases its report alleging that Japanese Americans on Oahu aided Japan's air attack on Pearl Harbor. Though the report will prove false, it heightens fears of sabotage and leads to increased calls for the removal and incarceration of those with ties to enemy nations.

January 29. Attorney General Biddle issues the first of a series of orders establishing limited strategic zones along the Pacific coast—zones which all enemy aliens will have to vacate by February 24.

January 31. The attorney general designates fifty-nine additional prohibited zones in California, mostly around oil fields, defense plants, and hydroelectric facilities, to be cleared of all enemy aliens by February 15.

February 1. The California State Personnel Board issues a directive that bars descendants of alien enemies from civil service positions.

February 2. Registration of all enemy aliens begins: each alien, in addition to supplying a photo for use in the pink I.D. booklet, must answer questions concerning employment, residences, relatives in Italy, and membership in organizations and carry the pink I.D. booklet at all times.

February 4. Attorney General Biddle establishes curfew zones in California from the Oregon border to Santa Barbara and extending as far inland as the Sacramento and San Joaquin Valleys, to take effect on February 24. Enemy aliens within the restricted zones must stay in their homes from 9 P.M. to 6 A.M.

February 9. Lieutenant General John DeWitt asks for a huge expansion of the prohibited zones—from which all enemy aliens would be removed—to include the entire Pacific slope (Oregon, Washington, and California) and parts of Arizona.

February 11. The Los Angeles County Defense Council approves a resolution calling for the evacuation to working internment areas of all able-bodied enemy-alien males; the same day, the Los Angeles County Board of Supervisors approves a resolution urging the evacuation of all enemy aliens.

February 14. Lieutenant General DeWitt sends a final memo to Secretary of War Henry Stimson recommending expanded zones from which he may exclude all persons of Japanese descent, including citizens, all enemy aliens, and any other suspect persons.

February 19. President Roosevelt signs Executive Order 9066, authorizing the secretary of war, or any military commander designated by the secretary, to establish "military areas" from which "any or all persons may be excluded."

February 21. The Select Committee Investigating National Defense Migration, known as the Tolan Committee after its chairman, Rep. John H. Tolan of Oakland, begins hearings in San Francisco to publicize the potential economic and social impact of the War Department's plan to exclude thousands of enemy aliens. The same day, FBI raids on suspected enemy aliens increase dramatically, with dozens of Italian Americans, including fishermen, farmworkers and laborers from San Francisco and Northern California, arrested and subsequently interned.

February 23. A requisition of purse seiners from Monterey and San Francisco cripples the sardine fleet; following a similar requisition on February 15th, which included tuna clippers from San Diego, this decimates the Italian American fishing fleet on the West Coast.

February 24. The deadline for more than 10,000 enemy aliens to evacuate their homes in prohibited zones eviscerates the fishing towns of Pittsburg and Monterey, as well as Italian American communities in Alameda, San Francisco, Santa Cruz, Eureka, and coastal areas from the Oregon border to Santa Barbara.

March 2. Lieutenant General DeWitt issues Proclamation No. 1, designating the western half of the three Pacific coast states and the southern third of Arizona as military areas and stipulating that all persons of Japanese descent will eventually be removed therefrom.

March 19. The Tolan Committee releases its preliminary report, distinguishing between the three alien groups and concluding that to evacuate German and Italian enemy aliens would have nationwide repercussions on the war effort.

March 21. President Roosevelt signs Public Law 503, making it a federal offense to violate any order issued by a designated military commander acting under authority of Executive Order 9066.

March 22. The first large contingent of Japanese Americans is moved from Los Angeles to the Manzanar temporary detention center.

March 24. The curfew zone is extended to Southern California, requiring enemy aliens and all people of Japanese descent to be in their homes from 8 P.M. to 6 A.M. and to limit non-working travel to five miles from their homes.

April 27. Lieutenant General Hugh Drum, commanding general of the Eastern Defense Command, announces his intention to establish prohibited and restricted areas covering the entire Atlantic seaboard and inland—to include sixteen states and 52 million people. The same day, Tom Clark, DOJ's man on the West Coast, writes to James Rowe, assistant attorney general, that Lieutenant General DeWitt fully intends a mass evacuation of Italian and German aliens as soon as he finishes with the Japanese.

May 5. President Roosevelt, alarmed by prospects of a mass evacuation of enemy aliens in the East, orders Secretary Stimson to take no action against Italian or German aliens there without first consulting him.

May 15. Secretary of War Stimson recommends that no mass evacuation of Italian or German aliens be initiated on either coast, but that commanders retain the right to exclude individuals, both aliens and citizens, based on military necessity.

May 25. The Joint Fact-Finding Committee on Un-American Activities, known as the Tenney Committee after its chairman, Jack Tenney, meets to investigate alleged Fascist activities in San Francisco, particularly among citizens beyond the reach of the enemy-alien program. Committee witnesses testify against dozens of Italian Americans, including California-born San Francisco mayor Angelo Rossi.

June 27. Lieutenant General DeWitt abolishes the prohibited and restricted zones in the Western Defense Command, allowing Italian aliens to return to their homes, subject only to curfew and travel restrictions.

September 16. Approximately 130 internees of Italian descent are transferred from the internment camp at Camp Forrest, Tennessee, to the more permanent internment camp at Camp McAlester, Oklahoma.

October 1. After being accused at the Tenney Committee hearings, dozens of naturalized Italian Americans from California are ordered out of the Western Defense Command, an order which excludes them from more than half the United States.

October 12. The attorney general announces at Carnegie Hall that all restrictions on enemy aliens of Italian descent are lifted; in California, the restrictions remain until Lieutenant General DeWitt lifts them a week later.

November 3. The transfer of Japanese American internees from temporary detention centers is completed with the arrival of the last group at Jerome internment camp in Arkansas from the Fresno temporary detention center.

1943
May 18. The War Department officially turns over control of enemy aliens to the Immigration and Naturalization Service; Italian American internees still in custody are transferred to the internment camp at Fort Missoula, Montana.

July 16. Attorney General Francis Biddle sends a memo to J. Edgar Hoover canceling and invalidating the use of the Custodial Detention List because, he writes, determinations about "dangerousness" cannot be made in the abstract but must be based on the actions of persons who may have violated the law.

July 25. Mussolini is ousted from power, leaving Italy in the nominal hands of King Victor Emmanuel and Marshal Badoglio, but with Germany's occupying army in actual control.

September 8. Italy surrenders to the Allies and begins to aid the Allied invasion against the German occupation. In the United States, this leads to the parole, in the next few months, of more than half of the Italian enemy aliens interned, as well as the return of most of the Italian American citizens excluded from military zones.

Appendix B
Map: Regulated Military Areas in California, 1942

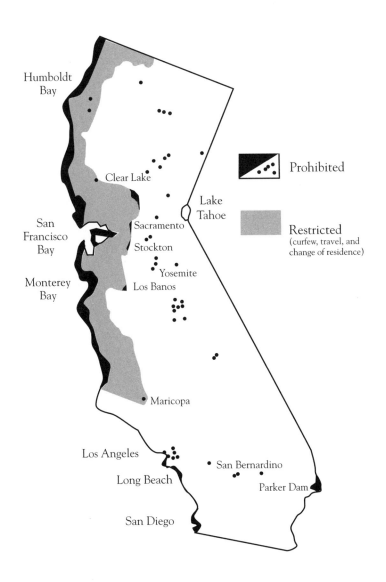

Humboldt
Bay

Clear Lake

Lake
Tahoe

San
Francisco
Bay

Sacramento

Stockton

Monterey
Bay

Yosemite

Los Banos

Maricopa

Los Angeles

Long Beach

San Bernardino

Parker Dam

San Diego

Prohibited

Restricted
(curfew, travel, and
change of residence)

Appendix C
U.S. Internment and Detention Facilities

This list does not include all temporary facilities, such as city jails and other facilities that were used by the Immigration and Naturalization Service (INS) in nearly every major city: Cincinnati, Syracuse, Niagara Falls, Omaha, Buffalo, Milwaukee, Denver, Tampa, Houston, Portland, Cleveland, and so on. PMGO refers to military sites run by the Provost Marshal General's Office. The major internment sites for enemy aliens of Italian descent were Fort George Meade (Md.), Camp McAlester (Okla.), Fort Sam Houston(Tex.), and Camp Forrest (Tenn.), all PMGO sites.

Location	Authority
California	
Ft. McDowell, Angel Island	PMGO
Sharp Park**	INS
Terminal Island	INS
Tujunga (Tuna Canyon)	INS
Colorado	
Ft. Logan	PMGO
Connecticut	
Hartford, Community Ctr. Bldg	INS
Florida	
Ft. Barrancas	PMGO
Miami, Border Patrol HQ	INS

---

* Signifies a permanent internment camp run by the Immigration and Naturalization Service.
** Signifies a site suitable for prolonged detention, also run by the INS.

Georgia
Fort Screven   PMGO

Hawaii
Sand Island   PMGO

Idaho
Kooskia**   INS

Illinois
Chicago, Home of the Good Shepherd   INS

Louisiana
New Orleans   INS
Algiers**   INS

Massachusetts
East Boston   INS

Maryland
Ft. Howard, Baltimore   INS
Ft. George Meade   PMGO

Minnesota
St. Paul   INS

Missouri
Kansas City   INS
St. Louis   INS

Montana
Ft. Missoula*   INS

North Dakota
Ft. Lincoln*   INS

New Jersey
Gloucester City**   INS

New Mexico
Ft. Stanton*   INS
Santa Fe*   INS

New York
Camp Upton   PMGO
Ellis Island**   INS

Oklahoma
McAlester   PMGO
Ft. Sill   PMGO
Stringtown   PMGO

Pennsylvania
Pittsburgh   INS
Nanticoke   INS

Tennessee
Camp Forrest   PMGO

Texas
Kelly AFB   INS
Crystal City*   INS
Kenedy*   INS
Seagoville*   INS
Ft. Bliss   PMGO
Ft. Sam Houston   PMGO

Utah
Salt Lake City   INS

Washington
Seattle   INS
Spokane   INS
Sullivan Lake   PMGO

West Virginia
White Sulphur Springs   INS

Wisconsin
Camp McCoy   PMGO

Suggested Reading

Benedetti, Umberto. *Italian Boys at Fort Missoula, Montana 1941–1943* (Missoula, Mont.: Pictorial Histories Publishing Co., 1991).

Biddle, Francis. *In Brief Authority* (New York: Doubleday, 1962).

Boehm, Randolph, ed. *Papers of the U.S. Commission on Wartime Relocation and Internment of Civilians* (Fredericksburg, Md., Government Printing Office, 1984).

Bosworth, R. and R. Ugolini, eds. *War, Internment and Mass Migration: The Italo-Australian Experience* (Rome: Gruppo Editoriale Internazionale, 1992).

California Legislature. *Report of the Joint Fact-Finding Committee on Un-American Activities in California* (Sacramento: State Legislature, 55th Session, 1943).

Cannistraro, Philip. "Fascism and Italian Americans," *Perspectives in Italian Immigration and Ethnicity*, S. M. Tomasi, ed. (New York: Center for Migration Studies, 1976).

——— "Generoso Pope and the Rise of Italian American Politics, 1925–1936," *Italian Americans: New Perspectives in Italian Immigration and Ethnicity*, Lydio Tomasi, ed. (New York: Center for Migration Studies, 1983).

———"Luigi Antonini and the Italian Anti-Fascist Movement in the United States, 1940–1943," *Journal of American Ethnic History* (Fall 1985).

———*Blackshirts in Little Italy: Italian Americans and Fascism, 1921–1929* (Lafayette, Ind.: Bordighera, 1999).

Commission on Wartime Relocation and Internment of Civilians. *Personal Justice Denied* (Washington, D.C.: Government Printing Office, 1982).

Corbett, P. Scott. *Quiet Passages: The Exchange of Civilians between the United States and Japan during the Second World War* (Kent, Ohio: Kent State University Press, 1987).

Christgau, John. "Enemies": *World War II Alien Internment* (Ames, Iowa: Iowa State University Press, 1985).

Daniels, Roger. *Concentration Camps USA: Japanese Americans and World War II* (New York: Holt, Rinehart and Winston, 1972).

————*The Politics of Prejudice* (Berkeley: University of California Press, 1962).

————Sandra C. Taylor, and Harry H. L. Kitano, eds. *Japanese Americans from Relocation to Redress* (Salt Lake City: University of Utah Press, 1986).

Diggins, John P. *Mussolini and Fascism: The View from America* (Princeton, N.J.: Princeton University Press, 1972).

DiStasi, Lawrence. "Dis-enchanted Evenings: Ezio Pinza's Wartime Ordeal," *Ambassador Magazine*, 41 (Summer 1999).

Fox, Stephen. "General DeWitt and the Proposed Internment of German and Italian Aliens during World War II," *Pacific Historical Review*, 57 (November, 1988).

————*The Unknown Internment: An Oral History of the Relocation of Italian Americans during World War II* (Boston: Twayne Publishers, 1990).

————*America's Invisible Gulag: A Biography of German American Internment & Exclusion—Memory & History* (New York: Peter Lang Publishing, 2000).

Gardiner, C. Harvey. *Pawns in a Triangle of Hate: The Peruvian Japanese and the United States* (Seattle: University of Washington Press, 1981).

Gillman, Peter and Leni. "Collar the Lot": *How Britain Interned and Expelled Its Wartime Refugees* (London: Quartet Books, 1978).

Grodzins, Morton. *Americans Betrayed: Politics and the Japanese Evacuation* (Chicago: University of Chicago Press, 1949).

Hillmer, Norman, Bohdan Kordan, and Lubomyr Luciuk, eds. *On Guard for Thee: War, Ethnicity, and the Canadian State, 1939–1945* (Ottawa: Canadian Government Publications Centre, 1988).

Iacovetta, Franca, Roberto Perin, and Angelo Principe, eds. *Enemies Within: Italian and Other Internees in Canada and Abroad* (Toronto: University of Toronto Press, 2000).

Inada, Lawson Fusao. *Only What We Could Carry: The Japanese American Internment Experience* (Berkeley: Heyday Books, 2000)

Irons, Peter. *Justice at War: The Story of the Japanese American Internment Cases* (New York: Oxford University Press, 1983).

Krammer, Arnold. *Undue Process: The Untold Story of America's German Alien Internees* (London and Boulder, Colo.: Rowman & Littlefield, 1997).

Lothrop, Gloria Ricci. "The Untold Story: The Effect of the Second World War on California Italians," *Journal of the West*, 35:1 (1996).

————"Shadow on the Land: Italians in Southern California in the 1930s," *California History*, 75:4 (Winter 1996–97).

Mangione, Jerre. *An Ethnic at Large: A Memoir of America in the Thirties and Forties* (New York: Putnam, 1978).

Pinza, Ezio, with Robert Magidoff. *Ezio Pinza: An Autobiography* (New York: Rinehart, 1958).

Pozzetta, George. "My Children Are My Jewels: Italian American Generations during World War II," *The Home-Front War: World War II and American Society*, Kenneth O'Brien and Lynn Parsons, eds. (Westport, Conn.: Greenwood Press, 1995).

————and Gary Mormino. "Ethnics at War: Italian Americans in California during World War II," *The Way We Really Were: The Golden State in the Second Great War*, Roger Lotchin, ed. (Urbana: University of Illinois Press, 2000).

Salvemini, Gaetano. *Italian Fascist Activities in the United States*, Philip V. Cannistraro, ed. (New York: Center for Migration Studies, 1977).

Scherini, Rose. "The Fascist/Anti-Fascist Struggle in San Francisco," *New Explorations in Italian American Studies*, Richard N. and Sandra P. Juliani, eds., (Washington, D.C.: American Italian Historical Assocation, 1994).

————"Executive Order 9066 and Italian Americans: the San Francisco Story," *California History*, 71:4 (Winter 1991–92).

————"The Other Internment: When Italian Americans Were Enemy Aliens," *Ambassador Magazine* (Fall 1993).

———— and Lawrence Distasi with Adele Negro. *Una Storia Segreta: When Italian Americans Were "Enemy Aliens"* (Berkeley: American Italian Historical Association, Western Regional Chapter, 1994).

Sheridan, Peter. "Internment of German and Italian Aliens as Compared with the Internment of Japanese Aliens in the United States during World War II: A Brief History and Analysis" (Library of Congress: Congressional Research Service, 1980).

ten Broeck, Jacobus, Edward Barnhart, and Floyd Matson. *Prejudice, War and the Constitution*. (Berkeley and Los Angeles: University of California Press, 1954).

U.S. Congress. *Report of the Select Committee Investigating National Defense Migration*, 77th Congress, 2nd session (Washington, D.C.: U.S. Government Printing Office 77th Congress, 2nd Session, 1942).

Van Valkenburg, Carol. *An Alien Place: The Fort Missoula Detention Camp 1941–1944* (Missoula, Mont.: 1995).

Weglyn, Michi. *Years of Infamy: The Untold Story of America's Concentration Camps* (New York: William Morrow, 1976).

About the Editor

Lawrence DiStasi has been the project director of the traveling exhibit *Una Storia Segreta: When Italian Americans Were "Enemy Aliens"* since its inception in 1994. The current president of the American Italian Historical Association's Western Regional Chapter, and a board member of the Before Columbus Foundation, he works as an editor, writer, and instructor in UC Berkeley Extension's Fall Freshman Program. He is the author of *Mal Occhio: The Underside of Vision* (North Point Press, 1981) and *Dream Streets: The Big Book of Italian American Culture* (Harper & Row, 1989).